100 years of the Ladies Scottish Climbing Club

THE SCOTTISH MOUNTAINEERING CLUB JOURNAL

| Vol. XL | 2008 | No. 199 |

EDITORIAL

Ladies Scottish Climbing Club

EARLIER this year the Ladies Scottish Climbing Club celebrated its centenary. We congratulate our kindred club on this significant milestone in its history and wish it all the best for the future. Given the nature of society one hundred years ago it is truly remarkable that the ladies set up their own club as early as they did. The three founders – Jane Inglis Clark, her daughter Mabel, and Lucy Smith – made their momentous decision just off the road to Killin near Lix Toll. The large boulder they were sheltering behind at the time can no longer be identified, otherwise it might be a place of pilgrimage today. We are delighted to include here a review of the club's first hundred years written by the LSCC President. *Last Seen Climbing Courageously* recalls some of the inspirational trips and climbs undertaken by LSCC members down the years.

Modern Technology

My predecessor left office sooner than he had planned and so missed the opportunity of saying his farewell. I thank him on your behalf for his toil over the last seven years. Colour photographs, which were introduced just prior to the start of his tenure, have become an important feature of the Journal. They have without doubt greatly improved its general appearance. Although this has entailed an increase in production costs it would be unthinkable now to return to the days of black and white. Charlie Orr was also passionate about having the Journal printed in Scotland. It is not my intention to break with this tradition.

I take on the job as the fifteenth Journal Editor in a time of remarkable change. (The previous Editor thought he was the fifteenth, but numbers weren't his strong point!) On more than one occasion the previous incumbent remarked in these pages that our Journal cannot continue to rely on a small group of ageing contributors for its content. He blamed

LSCC Members outside the Kingshouse Hotel. (Date unknown). Photo: SMC Archives

this state of affairs largely on the monthly climbing magazines, which he suggested the younger generation find a more immediate, and hence more attractive, outlet for their tales of derring-do. I'm not sure if this is any longer the case. The extraordinary speed of communication today means that even the magazines struggle to compete with internet forums and blogs. If you're not familiar with these terms (and yes, isn't 'blog' an awful word?) you're probably content to get along without using the superhighway. However, the Internet is certain to be an increasingly important way of communicating and Ken Crocket our webmaster, ever keen to keep us up to date, has recently set up a private internet forum for Club members. I encourage you to use it.

Such is the state of modern technology that nowadays a picture of a first ascent, taken with a mobile phone, can appear on the Web and be seen by millions around the world before the pioneering team is even off the hill. As Robin Smith wrote, 'You got to go with the times'. Although much of the traffic on open internet climbing forums is banal and illiterate, there are occasional posts of great interest. While lurking on a popular forum last autumn I was astonished to see the name Gordon Smith appear. He seemed to vanish from the face of the Earth in the early 1980s. When I made contact with him by e-mail he was in a boat riding out a typhoon off the Philippines. It didn't take much cajouling to get him to write for the first time about his amazing exploits from thirty years ago. So modern technology does have its advantages.

One of the important tasks of the Editor as I see it is to produce a Balanced Journal with a broad range of content. This year for some reason we've got a slight bias towards the faction/fantasy genre. While I hope readers find these very worthy and enjoyable articles, it would be good to have more tales about actual events, preferably from the present day. I would also put in a special plea for contributions from our female members.

Your Editor hopes he doesn't have to do a lot of pestering for articles. I've no reason to believe that my predecessor had become bitter and twisted by the time he left office, but the various manuscripts he forwarded for this year's Journal cost me a small fortune because of insufficient postage. It may take some of your precious time and a little bit of inspiration to compose an article for the Journal, but if you send it to me by e-mail it won't even cost you a stamp.

To finish I would like to record my thanks to the New Climbs Editor, Andy Nisbet, and to the Clerk of the List, Dave Broadhead, for collating and presenting their material for the Journal in such an orderly manner. I also thank Andy Tibbs for rooting out much of the photographic content. Last but not least, I thank Robin Campbell for his meticulous work on the index to the last volume, as well as much general encouragement.

LAST SEEN CLIMBING COURAGEOUSLY

By Helen Steven

I SUPPOSE the Ladies Scottish Climbing Club owes a debt of gratitude to the SMC for the fact that for so many years they didn't allow women to join their august body. Otherwise a hundred years ago three determined women might simply have joined their menfolk and been quietly absorbed into the SMC fraternity. As it was, in the year 1908 Jane Inglis Clark, her daughter Mabel, and Lucy Smith were all huddled in the shelter of a mighty boulder near Lix Toll. History fails to relate why they were in such an unlikely place – were they sheltering from a blast of April sleet, were they waiting to be picked up by a passing horse and trap, or were they – dare it be said – waiting impatiently for their men to come off the hill? At any rate, they fell to plotting. All three were keen climbers, experienced alpinists, and not allowed into the SMC. So they decided to start a women's club of their own. The SMC Journal of that year takes up the tale:

> The Ladies Scottish Climbing Club. The Victorian Era has seen the rise of many things, and the lot of man, collectively, has improved beyond conception. Sport in its many aspects has advanced with rapid stride, and woman, making up the leeway of centuries, has jostled to the front to take her place alongside man in the many active pursuits so long considered to be alone suited for the masculine persuasion. But although women had shared in the joys of mountaineering with their husbands, brother or guides, it has been left to the present gracious reign to find lady climbers banding themselves together into Clubs with the same aims as those of the various male Climbing Clubs. Last year the Ladies Alpine Club came into existence, and now the Ladies Scottish Climbing Club has not only been formed, but has carried out several highly successful meets.

It is hard nowadays to imagine the amount of courage it took those founder members of the Club to face up to the amount of prejudice and criticism they must have encountered. Consider this example of male chauvinist opinion as quoted by Nea Morin from Samivel's *Amateurs d'Abimes*:

> Well do we know them…lonely crows, who, aping men, haunt the huts and great mountain faces and ply the harsh tools of the mountains, baring their faces to the winds in ecstasy and straining to their bosoms the unfeeling rock with the ardour of lovers.
>
> No! True women are too tender for the rigours of the mountains, and men will not accept that they should penetrate their domain.

Fortunately such attitudes were not at all typical of the SMC (at least we sincerely hope not) and right from the start the LSCC was given wholehearted support by their mountaineering menfolk. The noted Harold Raeburn was the brother of founder member, Ruth Raeburn and was a stalwart supporter of the new club. He introduced them to the rock climbs on Salisbury Crags, and soon the women were setting off on their own early in the morning to do their own pioneering routes. Lucy Smith's hand-drawn map of the routes is still in the Club archives, and one of our best-known photographs is of Lucy, complete with hat and long skirt, making an impossibly long reach for a hold.

Jane Inglis Clark acknowledges the support given by members of the SMC after, as she says, she took 'climbing fever' rather badly. She speaks of eleven years of wonderful summer seasons with her husband in the Alps, when they did many first ascents together in Switzerland, the Chamonix area, and in the Dolomites. The joys of mountaineering in Scotland were only just being discovered at the turn of the twentieth century, and she talks of catching the 4.0 a.m. train to Crianlarich or Tyndrum and enjoying long winter days on the hill, returning long after dark. All the time the help of the SMC is duly acknowledged:

> We also had the privilege of making first ascents in Scotland under the brilliant leadership of Mr Harold Raeburn and other members of the Scottish Mountaineering Club.

Club records also give examples of more mundane assistance offered by the men. The Inglis Clark's chauffeur-driven car was often conveniently at hand at the end of a long day; one record tells of 'Mr Sang' being discovered in a corner of a field brewing up a welcome cup of tea. Men had their uses! And such practical help has continued over the years. Indeed the LSCC huts at Blackrock and Milehouse might well be in a sorry state without the willing help of our menfolk.

One has only to look through the list of members over the last hundred years to see the strong ties between our two clubs. A.E. Robertson, J.H.P. Bell, Harold Raeburn, Scott Johnstone, Tom Weir, Trevor Ransley, Graham King, Chris Gilmore, Bill Murray, Alan McNicol, John Higham, Campbell Steven (my own father), and many, many others linked to the LSCC by ties of marriage or family.

And, as in all families, there were occasions when the links with the SMC must have been strained to the limit. Take, for example, the Lagangarbh Incident. For many years prior to 1947 the Ladies had been looking for a 'home of their own' and, just before World War II, they were given to believe that Lagangarbh would soon be theirs for the asking. Indeed they were practically choosing the curtains. Imagine their chagrin when Lagangarbh did indeed become available and the SMC was given first refusal. There must have been some grim mutterings over the breakfast table in some families. Fortunately, in

1947, Blackmount Estate agreed to lease Blackrock Cottage to the Club and it has been a happy home for the Club ever since. (Dare we say that we prefer it!)

But enough of all this. Should we not just call the LSCC 'Daughter of the SMC' and be done with it? Perhaps, but only in the sense that a daughter grows up, throws off the ties and becomes independent. In fact right from the outset these women were pioneering climbers in their own right. Some of the distances covered during the long summer breaks were remarkable. In June 1919, one such stravaig took three LSCC members from Dalwhinnie to Glenbrittle, taking in Ben Alder, Creag Meagaidh, over the Corrieyaraick, through Glen Affric, and over to Skye, where they climbed the Cioch (the climbing was 'very entertaining and at times almost sensational'), ending up by taking in the Pinnacle Ridge of Sgurr nan Gillean and the Bla Bheinn/Clach Glas traverse.

Soon the obsession with Munro-bagging exerted its grip. An LSCC member, Mrs J. Hirst, was the first woman to 'compleat' all the Munros, then in 1980 Anne Littlejohn did all the Munros, all the tops, and all the Munros furth of Scotland, and in 1967 Mora McCallum was the youngest 'compleater' of her day. Kathy Murgatroyd was the first woman to do all the Munros in one expedition without using any public transport, apart from the ferry to Skye. Nowadays, it is quite commonplace to be present at an LSCC member's last Munro, or last Corbett, or last Graham party. Indeed this could become the latest challenge. A Munro only counts if it is someone's last one!

Lest an impression be given of addictive top-ticking it might be appropriate to recall the sheer pleasure of walking the Scottish hills with this passage from one of our Journals:

> Scotland's Munros are unrivalled anywhere in the world for delightful variety of weather, colour, birdsong and situation. The joy of crampons creaking on firm snow and the blue-green hole left by the ice-axe; the weary boots, dusty with heather-pollen on bee-droning evenings in the Rothiemurchus pine; the quiet satisfaction of navigating to the cairn in the right place after long-staring through moisture-rimmed eyelashes in the muffled closeness of the mist; the hooded isolation of a head-down battle against a West-coast blatter; or the delicate wrinkles of sun-warmed rock with Rannoch Moor at your back.

From the earliest days, however, the LSCC members were not content with going the easiest ways up mountains and often sought the 'most sporting' route. Three years before the founding of the Club, Jane Inglis Clark made the first woman's ascent, and the second ever ascent, of Abraham's Route on Crowberry Ridge in the company of her husband and, of course, Harold Raeburn. Known at the time as 'the most difficult climb in Britain' she recalls the thrill by quoting in part from the SMC Journal:

'To the left the ridge fell in an appalling vertical cliff for about a hundred feet to a hundred and fifty feet. To our right the deep-cleft gully was walled in by precipitous cliffs.' We turned to the left and braved the dangers of that appalling precipice....

I have accomplished some very difficult rock climbs such as the Kleine Zinne and the Winkler Thurm in Tirol, but it was the absence of holds, the trusting to mere hollows for support, the squirming and wriggling up that rock face of Buachaille Etive that I can never forget.

The photographs show her still wearing a hat!

Soon the long classic routes on the Ben and the Buachaille were being tackled in both summer and winter. Nancy Forsyth climbed Eagle Ridge on Lochnagar (another first for women); Anne Littlejohn made a solo traverse of the entire Cuillin Ridge in a record 17 hours 22 minutes; and Esme Speakman put up the first ascent of January Jigsaw on Rannoch Wall. Although the LSCC has never specialised in extreme rock climbing, there has always been an active core of keen rock climbers who keep pushing up the standards, and some very good routes have been accomplished. Summer evenings see regular outings to Craig y Barns, Polldubh, Ben A'an, and the infamous Whangie, and even quarries and railway embankments provide sport for enthusiasts. Sea-cliff climbing has become popular, with the warm rocks of Reiff in Coigach a favourite spot. Cynthia Grindley had an epic climb on the Old Man of Hoy, where being partially blinded by her cagoule blowing over her face made the crux move rather more challenging.

More recently, with the advent of cheap air flights, LSCC members have been migrating to Spain, Sardinia or even Jordan to be assured of sunshine and absence of midges.

After a gap of some years from the traditional Alpine meets, in 1985 regular Alpine Meets once again became a feature and many classic routes enjoyed. The Grandes Jorasses, the Mitteleggi Ridge on the Eiger, the Midi–Plan Arête, the Dent de Ruth, the Lauterbrunnen Breithorn and the Haute Route on skis all gave thrilling days out, so that an annual Alpine Meet is almost a must nowadays. An exception was made in the year 2000 when a grand expedition to Ladakh took place and 16 members celebrated the Millennium by standing on the summit of Stok Kangri, a peak that was well over the required 20,000ft.

In the 1950s SMC members such as Douglas Scott, Tom McKinnon and Bill Murray were making their names in the Himalaya. The LSCC was determined not to be left behind. In the days before guides, trekking companies and organised tours, maps were hard to obtain, whole areas unexplored and many peaks still unclimbed. In 1955 Monica Jackson, Betty Stark and Evelyn McNicol started planning an expedition to the Jugal Himal. It was a remarkably ambitious undertaking. Women had climbed in the Himalaya before, but always as part of expeditions led by men. This was a first for women. Nor were these three, by their own admission, particularly hard climbers. A remarkable feature of the expedition was not only the modesty of the climbers themselves, but also the modesty of their means. They couldn't afford to put up fixed camps all the way up the mountain, so they simply carried their old 'Palomine' tents up with them from camp to camp, having to wait each morning until the tents had thawed sufficiently to be able to take them down and pack them.

They were all very competent climbers and soon gained the respect and confidence of the Sherpas who were their companions. Not only did Monica and Betty, and the Sherpas Mingma and Ang Temba reach an unclimbed 21,000ft summit – which they named Gyalgen peak after one of the Sherpas – they also had to guide two of the Sherpas who had become snow-blind over knife-edge snow bridges and teetering seracs. Monica concludes with typical modesty:

> We had not accomplished anything spectacular, but then we never hoped to do so with such a small party. We *had* succeeded in doing what we had set out to do, which was to explore the Jugal Himal, the last large unexplored area of Nepal Himalaya. That we had managed to climb an unknown peak of over 21,000 feet was really beside the point – a kind of bonus.

There has always been something particularly enticing about the Arctic, and over the years Club members have travelled in Arctic Norway, Lapland, the Canadian Arctic, Greenland and also the Antarctic. The *Sunday Dispatch* of 1954 describes one such trip:

> Five Scots girls [*sic*] dressed in mountaineering outfits left Glasgow yesterday for the Arctic Circle. Their trip will make history – it is the first time an all-girl expedition has ventured so far north.

Others soon followed, and the Lyngen Alps became a favourite climbing area.

In 1968 Club members Eilidh Nisbet and Esme Speakman took part in the Women's East Greenland Mountaineering Expedition – the first ever women's expedition to east Greenland. Although they were not able to achieve any notable peaks, they paved the way for another expedition two years later, when twelve LSCC members took part in the Ladies Scottish East Greenland Expedition. Once again the SMC played its part, as Donald Bennett and Malcolm Slesser were encouraging and helpful with recommendations about the Staunings Alps, and organised a charter flight for several expeditions to Mestersvig. However, once there the women were on their own – as Malcolm Slesser informed them in no uncertain terms! Prevented initially by pack ice from launching their inflatable boat, a long trek up the Berserkerbrae was made and from there the first women's ascent of the dramatic Berserkerspire. The second half of the expedition then visited unexplored Nathorstsland, where they made three first ascents and a second ascent of Ardvreck. It seemed that the LSCC had acquitted itself well, and since 1970 many other trips to Greenland have been made, including a highly enjoyable Club Meet to North West Greenland in 1998.

Perhaps the main characteristic of the Club, however, is not so much its technical achievements as its pioneering spirit of adventure. Thus the highlight of the LSEGE was not so much in the climbing, but rather in the sheer adventure of threading a little rubber boat past glacier snouts and through ice floes. Some trips are undertaken for the plain good fun of them. Trying to find a comfortable billet in one of the Bonnie Prince's less regal dosses in Glenmoriston; having a good ceilidh in a snow-hole on Cairngorm; a moonlit traverse from Stob Ghabhar to Meall a' Bhuiridh; canoeing into Knoydart; dodging the Edinburgh constabulary to climb Edinburgh Castle Rock – these are just a selection of hair-brained adventures that give the LSCC its zest and savour.

So now we are a hundred years old! Our Centenary is being celebrated in fine style. In April we revisit our inaugural Boulder, where numerous toasts will be drunk. This to be followed by a dinner and ceilidh (SMC warmly invited). In May the Buachaille will be scaled by a variety of routes by members attired in clothing reflecting changing climbing fashions over the years (who's queuing up for the long skirt and nailed boots?). Thereafter some of us will head off on the 'Great Stravaig', beginning from Glencoe and ending up three weeks later in Dundonnell, having (we hope) traversed many peaks and passes en route. July sees some of us going off to Bolivia where it is hoped to climb a 6000m peak. Then in October we do some conservation work for the National Trust for Scotland in Glen Coe. Throughout the year an excellent photo-graphic display of our history will be on tour. Altogether a busy year.

So why do we continue as a women's club? Why did more of us not rush to join the SMC? Perhaps because the whole point of a women's club was to encourage women to take the lead themselves, to be pioneers, to be adventurous, confident in the knowledge of their own independence and competence. There has always been encouragement and support from the SMC, but the LSCC has helped women have their own adventures. And what's more, we actually enjoy each other's company.

In the 21st Anniversary Journal, Jane Inglis Clark wrote:

Mountaineering for women is the very best of sports, for there is no rivalry, no seeking applause, no possibility of heart-sickening sense of defeat. We leave our differences behind, and when climbing there is time to feel, to think, to be oneself. Mountaineering for women seems to have come as part of their emancipation, especially from the old conventional restraints.

We are looking forward to the next hundred years.

A GHOST OF CHRISTMAS PAST

By Graeme Morrison

'Visitors staying at the huts have no authority to allow casual persons to use the huts, whether they are members of other mountaineering clubs or not, except in cases of emergency.'

IN THE Eighties we habitually spent the weekend before Christmas at the Hut. Some years gales and rain were our lot, but more often than not we were favoured with good conditions on Creag Coire na Ciste or the Indicator Wall. On these pre-Christmas meets Crocket and Richardson were usually present, and in the long, convivial evenings the Climbs Book and Visitors' Book were spread for their scrutiny on A. E. Robertson's table. I do not know whether I derived more delight from Ken eruditely dismissing a recently-claimed route or Bob pronouncing doom upon some wretched university club who had left the dishes unwashed. For all his magisterial manner, Bob as custodian was not uncharitable, and no one could have been more solicitous for the well-being of an injured climber; but woe betide any nyaff who tapped too loudly on the window or sought to cross the threshold without invitation, because Horatius on the bridge was not more intimidating than Richardson at the door. He was my exemplar, should it ever fall to me to answer the opportunist's knock at the portal of the Charles Inglis Clark Memorial Hut.

The fly in the ointment was the food. At first our Saturday dinner was modest, but over the years it swelled to a feast, with table napkins (I ask you!) and even the ceremonious roasting of a chicken. Arguments began to arise: should Chablis or Sancerre accompany the fish course, and ought the Stilton to precede or follow the Christmas pudding? These hedonistic excesses reached a climax around 1987, when printed menus adorned a linen-clad table, and the talk was turning to a turkey for next year. Furthermore the climbing now had second place, for few can face a pre-dawn start after a night of surfeit.

The following year I resolved to spend Christmas itself at the Hut, alone. This would be a refreshingly Spartan alternative to the pre-Christmas banquet of Britain's highest dining club and would also avoid the humbug of a family gathering at home. Containing only the most frugal provisions and packed for solo climbing, my sack was easy on the shoulders as I crossed the golf course at first light on Christmas Eve. By 10 a.m. I had entered the shuttered Hut and lightened my load, before venturing into Coire na Ciste. The clouds were parting nicely, and the cornices sparkled against a blue sky. On the snowy steps of Three Gully Buttress the climbing was technically straightforward if occasionally thought-provoking for an unroped climber, and on reaching the sunlit plateau I had ample time to visit the summit before following the Arête to Càrn Mór Dearg and descending at dusk to the unoccupied Hut.

In the evening the wind got up, but within the Hut the fire was going well and the temperature had risen nicely. I had just finished my solitary meal of re-hydrated soya with Smash, and was looking forward to a dram of William Low's Five-Year Old (half the price of Hundred Pipers and little worse), when there came a knock at the door. By the time I had got to my feet, squared my shoulders, and affected a Richardsonian scowl, the blighters were trying the latch. I drew back the bolt and admitted a blast of cold air.

'What do you want?'

Outside stood a young red-haired couple, the man a little taller than the woman and both carrying monstrous packs and flap-about map cases. The man spoke with a Canadian accent.

'We are crossing to Steall, but my wife is stumbling in the dark and getting tired. In fact there is a baby on the way, and she's kind of nauseous. I wondered if we could come in and rest.'

'I am afraid this is a private hut. You have to book it through a club secretary.'

'May we shelter in the porch?'

Christmas Eve and all that. What would Bob have done? Give an inch and they'll take an ell.

'No. That is against the rules.'

'Is there any other hut nearby?'

'Nothing until you reach Steall. Well, I suppose there is the metal bivouac shelter in Coire Leis. Give me your map and I'll show you where it is located, but you will find it very draughty.'

'Thanks a million. My MacPhee granny at Cape Breton used to tell me about Highland hospitality, but we ain't seen too much of it so far.'

I bolted the door and returned to the genial whisky-toddy. Hailstones were bouncing noisily off the roof. Above the window hung the Great War photograph of Captain Inglis Clark, sepia-toned and ghostly in the gaslight, with its harrowing legend, 'Died of wounds in Mesopotamia.' What agonies had that young man suffered in the Iraqi desert, before eventually expiring? And what pre-war memories had risen to succour him, of joyous days on this distant mountainside? Was he once again roped to McIntyre and Goodeve, sure and tireless, as they plied the axe through a long December night?

My reverie was interrupted by the mouse as it scurried across the concrete floor. Before turning in, I strewed poison generously around the wainscot.

* * *

Christmas Day was clear and bright, though the wind remained blustery even down at the Hut. In hindsight Tower Ridge was a foolhardy choice, but I knew the route well, at least in summer, and moving unroped could expect to finish it comfortably in the short midwinter day. Indeed all went smoothly until in the early afternoon I reached the Great Tower. The Eastern Traverse, so often a well-trodden trench, was today a wall of iron-hard névé, thoroughly intimidating to a solo climber. By contrast Bell's direct variation, which was familiar from a summer visit, appeared from below almost snow-free, and might give a relatively safe rock climb to the top of the Tower. Upwards I therefore went, gloveless and with front points nestling on the little holds, until it became necessary to make a wide step rightwards. In rock-boots on a calm summer evening, I had skipped blithely across; today, clumsy-footed and buffeted by the winter wind, I hesitated. And the longer I hesitated the more intimidated I became, until at last conscience had made a coward of me and I began to climb down.

Perhaps my fingers had been weakened by cold; I am not sure. When the next gust caught my rucksack it knocked me off balance, so I fell backwards down the steep slab. I remember thinking, with complete detachment, that this would be fatal. In fact it was not, but when I regained consciousness darkness had fallen, and I was lying cushioned in a bed of drifted snow at the foot of the Great Tower. Blood had trickled over my eye and glued it shut, and though mercifully out of the wind I was numb with cold. One crampon was broken beyond repair and had to be discarded. Feeling sick from concussion I nevertheless forced down a couple of biscuits and fetched out the headtorch. To my surprise, it disclosed a line of footsteps leading westwards round the foot of the Tower, offering a possible escape from what was otherwise a very serious predicament. I picked up the axe and moved off.

Having only a single crampon I was glad to find the steps well made, like those cut by an alpinist of the old school, and I made rapid progress along this 'western traverse' until halted by a gully that plunged downwards into the gloom. Here was the fragrance of pipe smoke, and voices coming from the far side. Two shadowy figures seemed to be belaying a third, who was climbing down the gully using a long axe – for once the ideal implement – to cut steps in descent. I called over, 'Hello! Is this Glover's Chimney?' Came the reply, 'By Jove, it's our fourth man again! Do come across and tie on.'

On crossing the gully I roped up with the youngest of the three, a mere teenager whom the others addressed as 'Charlie'. By some trick of the torchlight he fleetingly resembled that sepia picture of the previous evening; but the face now appraising me was younger, and it lacked a military moustache. Like the others, Charlie carried a long axe and was dressed for a pheasant shoot *circa* 1907 rather than a winter climb. He explained that they were spending Christmas and New Year in Fort William and in spite of an early start had been overtaken by darkness at the foot of the Tower. Now by starlight they were engaged in a protracted struggle to escape to easier ground; and with frost-nipped extremities their jolly outing had turned into something of an ordeal. The trio had become convinced that a fourth climber was present, so were unruffled by my materialising from the darkness. (Would I care for a sandwich – roast ptarmigan with claret jelly *à l'Alexandra*? It was excellent, and I wolfed it down. Good woman this Alexandra, if a trifle extravagant.)

Given a few abseil slings and a longer rope we might have successfully descended Glover's Chimney; but lacking these modern luxuries we presently had to abandon the attempt, above a seemingly bottomless ice-pitch. Wearily we reascended the gully and took to the snowy rocks on its true left bank, where we eventually forced our way upwards to the cornice and emerged after midnight on the plateau. Here we re-roped as two pairs. My torch had long ago petered out, rendering map and compass unusable, but unerring instinct led us over the summit and down to the Arête. Now Charlie and I realised that we had lost touch with the other pair; moreover my head was hurting and double vision setting in. Descent to Coire Leis and its bivouac shelter was imperative, and Charlie would have to take charge. Baffled by my mention of the abseil posts, he nevertheless piloted us safely into the corrie. Near the tiny lochan a light was visible, towards which he steered.

The light came from a primitive sheiling, little more than a pile of stones and turves. Peat smoke percolated through the roof, and all around a herd of goats lay asleep in the snow. I turned to express my surprise to Charlie, but he had disappeared. Pushing aside a goatskin curtain, I crawled into the shelter and found it occupied by a red-bearded highlander, his wife, and a tiny infant. The man greeted me in Gaelic, but switched graciously to English on hearing my faltering reply. He was one Ewen MacPhee, well versed in goat-lore, and he had tended his flock peaceably on the good grazings of the Spean until evicted from cot and croft by Cameron of Corriechoille – or Corry, as he called him – at Lammas Day past, eighteen hundred and thirty-four. Now he was forced to overwinter with wife and bairn in this thankless boulderfield, where the beasts grew daily thinner. Would I take a bit bannock and cheese? It was all he could offer by way of sustenance.

The cheese was like Pecorino, but pungent and leathery, and the plaid in which the woman wrapped me stank of goat-urine, yet I accepted bed and board gladly and fell instantly asleep. In my dream I was blind, and Charlie was leading me short-roped over interminable screes, now bare and now blanketed in snow; yet in all our wanderings never did we leave this corrie.

When I awoke, the shelter was no bigger but its walls were of corrugated metal, and beside me crouched the Canadian couple. My head had been bathed and bandaged, and I lay cocooned in a down bag. How was I feeling? Could I manage a hot drink? Would I not do best to sleep some more?

It was broad daylight when Charlie and I left the bivouac shelter in Coire Leis and began our descent towards the Hut. From the sun's elevation this was certainly midwinter, but no trace of snow could be discerned on the Orion Face or the cliffs of Coire na Ciste, and the breeze was unseasonably soft. What is more, as we neared the CIC Hut its altered character became apparent: the building, faced with local stone, stood three storeys high and reminded me of the Britannia Hut at Saas. From a flagstaff on the roof fluttered a stylised rope and crossed axes, while high on the gable glowed a giant fluorescent-tubed snow bunting, powered no doubt by that coppice of wind turbines across the burn. As I approached the building, I could read the tariff displayed at the side of the door: besides bed, breakfast and Christmas lunches was advertised *local compost, ideal for mushroom cultivation, €20 per kg.*

The portly custodian standing in the doorway was seasonally red-suited and tassle-hatted, Peet-like at first glance but whiter of beard. I approached him up the wheelchair ramp.

'What can I do for you?' he asked.

'I'll be staying a night or two. Perhaps you don't know me, but I am a member actually.'

'I am afraid that's a thing of the past. We are full tonight: an elderly Canadian pair have just taken the last room. And don't even think of kipping in the radio shack.'

Turning despondently on my heel, I overbalanced and tumbled off the ramp.

* * *

It was just as well I had slept in the lower bunk, for the floor felt very hard. When I opened my eyes the grey light of dawn was filtering through the windows. On the table stood the economy blend, still half full. Outside the Hut I could hear voices and the mustering of ice screws, as an early party took a breather after the travail of the Allt a' Mhuilinn.

Perhaps they would like a cup of tea.

FOR OUR EYES ONLY

By Guy Robertson

ONE OF the great things about going winter climbing in Scotland is the delectably fickle nature of the conditions. On the one hand, they mock the dogged weekender with all shocking regularity, but on the other they dispense to the vigilant some of the most outrageously ephemeral and unique climbing experiences our planet has to offer. Keep taking your chances, stay optimistic, and eventually you'll find yourself something you'll know in an instant is for your eyes only.

I suspect that's exactly how the other pair felt looking up from the CIC hut on the first Saturday of February 2008, the pre-dawn murk slowly dissipating into light. The previous day, the Arctic Pipeline had opened up like a popped Champagne bottle, a vicious 'flash' storm freezing anything liquid along the full length of the Western sea board. The result was a sight to behold. It was like a scene from some great science fiction epic, first impressions suggesting everything was sodden and running with water, but closer inspection revealing the world had in fact been cryogenically suspended. Benson and I first noticed it when we arrived at the hut, the southern aspect completely smothered in fully eight inches of what appeared to be frozen semen. 'Hah! Imagine if this stuff's all over the crag!' we'd joked. Rather prophetically as it turned out.

The other pair were Steve Ashworth and Viv Scott, well known winter obsessives, and on this occasion overnight residents at the Ben's own *Haute Hotel*. We didn't clock their presence until I looked over my shoulder near the foot of the crag – 'Hey Pete, there's a couple of knights in armour heading up behind us!' Heading up they most certainly were, and with a clear urgency about their demeanour. They must be heading up into Coire na Ciste, I assumed; crazy bastards given all the precarious new snow. Negative. As we spread out our kit below the towering, plastered fissure marking the line of Centurion, the intrepid duo presently arrived, inquiring politely as to our day's objective.

I guess it was maybe a rhetorical question. Whatever, with a metaphorical piss on our lamp post, I expected their psyche to shift keenly, to re-engage with something else amongst the myriad of possibilities that the storm had bestowed on us. But no, they stood firm, speechless but expectant, as if waiting for compensation. 'You're not seriously going to wait it out and climb up behind us are you?!' I stabbed. It was a vicious but necessary blow, delivered with conviction.

Once our comrades had numbly departed, and with our bowels routinely emptied, we got to the business of working out who was on the starting blocks. As ever this was simple; whoever had not lead the previous pitch. That's the great thing about a regular partnership – no egos, no faffing, and no avoiding one's duties; just take it in turn and get on with it. Unfortunately for me this meant on this particular occasion Yours Truly was in the hot seat, a not entirely enviable position given the horror that lurked above.

Those first impressions at the hut had been a sampler for what now overhung us, and we couldn't quite believe it. Every inch of the crag, in all directions, was completely draped in ice. Some of it looked useful, some of it didn't. Huge drooling fangs hung menacingly from the belly of the great roofs under the Bat traverse, almost tricking the imagination into thinking a winter way was possible. Under normal circumstances, for the majority of winter climbers, such a copious icy carpet would be pure eye candy, but to us pair of mixed tricksters it set alarm bells ringing. It might assist upward progress, but would we be able to find protection?

Centurion in summer is a long, sustained Hard Very Severe, so clearly in winter it wouldn't be easy. The idea of just 'knuckling down and running it out' – acceptable enough on steep ice – wasn't something either of us felt inclined to explore on a mixed route such as this. As I started out, the points of my picks biting keenly into sticky slots on the cracked left wall of the corner, a distinct air of indecision and uncertainty wafted tangibly between us. It was immediately steep, but the placements were good; a tentative pull, then another, crossing through, mono-points biting into a thick sheen on the rock. Twenty feet up and a mild panic began to evolve, warm ripples of lactate swelling surely in my forearms, threatening to creep out terminally towards frozen, fumbling fingers. Fortunately at this point a generous foothold appeared, coupled nicely with a winking crack just the width for a nut. A wide bridge, a shake-out, some deep breadths and a bit of positive banter sent the doubts of the previous ten minutes whistling off down the glen. We were open for business, and battle had commenced.

The route now unravelled slowly, majestic and beautiful. A precarious step right popped me back to a perch at the base of the corner proper, where the steepness intensified and frozen glue clung all around. From here, the second pitch soared up into a feast of overhangs, powerful and uncompromising. I hoped it might prove easier than its brutal appearance suggested. The Benson motor dropped a gear as he swung assuredly past my stance, firing head-on with vigour into a series of torquing laybacks up a succession of chimney slots. It was a big pitch and a lengthy lead. By the time Pete reached the sloping belay the weather was revealing its colours for the day. Bemoaning the extra gravity of our shared rucksack, I joined him at the belay in flurries of spindrift.

Pitch three was sheer gold. A delicate traverse led out left, largely footless, but with good snow-ice across a series of flat edges at shoulder height. The exposure exploded in and out of swirls in the mist, until finally clearing as I swung into a series of grooves tucked in behind the left arête. For the first time now I could pull the throttle back, scurrying up past the odd runner like the proverbial Arctic rat. Ten metres or so up and the brain game resumed, the corner line reforming to my right above a sea of giant overhangs. The guidebook said step right, boldly out over the overhangs, but I couldn't help thinking going direct looked like the option. Experience told me to trust my instincts, but I followed the summer line, some sketchy teeters and short breaths taking me up right as instructed. The dubious sanctuary of a hanging stance was secured, and I called down to Pete to get his skates on.

Down below, on the screes, I could see two frustrated-looking little figures pottering about, making their way down slowly, but stopping every now and then to cast a glance back up at our progress. It was Ashworth and Scott. I was temped to shout something irreverent but thought better of it – they'd suffered enough, I reasoned. In any case, no doubt as they felt the unmistakable nip of a gathering storm against their cheeks, they were reasoning to themselves that perhaps it had not all been bad fortune that had rebuffed them from their objective. Or maybe they were just sticking pins into little *Berghaus dolls*. I thought briefly about the climbing still above us. The next pitch would be hard, then that should largely be it. We'd probably make it to easier ground by nightfall, but then we'd have to fight it out in darkness. I'd climbed three other big routes in the previous two weeks, and all of them had involved some form of torch-assisted finale; standard fare for hard mixed climbing in a Scottish January. No surprise then that here I felt confident, slightly cocky even, whistling merrily to the tune of 'Two Little Boys' as Pete whipped out my runners and scampered up below.

I can't really remember precisely when it all kicked off, but it must have been just after I'd seconded the fourth pitch. Things tend to go a bit fuzzy in the strange, lonely stupor of climbing into the night. Pete had faltered a bit on that pitch, though not unduly, as much torn between choices as anything else. But soon enough he pulled the rope tight, as I stretched left to the arête, feet cutting loose and swinging down before being thrown away up high onto the only lonely foothold. The last glimpses of daylight were dissolving over my shoulders, and the flutters of snow were becoming more frequent. I don't think we noticed that the wind was gathering strength.

Half an hour later, ten metres into the fifth pitch, it was dark. It was now snowing hard, and the wind was gale force. We'd been on the route for about nine hours at this point, with the most technical climbing behind us, but a growing awareness of the scale of the challenge ahead

Guy Robertson and Pete Benson on the third pitch of Centurion, Ben Nevis. Photo: Viv Scott.

quickly eliminated any thoughts of celebration. To make matters worse, an easing of angle meant there was now two feet of snow obliterating the rock. Stupidly, I had left my headtorch in the belay jacket below. I couldn't find any protection, and verbal contact was severely curtailed. This was the first of our three 'easy' exit pitches, and here I was, screaming, utterly desperate.

The next pitch would take us up to, and then across, the famous Route II traverse, and would undoubtedly involve lots of digging and soul searching across thickly plastered slabs. Then a further pitch would skirt right under the steep upper section of the buttress, into grooves in the crest. From above these, something like a hundred metres or so of grade II-ish ground should lead finally to Ledge Route, and our proposed line of descent. As I clung above a limp rope, face pressed hard into the snow, adding all this painful detail up in my head, I felt a bit like the boy in the sweet shop who's just realised he doesn't have money. Our adventure was just beginning, and the fact had got stuck in my throat.

'TIE!...IT!...ON!...TO!...THE!...BLUE!...ROPE!!!' Again and again I screamed the instructions into the murk, my shouts becoming softer as my throat dried out. Each time, nothing. Pete either disagreed, or misunderstood my request. I couldn't move without that bloody torch, and right now I felt like jumping on his head, stupid bastard. Eventually I deciphered a muffled 'OK!' and started yanking the blue line, praying the axe in my other hand would hold. The torch appeared on a knot in the rope. Jesus, was that so difficult?

With the torch on, protection was forthcoming, but typical of such predicaments it wasn't particularly inspiring. I remember a limp Hex, rocking alarmingly, but too deep in its seating to be hammered into place. I was stuck fast between two parallel grooves, clinging to a sort of bulging rib between them, with one axe placed in either side, holding a koala-like pose. It was precisely the kind of inefficient and precarious lodgement one attains when climbing frantically without thought. I kicked myself inside, furious with my carelessness. Very gingerly, I crossed first right foot then right axe over into the left-hand groove, quickly stamping my left foot out onto some deep snow to stabilise my position. Wiping the memory of the Hex from my mind's eye I continued, battle-frenzied now, hacking and mantling into the driving sleet, my feet up by my axes. A few more feet and a little stance afforded a belay. I tugged at Pete to follow on the rope.

We weighed up the options, or so we pretended. In reality, there were two – abseil off, or keep going into the thick of it. We were already battle-weary, and with at least two roped pitches to go the climbing was far from finished. A deafening storm raged about us, huddled fast in our nook, nibbling energy bars and searching for inspiration. 'Listen, I've been here before. It's not difficult, we might as well keep going!' Pete

Pete Benson on the fourth pitch of Centurion, Ben Nevis, 2 February 2008. Photo: Guy Robertson.

screamed at me assertively, 'I'm pretty keen to bag this little beggar after all that effort!' I mumbled in agreement, though in truth I wasn't convinced. It seemed to contradict my instincts to climb wittingly up into the teeth of a blizzard, knowing full well that even once we got to the top our descent would be highly dangerous. And all for the sake of a few pitches of grade V at most. On the other hand Pete was right – the first ascent party had bivouacked just below this point, so to turn back now would mean unequivocal failure. He led off briskly, whistling to himself. I slumped onto the belay, turned my headtorch off, and shut my eyes from the maelstrom. My eyeballs burned with a searing white light.

The rope had been static for about half an hour when I switched the torch back on. Shuffling round and trying to look up between gusts, I could just make out the dancing shadows from Pete's torch. He had gained maybe ten metres or so in an hour and a half. The storm was still gathering force, and the temperature was rising. I slumped back again, only this time I felt water running down my chest, across my belly and down inside my shorts. It couldn't get any worse. Then Pete was shouting from above, but I struggled to interpret him, until after ten minutes or so I gathered he was proposing I used a back rope. He could clearly see a hard traverse right without the promise of protection, and was looking out for me on the blunt end. Perhaps he sensed my apathy crawling up the rope. Whatever, in my frozen little penance it was a nice, warm thought.

I think we would have reached the junction with Ledge Route at around 11 p.m., but the chaos and darkness combined with such ferocity that we couldn't identify it. By that time the thaw had well and truly set in, and what we previously knew to be a perilous avalanche risk all of a sudden had worsened. The situation was grim. Every tired step created giant sludge balls on the base of our crampons, slowing us up further and threatening to skitter us off the mountain. Descending on this side wasn't an option – even if we could have found the way – as the snow was in such condition now as to release at the faintest trigger. Resigned to our fate, but uncomfortable with it, we trudged on, untied. Memories of the hard climbing were remote up there, and I giggled inwardly at the insanity of this compulsive desire, sensing the descent was near and allowing a fleeting moment of humour. Then Pete fired down his shot from above, 'Guy, have you got a compass?!'

His words arrested me, igniting a sudden panic like that of a bride jilted at the altar. A compass. A little piece of magnetized plastic that helps you get down safely. One of those bits of kit that very rarely gets used but in certain situations separates life from death. Of course, I didn't have one, or at least I was pretty sure of it, remembering it had lived in the map pocket of my old shell jacket. I'd given the jacket away, but hadn't replaced the compass. In a rather desperate and futile bid to restore order I asked the same question in return. No he didn't have one, why on earth would he have asked?

We sat fixed to the summit cairn, exhausted and vulnerable, the freezing rain building thick rime across the lee of our sodden bodies. Visibility was zero, but our eyes were clamped shut. We couldn't hear beyond the howl of the wind, but didn't care to listen. In total whiteout, with creeping damp, and no firm grip of what might come next, the cairn was soon our only reference in a swirl of impossibilities. We clung there a while, unwilling to let go and unable to commit. It was now well after midnight, and I reckon in retrospect I'd have survived maybe an hour at most. My 'wardrobe malfunction' had left me soaked to the core and I was shivering uncontrollably.

Beside me, something barked loudly, awakening my fuzzy head. I turned to see Pete kneeling, head hung low, shouting at the rock, pounding an axe in frustration. It just shouldn't have happened, that was it and we both knew it. We also knew that getting going was now critical, as our wet clothes had began to freeze and our core temperatures were plummeting. Yes, get going, but where? We assessed then re-assessed the guidebook's little sketch map, trying to retain perspective on which direction we'd come up from. Straight ahead and slightly rightwards, but not too far right. Be wary of anything at all steep. Just a steady, even descent to the top of the Red Burn, from where we couldn't really go wrong. We knew the overhanging crags of the Castle Face lurked just to our right, precisely the direction the hurricane would be blowing us.

Our first attempt failed in blind panic, the steady descent we were praying for ending abruptly where the rocks underfoot disappeared, replaced instead by nothingness, just pure white space. More than twenty hours in, with empty tanks and dying limbs, our imaginations needed no catalyst to have us wandering terminally off into the abyss. We were lucky to regain the cairn, our footprints painted out behind us within seconds of each step. Going back down the face was again touted as an option, but I sensed Pete's desperation. Don't get side-tracked, stick to your bearing (or whatever you have in its place) and move steadily and confidently. It was becoming increasingly difficult to grasp any sort of safe, rational strategy; psychologically, we were stumbling.

On the second attempt we stayed further left, embracing the consensus that a long walk out from Glen Nevis was daunting, but safe. Twenty minutes down and it happened – we were spared. The clouds parted below us. Ahead and to our right the soft lights of Fort William beckoned, their ochre twinkle shooting warmth into our souls. The mouth of the Red Burn was immediately below us, full of nice soft snow

– we were home and dry at last. Two hours or whatever still to go, through drenched bog, raging torrents, and away off down the forestry track – I'd have happily ran the lot, down and back if that's what was needed. We had reached salvation, and would have given anything for it.

Just beyond the halfway lochan, we stopped and festered, drank a bit, and dozed. It was 3 a.m. I noticed Pete was talking on his mobile phone, but thought nothing of it, my brain melted through an overdose of relief. Flushed of emotion, I couldn't think. Throwing a glance over my shoulder, back up the Allt a' Mhuilinn and on to the crags where we had climbed, I could make out the bottom of Carn Dearg below a quilt of mist. It was stripped bare, jet black and no doubt running with water. Snaps of the route flickered through me – the white and the cold, sticky ice. The anticipation of walking in, the excitement of our first glimpse, and then all the relieved bravado of climbing surely through the crux pitches. It was still there, just overshadowed temporarily. But gone was the route, washed away, quite literally, and within the space of a single day. It might wait for another twenty years, or even more. I ponder this thought quite deliciously now, in the knowledge that something amazing has been gifted to us. Something exciting and totally unique, that had stretched us beyond reason. For our eyes only.

FATAL ERROR

By John Burns

THE LEADER confronts his demons head on but the second man on the rope suffers a much sterner ordeal; trial by imagination. Steve had been a long time on that freezing stance watching the yellow ropes snake away into the spindrift. Far too much time, wondering about how secure the belay was, considering the possibility of plunging down the icy face and into the corrie below, enough time for his mind's eye to replay that horror show several times over and, worse, to imagine its consequences.

Now and again a few words would be carried down the route by the wind, 'London's burning with boredom now!' Sandy sang as he battled with gravity, ice, spindrift and fear.

'Please God, no more punk,' thought Steve, with vivid recollections of his drive to Ben Nevis in Sandy's ancient Mazda.

'It's an amazing thing the Internet, isn't it?' Sandy had said, his huge shoulders filling the doorway of Steve's flat. Moments later Steve was embarking on the longest car journey of his life. Two and a half hours of nerve jangling driving followed as Sandy raced the dawn up Loch Lomond side. Sandy was no conversationalist and filled the car with deafening seventies punk rock, slamming tape after tape into the old squealing cassette player, pausing only to curse to himself as he rummaged on the car floor for the adolescent outpourings of his long-dead heroes.

This he accompanied by occasional tuneless outbursts and clouds of acrid smoke emanating from the small brown roll-ups he manufactured whilst overtaking lorries on blind corners. The car had barely stopped when Steve leaped out into the sweet, cold air of the early morning – his eyes streaming and his ears ringing. Sandy's comment about the Internet had been the only phrase to pass his lips during the whole drive up from the Central Belt and Steve was now seriously doubting the wisdom of locating climbing partners over the Internet. His mind returned to nights in the pub and dire warnings from his friends about the people you meet on the information superhighway. They had gleefully regaled him with stories of Internet brides whose age, physical attributes and even gender had proved to be fiction once the glowing screen had shut down and the revelation of an airport meeting had turned into stark reality. Steve fumbled desperately in his sack for his water bottle and was flushing away the dry taste of fear from his mouth when Sandy's voice tore through the stillness of the morning air.

'No future,' he sang, with a great deal more enthusiasm than talent. Steve turned to follow the sound of the vocals and was able to study his companion for the first time that morning. He was a powerful man, that much was evident, tall and broad-shouldered, his features gaunt and his mass of dark hair flecked with grey. It was hard to say how old he was, forty perhaps, maybe fifty or even older, his ears and eyebrows pierced by rings. His accent, what little Steve had heard of it, was east coast Scottish, possibly Aberdonian in origin. It was an educated accent but there was an unmistakable roughness to the voice. Steve had climbed with a handful of partners; his shift work had made finding a regular partner difficult. The Internet had seemed the obvious solution to mid-week days off, now he was less certain of its benefits. Suddenly Steve realised that his companion was already heading off across the golf course towards the looming mass of the Ben. He struggled to push his feet into resisting boots and was halfway across the golf course before he began to wonder why they were not using the new North Face car park as he had always done in the past.

The drive and the walk up into the corrie were history now as a sudden tug on the rope brought Steve back from memories of the morning. Whatever his doubts about his partner, halfway up a route on the Ben, with the weather breaking and darkness coming the word commitment carries a potency it lacks in everyday life. There was no choice but to follow the rope wherever it led. Sandy was a strange guy, Steve decided, reflecting on climbing's ability to attract the renegade, the odd, and the downright peculiar. Day trippers in a land where only the laws of life and death are revered, some find the journey back to normality difficult to make. Days on the hill are Technicolor, days in the street fade to black and white.

Soon movement had brought life back into frozen fingers and the demands of the climb drove all other thoughts from Steve's mind. The route was harder than he had expected, not desperate, within his abilities but nevertheless the fragility of the ice held his attention. Minutes later he was gasping on the stance beside Sandy and noticed the letters SM written on the old slings passed to him by Sandy. Clearly Sandy was a man who held on to everything, his climbing gear was the same vintage as his car.

'What's the M for,' Steve asked in an attempt to encourage some conversation from his taciturn companion.

'Murder,' Sandy grinned, and for the first time seemed to show a little humanity in an otherwise dark countenance. 'Madison, that's my name, like the avenue, man.' Sandy seemed relaxed, confident, and his attitude eased Steve's concerns at climbing with this 1970s relic. Steve led the next pitch, an easy snow slope, until Sandy's bulk again joined him on the small stance, crushing Steve's smaller frame against the rock. Above them loomed an awkward-looking crack with a short fierce overhang at its top. This was obviously the crux of the climb. 'That crack looks hard,' Sandy said, in a hoarse whisper, more to himself than anyone else.

He grabbed a friend from Steve's rack and paused for a moment examining the movement of the cams, fascinated, like a small boy watching a fly drowning in a jam jar.

'I'll lead it if you like,' Steve offered, sensing an uncertainty in his companion he'd not seen before, 'I think I could …' Steve's conversation was rendered pointless as Sandy lurched away towards the next pitch. Steve was growing tired of his taciturn partner, a man who seemed determined to shrug off any human contact, and disliked being treated like an film extra in what Sandy obviously saw as his starring role in a personal battle with the route.

By now the spindrift avalanches were blinding and Steve stood for what seemed an age on the small stance while Sandy struggled with the crack. 'I'm coming off!' Sandy shouted down. Steve peered up into the falling snow expecting Sandy to come careering down the face, but no flailing body appeared through the spindrift. Steve started to relax; at length the rope moved on and he soon followed finding the friend Sandy had taken from his rack twisted and battered in a crack.

Minutes later, as darkness settled on the mountain, both men stood on the summit coiling their ropes and allowing the tension of the hours of climbing to trickle out of them. 'What happened to this?' Steve asked, holding out the battered friend. 'Sorry,' Sandy replied with a wry grin, 'I had a few problems there.' At that point the wind eased and the snow cleared and suddenly the summit of the Ben lay before them glittering in the moonlight. It was as though the mountain recognised their efforts and now, having paid their dues, it gave them a reward and showed them a sight few men see. Even Sandy was moved by the sight. 'Look at that,' he said, 'I can die happy now.' He stood up, hauled his sack on his back, and turned to Steve before they set off down the hill, 'You know that guy who said all we have to fear is fear itself. Well he never climbed on the Ben, I'm sure of that.' Both laughed, and Sandy belched lungfuls of acrid smoke into the night air. The tension was gone between them now, all danger passed, and they walked down towards the twinkling lights of Fort William, travellers in another world, suspended somewhere between the stars above and the man-made lights below.

It was the early hours of the morning when Steve finally hurled his sack into a corner of his small flat. Unable to sleep and with no work the following day he unwound with beer, pizza and late night TV. His mind replayed the day's events and, for some reason he couldn't tie down, Sandy's name kept coming back to him with an odd familiarity. Finally tiredness overwhelmed him and he fell into a restless sleep in his armchair before the flickering TV. It was perhaps five in the morning when he awoke with a jolt numb from sleeping in the seat. Sandy Madison, he had heard that name before! Half an hour's frantic search through climbing magazines found the article he was looking for. There it was; Alexander Madison, the article stated, killed some thirty years ago on the very climb he had just completed with a man of the same name. He just had to tell Sandy, even the morose ageing punk would laugh at that; he quickly rattled off an e-mail to the man he'd spoken to more over the Internet than face to face. Clicking 'send' he rose and stretched, now ready for bed, leaning over to switch off the computer he noticed an e-mail pop into his inbox. It was a response to his e-mail to Sandy. He read it through bleary sleep-filled eyes.

'Mail delivery failed, address not known, fatal error.'

A TALE OF DANGEROUS OBSESSION

By Gordon Smith

KINGY, Terry to everyone else but me, and I had planned a summertime in the Alps for 1975. We had planned this as we defrosted in the warmth of his caravan after some very cold nights spent curled up like husky dogs in the snow outside the CIC hut. We did indeed go to the Alps that summer for our first season together, and we climbed this and that, including the Shroud on the Grandes Jorasses with Dirty Alex. For some reason, which escapes me after thirty years of doing other things, instead of climbing up the ice chute leading to the great ice field of the Shroud we climbed up very steep and very difficult rocks littered here and there with sections of faded fixed rope, soft steel pitons and old bits of tat. And then, after a five or six pitches of this, we traversed wildly into the top of the left-hand chute (or right-hand chute if you are one of the French guidebook writers who always are looking down when we Brits are looking up – leaving us enormously confused). What we climbed, entirely free as far as we went, by skirting round the hard bits on the left or pushing Kingy, our secret weapon, up them on the sharp end, was the start of René Desmaison's route on the North West Face of the Walker Spur. Thus began an obsession with the climb, for I had seen pictures of Desmaison and Serge Gousseault, his doomed companion, stormbound on the first attempt, and Desmaison with his nephew Michel Claret and the Italian guide Giorgio Bertone on the successful ascent in 1973, in Paris Match while a schoolboy in Scotland. And now I had seen the climb itself. Kingy wasn't interested. He wanted us to go to Afghanistan with our Polish friends. Dirty Alex wasn't interested. He wanted to go to Afghanistan with Kingy and the Poles instead of me and, seeing as he had money and I only had a broken leg and a sore head after a debacle on the Ben, he went and I got left behind to my own devices.

Black Nick Colton was around, however, and without a partner, and he agreed to come with me to climb Desmaison's Route on the Walker Spur. And he agreed in the full knowledge that I was still then gimping along on a bionic leg full of titanium rods and screws after that little mishap on the wintry slopes of Ben Nevis. Ah, Black Nick. Now he may be a Respected Mountaineering Bureaucrat but in those days he was a black haired, black moustached young hooligan, one of the bad boys of the Biolay campsite along with Kingy, Dirty Alex, Blond Nicky and me. As a gang of thieves we had, directed by our indomitable leader, 'Our Man From the Petits Charmoz' Colin Somebody or Other, raided a building site in the centre of Chamonix and walked away like a gigantic centipede with an enormous roll of thick and heavy polythene on our heads. Through the centre of town. In the middle of the night. Without being caught. Enough polythene to provide the Biolay campers with kitchen shelters for many years to come. Black Nick, good lad, he would come and do the climb with me.

We huddled together in the early June rain in 1977, under a polythene kitchen shelter, and made our plans. We didn't have much gear, for a climb reputed to be one of the great routes of the Alps, graded EDsup, and on which the first ascentionists had used over three hundred pitons. But we both had Terrordactyls and the confidence, nurtured in the Scottish winter, to climb in any weather on just about anything just so long as there was some ice around somewhere. We packed our sacks and coiled up our ropes and took the train up to Montenvers, being lazy buggers, and walked along the Mer de Glace and the Leschaux Glacier moraines up to the hut below the North Face of the Grandes Jorasses.

Alain, the Leschaux Man, guardian of the hut and my pal from seasons past, was concerned at our sacks for such a 'grand excursion' and concerned that, as usual, we had no guidebook or route description. Oh well. We had done 'Le Linceul'. We had done 'Le Walker'. We had done 'Le Croz'. We knew Les Grandes Jorasses and what we were doing, or so we all thought. We promised him, though, as we left the hut sometime after midnight filled generously with his chocolat chaud, that we would signal with a head torch every night so that he could monitor our progress. And so we intended, although we didn't intend to spend more than one night on the climb.

We couldn't be bothered to go around the corner and start up the same way that Kingy, Dirty Alex and I had started the Shroud. There was a better way. Closer. In the rimaye at the very bottom of the crag.

The first pitch of the route we chose to climb, after a tenuous and sugary creep out of the rimaye and up the little snow slope above it, was a loose wall topped by an overhang. I had led the climb out of the rimaye so I declared that it was Nick's job to lead up the loose wall and over the horrible roof. And so he did. It was not that he didn't whimper a little. It was not that he didn't drop a few rocks, including most of the holds, on top of me. It was not that the ropes didn't shiver, electric, with the expectation of a tumble. It was that he led the thing without falling off and with such a spirited burst of Elan Anglais that Desmaison himself would have been proud to be called English.

He tied himself to something a little less loose than most of the bits of rock up there and then he dragged me up after him. We climbed on and on up mixed ground that wasn't hard and that wasn't easy until we reached a fine looking channel of green ice, shaded at this time of year from the sun and therefore hard and brittle. I wandered up the ice to a large flake, where an old and faded bit of fixed line came in from the left. I tied myself to the flake and thought to myself that this thing was big so it shouldn't fall down. I mean, it didn't tremble at my touch. It didn't squeak. It didn't give any other sign of being anything other than a big, solid belay. But just in case and because it cost nothing, and everyone knows that if it doesn't cost anything a Scotsman is well likely to look for at least some benefit from it, I clipped a jumar that I carried for just such things onto that old, faded bit of rope that Desmaison had left there years and years before.

The route ahead looked like a doddle mostly, I realised later, because of foreshortening and not because it was easy. Nick crunched and banged his way up the brittle green ice. As his black moustachioed face hove to between my legs I moved aside, as a gentleman should, to let him pass. And as I moved, so did that great big tombstone flake. It gravelled and ground around like a bloody great molar ready to pop out. And pop out it did. Rolling right over my foot and squashing my expensive chrome-moly steel crampon flat. And rolling right over the expensive ropes. And it carried on rolling down, Nick scrunching himself quick as a cat into the smallest ball you ever saw and out of its way, with a great rumble like a clap of thunder and a cloud of black smoke shot through with sparks that looked and smelled like Trafalgar or Jutland being fought on the flanks of the Grandes Jorasses.

Down the way we had come it rolled and roared, a sight that entertained our friends climbing on the Petites Jorasses five miles away, disintegrating into millions of pieces that soiled the snow fifteen hundred feet below us in a vast, dirty triangle that disappeared over the edge of a crevasse. I was left dangling from that tatty old bit of rope while Nick, who didn't know about the jumar and the tatty old bit of rope, was left wondering when I would start to roll down our route in the wake of the tombstone and pull him down with me to a place where we could begin to climb the heavenly mountains partnered by angels. Or, in Nick's case, down to stoke the devil's furnaces with shovels full of black coal.

The pair of us were left shivering with shock, and we still had to abseil back down our fifteen hundred feet of climbing with the ropes all chopped up, and me with a gammy foot as well as a gammy leg. Fortunately the foot and leg were both on the same side, leaving me one entirely good leg to hop on. We got back down to the glacier because we had to. And the little nicks in the ropes became long sections of bare insides, where only a few of the strands remained intact.

Now, instead of going back down our own route we nipped around the corner and down the line of stuff on the left, the stuff that Kingy, Dirty Alex and I had followed for some way coming up years before. We even found a faded Millet sack on the way down, not far below our high point, filled with old soft steel pitons and Camping Gaz canisters. So, being poor Brits as we were, we cut it off intending to pick up the old pitons and gas canisters at the bottom of the face. Unfortunately it, too, burst into a zillion pieces like the tombstone before it and almost all the pieces followed the tombstone down into the depths of the crevasse. We carried on abseiling down, tying off bits of bootlace and jamming the knots into cracks as abseil anchors wherever there were no old pitons conveniently in place.

Down on the glacier my foot hurt like hell when I tried to walk on it and so I took my boot off to have a look and to see if it was broken. Instantly the foot swelled up like a bullfrog preparing to mate or like a blowfish in a tizzy, and I couldn't for the life of me put my boot back on.

There I was stuck on the glacier with only one boot on, and the other foot looking like a barrage balloon in a dirty sock. But I was friendly in those days with Schmutz of the Peloton de Gendarmerie de Haute Montagne (PGHM they called themselves) and I told Nick to run down and see if Schmutz would come up with his helicopter and give me a ride down. Nick ran off, filled with good intentions, and I settled down in the snow, admiring the blue sky and the lovely, snowy peaks all around, to wait for my ride.

I waited for a long time. I brewed up the occasional cup of cold water. I nibbled on our bivouac food. I chatted with climbers, lots of climbers, walking past filled with resolve to climb their climbs with derring-do. Without exception each group asked me what climb I was headed for. How embarrassing. 'Well, actually, I was going to climb up there, but a rock landed on my foot and now my foot's swollen up, see, look at it, and I can't put my boot on, and I'm waiting for my friend to come and get me with his helicopter, and my partner left quite a while ago and I've been sitting here for bloody hours. And no-one has come!'

They all shrugged and went off to do their respective things. As the sun fell below the horizon, and as the cold tendrils of night started to darken the glacier I prepared myself for a lonely bivouac lying on my polythene bag in the snow. And I made my plans for a long crawl down the glacier, like Doug Scott on the Baltoro, on the morrow. But with the last of the light Schmutz came for me with his helicopter and whisked me down to the valley.

I wanted just to get out of the helicopter and hobble back to the Biolay campsite to lick my wounds, but they were having none of that. Journalists flashed their flashbulbs and wrote little notes to themselves, and Very Big French Gendarmes escorted me into the hospital where the nurses, for reasons known only to themselves, put me into the maternity ward among the babies.

Lots of nurses came to look at M. l'alpiniste Anglais (I chose not to correct this presumption) lying in his bed in the maternity ward, among the babies. It was actually rather fun. Lots of pretty young nurses came to see.

The next day Nick came to visit and explained, very sheepishly, that he'd seen a helicopter flying up the Mer de Glace and had assumed that Alain from the Leschaux Hut had seen what had happened and that the helicopter was for me. When he'd come in the late afternoon with Blond Nicky to visit no one had heard of me at the hospital, so they had realised Nick's error and had run off to explain what had happened to my pal Schmutz.

I was booted out, after a couple of days fretting about the bill, with a plaster cast on my leg and a pair of crutches that I had to promise to return. I spent the next several weeks hitch hiking between Leysin, where I once was one of those notorious ISM instructors, and Chamonix. Keeping an eye on my route. And the border guards became so suspicious of me passing the frontier to and fro with a cast on my leg that they took to yelling at me about drug smuggling and poking long sharp things down my cast, with scant success in the search for drugs except that the long sharp things scratched the itchy bits down my cast that really wanted scratching and caused me great pleasure.

As the days passed I became more and more obsessed with the climb, however, and with the gear that I was sure was stashed on it close to the top, until eventually I cut off the cast myself with a penknife and hitch hiked back to Chamonix and persuaded some fool to come with me to do the climb and recover all that mythical booty. Three times I hobbled to the foot of the climb with different fools whom I had suckered with my stories, and three times my foot hurt so much, with the bones grinding around inside, that I gave it up as a bad job. In the end I hitch hiked back to Scotland and went to visit my friendly ortho doctor at Bridge of Earn hospital who had looked after my broken leg with all its Raigmore pins and needles four months before. By that time the bones in my foot had already fused into a lump and the doctor said he couldn't do anything for me and just sent me home with a flea in my ear for being such a burden on the NHS.

Of course, the minute I was home I was packing up my stuff and away I went, hitch hiking with a will in the direction of the Grandes Jorasses. When I got back to the Biolay at the end of September, however, Black Nick had already gone off with RBJ onto the Whymper Spur. So I was left again partnerless. But someone knew someone, who knew someone, who had come across an American who didn't have any gear but who was looking for someone with whom to climb an Alpine North Face. And that was how I met Tobin Sorenson, the wildest, looniest, luckiest climber alive. Until the day he unfortunately fell off from high up some mountain face in Canada while soloing, which is never a lucky thing to do.

I'd seen a photograph in a book, some time or other, of Tobin laybacking under a flake on hand jams, or so the caption said, and looking as if something nasty had approached him affectionately from behind. I knew, from that book, that Tobin was one of the top rock climbers in the US, one of the Stonemasters. What I didn't know was that the expression on Tobin's face was characteristic of the kind of trouble that Tobin constantly got himself into while climbing.

According to John Long, another Stonemaster, whose article 'The Green Arch' I read many years later, no-one was better than Tobin, who tended to rush pell-mell at any climb, on a straightforward route that was just plain hard. But no-one was worse on any climb that required devious thought and cunning. He took the most appalling whippers, astounding his climbing friends that he could walk away from them and still come back for more. But the very fact that Tobin had arrived in the Alps without any equipment at all and looking to go straight onto a big Alpine North Wall never having climbed in the Alps before warned me straight away that here was a climber just like me. There was just one, small, issue given that we managed to solve the gear problem. Tobin knew nothing about alpine mixed climbing. And my route (for it was now 'my route' in my head and to hell with Desmaison) was a big alpine North Face route with lots of alpine mixed climbing and not some sun-drenched granite spire.

Of course we got along famously once we had met each other, seeing as we were so alike in our attitudes. And yet Tobin was quiet and very shy allowing me to babble on and on enough, in the way that I had, for the two of us. I suggested that we should do a training climb and then tackle 'my climb' on the Walker Spur. Naturally Tobin agreed, like a horse that has been tied in shackles for far too long.

I chose to approach a couloir climb, an ice climb, on the West Face of the Plan which I knew would be in condition after all the bad weather I had missed. Tobin borrowed a Chouinard ice axe, hammer and pair of Salewa crampons from some generous American who wasn't using them just then, probably Rick Accomazzo, another of those Stonemasters. He was equipped. He had his tartan shirt, or 'plaid' shirt as he preferred to call it because he wasn't a Scotsman and therefore ignorant, and he had an anorak, blue jeans, and an old pair of climbing boots that he had worn into Eastern Europe while smuggling bibles, or some such foolishness.

Our route had an easy approach from the meadows at the half way station of the Midi Telepherique. It also had an easy 'descent' along the Arête Midi-Plan to the Telepherique station on top of the Midi. Yet the climbing would be quite hard. That I knew from earlier adventuring on the West Face of the Plan as the butt end for Kingy's jokes in his scribblings for Mountain Mag. It would be the perfect training climb for us. And it would be new.

The start of our training climb was a granite slab, thinly covered with slush, that led up into a narrow gully blocked by an ice bulge that well could have decorated Green Gully on Ben Nevis. We set off at midday, creeping up through the slush to a spot at the bottom of the bulge equipped with a rock crack for providing a belay. I led the bulge, which was indeed just like something out of Green Gully, not too hard, not too easy, and I tied myself to a spike at the top. Tobin followed. After one or two jerky moves the rope twanged tight as a bowstring. Tobin started again. After another one or two jerky moves the rope twanged tight as a bowstring. Tobin started a third time and a long time later he appeared covered in powder snow, sweating profusely and smiling innocently, as was his wont. Hmmm. I figured that this chap, famous rock climber though he might be, doesn't have a clue about climbing ice.

We continued up the couloir, leading through up steep ice and over difficult and loose rock. We bivouacked somewhere in the middle. Now, Tobin didn't have a sleeping bag so, being the Hardy Scot and believing Tobin to be nothing more than an American Softie, I had elected to leave my bag behind in order to climb light. In the middle of the night it froze very hard and I cursed Tobin for a fool for coming to the Alps without a sleeping bag, and myself for an even bigger fool for having a sleeping bag but leaving it behind, useless, in the tent just because Tobin didn't have one.

In the morning the final pitch of the goulotte Smith-Sorenson, when we reached it, reared up before us. Horrific. A vertical rock corner sporting an evil off-width crack, encased in ice and verglas and topped by a large roof dripping icicles. Tobin led it, for it was his turn and he never was one to shy away from a challenge, with all the histrionic and noisy brilliance that I later came to expect from him. And that was the end of our training climb. At the start Tobin didn't seem to have a clue about how to climb an ice bulge. At the end he led one of the hardest ice pitches I have ever seen. It was a bit strange, all this falling off, but then Tobin did have a reputation as a practical joker…. Anyway it had proved to be the perfect training climb for us. Or almost.

Back at the Biolay we prepared to assault one of the great walls of the Western Alps. We bought our bivouac food, a couple of small, heavy loaves of bread called 'pains', a lump of Swiss cheese full of lightening holes like a Chouinard bong fit for a four inch crack, a tube of Nestlé condensed milk, and a packet of chewy sweeties – Yoplait. Someone on the Biolay campsite generously donated a packet of Knorr Fish Soup Powder to complete our rations. We had a stove, but only one cylinder of gas, for melting snow to drink en route.

We gathered together our equipment. I had some slings, a bunch of nuts, three or four pitons. Tobin, of course, had nothing other than the axe and stuff that he had borrowed. I also had, at that time, two two-hundred foot, eight mm old fashioned laid nylon ropes, ropes better suited to retreating from moderately difficult Scottish winter climbs than assaulting one of the greatest bastions of the western alps. Ropes terrible for getting into impenetrable fankles because they were twisty old laid ropes rather than soft and supple modern kernmantle. We packed our sacks and set off for the Leschaux Hut and my friend Alain the Leschaux Man. Alain, again concerned about our intentions, for he had heard about my previous misadventure after leaving the hut through the grapevine, insisted that we signal him every evening with our head torch. And so we intended, though we didn't intend to be on the climb for more than one night.

We started our climb at the bottom of the same rimaye as my previous attempt with Black Nick. This time, however, instead of a loose wall of crumbling granite topped by an overhang there was a magnificent icefall, something that could have come directly from Hadrian's Wall on Ben Nevis. We climbed up that, and the mixed ground above that was not too hard, not too easy, and back into the chute of green ice that led to my highpoint with Black Nick. I went up the chute in one two hundred foot pitch and tied onto lots of flakes and blocks and pitons and nuts at the top. Everything I could find that looked remotely solid I tied on to. I even clipped a jumar onto that same bit of old, faded and tatty string that Desmaison had left. Tobin followed without falling off, as he had by now already proved his worth on ice, and then led on into the unknown.

We had been following the first great ramp of the climb from the very bottom, in the rimaye at the foot of the face. Now Tobin wandered up the ramp towards an enormous overhang dripping icicles, a great rock that rested across the corner between the ramp and its retaining wall on the right. I turned that block of rock on the right by scrabbling up the icy crack between it and the wall, bridging out as wide as my little legs would go and laybacking with jolly abandon over three little overhangs. It was one of those pitches where once you start you either finish it or you fall off. You can't just stop and pass the time of day or have a cup of tea in the middle.

I suspect that this block is no longer there. That it remained transfixed while I clung to it and grappled with it I shall remain forever grateful. I didn't always have such luck, however, although not following that old tombstone flake down to the glacier on my attempt with Black Nick must constitute luck of the highest order. Tobin, I noticed, never seemed to have any problems leading, or following anything that I led, on rock or ice.

By the time that we had finished struggling with the big block the light of the short autumn day had faded. Tobin led a spectacular rock pitch up the retaining wall to our right by torchlight because I was sure I could see a ledge at the top. And so it proved, though Tobin had been doubtful. Tobin, my friend, shone our head torch down so that I could

Top: Looking south-east from high on Ben Nevis, December 2007. Photo: Noel Williams.
Bottom: Traversing Beinn Alligin, March 2008. Photo: Des Rubens.

have some idea where I was going and what I was doing as I followed him up.

Then we settled down for the night on our comfortable ledge having melted some snow for water to drink, and having chewed each on a lump of heavy bread garnished with cheese, decorated with Swiss Holes. And having exercised our jaw muscles on frozen Yoplait chewy sweeties for afters I remembered to signal Alain with our head torch, but as I never saw him again I don't know if he saw my signal or not. Tobin wrapped himself up in my nylon bivouac bag because it was cold and I had my little red down sleeping bag, that only lacked down, to keep me theoretically warm.

The next morning, because we were where we were I suppose, we continued on up the steep slabs and cracks above us until the climbing became very hard rock climbing and completely lacking in snow and ice. And it also became obvious that our route lay far below us on the ramp system where there was plenty of snow and ice covering the difficult rocks. We abseiled down again, all the way back down to the ramp. From there we climbed up slabs and corners covered here and there in plates of ice and lined with snow, leading out the rope in long bald pitches.

On and on we climbed up the ramp, moving fast and taking chances again and again with dodgy moves and not bothering about putting in runners. We were as bold and as bad as each other and each egged the other on to climb faster. We were so alike. Caution we threw to the winds. Here I would lead up a thinly iced groove. There Tobin would scrabble gung-ho over a little rocky overhang dripping with icicles. Together we reached the end of the ramp up a long tongue of hard, black winter ice that squeezed between the headwall on the right and a giant shark's fin of granite on the left.

Then we turned right and started up the headwall of the climb. I led, swinging up icy grooves and over snowy blocks, and Tobin led swinging up icy grooves and over snowy blocks, until I came across an empty Millet rucksack stuffed behind a flake of granite. Aieee! The mythical horde! My dream of riches! The treasure trove! Empty! There was nothing there! Not one tiny little piece of inexpensive anything. But I was there, and at least I was getting close to the top of the route, my route, my obsession! And the long, cold autumn night was drawing in.

We decided to bivouac there and then even though it was quite early because we were tired and because we hadn't seen many ledges on the route so far. I would lie jammed behind the flake in my little red sleeping bag and Tobin would sit wrapped up in my nylon bivouac bag on a little ledge above me. We chewed on the last of our bread with the last of our cheese, and with the last of our Yoplait sweeties for afters, and then we melted a little water to drink and to fill our water bottles for

Tom Lee on Stone of Destiny F6c+, The Camel, Inverness-shire. Photo: Dave 'Cubby' Cuthbertson.

the morrow with the last of our gas, and finally we prepared ourselves for the long, cold night. Then, with the setting of the sun, the sky flamed brilliant green and a crowd of little lenticular clouds appeared milling ominously around the summit of Mont Blanc. Tobin, the ignorant fool, stood tall, still wrapped in swathes of nylon. With his arms stretched out to the sky he cried in his ecstasy, like some Moses standing on his mountain and holding aloft the ten commandments: 'Praise the Lord! Look at the sky! It's so beautiful!'

I gibbered in my little red sleeping bag, trying not to think about the storm working up to dump itself upon us and terrified at the sight of that anachronistic figure stood before me.

Two hours later, in the blackness of the moonless night, the storm hit. First the wind got up. Then a few snowflakes. Then more wind and more snow and wet, until at length I could not stay warm in my sodden pit and so got out into the storm and put the dripping thing away in my sack and went to join Tobin, sitting on his ledge, in his wrappings.

We sat there, wrapped up together, for long hours as the wind howled about us and the snow covered us up. Until the black changed to grey. Then, unwilling to stay another moment in that place, we went out from our wrappings and our covering of snow into the foul and blizzardy morning.

With empty stomach Tobin led off up through the stour onto a steep pitch of granite covered in fresh snow. I shivered hungrily in the bitter blast and thought long thoughts of faither's hot tattie soup. There was much scrabbling of crampons on rock for a long time. Then without warning out of the storm flew Tobin, arms outstretched and jangling and clanking like a carillon. Those long, thin ropes stretched longer and thinner, but they held and stopped Tobin on his downward plunge.

Without a word he gathered himself together and went right back up. This time he wailed for a skyhook for a long moment, but I had none to give him, and again he flew out of the murk, a black winged creature of the storm. When again he had jangled to a halt, with the ropes stretched longer still and thinner, he gathered up what little wits he had left and went back at it furiously. Third time lucky for Tobin, and this time he made it to a little foothold where he could bang in a solid piton and he yelled for me to follow. And follow I did, buffeted by the wind and by the swirling snow and climbing through the storm to join him on his little, lonely foothold.

I led on through, tenuously swinging around to the left and across a shattered wall of frosted marbles to reach a flake attached to a rock sticking out of ice. That flake I pulled off as I laybacked up and I threw it down at Tobin to keep him in focus. The next flake I laybacked up I also threw down at Tobin to ensure that he was paying attention. The third flake I laybacked up I also threw down at Tobin, and that was the last of the flakes for I managed to get off that horrible arctic wall of frozen biscuit flakes and into a lovely bank of fresh fallen snow resting on a little spur. Tobin, when he followed, followed slowly complaining all the while that I hadn't left him much to climb on.

We climbed through the storm, following our noses for we had nothing else to follow and we couldn't see damn all, until I got a nice place to sit in the snow on the top of a block. Tobin led on towards the snow streaming over the summit ridge which we could vaguely make out through the murk. Then the ropes ran out and I had to follow, hoping that somewhere along the way Tobin had arranged for a running belay to stop us both if he decided to fall off again. And he did fall off. Again. And the ropes stretched long and thin but stopped him, hanging from a sling looped around a cracked block that stuck out of the snow. Around he flashed. Up again he flew at it, his axe arm flailing, his hammer poking and prodding. And yet again he flew off. As he hung from his cracked block that stuck out of the snow I got close enough to shout at him and ask him what the hell the matter was.

'There's an overhang of soft snow up there and I don't know what to do to climb it. I can't get my ice axe to stick.'

Of course I hadn't taught him how to deal with a cornice before because on the Plan there had been no cornice, only that tremendous iced corner with its roof dripping icicles. So now I yelled at him to cut the crap and flog the bloody thing down with his axe and be done with it. Tobin was obviously stung by my words, for he never cursed nor did he ever say harsh words. He flew again at the cornice and cut it down just as I had told him, and he rolled over the crest onto the top of the mountain. I followed like a dog on a leash, and the climb was done.

We gathered up our stuff and packed it all away and rolled up one of the ropes into a giant knitting and stuffed it in my bag. Then we ran down the hill through the storm until, just before night time caught us out, we reached the Italian hut. There I took off my boots to find there were no feet there. At least I could see feet, but it didn't feel like the feet belonged to me.

They stayed frozen until we set off down for the valley the next day, and I ended up hitch hiking on my rotting stumps, which included walking miles and miles through London in the middle of the night, until I got back to Scotland and my mum, who fainted clean away at the sight and smell of my necrotic feet. Then back to Bridge of Earn. There they saved my toes, but my old friend the ortho doctor came to visit me in the Plastic Surgery Unit and gave me another flea in the ear about being such a burden on the NHS.

Now, if the truth be told, back up on the mountain when I said 'we ran down the hill through the storm' of course we didn't just run down a simple snow slope. Straight away we got lost in the storm, and fell down countless little snow gullies, and set off little avalanches and slid down in them until they got too big to manage, and once we jumped a long way down off a serac into a crevasse and then had to climb out of the other side. Finally, just before it got dark and desperate for a drink of water, we found the hut. Thank goodness.

Then in the Italian hut we had been very, very hungry and thirsty with nothing to eat but that packet of fish soup and no gas left. But we found a canister hidden somewhere in a cupboard which I stole immediately, us being very poor and very hungry and Tobin being far too honest to contemplate such an action. And I boiled up that horrible fish soup and we supped it down. And it was so delicious that the best restaurant in town would have been proud to serve it. The next day Tobin walked and I hobbled down the long snowy path into green meadows and trees under a beautiful Italian sun. And behind us the mountain's Italian face looked so very high and so very beautiful against a cloudless blue Italian sky.

That is the end of the story of my dangerous obsession for Tobin didn't wait for me to come back but went off with Dirty Alex, and my long two hundred foot ropes, and did the Harlin route on the Eiger Nordwand. Thirty years post hoc I discovered from Rick Accomazzo that Tobin had already climbed the Dru Couloir Direct, the 'hardest ice climb in the Alps' with him the summer just before I met him, and that they'd 'swapped' leads. And there, I'd thought that I'd taught the wildest climber in the world how to climb ice, leading him on to doing some of the greatest Alpine routes in the world. Oh well, at least I did teach him how to cope with a cornice, that cornice at the top of the Desmaison when I'd spurred him on with my harsh words, 'Cut the crap and flog the bloody thing down and be done with it.' That was my lesson to Tobin Sorenson. Oh, and thirty years later another Scot, two Scotsmen in fact, who'd scarcely been born at the time of our great adventure, did that climb again and cleaned up the last few pieces of aid that we had left for them to clean up*. That was a very fine effort on their part, but it is a tale for them, not me, to tell.

* [Guy Robertson and Pete Benson, October 2007, VI 6c M5/M6—Hon. Ed.]

BEFORE THE MUNROS

By Hamish Brown

SIR HUGH Munro's historic *Tables* of hills over 3000 feet appeared first of all in the 1891 *Scottish Mountaineering Club Journal* (and later as a separate publication) thus setting in motion the great hill game we know today.

Before that time the general knowledge about Scottish hills was meagre and did not have anything to do with the magic plimsoll line of 3000 feet. I've several Victorian guidebooks and none list more than thirty 3000-ers.

Recently I went to my set of Groome's *Gazetteer of Scotland* of 1882, six large and useful volumes for giving the picture of Scotland at that period – and my eye caught the name Ben Hutig. I would hazard most readers are saying 'Ben What?' and the rest 'Ben Where?'.

I just happened to be writing about that hill which I discovered on one of those serendipitous walks that happen now and then, and here was Groome giving all sorts of surprises, whole pages of Bens before 'Munros' erupted on the landscape.

You might have fun recognising some of the names he gives: Ben Auler (Alder), Bentealluidh (Ben Talaidh, Mull), Bensliabhoch (Slioch), Benavere (Beinn a' Bheithir), Bendeanavaig (Ben Tiannavaig, Skye), Benkitlan (Beinn Ceitlein), Ben Loy (Beinn Laoigh), Benspenue (Spionnaidh), or Benfile (Beinn Eighe).

This last is a delightful mess for elsewhere 'Ben Eay' is also listed – and the Gaelic translation is *file* of course. The description is all right '... a stately base and a lofty altitude; it terminates in two sharp lofty peaks of snow-white quartz; and makes a dazzling appearance under a play of sunshine'.

Descriptions are given for the hills which, then, obviously had popular appeal, some perhaps more looked at than climbed.

'*Ben Nevis* ... accessible by a new carriage drive of seven miles to the head of Glen Nevis, opened in 1880 ... 4406 feet, the highest mountain in Great Britain.

'The ascent is usually made on the W. side, from Fort William or Banavie, and occupies 3½ hours; but it cannot be made without considerable difficulty and some danger, and ought never to be attempted by a stranger without a guide ... In 1881 an observatory of the Scottish Meteorological Society was established on the summit.'

The geological description is interesting and the view from the summit, while 'sublime', I'm doubtful about the claim one can see the 'Atlantic and German Oceans'. Ben Nevis had obviously taken its rightful place as highest, usurping Ben Macdhui.

'*Ben Macdhui*, 4296 feet, *mountain of the black sow*, only 110 feet lower than Ben Nevis, a far less conspicuous figure ... The ascent (18 miles) is from Castleton [Braemar] by Derry Lodge and up either Glen Derry or Glen Lui. The glorious view from the broad flat summit extends to Ben Wyvis, Ben Nevis, and Ben Glo; but Benabourd shuts out prospect of the German Ocean. The Queen and the Prince Consort made the ascent on October 1859 and August 1860 as described in the *Queen's Journal*.' (Benabourd was climbed by the royals in 1850 – so was Cam a' Chlamain but Groome omits those royal Munros.)

Ben Wyvis is translated as '*stupendous mountain*' but likened to a haystack, 'the ascent very tedious and fatiguing, impeded by spongy moor, but can be facilitated by the use of Highland ponies ... Its upper parts, even in warmest summers, are almost constantly sheeted or flecked with snow".

Schiehallion, 3547 feet, ... its outline is, on the whole, curvilinear and has fewer angles and breaks than most of the monarch-heights...' The view however is 'tame' and 'disappointing', so much 'a tumultinous sea of wild elevations, among which the eye traces few striking forms'. However, 'Schiehallion is known throughout the scientific world as the scene, in 1772, of curious observations by Dr Nevil Maskelyne, astronomer-royal, to ascertain the density of the earth ... The name is said to be a corruption of the Gaelic *Ti-chaillin*, the Maiden's Pap' – a new one on me.

Obviously the view from the summit was the key to popularity for many in Groome are given the accolade as being the best, most sublime, most striking, impressive, majestic, commanding, and other superlatives.

Ben Lomond, 3192 feet, not surprisingly, comes into this category. 'The views from the top has less breadth, less force, less gorgeousness than Ben Lawers, but in aggregate diversity, brilliance, and picturesque magnificence is equalled by no view in all the United Kingdom.' The 'most curious' ascent was made in 1796 'by the Rev Charles Simeon and James Alexander Haldane who on the top, impressed by the grandeur of the surrounding scenery, kneeled down and solemnly consecrated their future lives to the service of Almighty God'.

Ben Lawers 'culminates at 3984 feet above sea-level, or 4004 if one includes a cairn built in 1878, and thus the fifth loftiest in all Scotland. It does not consist of a single mass, but rising from a broad base, in fusion with contiguous mountains, rolls up in a series of shoulders and terminates in a noble cone that towers above all eminences ... . On its summit are found the small gentian and other alpine plants. The ascent is generally made from the Ben Lawers Hotel, so easy it can be made on horseback'. The view is excelled by no other except perhaps Ben Lomond.

'*Ben Liughach*, a grand mountain in Gairloch parish, 1½ miles from Loch Torridon and 4 miles SW of Ben Eay. Its height is about 3000 feet.' Liathach was actually the easy to remember 3456 feet before metrification.

Skye is very well covered with nearly every notable hill mentioned (even Ben Aslak, another mighty neglected viewpoint) but in the Cuillin there is no Sgurr Alasdair, no Sgurr Mhic Choinnich, no Inaccessible Pinnacle for these had not been so named. By whom and when were certain Cuillin summits given people's names I've often wondered. Such namings would not be tolerated today.

'Benveedan or Beinn Fhada, a mountain separated from Buachaille-Etive by the mountain pass which leads from Glen Etive to Glen Coe ... A stupendous mass, it attains, in its highest point, Bidean nam Bian, an altitude of 3766 feet', which is the highest in Argyll.

Other Munros that receive some description include Cruachan, Beinn Laoigh, Ben More in Mull (likened to Vesuvius), Starav, Lochnagar and Benmore-Assynt while many are just listed with their location: Dorain, Achallader, Chreachain, Vane, Ime, Vorlich (both), Attow, Ben Avon, Ben-a-Chroin, Benalligin, Beinn a' Chochuill, Chonzie, Benclibrick, Dearg (Loch Broom and Athole), Ben More and Am Binnein, Hope, Tulachan, Aighean (Aighenan), Scrial, Udlaman, Sguliaird, Bensheasgarnich, Beinn-a-Chleibh, Benbui (Glen Fyne), Cam Liath (Benglo), Carn Mairg.

This is a surprising number considering the paucity generally at that time. Corbetts were well represented as well and among the weighty text are found nuggets like the note that Arthur's Seat can be seen from Ben Vrackie. But Groome is murder on the spellings we know today.

Ben Ghulbhuinn (Gulbain) at the head of Glenshee 'is held by tradition to have been the scene of a hunting-match which proved fatal to Diarmid, one of the Fingalian heroes and on it, or adjacent, are the alleged grave of Diarmid, the den of the boar which was hunted, a spring Tobas-nan-Fiann (Fingalians' well) and a small lake, Loch-an-Tuirc (*boar loch*)'.

Ben Venue rises 'almost murally from the margin of Loch Katrine, it surges upwards to 2393 feet ... in the territory celebrated in the *Lady of the Lake*'. The description is worthy of Scott: '... shows rich flecking and interminglings of verdure, natural wood, and naked rock; it exhibits a lofty terrace-pass and a stupendous corrie ... and combines the characters of grandeur, romance, and beauty, its aggregate configuration answering closely to Sir Walter Scott's "Craggs, knolls and mounds, confusedly hurl'd / The fragments of an earlier world"' .

The Cobbler is another described as both difficult and dangerous but 'when scaled by a daring mountaineer on a clear day it rewards by one of the most extraordinary prospects anywhere seen in Britain, over a bewildering expanse of mountains, glens and lakes'.

Ben Loyal 'curves gracefully upward from rounded loins to splintered summit, terminating in four massive peaks, the most picturesque of any Highland mountain'.

Ah well, as they say, one photo can save a hundred words, but what fun they had heaping up these wordy peaks of language – a long way from 'the dreary and dreadful' of a century earlier by Dr Johnson and other travellers or today's shopping list prose descriptions.

Other Corbetts listed (Groome spellings) include Mhic-Mhonaidh, Benmholach, Farragon, Pharlagain, Resipol, Rinnes, Tee, Benshianta (Jura). Trilleachan, Ben-a-Chroin, Ben-a-Chaisteil, Ben Odhar, Ben-an-Lochain, Bheula, Donich, Ben-derg-veg and Ben-derg-vore, Benhee, Ledi, Leoid, Benchait (Bhreac), Benevachart (Beinn a' Bha'ach Ard) and Ben Larig (Lair).

One entry intrigued: 'Beneaddan or Ben Yadain ... flanking the southern shore of Loch Sunart, rises to 1873 feet; towards the summit is an excavated flight of steps, called Cenmanan Fhin or Fingal's Stair'. This I take to be Beinn Iadain on the current OS map but I've never heard of it before. Are there steps on top? 'Ben Fin, a mountain overhanging the S side of the head of Loch Fannich' has me baffled, especially as the Fannichs are barely mentioned. 'Benwhat' near Dalmellington puzzled but today is attired as Benquhat (with Craigdonkey on its north slope).

The Bartholomew map at the end of volume 6 has more hill details than the text in fact. The hill information was there: it was just slow in being studied by outsiders or disciplined in the listing of Munro. Many other Groome names appear under parish headings. OS maps existed.

Lastly, some of Groome's lesser hills, working south-north: Benbeoch, Ben Varen (Bharrain) and Bengnuis (both Arran), Ben Avon (A'an), Benarty, Bencleuch, Ben Buy (Mull), Benhiand (Ardnamurchan), Ben Cailleach (the Skye 'Vesuvius'), Ben Killilan, Bennochie, Ben Goleach (Ghobhlach), the Ben Griams, Ben-a-Bhragie, Ben-an-Armuinn, Ben Stack and Ben Thutaig (Hutig) – beyond which we run out of Scotland and you can imagine why I found it a special hill: it is sublime, with a gorgeous panorama, scarce excelled in all the length and breadth of the land, or from the western horizon to the German Ocean. You can quote me on that.

HAROLD RAEBURN – THE FINAL JOURNEY

By Mike Jacob

Who are these? Why sit they here in twilight?
Wilfred Owen, 1917

MOST mountaineers will surely be familiar with the name of Harold Raeburn, perhaps having repeated one of his routes or having read about the impact that he had on Scottish mountaineering in the early years of the twentieth century. His climbing accomplishments, technical ability and indomitable character are well documented but it would seem that other biographical information is rather scanty. Raeburn was an assiduous record-keeper and although a few climbing notebooks survive in the SMC archives, I suspect that, after his death, his sisters destroyed any personal letters or diaries, perhaps out of a sense of loyalty. Briefly, Harold was born in 1865, the eighth child and fourth son of William and Margaret (Jessie) Raeburn of Edinburgh. He left Merchiston Castle School in 1881 and studied chemistry at the Watt Institution, Edinburgh, before joining the family firm as a brewer.

In the 1997 SMCJ, John Fowler described his search for Harold Raeburn's grave, a quest which led him to an overgrown corner of Warriston Cemetery in Edinburgh. He also wrote that Raeburn's health, 'already chronically weakened by overwork during the Great War', failed during the 1921 Everest Reconnaissance expedition and that he was admitted, on 8 February 1922, to Craig House in Morningside, a sanatorium for the mentally ill. There he remained for nearly 5 years, dying on 21 December 1926, aged 61. His death certificate states that the cause of death was 1) Exhaustion from melancholia 2) Endocrine insufficiency.

All this left some niggling questions in my mind. Was there any evidence to support the notion that Raeburn's health **was** significantly affected by overwork during the First World War? What was the state of medical knowledge, then, about the human endocrine system, which is responsible for hormone production and regulation, and was any attempt made to treat his 'insufficiency'? But most crucially of all, I was intrigued by those three words – 'exhaustion from melancholia'.

How could this be? Surely, 'melancholia' couldn't cause death – could it? Not to such a tough character as the great Harold Raeburn, described by Sandy Mackay as physically and mentally hard as nails.[1]

---

[1] *Vignettes of Earlier Climbers* by Lord Mackay. *SMCJ* 1950, XXIV, 141, 169–80.

Perhaps he had contracted some disease on the Indian subcontinent, had been a bit dejected and an awful mis-diagnosis had caused him to be unjustly incarcerated in a ghastly asylum, little changed from an eighteenth century mad-house. Or so I thought, partly because, over the years, the facts of his death have been somewhat distorted by a process of omission and several sources do ascribe his death to 'disease contracted on Everest.'

It is hardly surprising that no mention was made of 'melancholia' as a contributory factor to Harold's death, given the universal stigma attached to any form of mental illness that existed at the time and, to a lesser extent, still does today. Perhaps, in deference to Raeburn's reputation as the most outstanding mountaineer of his generation, the possibility of mental disorder was just too embarrassing to be talked or written about and the awkward matter was thereby swept under the carpet. An obituary in the *Scotsman*, on 23 December 1926, outlines Raeburn's sad decline but attributes this to an attack of dysentery and his arduous physical exertions during the Everest expedition. It is clear that other authors over the succeeding years have relied heavily for their information about his death, directly or indirectly, on what was written in the aforementioned obituary.[2] It is even possible to detect the same words and phrases being repeated. In this way, the impression given is of a man, severely incapacitated by illness and overwork, who overcomes adversity by sheer will-power and who never really recovers his health, gradually weakening to the point of death.

Further, although held in high regard by the mountaineering cognoscenti, Raeburn has been somewhat air-brushed from the general historical records, as the following two examples demonstrate. One; in a recent exhibition[3] at the National Library of Scotland in Edinburgh, the section about Himalayan mountaineering inexplicably failed to even mention Harold Raeburn whilst featuring fellow SMC members Alexander Kellas and Dougal Haston. Two; the expedition book[4] describing the search for the bodies of Mallory and Irvine in 1999, whilst giving a coherent account of the early Everest expeditions, overstates the significance of an 'old boy network' within the Alpine Club, which most certainly promoted mountaineering experience and skills in its choice of candidates. To be chosen as the leader of the mountain party for the first Everest expedition, which was always

---

[2] Slightly fuller versions of the same obituary, written by W. Ling, appear in both SMC and Alpine Club Journals.

[3] *Tea and Tigers: Stories of Scotland and South Asia* (30 June – 5 September 2007) – The story of why, for over 400 years, Scottish travellers have been drawn to India, a land of opportunity for soldiers, doctors, explorers, and adventurers.

[4] *Ghosts of Everest* by Hemmleb, Johnson and Simonson. Macmillan, 1999.

primarily intended as a reconnaissance trip, was considered as a crowning achievement by Harold Raeburn, and his choice was based purely on the fact that there was no able-bodied climber in Britain who could match his exceptional record. Both Raeburn and his Scottish compatriot, Alexander Kellas, worked tirelessly for the good of the group but they are casually dismissed without even being named '...of the two most experienced Himalayan explorers on the expedition, one dropped out due to illness and retreated to India, and the other dropped dead and was buried on route...' a summary which treats them like a pair of decrepit yaks.

I wondered what a modern medical re-evaluation would make of Raeburn's symptoms, but this was impossible without his doctors' notes, surely now long gone, and Craig House itself had been closed as a hospital in 1993. Even if they had been kept, there was a restriction on their release[5] to non-medical personnel which meant that they could not be seen until December 2001 at the earliest. Some enquiries in early 2002 revealed that the records had been retained but, due to Raeburn's status, and the sensitive nature of the details enclosed within the case file, my request to have access to them was passed to the Director of Public Health.

The decision was made to release the file and I was sent photo-copies of the case notes. The documents give the medical condition of Harold Raeburn from the day of his admittance on 8 February 1922 until his death. There is information about his physical appearance, medical history, progress notes, doctors' letters and charts detailing pulse, temperature and weight. I am conscious that it could be argued that this information is private and should remain so; on the other hand, Raeburn had no family descendants and I do not intend to reveal any great detail from the notes. It was written[6] of Raeburn that he was absolutely fearless in challenging erroneous notions and, therefore, I feel he would have been content that, from his sad ending, we would come to dispute that there should be any humiliation or shame associated with succumbing to mental illness.

*

It is clear, after a first reading of the notes, that he was suffering from more than just post-Everest 'blues' or, given his age of 56, what might these days be called the male menopause. He had been suicidal:

[5] At present the Freedom of Information (Scotland) Act 2002, which came into force in 2005, has an 'exemption' whereby the health records of deceased individuals are closed for 100 years. In practice, NHS (Scotland) operates under a guideline which lays down a 75 year closure period for adult patients.

[6] W.W. Naismith in his review of *Mountaineering Art* by H. Raeburn. *SMCJ* 1920, XV, 90, 346–8.

...on Sunday, February 5th he threw himself on the road in front of a taxi-cab in a deliberate attempt to commit suicide. He was then removed to Comiston Nursing Home and during his first night there he got out of bed, seized a poker and attempted to smash in the vault of his skull. Fortunately he only contrived to raise a few weals. He was then transferred to Craig House.

I soon discovered that institutional care in those days had, in fact, progressed profoundly. Long gone were the days of chaining patients to beds in grim City Bedlams. In the nineteenth century, the Royal Edinburgh Asylum, under a succession of enlightened doctors, led innovative approaches to the treatment of mental illness, such as encouraging patients to pursue recreational interests, and aimed to provide a 'home' with comfortable wards and good food. To cope with increasing demand, Craig House (a sixteenth century mansion with a 60-acre estate) was acquired in 1878, and when it opened in 1894 it was the largest and most progressive asylum of its kind in the country. By 1922, the year of Raeburn's admittance, an Act of Parliament allowed the asylum to become the Royal Edinburgh Hospital for Nervous and Mental Disorders, to reflect the 'hospitalisation' approach to treatment. The purpose, in Edinburgh at least, was to provide humane, sympathetic treatment for patients and, contrary to what has been thought by some, Raeburn could not have been in better surroundings.

There is mention in the medical history, written shortly after his admittance, that:

Mr. Raeburn had an attack of melancholia about ten years ago and was treated at home.

This would have been some time around 1911 or 1912. These are precisely the two years when, according to Ling's obituary, '... owing to an accident his energies were restrained.' The accident was confirmed in Raeburn's journal for 1910 when, referring to his summer trip to the Alps, he wrote:

...proceeded down the valley to the Satarma Needle, a most extra-ordinary needle of rock. It quite overhangs on one side and is very steep and also at one part smooth on the other. I preferred to do it in stockings and consider that with worn nails in boots it is not a safe climb. There is a rope ring which makes it quite easy to descend. It was my first climb since the end of Feb. but I did not feel at all put out on it so the affair of Feb. 27 can have had no nervous effect. Of course I still feel muscularly weak and am 9–10lbs underweight still.

I had been unable to discover much about the circumstances of the 27 February incident until I mentioned it to our Hon. Archivist, Robin Campbell, who had never heard of it. Subsequently, some diligent research by Robin was rewarded by the discovery in Ling's diary that the accident occurred on Stuc a' Chroin. Raeburn, in attempting to hold the combined weight of three falling companions (R.P. Hope, Miss Smith and Miss Gray), was plucked from his stance at the top of a slab of rock and they all fell away down the steep snow slope below. Ling, who was on a separate rope with Ruth Raeburn, Harold's sister, witnessed the event and found Raeburn lying head down[7] and barely conscious. A long, cold rescue followed, which would not have been possible without the assistance of two long-suffering shepherds from Glen Ample. Raeburn clearly suffered debilitating injury, including broken ribs, the recovery from which was to take several months. However, they were not sufficiently severe to curtail his formidable summer Alpine season and, later, at least one strenuous excursion to the Lake District with W. Ling and G. Sang.

So, 1910 was an active year by any standard and it would appear that Raeburn's inactivity in 1911/12 cannot readily be explained by his accident, at least not physically, despite the assertion in the obituary. It is open to conjecture whether or not the injuries he suffered contributed in any way to the attack of melancholia referred to in the medical history. Raeburn was a chemistry graduate and brewer by profession and it is possible that the demise of the family brewery at Craigmillar, which was sold in 1913, could have been a contributory factor to his depression. However, this is mere speculation. His doctor would have treated him by recommending plenty of rest and gentle exercise and, by the end of 1912, this seems to have worked for he was, once again, his tireless self. In September that year he had another visit to the Lakes, 'accompanied by his motorcycle on board coal train for Carlisle', and then soloed up North-East Climb[8] and down Central Jordan on Pillar Rock.

Raeburn looked further afield for his adventures in 1913 with a trip to the Caucasus with W. Ling. Here they had an unsuccessful five-day battle with the twin peaks of Ushba – the 'Matterhorn of the Caucasus' – but climbed seven other mountains including five very difficult first ascents. Raeburn was back in the Caucasus in 1914 with another four first ascents but this expedition was curtailed by the outbreak of war. John Mitchell wrote a full account of the return journey, as Europe prepared for War, in the 2000 SMCJ.

Patriotically, Raeburn tried to enlist in the Royal Flying Corps but, at age 49, was considered too old and, instead, worked long hours on the 'home front' in a factory, probably at one of the Clyde shipyards sub-contracted to manufacture aeroplane parts. He had the occasional trip away but such visits could hardly be justified whilst others were dying

---

[7] Harold's hat was lost … however, sociable SMC members will know that our Hon. Archivist is now in possession of a replica.

[8] Like most of the routes hereabouts, this rock climb (now graded Mild Severe) becomes considerably harder (unless you care to wear nailed boots) when wet.

daily by the thousands and, in any case, the economic strictures of a country at war would have imposed many constraints upon travel. Almost certainly, he used this time to prepare the manuscript, the fruit of several years work, for his book *Mountaineering Art* which was eventually published in 1920.

After the austere war years, with Europe still in turmoil, in 1919 Raeburn still managed to travel to the Dauphiné where he made a solo traverse of the ridges of the Meije, '... perhaps the most daring of all his expeditions' as Ling says. Then, in 1920, the SMC held an Easter Meet at Fort William. This saw a party of three – Goggs, Mounsey and Raeburn – making a first ascent of Observatory Ridge (of which Raeburn had made the first summer ascent, solo, in 1901) in full winter conditions, with 100ft of rope between them, no crampons and only a long ice-axe each. Goggs wrote an account of the climb for the SMCJ which captures the drama and tension of the day as the conditions worsened. This was a real tour de force by all three, especially the 55 year-old Raeburn who led the entire route in just under six hours.

That same year he made his first trip to the Himalaya. Two approaches were made to Kanchenjunga with different companions, with a camp at 20,000ft, but weather conditions were poor. There is a very full account of this expedition, as with several other trips, in Alpine Club Journals of the period and these retain snatches of his dry sense of humour:

> ...we passed several bears within smelling distance – I mean of our noses, not bruins.

SMC traditionalists may be saddened to learn that the ice axe given to in-coming Presidents is not the same one that cut its way up Green Gully or Observatory Ridge. That axe, a present to Raeburn from Harry Walker of the Alpine Club, was swept away in a flooded Himalayan river, much to Raeburn's chagrin.

All of this intense post-war activity is hardly consistent with the notion that Raeburn had damaged his health by over-work. On the contrary, around this time, the medical notes state that:

> Mr. Raeburn was described as being somewhat above himself, full of energy and enthusiasm and not nearly as reserved as was his wont. About the same time he published a book on Climbing, which is said to be one of the recognised authorities on the subject. As an indication of the tireless energy which characterised him at this time it may be noted that the MS of the book was lost and the fruit of several years' labour seemed to have been lost with it. After communicating with his publishers, however, Mr. Raeburn undertook to re-write the book, a task which he accomplished within three months. Eventually the book was published at the right time.

Raeburn was immensely proud to be selected as the climbing leader for the proposed Everest Reconnaissance Expedition of 1921. The details and significance of this Expedition can be reviewed in any one of the ship-load of books about the history of Everest – and it makes interesting reading – but I can give only a brief account of the affair here. Less than a hundred years ago, say three or four generations-worth of memories, yet the time of these men is as difficult to imagine now as trying to retain the glistening colours of a sea-worn pebble from the beach as it dries slowly in your hand.

The team and its mighty train of porters and pack animals departed from Darjeeling, in May 1921, en route via Sikkim and Tibet to the mysteries of Mount Everest (Chomolungma). It should be remembered that virtually everything about the mountain and its environs were unknown and that, for most of the Tibetan villagers, these strange white men were the equivalent of aliens from Outer Space. But already tensions had surfaced between three of the most unyielding, self-confident characters on the team – George Mallory, Harold Raeburn, and Charles Howard-Bury (the overall expedition leader). Of the three, Raeburn is the only one to have left no books, private letters or diaries and, as a consequence, the words and opinions of the other two men have carried weight through the succeeding decades, to Raeburn's detriment. During the approach trek, nearly all the members – both Europeans and native porters – became ill with food poisoning and, most unfortunately, fellow SMC member Alexander Kellas succumbed and died. Raeburn, suffering from similar symptoms, was forced to return to India to begin a slow process of recuperation. Thus his place as the foremost mountaineer on the team was inherited by the much younger Mallory who, along with Guy Bullock, made a brilliant job of the mountaineering reconnaissance. Raeburn eventually recovered sufficient strength to return, in monsoon conditions, by an arduous and flooded route to rejoin the Expedition. However, he was no longer needed, or wanted, by his team-mates. His position on the mountain had been usurped and he was now superfluous to requirements.

The tide had changed. It was clear, back in Britain, that he had no part to play in the celebrations and flag-waving that accompanied the return of the Expedition and he was effectively side-lined as yesterday's man, with perhaps even the subtle whiff of a malingerer about him. The Mount Everest Committee and their devious secretary, Arthur Hinks, were committed to a return to Everest in 1922 and realised that, in order to raise public awareness and much-needed funds, the future lay with George Mallory. Raeburn could be put out to grass and he took this perceived humiliation very much to heart.

There is nothing in any of the archive material which I have seen to suggest that Raeburn's mental illness actually started while he was on the Everest Expedition. Although he may have shown some very non-specific indications, such as irascibility and obstinacy, they could be as equally attributed to the effects of altitude, physical illness and disagreements – or even his normal stubborn nature. However, since it is rare for any depressive episode to be totally devoid of external precipitating factors, it is highly probable that his breakdown can be traced back to the events of Everest and its aftermath.

After the Everest expedition, Harold returned to Edinburgh where, initially, he stayed with his sisters. However, he was a troubled man for he was being badgered by Secretary Hinks for various reasons and the relationship between the two men had degenerated so far that Raeburn asked his SMC friend and lawyer, George Sang, to deal with matters for him. I am pretty certain that this was the final trigger in the series of catastrophically disappointing events that had befallen Raeburn who, in low spirits, was sufficiently run down that he had been advised by his doctor to recuperate at a nursing home in Colinton. In February 1922 Harold Raeburn was so depressed that he tried to kill himself in front of the taxi-cab.

*

Upon admittance, on 8 February, he was given a full medical examination. Physically, he was described as *well built*, muscularly *very well developed*, with *grey/blue* eyes and *grey* hair, *bald on top*. He was 5ft 10in (178cm) tall and 9st 10lb in weight. This was about 11 pounds less than his usual weight and it is surprising that, in the 'fatness' category, he was given as *well covered*. There was no evidence of injury or disease, thus rebutting the idea that he may have been suffering from an illness such as TB and this is confirmed by his satisfactory pre-Everest medical check-up.

The doctors at Craig House interviewed Harold's surviving siblings at length and compiled a history for their medical notes. This extract confirms his dejection:

> What he regarded as the crowning point of his whole career was his selection as a leader of the climbing-party in the Mount Everest Expedition … Naturally he was very crestfallen owing to the collapse of his ambition, and though he made a good physical recovery from the ptomaine poisoning his friends were conscious that he was somewhat depressed and that he needed a prolonged rest.

And so began weeks and months of a slow decline into a world of demons, in a quiet Edinburgh suburb, as the rest of the world moved on. While the second and third Everest expeditions were organised and mounted, while Mallory and Irvine climbed into oblivion, Harold Raeburn was stuck in a mindless time-warp. The medical notes reveal that Raeburn was tormented by feelings of guilt and murder, which

First winter ascent of Grand Diedre (VI, 6), Coir' a' Ghrunnda, Skye.
Climber: Pete MacPherson. Photo: Graham Briffett..

probably related to the death of Kellas. At one stage, he had successfully persuaded Kellas that he was too weak to travel any further but Howard-Bury had dissuaded Kellas, convincing him that it was better to continue the journey. Raeburn, in his tortured mind, must have felt that he was responsible for the death of his friend by his inability to protect him, and this may have translated itself into the notion of murder.

Harold's health remained a cause for anxiety and the doctors had no idea how to treat his depression. He often refused food, necessitating tube-feeding, and was usually quite silent. We will never know exactly what Harold thought about as the minutes ticked by in this state of total collapse. The only clues come from others who have described what it is like to go through such periodic bouts of intense emotional pain, the mind spinning in intertwining circles of guilt and loss, despair and recrimination. Harold's fearful desolation, however, was unending. In name and appearance this was Harold Raeburn but it wasn't Harold Raeburn the legendary mountaineer. His weight now fluctuated around the 8 stone mark.

Yet another year went by, turning to 1925. His condition was unchanged; there was only one medical note recorded, in March, and it is apparent that the doctors were still baffled by this enigmatic case. Given his general demeanour and refusal of food, it is notable that Harold's overall physical condition was not a lot worse. Undisturbed by the urgency of physical activity, he had the time to suffer the worst mental torture; to dwell upon the misdeeds, real or perceived, that had been perpetrated against him, perhaps to suffer the anguish of nostalgia and the lack of a loving relationship. This, now, was Raeburn's world. It is a miracle that he fought the battle for so long; another, sadder, reminder of his remarkable tenacity.

It was over yet another year before the next medical note was recorded, in April 1926. However, there is now an ominous tone as it was registered that Harold's physical condition was deteriorating and his weight had fallen to 7 stone, largely because he vomited his food, which was still tube-fed. His vital organs were now irretrievably damaged and, a few days before Christmas 1926, Harold Raeburn died.

All of the foregoing leaves a bewildering set of questions about the nature of depression (melancholia); its causes, effects and treatment, and the involvement of the endocrine system. Accordingly, I asked Dr Eric Wood, a Consultant Psychiatrist, if he would kindly have a look at Raeburn's medical notes and give a modern diagnosis and treatment should he encounter a patient with similar symptoms today. Basically, he considered that Harold Raeburn was suffering from a severe psychotic or delusional depression, his physical condition at the time of admittance ruling out other diagnoses such as delirium or dementia. A limited number of routine tests and investigations were done which

First winter ascent of Commando Direct (VI,6), Beinn a' Bhuird.
Climber: Pete Benson. Photo: Ross Hewitt.

excluded kidney damage, diabetes and, quite importantly, neuro-syphilis. In short, Harold's delusional depression and weight loss was so severe that, in the end, his heart and other organs were fatally weakened. Dr Wood was of the opinion that a patient suffering similar symptoms these days could, in all likelihood, be successfully treated by Electro-Convulsive Therapy (ECT) and/or the use of modern anti-depressant and anti-psychotic drugs, along with one or more 'talking remedies' (or psychotherapies).

The other cause of death on the death certificate was *endocrine insufficiency* – a bit of a cover-all given the state of knowledge about hormone production and regulation at the time. Although the complex processes of the body's biochemistry may still be incompletely resolved, modern sensitive blood tests enable doctors to prescribe relatively straightforward and effective therapies.

My original doubts were only partially resolved for, although I now understand more about clinical depression, most perplexingly, how could someone like Raeburn suffer such a complete reversal? Harold was very much a man of drive and practical achievement, and it is probable that his melancholia, some ten years earlier, coincided with a period of impatient inertia when he was unable to participate in his usual activities after his accident. Was this impotence a precipitating factor, and a common denominator, between the two attacks?

He had lost everything; his dream, his hopes and rewards, his influence and ability to act, his position as an important leader, and his authority and reputation – all gone in the maelstrom of the Everest wind and its back-eddies. Freud proposed that an unwilling loss and betrayal resulted in an unconscious loss of self-esteem as the ego became bereft and, in the distressed melancholic mind, accusations against the outside world were turned in on itself:

> …everything collapses and disintegrates around me, the scenery, the walls, the people, while the anguish becomes more intense and more precise. Now everything has changed to chaos; I am alone in the centre of a grey and turbid nothing…

> Primo Levi 'The Truce'

*

My own voyage of discovery, which started several years ago with a casual inquiry and ended in contemplation at the two Raeburn family memorials[9] in Warriston Cemetery, is now almost ended. On the way, I

[9] Warriston cemetery was compulsorily purchased by Edinburgh City Council in 1994 to prevent its continued degeneration. However, hundreds of headstones were officially pushed over on safety grounds and drug-addicts and other 'undesirables' were abusing the site. By 2007, this state of affairs had been

have called in at the National Museum of Scotland in Chambers Street, when I had a bit of spare time, to discover that they had, unbelievably, a ptarmigan from Ben Cruachan amongst other avian paraphernalia once owned by Harold Raeburn; I have cradled the egg of a golden eagle, that Harold removed from an eyrie in a remote Angus glen; I have hunted through old papers and letters in the archives of the Royal Geographical Society in London and held a letter written by Raeburn with a fountain pen in the Kharta Valley of Tibet as his Everest hopes fell apart; and I have sat shivering through cold, wet winter days trying to compile it all as my contribution towards a book. I continue to marvel at the life of this extraordinary man and am saddened by the manner of his death, which echoes that of the poet, Robert Fergusson, some 150 years earlier. There is something, though, that I am inspired to do. One of Harold's shattered memories, floating through the cosmos like a spore, has germinated into a dream … a dream of repeating an 1890 rock climb, the first he ever described; it's not on Salisbury Crags or the Lakes or on a mountain, and to do it in the same style I'll need a boat and a length of cod-line.

---

improved and access is permitted from Warriston Gdns, off Inverleith Row. Harold Raeburn was buried, two days after his death, in the family grave in position Q57. On the other side of the wall is the burial site of his mother and other relatives.

BY THE WAY

By Iain Smart

ONE FINE day in June 2003 I was walking through the oak woods on the lower slopes of Ben Airidh Charr. My intention was to trace the old postman's path that ran along the lochside in the elder days from Ardlair to Letterewe. It was warm work travelling across the grain of the country. About noon I stopped for a rest under a spreading oak shading a pleasant patch of greensward. In the restful shade, I set out my lunch of bread, cheese, honey and milk – a meal of ancient simplicity still on sale in village shops. After half an hour I started reluctantly to get ready to go on. On a hot day like this it would have made more sense to drowse away the afternoon in the dappled shade playing with the tangles of Neaera's hair. In spite of this sensible call to sun-dappled slumber, I continued to put the remnants of lunch back into my rucksack. The Protestant Work Ethic is strong. Unless you are actually doing something all the time, preferably something difficult, you feel you are failing in some way. It's a terrible curse; I have been fighting it all my life. Suddenly over a few seconds the air became colder and I felt a friendly presence. I looked up and there was a twelve-year old sitting on a branch swinging her legs in the air. She was dressed in some sort of mossy green gossamer.

'Hello,' she said, 'why are you in such a hurry?'

I thought she must be some child playing at make-believe. How did she get to this remote place all by herself? I decided to make a run for it. It doesn't do for an old man to be alone in a wood with a twelve year old. I could already see the newspaper headlines: 'Elderly beast molests child in lonely wood.'

I looked at my watch. 'I'm late.' I said, 'I must get going.' I started to hurry, stuffing things willy-nilly into my rucksack.

'Don't go,' she said 'I haven't talked to anyone for years and years.'

She seemed older, more serious than a romantic child, consequently probably more, rather than less, dangerous. She might be a professional nymphette with her lawyer hidden in a nearby bush. We live in terrible times. Nevertheless, I don't like being rude, so rather than get my things together in silence I asked, 'Where did you come from?'

'Nowhere, I live here.'

'Where? Up there in that tree? Do you have a house or a nest up there?'

'No, I live right here within the tree, you daftie.'

I ransacked my mind for something else to say while I put more things in my pack. I decided to play along.

'You must be a tree spirit – a dryad, perhaps?'

'No, as it happens I'm a hamadryad.'

'Is there a difference?'

'Yes, I am part of the tree. I live in this tree all the time.' She patted the branch affectionately. 'Dryads are free to wander around. We hamadryads are stuck in one tree for its life span.'

I was silent; I am quite out of my depth with loonies, particularly loony children.

'Well say something' she said. 'Tell me your name?'

I wasn't going to fall for that one. Once they had your name you were done for. If she was real her lawyer would use it to identify me and if she was a genuine tree spirit she would have power over me. The latter is a well-known fact. I have read about it in books.

I changed the subject. 'Aren't you lonely up there all by yourself?'

'No, the trees are good company and I chat to the other hamadryads. We network through the interlocking root systems of our trees. We are always in touch. We often have parties and when there is a wind we sing together.'

I didn't reply.

'What's wrong with you people,' she asked, 'haven't you anything interesting to say?'

'I am sorry', I replied, 'I'm just not used to chatting with supernatural beings.'

'I am not supernatural. I am entirely natural. I am made from the same material as the tree and the same material as you. We're all based on carbon chemistry. It's not too difficult for me to emerge from my tree from time to time. I just re-configure some of the material of the tree to clothe my spirit and use some of its moss for a dress. All hamadryads can do it. I have forgotten the details of the theory behind it but I know it's something to do with managing probability.'

'Probability is something that can be managed?' I queried in some surprise.

'Yes, didn't you know that? You must have heard of quantum tunnelling, surely? You know an electron has only a probability of being at any particular place?'

'Well yes, but that only applies to electrons in the subatomic world – not to big molecules out here in the real macro world.'

'Well, put it this way: from your point of view it is very improbable that part of a tree can come out and re-assemble itself into a likeness of a hamadryad.'

'The likelihood is vanishingly small.' I agreed. It was getting very wearing having this heavy conversation with a ken-it-all *enfant savant*. It was a ridiculous scene. There I was on my knees with my half-packed rucksack before me being lectured on nuclear physics and probability theory by a hamadryad sitting airily on a branch of her oak tree.

'Well,' she continued, 'if you know how to manage probability it's easy to make what you would call improbable things happen. I am using the technique we were all taught when we became hamadryads. Like everything else manipulating probability needs energy. You must have noticed that before I came out the tree the atmosphere was quite sultry and now it is cool and fresh. The cooling results from my mobilisation of energy from our surroundings to configure my present form. It's easier to do on hot windless days like this: there is more ambient heat energy around. Even so, I can't keep up maintaining this improbable state for long. So let's get on with our conversation. How old are you?'

'Almost eighty.'

'Almost eighty! Gosh, you humans don't wear very well. I'm over twice your age. It's a hundred and sixty years since my tree and I were an acorn. My tree can probably do the same again before old age really sets in. I don't age fortunately. I'll just get another acorn from somewhere when my tree's time comes.'

'Does every tree have a hamadryad?'

'I think so, all the trees in this wood do, at any rate.'

'Where are they?'

'They're still in their trees. No point in them coming out. You are under my tree. You belong to me for the moment! But they are listening to us.'

'What puzzles me,' I said, 'is how a hamadryad speaks Academic Scots with an Edinburgh accent?'

'Because that's the way you speak. Before you noticed me I tested you for Gaelic but without sufficient response so I had to lapse into your speech.'

This child seemed to have all the answers. I changed tack again.

'You say you all can sing when the wind blows?'

'Yes we just adjust the angles of incidence our leaves make with the wind.'

'You mean you can control the leaves like reeds in a wind instrument?'

'Yes, why not? We are the original woodwinds, after all. What's more, our singing doesn't have stupid arrangements like beats to the bar. Millions of leaves precisely adjusted to the wind generate complex harmonics. Our melodies are huge and our rhythms immense. Your music by comparison is like a bird in a cage. It can't escape for the bars. "Beats to the bar" is a terrible concept; it is equivalent to corporal punishment. I think it comes from the way you have of writing music down. Before that your music was free. The pipers in the old days knew how to play in the free way. That was when tunes were passed on from piper to piper by ear and each tune had its geneology. Traditional pipers still say, "I got this tune from … and he got it from …." and so on back to the tune's origin. The old music was much more sensitive to the great natural rhythms of wind, sea and running water. If music is to respond to these elemental forces it can't be imprisoned in a cage, however golden. Such sophistication leads to deafness and too much sophistication to stone deafness. Everyone knows that.'

Then changing to something less intellectually demanding (I think she noticed I was struggling), she said 'But usually we only sing at night.'

'Only at night? Why?'

'Because during the day the leaves are adjusted to catch the radiant energy from sunbeams. This has priority. The trees need energy to grow. But on a good sunny day there are plenty of spare leaves and we do a bit of daylight singing. But at night we have all the leaves to play with; we are a massed choir. Well worth hearing. If we get a decent wind at the next full moon we are having a big concert. We have been rehearsing for months. We expect a lot of dryads will visit us. As I explained they are free to move around. I am on the waiting list to become a dryad,' she added.

'What do you sing about?'

'Different things, it depends on the wind and the mood we are in. In gentle breezes we do lovely sussurating lullabies, in boisterous weather we do the equivalent of strathspeys and reels and in a full gale we do jigs and headlong gallops. We also do serious stuff, praising whoever it is who runs the universe – equivalent to your hymns and oratorios – and during storms we usually do a paean. In winter when our leaves have fallen our bare branches are more like a stringed instrument. We can't adjust them so the wind plays its own music. We learn some interesting things from the wind when the breezes whisper through our branches.'

'You know, I have always suspected something like this was going on,' I said. 'I will listen more carefully in future. Tell me do you appear to everyone that rests beneath your tree?'

'No, of course not. As I have explained it takes a lot of energy to come out and talk. Usually it's not worth the effort. You just looked less dozy than most humans so I decided to give you a whirl.'

'Have I been a disappointment?'

'So-so. At least you haven't run away screaming like most of them and you seem to be interested in our singing which is something. Now look, I can't keep this up any longer. I see my leaves are beginning to droop. I have only a minute or two left. Tell me something interesting. Quick.'

'All I can say is I find the world a much better place now that I know for sure that hamadryads actually exist and trees can sing and some pipers are still playing the real un-caged music. I will listen more carefully in future.'

'Well, if I've managed to pass on that message, the effort of materialising has been worth it. Goodbye now.'

She faded and a couple of handfuls of moss floated down from where she had been sitting. I carefully replaced the moss on the branch in case she needed it again sometime.

But that is all by the way. What I am really trying to tell you about is the postman's path from Kinlochewe to Letterewe along the side of Loch Maree. The ground is steep and rough and at times precipitous right down to the waterside. The path is not obvious; it offers multiple choices with unavoidable detours both up and down. By mid-afternoon I had drifted fairly high on an intermediary ridge. I was probably sitting at the very place where on another June day exactly 200 years ago the writer, poet and shepherd James Hogg of Ettrick paused on his journey in the opposite direction. His party had been driven similarly high by the lie of the land. He looked back towards Letterewe and saw,

> …a lady of most delicate form and elegantly dressed … climbing over the dizzy precipices in a retrograde direction, and after fixing one foot, hanging by both hands until she could find a small hold for the other.

This spirited lady who understood the elements of rock climbing, was a Miss Jane Downie, daughter of the Manse of Urray near Dingwall. She was on her way to the Lewes to visit relatives. She, Hogg and two locals had tried to row down the loch from Letterewe but had to give up because of the headwind. Leaving the boat they had continued on foot into the teeth of the wind. Hogg goes on,

> [Her] clothes were partly torn and otherwise abused, and the wind had carried off her kerchief altogether. For upwards of a mile we were forced to scramble in this manner, making use of all fours.

He continues,

> I was in the greatest distress on account of the lady. The wind which had grown extremely rough took such impression on her clothes, that I was really apprehensive that it would carry her off, and looked back several times with terror for fear that I should see her flying headlong toward the lake like a swan.

Miss Downie was a spirited lady:

> Being the daughter of a respected clergyman, she had received a genteel education, a circumstance to which the utmost attention is paid by all families of rank in the north. To this she added a extensive knowledge of the world, of which she had seen a considerable part for one of her age and sex, for besides her acquaintance with both the Highlands and the Lowlands, she had resided some years in St. Petersburgh with a sister, who was there distinguished by royal favour and protection.

After this 200 year old, wind-buffeted foursome had passed by I felt a sense of anticlimax. I could see the rest of the route to Letterewe – miles and miles of repetitive, tree-clad ups and downs. On a day like this when the sky was blue and visibility only limited by the curve of the earth's surface, it would be more interesting to wander among the breezes of the upper air exploring the summit ridges of sunlit Beinn Airidh Charr.

It was the right choice. What a viewpoint! Don't take fright – I am not going to describe it to you as it deserves, but I must record the blue of the lochs in the brown heathlands and away to the west the blue-grey patterned sea edged by the Long Island, and leaving Gairloch was a boat with a brown sail – probably bound for the Lewes with Miss Jane Downie aboard.

The day was still young so I descended into the complicated territory on the north side and identified the main feature, a steep buttress rising to the summit where Glover and Ling had made a Diff route in 1910. In that year Osgood Mackenzie must have been an active stripling of sixty-six busily engaged in building the celebrated garden on the once barren peninsula next to Inverewe. The Ling-Glover duo were not the first to climb these rocks. Osgood mentions that when he was 'not more than seven or eight years old' the sea eagles nested on,

> …that stupendous precipice at the back of Beinn Airidh Charr just above Carn nan Uamhag (*the Cairn of the small Caves*) – that wonderful cairn and stronghold of foxes and wildcats where the last of our martens was killed.

He continues on his deplorable way to raid the sea eagle's nest,

> '…away we went on pony back with an expert rock climber and ropes etc.'

So rock climbing using a rope has a long history in the Gairloch area.

I also tried to find the site of the first recorded traverse of the summit crag. It was made long ago by a shepherdess looking for the spindle she had let fall from the summit. She fell to her death, alas. I didn't investigate too closely; she might still have been there and in a chatty mood. I had had enough female epiphanies for one day.

LYME DISEASE AND YOU

By Iain Thow

As AN active hillgoer who has been affected by Lyme Disease for the last year and a half it has been suggested to me that some information about the disease might be of interest to Club members. Lyme Disease is a tick-borne infection, first diagnosed in Lyme, Conneticut in the 1980s, hence the name. Recent milder winters have led to both an increase in the number of ticks and a lengthening of their active period, and in addition more of them are carrying *Borrelia Burgdorferi*, the Lyme vector. In some areas as many as 30% of ticks are infected, and confirmed diagnoses in humans in Scotland have risen from 16 in 2005, to 300 in 2006 and 250 in the first half of 2007. Part of this is explained by greater awareness among both doctors and the general public, but it seems likely that there has also been a genuine increase in cases.

Ticks lay eggs on the ground in spring and autumn and when they hatch, the larvae feed on small mammals and birds, then lie dormant for a few months to become adults. At this point, by now April/May or October/November, they attach themselves to larger mammals, including humans, and can now transfer any infections they carry to us. Lyme (*Borrelia*) is the commonest of these, but there are also several other possible delights. In my case I also received a fun nematode worm known as *Cryptostrongylus*,[*] first identified by Harvard Medical School in 2003, possibly the same as a parasite in sheep. This affects my ability to absorb oxygen and leaves my lungs only half as efficient as before. Some doctors think these worms don't exist, but given that they have turned up in my blood samples I find this a difficult argument to sustain.

If ticks are removed quickly they are unlikely to transfer any infection they carry to you, so regular checking is recommended. I still often wear shorts, but check my legs any time I stop. Ticks will crawl up your legs and clothing to find warm places where the blood is near the surface before biting. Conventional wisdom has it that if a tick has Lyme Disease you will get a target-shaped rash around the bite, but in fact the rash can be any shape and at least 10% of people (40% in one study) get no rash at all. Certainly if you get a rash or swelling around a bite you should get a course of antibiotics. If treated within 3 weeks or so then the bacteria are easily killed. Problems arise if it is left untreated. I had no rash, and no real symptoms for 4 months, apart from feeling a bit more tired than usual, which I just put down to *Anno Domini*. My joints then stiffened and developed sore spots, I got so tired that I needed a rest

---

[*] [These creatures are tiny; the male is approximately 0.3mm in length; the female is a little less than one millimetre in length—Hon. Ed.]

after walking upstairs, I needed 10 hours sleep a night, had a permanent cough, flu-like symptoms, difficulty concentrating, sharp headaches located in very specific spots on the outside of the skull, and what I can only describe as 'washes' of tiredness. Both the headaches and the tiredness felt different to any I'd ever had before. Over a few weeks I went from doing 15–20 hill miles a day (I work as a walking guide) to barely making it upstairs. It felt like living permanently at 4000 metres! As I know a number of people who have had Lyme recently I thought that it was likely to be what the problem was, but the doctors I saw were very reluctant to conclude this and just kept sending me for more tests.

The usual tests for Lyme Disease look for antibodies, but the Lyme spirochaetes seem able to 'hide' inside other cells, so after a while the body just accepts them and stops producing antibodies. The tests therefore often produce false negatives. Doctors are therefore advised to diagnose on the symptoms rather than the tests. Without the rash, though, these are easily confused with a number of other syndromes, so doctors are reluctant to diagnose Lyme. Two out of the three doctors I have seen didn't think Lyme was the problem as I had had three negative tests, despite the fact that my job makes me a prime target for the disease. It wasn't until I had a different sort of test, basically looking for the spirochaetes themselves with a microscope, that I had a confirmed diagnosis. Unfortunately these tests are not available on the NHS and are not widely carried out. Dr Andrew Wright at the Fatigue Clinic in Bolton did mine.

In summary, Lyme Disease is an increasing risk in the Scottish hills. Check regularly for ticks and seek early treatment if bitten, especially if there is any sign of a rash around the bite.

[Iain tells me that he has now largely recovered from the worst effects of his infection. The Lyme disease was treated with a two week course of antibiotic (*metronidazole*). However the worms in his lungs still give him problems. He cannot absorb oxygen as efficiently as previously, and so has difficulty running or performing strenuous exercise. In some countries this worm in humans is treated with *ivermectrin*, but this drug is only approved for use on animals in the UK. Iain hasn't yet found a vet who is prepared to treat him—Hon. Ed.]

WASPS ON A STRING

By Mike Dixon

THE DAY began ominously.

Brodie rang the bell for Taylor's flat twice but there was no answer. He paced about then threw some chippings at a first floor window. A dishevelled, startled figure appeared from behind a curtain. Taylor was half dressed, unfed and his sack not yet packed. He tried to make light of the situation as Brodie passed the time watching breakfast TV. He grunted in response to Taylor's excuses. The day was now soured for Brodie. He couldn't help noticing Taylor's greying hair and slight paunch.

Two nights ago in the Market Bar, things had seemed promising for the pair. They'd decided upon a route in the Loch A'an Basin; conditions permitting, something on Hell's Lum.

At 34, Brodie had come late to mountaineering. His past career as a rugby player had left him with a heavy, bull-like physique and a rather clumsy gait. Since catching the climbing bug he'd devoured the literary canon of Scottish winter mountaineering and the words of Collie, Smith and Mullin had left him inspired and thirsty for adventure. He was relatively new to the sport and needed someone with a bit more experience to point him in the right direction and help push up his grade. A regular climbing partner had not materialised. He'd known Taylor, a local Inverness climber in his early forties, for about six months. They'd drunk, joked and talked climbing together without actually doing a route. Winter climbing is a rigorous test of any friendship.

Despite Taylor's experience, little of his climbing had been of a recent vintage. It's easy to forget the hardship and the raw fear of winter climbing under the euphoria of alcohol. Taylor had returned to climbing, as many do, following the breakdown of his marriage, seeking the familiarity of old companions and the excitement of his younger days. Even talking about the hills was an escape for him although he was inclined to forget that the triumphs he relived were separated from the reality of today by eight years of relative domesticity. However, three weeks ago he'd climbed Emerald Gully, when other parties had retreated. He was back.

His attitude was too laid back for the rather intense Brodie who thought him smug and living too much off his back catalogue of routes. It was quite telling of Brodie's perceptions that no one else read Taylor's character in this way.

Brodie reassured himself with the facts:

Taylor's climbing CV was enviable.

He'd often pulled off respectable routes after a long lay-off. Once embarked on a route, Taylor rarely failed to finish.

Brodie was frustrated by his failure to establish himself as a climber. Tomorrow he would be back in the classroom. He needed a good route and he needed it quickly, and very much wanted to out-perform the older man.

Taylor quite liked the idea of having an apprentice. The only thing that grated was Brodie's tendency to pepper his speech with phrases from Monty Python. During the short journey down the A9 Taylor became increasingly excited about the prospect of a climb. Brodie had been a bit prickly this morning, noted Taylor, but put it down to the nerves he was experiencing before his first hard route.

The orange glow behind Ben Rinnes lifted Brodie's spirits fleetingly but his mood had dropped again by Aviemore. The upper car park was almost full and had all the allure of a supermarket compound. He found a space between a luxury 4WD people carrier and an old hatchback much the same as his own.

'We need to get a move on,' he muttered.

Taylor responded by stretching out on the passenger seat and rolling a fag. At least three pairs of climbers who arrived subsequently were to beat them to the off. Then there was the usual debate over which pieces of gear to take and how to equalise loads. At last they joined the line heading towards Cairn Gorm. Brodie had deferred to Taylor the night before and agreed to take up the offer of a complimentary ride on the chair lift. Queues were lengthy, Brodie's eyes rolled upwards.

'Shall we go to Sneachda instead?' he ventured, anxious to get on a route and aware of the shortening day.

But Taylor was inflexible. He was also not fit. He was sweating in the relatively short rise to Cairn Gorm and demanded a rest en route. He at least enjoyed the arctic vistas which was more than could be said for his companion. Brodie was already wishing he had a viable excuse to abort the trip. Why on earth were they approaching by this indirect route?

A solo climber emerged from one of the gully exits in Sneachda, all smiles and enthusiasm about conditions. Upon peering over into the coire Taylor became acutely aware of how popular the sport had become in the last few years. Crampons were donned before the descent into Coire Domhain. The cliff was sheeted in textbook ice. All the classics were occupied including their intended route. There were however a few vacancies. Still no urgency from Taylor. He jettisoned his sack and proceeded to inspect the crag's left hand side. During his absence another pair had arrived and staked their claim at the foot of a free route. While Brodie simmered, Taylor rolled another fag. At least he was now starting to gear up.

'What do you fancy?' enquired Brodie.

'Not sure yet. Don't want to be behind anybody. Chuck us over that guidebook.'

After thoughtful study, alternating with upward scans of lines on the cliff, Taylor promptly sat down again. His next major action was to reach into his sack for a pork pie. Brodie erupted at the prospect of another delay.

'For fuck's sake! We're here to climb, not fucking meditate! How much longer are you going to be?!' He'd had enough of all this indecision. His body language became belligerent, pointing to his watch like an irate, delayed rail traveller. His outburst seemed so out of place in the hallowed setting of this frozen sanctuary. Brodie spat out another torrent of abuse, but felt he'd been diplomatic beyond the call of duty. After all, surely winter climbing required more of a commitment than Taylor was offering? Letting off steam only temporarily alleviated his angst. More importantly he'd lost his head and thus now suffered from loss of face. An instant apology or some ironic laughter could have defused the situation, but it was not forthcoming.

In the face of this onslaught Taylor remained composed, affected a wry smile and coolly replied, 'I'm not going to be dictated to by a novice.' The precise but unnatural enunciation of clipped syllables added extra bite. 'You don't half remind me of my ex-wife,' added Taylor, spitting out fragments of pork pie with his words. Brodie had been niggling him all day. It was like being tethered to an angry wasp on a short string. 'You've had more climbing partners in the last two months than I've had changes of underpants,' he pointed out to the younger man, with all the poise of a matador delivering the final, fatal blow.

'Perhaps you ought to consider why that is, before you go on yelling at me. Learn a bit from experience before you go shouting the odds.' It was Taylor's controlled delivery which gave his verbal barbs the extra sting. In reality neither could afford to be choosy about climbing partners.

The image of a banana pick embedded in a skull began to evolve in Brodie's mind. Violence seemed an option but he kept his mouth and fists tightly bound. The intensity of his stare threatened to reduce the Shelter Stone to dust.

'Ah, the camaraderie of the hills. There's nowt like it,' drifted down in a thick Geordie accent from a climber on Devil's Delight. It triggered a chorus of laughs from all over the cliff.

After what seemed like an eternity, Taylor said he didn't feel like doing anything now. It was his first decisive act of the day. Lack of time was now a more reasonable excuse, but things had been said and minor annoyances from the past began to fester and magnify. There would never be a return to the genial conviviality of the past.

As if to mock them, the weather was now quite flawless. It should have been a simple return to the car but Taylor felt he hadn't yet finished with his partner to his satisfaction. Brodie wanted to speak but couldn't decide upon a suitable entrée. Any eye contact would have been too painful for him. Taylor was too good at dealing with awkward customers. He encountered them every day at work through his job at the benefit fraud office. The time was right to engage in some mind games. Brodie swallowed the bait. It began with Taylor picking up the pace ridiculously and revelling in the sound of Brodie's exertions to try to keep up with him. Brodie moved like a wounded animal after the verbal assaults. Then Taylor dropped several gears. Indeed he had no choice with his level of fitness. He knew he was succeeding when Brodie knocked into his heels several times and then overtook him with an audible sigh of frustration. Taylor let him get right ahead then decelerated further, so that his companion would have to wait even longer for him to catch up. He correctly surmised that Brodie didn't have the balls to bolt off without him.

On attaining the rim of Sneachda they were greeted by hordes of climbers delighted by their routes and the fabulous conditions. Most had completed lower-standard routes. Those successful on harder routes wore expressions of more controlled emotion. One climber tried to engage in conversation with Brodie. In a forced interaction, all he could say was that they'd been to look at something over at Hell's Lum. He kept back from the corrie's edge to discourage any more enquirers. He passed a work colleague, an occasional hillwalker, his face a picture of divine revelation after a walk out to Macdui. There was just no redeeming feature of the day for Brodie.

Taylor held back and was more sociable. 'Great day, shame about the company,' was his comment to one passer by, with a wicked grin in Brodie's direction. Still the younger man plodded on in silence, picking up vague snatches of conversation, adding to his paranoia. More was to come. Taylor announced he wished to make the most of the superb day by re-traversing Cairn Gorm. A full moon meant he could prolong the day even further, but he kept this thought to himself. Brodie was relieved to escape him and sat down for a rest. His return route was significantly shorter than Taylor's. If there'd been no one else around, he would have burst into tears. He knew what Taylor's strategy was, but felt he should endure it as a penance. 'Never again,' he mumbled.

He wondered how to deliver the day's events to mutual friends. What decision would the kangaroo court in The Phoenix Bar come to over this debacle? It would certainly provide no shortage of amusement and psychological profiling for them. He was already dreading having to stop for the obligatory pint at the Winking Owl which Taylor would insist upon. Not one metre of ice had been climbed on the best day yet of the season. Brodie consoled himself that he'd learnt nothing about front-pointing, though at least something about life, but an aspect of life that he could quite happily do without. Despite the crowds, Brodie felt completely alone as he traversed round the lip of the corrie. Over and over he replayed the day's events. Guilt had finally entered his mind. Perhaps he should have forgiven the lateness and the slowness of pace? They could easily have abandoned climbing and still enjoyed a hill walk. It would have been one of his finest days weather wise since moving up north. Emotionally, it would at least have ended in neutral. Pride had caused him to offer no apology but he vowed to rectify this as soon as they were reunited. He really couldn't afford his meagre social circle to diminish any more. That was another thing they both had in common.

Approaching the summit of Cairn Gorm, Taylor's thoughts were not as conciliatory and he decided to continue with his lesson. Make him wait, he thought. Make the little bastard wait. His footsteps became slow and deliberate. He visited several obscure, satellite tops and savoured the frozen solitude. It was as good as daylight under the neon moon. He took lengthy stops to absorb the whole scene at leisure. Life was so simple and uncomplicated up here.

Descending from the summit plateau Taylor was looking forward to the cosy nest of the warm car awaiting him and inwardly gloated over his handling of the situation. As he approached the lonely vehicle at the bottom end of the desolate car park he began to whistle then deliver the lyrics of a familiar song in an overly cheery manner,

'Always look on the bright side of life ...'

He was more than surprised when his taps on the roof elicited no response. The car was frozen up. He scraped away frantically at the driver's window. There was no one in there! Suddenly his heart started racing. Where was Brodie? Fallen through a cornice? Lost? Lying injured? Committed suicide? Dead? Oh Jesus! He should never have left him. He felt responsible, being the more experienced of the two. Waves of concern flowed over him. He scanned the hillside for any sign of a headtorch. The wind was picking up and the moon was becoming obscured by falling snow. 'Brodie! Brodie!' he howled into the blackness. He was just about to head up to the phone box to make a 999 call when he became aware of the sound of a car engine behind him. He turned round to see Brodie grinning from ear to ear.

'Isn't that amazing,' he said laughing, 'an old hatchback just like mine!'

Dougal Haston (on the Eiger). Photo: John Cleare.

MÖNCH NORDVÆG

By Ole Eistrup

This article describes the first ascent of the Haston-Eistrup route on the North-West face of the Mönch (TD+, September 1976). This was the last new route made by Dougal Haston before his untimely death. It is a translation of an article written by his climbing partner, Ole Eistrup, which was originally published in Danish in 1977 in the Magazine of the Danish Alpine Club, Dansk Bjergklub.

Ole was the first student Dougal had at the International School of Mountaineering (summer 1967) after taking it over from John Harlin. Over subsequent years Ole became a personal friend of Dougal and his wife Annie, working occasionally as an instructor for the ISM.

IT WAS a day at the end of August. I was in my office trying to forget how nice the weather was when the phone rang from Switzerland. It was Dougal Haston. After sharing a few pleasantries with me, he, as casually as possible, enquired whether I would like to come down and climb with him. He had a fortnight off and so on. At first I was non-committal but I promised to phone him back in a couple of days. I had recently, with much effort, repaired the damage caused to my family, my work and my sense of duty as a citizen, by my 7 week long trip to Peru. On the other hand, something big must have been afoot.

This could potentially be a chance for me to progress beyond the Alpine trade routes, since Dougal never repeated an established route without being paid to do so. In a short space of time I had managed to justify another period of absence, at least to myself, and a couple of days later I was on the train. The situation was quickly made clear to me: some of Dougal's young instructors, Terry King, Gordon Smith, and Alex McIntyre, who during the last couple of seasons had been bagging classic routes, were now looking for recognition and fame – that is, new routes. Dougal, whose 10 year experience of Switzerland naturally gave him the advantage of knowing which lines remained to be 'conquered', was starting to worry that the ambitious youngsters would try to overshadow his past triumphs. That he, in that particular situation, decided to request Danish assistance, probably says more about professional rivalry than about my climbing qualifications.

After a couple of training trips to Tour d'Ai above Leysin, and some rainy days, we were ready for Mont Vélan in Valais. Here, Dougal had chosen a long, narrow ice couloir on the north face; an obvious and aesthetic line which I hereby recommend to the Club's alpinists as it

Top: North Face of the Mönch (left edge of shadow approximately corresponds to Haston-Eistrup Route). Photo: John Cleare.
Bottom: North Face of the Mönch, 10 October 2007. Photo: Nick Csakany.

remains unclimbed. That's because when, after a sweaty day and a half, we stood at the start [of the couloir], we agreed that we should take advantage of the beautiful weather and clear sky to attempt what Dougal really had in mind: a new and more direct route on the north face of the Mönch. Down again, back to Leysin, shopping, bath, check equipment, and the next evening we were, once again covered in sweat, sitting in the Guggi Hut enjoying the solitude, lemon tea, and an amazing sunset. At 4 a.m. we left the hut behind us and stomped up the Nollengrat, until we reached a point from where we could abseil down into the basin above the icefall and under the north face (or more accurately: the North-West Face, to the right of the Lauper route). We kept to the basin's westerly edge to cross the bergschrund, and finally traversed a bit to the east directly under the face. When Dougal stopped and suggested a cup of tea, it occurred to me that we were still short of where we would be able to start the obvious central line we had decided upon when studying Mountain 27[1], which would take us directly to the top[2]. However, I did not feel it was my job to make any demands and, although I felt physically fit, I knew that my task was to belay and to follow.

We expected to find the biggest technical difficulties at the beginning of the face. Here, a broad rock band rose out of the basin, and the ice conditions would be crucial in deciding how far we would be able to go. From the stance I listened to a commentary of crude Scottish vocabulary. For an hour or two, Dougal was out of sight, and when I was finally able to follow I understood the meaning of his description 'fuckin' unconsolidated ice on top of nothing'. The ice was brittle and thin, and frequently gave way under my crampons. The terrordactyls only occasionally found a centimetre to bite into. It was truly mixed climbing, and the angle sometimes approached 80 degrees.

Feeling relieved, we continued going upwards for another couple of rope-lengths. The time was approaching midday and small avalanches and rocks were starting to fall on both sides of us. Despite the snowfall of the last week, which made the outing appear to be happening under almost winter conditions, it was uncomfortably hot. It must have been the latter which compelled Dougal, when faced with a sheer rock band, to veer to the right on the rock face rather than taking the direct line to the left of the face. By mid-afternoon we had reached the very wide ice couloir which separates the north-west face from the Nollengrat, and we stuck to the very left of this whilst looking for a suitable place to make our bivouac. When we thought we'd found the right spot, sheltered from avalanches under a rocky overhang, we both in turn and involuntarily got doused by great showers of water. We now faced the option of either

---

[1] [The reference to *Mountain* 22 in the original article is a mistake—Hon. Ed.]

[2] [First climbed by Renshaw and Wilkinson 3 months later—Hon.Ed.]

hoping for icy conditions to freeze the water before we became entirely soaked, or continuing upwards. We decided upon the latter, but before finding the appropriate spot, two rope-lengths further up, Dougal managed to break the tip of our only ice axe (he was making use of two terrors, a hammer and an ice axe); meantime the night was upon us and our clothes were frozen. We both hacked out a small platform. In record time, Dougal had disappeared into his bivouac sac, and I quietly cursed him while I frantically and unsuccessfully attempted to keep clear of the increasing spindrift.

My mood improved, however, when a long arm suddenly reached up and handed me a mug of hot soup. Instead of indulging in a description of the menu, I would like to offer some advice to other Danes who might embark on climbs with Brits; take charge of buying the food. Although I am aware that fat contains the necessary calories, and despite normally enjoying bacon fried with eggs, I have rarely eaten anything more nauseating than raw bacon, served as starter, main course and dessert.

The night was long, and, although from a climbing point of view it would have been preferable, I found it difficult to wish it any colder. We left the couloir and went about 3–4 rope-lengths up a difficult rock rib in the wall[3]. It had started snowing, and we now had to contend with very strong gusts of wind. Strangely it was not until this point that I started to take pleasure from the thought that no other human being had been here before; there were no chocolate wrappings, no matches, and no bolts. The change in weather was evident in Dougal's runners: some of them were purely psychological. The opportunities for protection were also much reduced by a change in the geology of the rock. It was Dougal who brought this to my attention; he had noticed this the year previously on the north-east face when he had put up a new direct route with Guy Neithardt.

Once again we moved out to the wider couloir[4] just above the obvious diedre, and from here it took only 3–4 rope-lengths to reach the shoulder where the Nollengrat ends, and where the descent to the Jungfraujoch starts. As I have never done the full journey on the Eigerbahn, I had been looking forward to reaching the Jungfraujoch. However, for some reason Dougal decided to descend via the Nollengrat. The weather was now turning into a full-blown snowstorm and the abseil, and in particular the subsequent unroped and rather random descent down the snow covered ridge, was almost literally lethal.

In the Guggi Hut, four inexperienced, ageing hillwalkers were sitting worrying about how to get back down again. We were not much help to them. Following the effort and the solitude of the wall, their hectic

---

[3] [On the left side of the couloir. See end notes—Hon. Ed.]
[4] [They moved right to regain the couloir. See end notes—Hon. Ed.]

conversation seemed almost blasphemous to us, so we went to bed, and left the hut before they even rose. Through the mist and the snow-fog, we made our way down to Kleine Scheidegg. Lunch in Grindelwald, dinner in Leysin, and, following the obligatory long night at the bar in Club Vagabond, I allowed myself to collapse into the train seat. I had scratched an itch, and now my thoughts were already returning to my son and my work. The season was over.

* * *

Additional notes supplied by Ole Eistrup (March 2008)

Our original intention had been to attempt the more central line [i.e. Renshaw/Wilkinson, Ed], but the warm conditions caused us to change our plan – a sensible decision given the subsequent frequent stonefall.

We started somewhat to the right (west) of the start of the Renshaw/Wilkinson Route. I would say midway between that and the prominent vertical line we are credited with in the photo on page 14 of *Mountain* 54.

The first part of the route went over difficult rock bands (to the left/east) of the couloir. Only after some 8 or 10 hours of climbing did we reach that broad ice couloir, and after 4 or 5 pitches did we dig two separate bivouacs in its left part.

Next morning saw us leaving the couloir again to climb a series of difficult rock pitches in deteriorating weather (snow). Eventually that same day we once more moved (right) out into the couloir again, and after 3 or 4 more pitches, we stood on the shoulder where the Nollen ends.

The current guidebook description (cf. the alternative start to the right/west of the couloir) is neither mine nor Dougal's. It must have been made by somebody who, due to the scanty information in *Mountain* magazine, thought they had repeated our route, while in reality they were making a first ascent!

The time given [7–10hrs] is what I would estimate for the ideal, straight-up line, whereas we spent two days on our version.

An interesting point is that the lower part of the couloir apparently had too little ice when the describer made the climb. It most probably also had too little ice at the time of our climb, in September! But no-one seems to have thought about that, or have there been whispers??

[Thanks to Susan Rasmussen of Stirling University for translating the original article into English. Thanks also to Robin Campbell for putting me in touch with Ole Eistrup, and also for giving the translation a final polish—Hon. Ed.]

TWO WORLDS

by John Mackenzie

IT WAS whilst stirring the marmalade and contemplating the dearth of Sevilles[1] that the words the Great Helmsman of the Journal spoke at the AGM bubbled through the boiling pot below. 'No articles equals no Journal; just a compilation (a constipation?) of 20m routes'. Being only partially guilty of the latter I decided to put the former at least marginally to rights.

Andy N's theory of every seven years bringing a cracking winter seemed in December at least promising. Neil Wilson and I were driving down Glen Strathfarrar in temperatures of -9°C; the frost rising and falling as we entered and left pockets of still cold air. We drove past Braulen Lodge, shuttered and empty, past the track to Sgurr na Muice and scene of so many jolly winter days, over the fine arcuate dam at the head of Loch Monar and past the little conical hill of Meall Innes an Loichel that separates the loch into two arms to finally come to rest at the pumping station by the Uisge Misgeach. The pump jets water over the bridge and now this was a platform of ice, covered in ice flowers, indeed a veritable forest of them; so we then drove over this hurdle (to save 300m of walking), got ourselves an ice wash and parked by the pipeline.

It was certainly cold but still, not a breath of wind and clear as a bell. Negotiating the verglas-covered concrete building to access the hillside was the first of the day's obstacles. The second was trying to keep up with Neil, fit and fast, a Snow Leopard compared to my ageing Chamois. Our game plan was to sprint up the first 200m to the spot height of Carn na Saile Leithe at 483m, gambol like lambs across the peat hags of the Garbh-choire, saunter up the open gully to the Bealach na Cloiche Duibhe at 796m and finally march up to the hidden coire of Creag na Lapaich, marked on no maps at all. I had surmised that due to a temperature inversion above the frost there would be only one place in the Northern Highlands fit enough for climbing on and that was here, tucked into the folded skirts of Sgurr na Lapaich, with a base of 900m and possibly protected from the inversion.

The initial sprint to the spot height was spoiled only by my rasping breath, forming small strato-cumuli behind me. At least the ground was rock hard. The amble-gambol across the peat hags was partially thwarted by spigots of bog oak catching and tripping us up, but led to the lower crags of Coire nan Each at 700m where both the peace and

---

[1] Seville oranges for those unfortunate enough to have to buy their own marmalade.

panorama of this deserted part of the Highlands started to make itself felt. The open groove-like gully that led up the right-hand side to the bealach was less of a saunter than a sauna. It was the first winter route of the season and my sac was transmogrified into an obese creature fed solely on black puddings and haggis and which dragged a pair of anchors behind. I noted that even Neil, ahead of course, was slowing slightly. Stopping for a breather at the bealach we could at last appreciate where we were. Huge views were all around, the clarity of the air crisping up distant horizons and also, pertinently, showing us that though Lapland Buttress across the way was clear of anything white, our secret coire was not only white but icy.

I had soloed a line one February not many years ago, near the centre of the crags above and couldn't help but notice a tempting slot to its right which had ice spewing down it. As we traversed into and down towards the base and the snow, would our gamble pay off this time? I saw that there was avalanche debris from a cornice collapse exactly in the same spot as there had been when there last, but would there be as much ice in the slot?

The snow was firm and crisp, the air temperature hovered around freezing and the slot ahead drooled a tongue of ice. So far so good. A convenient cave lay to the right of the slot and knowing how narrow the second pitch would be we left our sacs there. Last year the slot was bottomed by blue ice flowing out beyond where it did today. It formed a flume hemmed in by narrowing walls that are initially open for the first pitch but then close dramatically. Then the would-be second pitch appeared to be vertical ice with a chockstone overhead which would need to be squeezed under; now it was leaner and less easy to see from below.

Neil was almost over-keen to lead the first pitch and was soon engrossed in the bulges of the initial pitch. I moved right from the cave to see what he was up to and saw that the upper chimney was a rather gap-toothed, icicle-fringed black hole. A wise choice of lead for him as he bridged and picked up the translucent bosses set amidst bare rock. He reached what looked like a solid belay and it was time for me to see if our gamble had paid off.

Without that sac hulking on my back, climbing became a pleasure again. The ice bosses were very brittle but my picks and crampons were sharp too and if above was not exactly big scale then at least it was precisely neat and concentrated, balancing across from ice to rock and back to ice again. Stepping across the corner I joined Neil at his decidedly cramped stance on ground that had looked almost flat from below and now turned out to be as steep as usual.

Geared up and ready to go, I headed towards the chimney, a black portal that had festoons of icicles blocking it just where the point of greatest difficulty would lie. Steepish ice led into the slot where the angle rapidly steepened to plumb vertical, the point in my photos that showed either a submerged chockstone or a rock rib under the ice. Now that that ice was no longer thick enough to obfuscate chockstone with rib, I could see it was a recessed rib lining the slot. Ice ran down either side of it with a serious fringe of icicles overhead and, well above, the tilted chockstone that marked the entrance to a yet deeper inner sanctum that appeared to end at another blank wall thus making for a perfectly enclosed rectangle save for its entrance. This was the sort of line that would make a popular route in the Cairngorms or other climbed-on areas but here probably wouldn't see a second ascent for another 20 years and perhaps was all the better for it.

Uncomfortably wedged at the base of the slot I was now anxious for some gear. I cleared away much of the overhead frippery of ice chandeliers, corkscrews, holes and other convulsions of solid water and concentrated on the rib set between walls little more than two feet apart. I moved up to an ice foothold, comfortingly flat for one foot but leaving me restricted in movement, a straitjacket pinning arms so only one could move at a time. The side wall to my left was smooth, the one to my right thinly iced. The rib between had a poor crack on the left but, with digging, a better one on the right at waist level. Due to the inversion and the fact that the ice was largely due to a healthy spring, the water now flowed slowly out to the surface when I had cleared the crack, thus wetting gloves and arms nicely. Convoluted efforts were needed to place gear whereas thicker ice might have offered a screw and less effort.

If I could but find a way of moving up a mere metre I could get an axe over the top of the rib and into whatever lay beyond. A clue was a frothy ice bulge at chest height and a precisely placed axe into the tinkles above that. This was done, given the thought of a solid Neil and runners below. Standing on the froth was one thing; moving up another. The slot now lessened in angle but the ice thinned, running glassily over mossy rock. So, good right foothold below, nothing above. Overhead, the ice seemed thicker to the right so a well-aimed axe sank into what could be described as a 'Thank God' slot. With a rock solid right axe but a scrape for the left the first attempt ended in a technical failure with both feet and left axe ripping, all held nicely by the right axe. Try again, clear a snagging icicle and pull; same result, so back on my foothold. 'Must try harder', as my school reports so often warned, so a really big heave up on the right axe resulted this time in a grovelling success, bum in the air and left axe waving around as if at some political rally. Not being easily fooled into releasing the right axe the only way I could figure was to mantle onto the adze with my knee and hope that the little flake of rock for the left axe would hold. Which it did and so a well-wetted and somewhat muddy self was dragged inelegantly into the Inner Sanctum.

The chockstone was now well overhead and the slot had narrowed so that progress was crab-wise, sidling up to an emphatic dead-end under another chockstone. A couple of metres above was sunlight, thick ice and freedom but I was happy to have got at least this far. A small nut under the capstone helped as I squinted upwards and so by dint of chimneying outwards towards the tilted chockstone, now level with me, I could fling a right leg against it and reach the thick ice at full stretch, to heave over into the full glare of the sun. I could now move my arms into whatever position they liked, so waved them around a bit, then climbed the generous ice towards that most perfect of belays, a deep square-cut spike well-glued to the mountainside.

Now it was Neil's turn. He's wider than me and cheated by wedging his shoulders across the slot and udged up, something a person of his build could do. However his progress ground to a halt within the Inner Sanctum, somewhat to my relief. Here his bigger frame took on the role of a reluctant belayer; secure when static but unwilling to leave when the time came. Massive blows of his axe produced some but not enough purchase to overcome gravity until he had reached the tilted chockstone and the leg trick which landed him on the ice above. The shortness of the pitch – a mere 20m – gave little clue to the amount of calories need to attain them.

Above was slightly anti-climactic and Neil led up easy ice whizzing arms and legs around like windmills just to show that a short period of solitary confinement never did a man any harm. He belayed when the rope ran out, so I followed through and did the same just reaching an isolated rock below the cornice, the rock having a good crack for gear and a belay. Neil by now fully restored to all motor movement charged up and hopped over the cornice and waited in the sunshine whilst I took a more relaxed pace to the same spot. Enthusiasm undimmed, he decided that the long gully on the left of the face would be a perfect way to finish the day. We would leave most of our gear at the top and descend to the base, pick up our sacs and then saunter up the gully to biscuits and tea at the top.

Apart from it being the Winter Solstice and being personally well knackered, I agreed that this was an admirable idea, rather hoping that Neil would carry my sac and possibly me up the gully too. First though the little problem of the descent. The cornice lay unbroken and stretched towards the final slopes of the east ridge of the hill. This meant a weary wander to where it ended and then a down climb of the steep headwall which gave way to an equally steep iron-hard slope which of course steepened into what looked suspiciously like another unclimbed line and so required yet another traverse right to avoid it. By the time we had collected our sacs and found a perfect ice grotto – with a blue hole of unfathomable depth in its base – we were ready for lunch.

After this rest, weight off the legs was now reversed and whilst Neil with undiminished speed sped off up the slope towards the gully of his dreams, I followed lamely in his wake, trying out all possible effort-saving combinations with crampons as the gully narrowed, steepened and continued without let or hindrance in a long straight line towards what looked like a little turfy pitch near the top. We were soloing up towards this feature, encouraged by Neil's shouts of 'Not far to go' and (later) 'Still not far to go' and finally 120m higher at the turf bulges 'Only fifty metres to go'. The turf steps were short, well frozen and provided a point of interest though still only Grade 1ish. A snow rib really did lead to the cornice-free top in what seemed like 50m and then there we were, back at our gear again.

The summit of Sgurr na Lapaich has a fine circular shelter and 360 degree panorama. The main focus was on Loch Monar and lonely Pait Lodge in its stand of frosted conifers, the fine cone of Bidean an Eoin Deirg, the plateau of Maoile Lunndaidh and to the right the Strathfarrar Munros with the huge triangular shadow of Sgurr na Lapaich rising ever higher up their flanks, reminding us that the sun was sinking fast and that the car lay 1000m below an ice bound north-east ridge. Of course there was no-one else around, not for miles, we had an entire range to ourselves and the sound of silence was everywhere.

3.30 p.m.; could we reach the car in a little over an hour? We had torches but the fading light had a greater magic than simply eclipsing it prematurely. Colours ranged through mauves then purples as we covered the frost-bound yellow grass below the top of Rubha na Spreidhe in our strides, before edging over An Leth-creag 300m lower and into the almost dark pit of the Garbh-choire aiming in the last light for the little point of Carn na Saile Leithe – our first port of call this morning. By now an almost full moon was helping our angry stumbles over the peat hags and the wretched bog oak that snagged and caught and begged us to be their bed companions for the night. A final uphill to the Carn and then down steeply for the last 200m, aiming for the ancient trees that dotted the slope and enthusiastically hanging off the rylock fence when feet skated off the ice flows that magically appeared whenever the slope disappeared over an edge.

Level ground with some light left but torches still unlit; a moon riding the sky and an intense frost covering the ground with white; then the final hurdle, the day ending as it had started, the large diameter concrete pipe separating us from the car had to be crossed. Neil threw his sac over the pipe, a feat of some strength but at that particular moment I felt more like Mr Bean and, finding a spot under the pipe, crawled through pushing my sac in front. We arrived at the car at exactly 4.30 p.m., one hour to the minute from the summit and 8 hours from when we had left the vehicle; satisfactory for the shortest day of the year and one of the best too.

Three weeks later after a good day out on Ben Wyvis's Coire Mor in more good weather, things changed. It snowed hard but remained icy. Andy and I had done, but not recorded, a summer Severe on Sgurr na Fearstaig's South Top and were ever so slightly anxious to try it this winter after an abortive attempt the previous one. We met just before the gate at the entrance to Glen Strathfarrar having survived black ice and snow on the drive in. The party consisted of Andy, Dave McGimpsey, Neil and me, but the weather consisted of lowering snow clouds and frets of a ragged wind. We were after the Grail again, hoping the previous frosts had done their work on the turf and that the steepness of the route had shrugged off most of the snow. The glen was quiet; no cars and the road, untreated as it was, was in a better condition than the one we had driven on to get here.

The familiar path up into Coire Toll a Mhuic was trudged up in ever deepening abominably soft snow and outbreaks of rain. It was hardly promising, what with forgetting my walking poles and how icy the Cannich road was compared to just how un-icy it was here. Ahead was white enough but the burn flowed like water with the path an increasing mire. There was a sudden temperature drop at about 400 metres and the rain turned abruptly to snow, not heavy but persistent. Never have I regretted not having poles with me so much. Whilst the indefatigable pair of Neil and Dave forged ahead, ploughing a footpath, Andy and I brought up the rear. The snow bore no weight, first ankle deep, then calf deep and finally knee deep at every step save for drifts and holes where it was thigh deep. Visibility gradually closed with the enigmatic face of where we hoped we were heading for hidden in mist. The final mile up the slope opposite the crag was purgatorial, as bad a going as I can remember. Finally we stood, knackered, opposite our crag – which waspartially obscured by shifting mists – and wondered if there would be any sort of climbable conditions at all. Only a close, hard look would tell as the route was entirely dependant on the turf being solidly frozen.

Ploughing up to the crag showed more snow than I had seen in twenty years, but that contrary to our gloomy thoughts the steep ground ahead began to look suddenly promising. The easy gully up to our right looked threatening with hidden cornices a real menace and what with the wind and snow only the steep stuff would be a safe option, which was just as well in the circumstances. We left our sacs below a bluff, geared up then climbed up and left, traversing into the base of our line and away from the line of the gully which I felt held danger. Safe in a recess above a possible direct start in leaner conditions, Andy prodded the turf; it was frozen solid. Andy and Dave would climb as a pair with Neil and me close behind with Dave appointed to climb the first pitch. The line was attractive, a long slabby edge rising more steeply near the top where it merged into the headwall. A complex summer line, we had every reason to suppose it would hold its interest in winter and it certainly looked as if it would.

Andy and I were having a wee chat about the snow conditions. I was dubious, he was uncertain. To clinch the argument, a roar from below announced the presence of a sizeable avalanche running the full length of Slanting Gully. We were safe here but our descent would be a problem later as would the short scarp slope below the cornice which we could see was small but like a healthy youngster, visibly growing. Out of the line of fire for the route, we could always abseil off if the exit proved too hazardous.

Dave meanwhile was getting on with the climbing and making steady progress up the edge above. It was a long pitch and he was soon lost to sight amidst swirling snow and mist. Andy in due course followed and then Neil, close on his heels. There is an initial tricky section to this pitch where a sloping foothold gives a springboard to move up left and round a corner where he disappeared for a while before re-emerging on the crest itself. He was soon lost in the murk and I had the crag, the wind and the eddies of spindrift seemingly all to myself; it was, in essence, a full-on Scottish winter day.

As usual when the rope went tight I began to move, no voice communication possible in such conditions; it was also cold and I was glad to get moving and see what this route was made of. A steep initial pull then up into a cracked corner to that downward pointing foothold where crampons had to be edged just so to stay on. Naturally there was a jammed nut to remove at this point of tenuous balance but it came out with a little effort. The steep moves above were strangely delicate with axes torqued horizontally and semi-mantled on to gain lodgement in an open corner, all nicely sustained without being desperate. Above and back right and then the very edge to follow, a big sweeping slab to my left bounded by the corner of The Sorcerer and to my right a drop. We were following the only line of weakness on perfect frozen turf and ice with dollops of snow to add interest. A short wall of thinly turfed rock, climbed on snibs and snubs, gave a foretaste of the pitch above where Andy could be seen having a great time clearing the snow hoping to find more nubbins of turf that he could join into a trail of possibility.

With all three of us at the stance, cramped but friendly, much advice was being suggested of going left or right or up or even down. In response he climbed even faster just to escape this verbal jostling but was soon back at clearing away the ubiquitous snow that hid the line so well. Another avalanche rumbled down Slanting Gully which changed the conversation to matters of weather, snow and winter climbing in particular in these days of climate change. The snow was falling steadily now that we were sheltered, though an occasional blast from above reminded us of the westerly gale that was evidently still in progress.

Andy was running out another long pitch, totally in his element. After an initial difficult wall he had moved right to a hidden groove then up to an overlap where a curious pair of rock ears jutted symmetrically. These pointed the way to a narrow runnel of turf that led to a right-facing corner and up into what looked like a dead-end. Another, bigger, overlap barred the way from the corner rightwards, save at the very rightmost end where the crag simply got steeper. Andy was now traversing close below the overlap and probably wondering just where we had gone in summer. I shouted up to him that there should be (I hoped) a hidden groove up and to the right that would be reachable. After a few steeper moves above the overlap the groove might be friendlier and I knew I had dismissed it as a summer way as it looked too easy, preferring a steeper but moss-free direct on knobbled schist. Andy's route certainly didn't look too easy now, but I also remembered it leading into a welcome alcove and groove leading to the top. He must have found it though as he was now out of sight and the rope was speeding up into the gloom.

With Dave now climbing above me I set off. The initial wall was getting a little bare of turf after the other pair but was delectably delicate, just in balance and protected by a fine small nut. Dave was settling into his role as unofficial photographer, keeping a steady five metres above me, whilst I made efforts not to appear flustered or to smile inanely. The climbing was surprisingly good and sustained but never too hard. The groove led to the pair of ears which Andy had draped with sling adornment and I found the narrow turf strip above them quite awkward, axes and crampons sharing the same cramped holes. One of the joys of this route was the excellent gear, spaced but solid and often slings around schisty gargoyles. Bumping up under the top overlap the delicate traverse right was the only option with just one tricky move to gain the groove. This, though steeper, was easier and soon led right to the spacious and almost weatherproof alcove that provided me with a perch, security and shelter. Andy was belayed higher on the right, tied to four separate belays just in case Dave avalanched the scarp slope beneath the cornice. I was out of the line of fire, safely off to one side but Andy wanted to field his man at closer quarters.

Whilst Dave ploughed up the short but steep scarp we all cowered waiting for the inevitable. Of course it went with a fine whoomph and the snow flew off overhead, much of it landing on Neil 50m below, unsuspecting and giving us some amusement. Dave, no innocent, had dug himself a fine trench to more solid stuff so when it went it was more like the parting of the Red Sea than a tsunami. Neil came up soon after, a little whiter, and, once Andy had cleared the top, proceeded to follow before the snow had a chance to build up again. By the time it was my turn on this evil little headwall there was no sign it had ever slid, the snow pouring over the lip of the cornice was building it up as quick as we were knocking it down. The cornice had now a sizeable breech and rolling onto the plateau the wind blasted horizontally. It wasn't too strong, just strong enough to be uncomfortable, but fascinating to see at first hand how quickly and efficiently snow is moved from one side of a hill to another. Snow seemed to be accumulating at a rate of 150–200mm per hour and this was the cause of those spontaneous release avalanches down Slanting Gully

A good route was done and now time to descend, but where? All the usual suspects were suspects and so a less lethal alternative had to be found. Fortunately the A team had been busy scouting and had found a steep cornice-free slope a few hundred metres away, well beyond the main cliffs by a nose near the summit of the South Top of the hill and had lowered a rope down it for a 'volunteer' to try the slope out. Neil as the heaviest was chosen and we expected waves of snow to career away but as they didn't, it seemed a well chosen site by the other pair.

I down climbed with Andy and we congregated at a little cave below the nose. To our right was a perfect iced groove, tempting but short and not for today despite a passing pang. Our next problem was to collect the sacs which of course meant climbing up to and crossing Slanting Gully which as we knew was spontaneously releasing every two hours or so. We descended as quickly as was possible through the deep porridge, which wasn't that speedy at all and then, for me at least, a tiring wade back up to reach the sacs. With Dave in front and the two hours up, nearing the now lethal battlefield of the formerly innocuous Slanting Gully we were trepidatious and sure enough another avalanche rumbled by, the fourth today, leaving a debris field about 100m across of soft blocks, quite uncompressed and looking as innocuous as a madman with a gun. Wading across this had all the essential qualities of a good honest-to-God nightmare, lead boots and all, trying in vain to hurry even though we knew our timing was okay since the slides seemed to be pretty regular.

Sacs were retrieved and so back across the dreaded gully, this time more quickly as it was downhill and no-one stopped for a bite until way beyond the danger zone. The wade out was much the same as the wade in but with the help of gravity to lessen the effort a little. If anything it was deeper, softer, and the holes (for there were plenty of them) found each and every one of us in turn and only lower down as the snow depth lessened did walking become more automatic again. In truth the climb had been the easiest and most relaxed part of the day and in perfect condition too. Now a light drizzle fell as we neared the car and I couldn't help but muse on the totality of difference in both weather and snow to that on Sgurr na Lapaich a few weeks before.

6000 METRES

by Derek Fabian

This article describes ascents of San Juan (5843 m) and Nevado Chinchey (6222 m) in the Peruvian Cordillera Blanca made by the 1958 Edinburgh Andean Expedition. It is dedicated to the memory of Bill Wallace.

Cold dinner on the Nevado San Juan:

FROM THE tent door a dramatic panorama spread before us to the northwest. At the head of the valley in which our base camp lay, some 1500m below, was an incredible spire of ice and rock, the Nevado Cayesh (5721m). We were able to confirm, in our lesser rights, the reported conclusions of two outstanding Alpine guides, Lionel Terray and Raymond Lambert, that it was probably unclimable from this, the south-west side. To the left of this spire and about 10km due north was a massive and beautiful pyramid of snow and ice, the Nevado Chinchey (6222m) – a six-thousand metre summit, we had noted, when its enticing vista had first come into view during our ascent to here. It had been climbed – according to our notes on the area – only once before, along its northern ridge by an Austrian pair (W. Brecht and H. Schweitzer of a German-Austrian expedition) in 1939. Perhaps we could attempt it along its west ridge which appeared steep but by no means impossible, for we were able from here to see its entire profile; or, perhaps, along its south ridge which ran out towards us, badly corniced but it looked to be of a lesser angle.

But – for now – all of our attention needed to be focused on the Nevado San Juan; and we had turned to our tasks. I was changing the film of my camera when Myrtle, rummaging through the primus bag in preparations for our evening meal exclaimed with a hint of stifled distress, 'Matches!' We both searched frantically … 'No!!' … somehow that vital item had been mislaid and was not packed – as of always – with the stove. Not one of us smoked and therefore the chances of Bill or Hugh having matches on them were slim.

How could we produce flame? A spark from the piton hammer striking metal? Sparks refused to fly! My folding camera was still lying open with the film removed. The rays of the sun focused to a pin-point through the lens of the camera? For over half an hour we tried but it was past 5.00 p.m. and the heat from the sun had gone; paper, celluloid, everything singed promisingly but refused to ignite!

The other two soon returned from their reccy above to learn the dismal news, shortly before 6.00 p.m. Our evening meal consisted of biscuits, corned beef and dried apple with snow. Our worst problem was dehydration, that unfailing effect of high altitude, and unable to melt snow we had been obliged to eat it – slowly melting it in our mouths. The discomforts of a night at high camp, with four of us crowded into a tiny B-Meade, were not in any way decreased by the lack of hot food and drink.

We spent a restless night and I lay in my bag recalling the events that had brought us to here: I was working at the time for a mining company in central Peru, Cerro de Pasco Corporation, in La Oroya, and was living with my family (Janet, also a climber, and our daughter Wenda) in a delightful hamlet called Mal Paso some 15km from there, along a valley green and lush and so like Scotland but drier. Work and home were only some 120km to the east of Lima but to reach there, in our 1956 Series-1 Land Rover, on the un-made-up road, we needed to cross to the east side of the Andean chain, over the Pass of Ticlio at an elevation of 4818m – higher than any mountain in the Alps!

For two weeks leave in August of 1958 I was enjoying the good fortune of joining the Scottish climbing team of Bill Wallace, Hugh Simpson and Myrtle Emslie (later to become Myrtle Simpson), who formed the Edinburgh Andean Expedition of that year, the first all-British expedition to the Cordillera Blanca. I had made contact through the SMC, before Bill and Myrtle departed from Scotland, now two months ago. Hugh had been, for the previous year, in the Antarctic, with FIDS (the Falkland Islands Dependencies Survey) and he had been the first to arrive in Lima, from where he'd reached – a week or so ahead of the others – our home in Mal Paso (Bad Step) named, we had learnt, after the canyon through which the track to there passed from La Oroya.

After a few days with us at nearly 3800m – and their first ever canoeing on the mountain river that streamed past our door – the three had departed for a further period of acclimatisation, as well as a spell of Hugh's medical research, in the central Sierra where they reached the summits of three unclimbed peaks above 5000m. They had then arrived in Huaras, the provincial capital in the centre of the Cordillera Blanca, during the latter part of July and, with the help of its well-known citizen Juan Manuel Ramirez, whose generous assistance and local knowledge never failed a climbing party that passed his way, burros (mules) had been hired to transport their modest pile of food and equipment to the head of the Quebrada Rurec. From this valley they had successfully attacked the virgin peaks of Nevado Rurec (5320m) and Nevado Huantsan Chico (5703m); the latter being a joint effort with two French climbers, Henri Chanzy and Yves Merle d'Aubigne, which had involved a planned bivouac at 5300m or so in an ice cave.

My having kept in touch with their movements and whereabouts, the late evening of 10 August found me arriving, with Janet and two-year old Wenda, at Quinta Los Pinos – a pension, high on the hillside east of Huaras, commanding a snow-mantled panorama ranging from the

Ranrapalca massif in the north to the majestic Huantsan due east. A timely telephone call from Hugh had brought the news that at 6.00 a.m. the very next morning the Scots were moving off with laden burros to establish a new base camp in the Quebrada Cayesh. Further contact had been quickly established and Bill Wallace had agreed to remain behind the main party to accompany me in, starting at the more leisurely hour of 8.00 a.m.

The morning had been fine and clear; a slight haze in the valleys emphasised the nature of those glistening white expanses of snow and ice that towered above them. Bill and I had set off promptly, optimistically expecting to make up time on the burro party, but – unaware of the excellent track that lay to the north of the Rio Quilcay, running due east from Huaras – we had chosen the south bank of the river; our path had soon given out and we had found ourselves struggling through undergrowth, making innumerable detours over and around bluffs. Finally we had been able to cross the river by a bridge at the point where it divides into two swiftly-flowing mountain streams, Quebrada Shallap and Quebrada Quilcayhuanca, and it had been mid-afternoon before we caught up with the advance party, encamped a short way up the Quilcayhuanca valley. They had reached this spot at midday.

Like most valleys of the Cordillera, it offered very fine camping in beautiful surroundings, but not for this reason had they camped down so early. Antonio, our 'arriero' in charge of the burros, had misled them into believing that he possessed the key to the only gate through which the burros could pass to the privately-owned upper pastures of the Quilcayhuanca. This, as we were to learn, was only one of the ruses that Antonio used to try and prolong the journey. He and his burros were being paid on a time basis.

An attempt had been made to find other ways through the wall, but there was nothing for it, we had been forced to wait until 6.00 a.m. next morning … 'manyana!' … when the 'portador' was due with the key. It had been well past 9.00 a.m. when he finally arrived and we had been able to continue our trek to the Quebrada Cayesh. By then we were fully aware and ready to encounter any of Antonio's go-slow attempts and had been able to make good time, arriving at a suitable site for base camp shortly after midday. The burros had soon been unloaded and Antonio paid off after much customary haggling. Camp had then been pitched and the afternoon spent relaxing and getting ready for a move upwards the following day. An excellent evening meal had been prepared by Myrtle from our stocks of dehydrated foodstuffs and we had retired early to our sleeping bags.

The mountain on which we were now encamped, in our Meade tent clinging at 5200m to the steep eastern flank of its north-west shoulder, was the Nevado San Juan. It was the peak that had been set out as

Top: Hugh Simpson turning an icy corner on the San Juan. Photo: Derek Fabian.
Bottom: Sunset on Nevado Chinchey from high camp on San Juan. Photo: Derek Fabian.

expedition goal in the programme approved and backed by the British Mount Everest Foundation in September of 1957. Since then however we had learnt that the summit had been reached in that same year by an American party (Norman Clinch and Robert Tidrick). They had attempted it along this, the same north-west ridge on which we were now tackling its ascent but, after being unable to make the climb 'go', had moved their camp and attack round to the Shallap valley, from where they had then found a route to the summit along its south-west shoulder. With the Scots trio we had decided to try our luck on this northern approach where the Americans had failed, making and following the north-west ridge. My joining the three had meant that, where hitherto they had been climbing as a rope of three, we were now the more manoeuvrable two ropes of two.

Base camp lay at about 3700m and our plan had been to put an assault camp as high on the northwest shoulder as would prove feasible. We had left base at 8.00 a.m. and had toiled, carrying packs of 20–25kg, first up a slope of steep grass and scrub that lay between two deeply-cut streams and then, as the angle eased, had made good time for the next 800m or so. Nearing an altitude of 4500m and beyond, I had been surprised to find myself holding the party up to some degree. Having lived now for six months in Mal Paso at nearly 3800m and rambling at weekends in the surrounding hills, I had expected that I would be sufficiently acclimatised for high climbing. My companions had spent nearly six weeks living high and climbing at heights above 5000m and they were proving to be considerably more adapted and fitter than me. Such it seems are the mysterious physiological aspects of altitude!

The grassy slopes had given place to moraines, from which we had gained a north-easterly rock ridge leading towards the long snow and ice summit ridge curving and glinting away southwards to our left. Good firm rock had brought us to a steep snow face, whose surface consisted of a sea of miniature ice pinnacles, the 'Zacheneiss' so typical of north-facing snow slopes in the Andes. Roping had been necessary to cross several large crevasses and the bergschrund. Bill and Hugh, making a fast-moving rope, had soon been well ahead and mid-afternoon had found them establishing a camp at about 5200m. They had chosen probably the only promisingly level spot in the steep slope sheltered beneath seracs and, though uncomfortably close to crevasses, these appeared to be stable. By the time Myrtle and I reached the site, they had cut out a sizeable platform and we quickly had our Meade tent neatly pitched.

Hugh and Bill had soon been ready to set off on a reconnaissance of the steep and complicatedly crevassed slope that lay directly above and, if negotiable, would give access to the summit ridge. Their recce had required first a traverse out to the left from where the bulge above the

Bill Wallace and Hugh Simpson on their recce (late afternoon) above high camp on Nevado San Juan. Photo: Derek Fabian

tent could be surmounted; Myrtle and I had briefly reconnoitred the alternative, a traverse out to the right, but we had quickly determined that the wall above where the traverse would end was even steeper than that on which Bill and Hugh were already cutting steps towards the ridge. We had returned to organise camp and to prepare a meal for their return. It had been then that we had discovered to our distress the missing matches!

Now, at 5.00 a.m. after dozing restlessly throughout the night, I forced myself awake to face the new dawn. Our breakfast was much the same as the meal the evening before: biscuits and jam, slabs of chocolate, and snow to quench the thirst. We set off shortly after first light at 6.00 a.m. The morning was cold and cloudless. The reconnaissance made by Bill and Hugh proved of real value in finding our way up that first complicated iron-hard snow slope. Some 200m higher we came over a shoulder to where steep, loose rocks on the north face swept down from the snow and ice of the summit ridge. For a while we were able to follow a convenient ledge formed by the junction of this fallen rock and the hardened snow, but were eventually forced up to the crest of the ridge.

We were travelling now with only light packs but I again began to feel the altitude. Bill and Myrtle, forming the first rope, were soon well ahead and my laboured breathing demanded a considerably slower pace from our rope, a pace which Hugh generously professed to be glad of. As a result it fell to Bill on the first rope to do all the step cutting, of which there were long steep stretches on both ice and iron-hard snow. This undoubtedly proved strenuous work for Bill but our rope was never sufficiently on the others' heels for Hugh or me to take over the work with the ice axe. These were the days before front-pointed crampons and short hooked ice axes.

The ridge became a series of giant cornices, on nearly all of which we were forced to traverse out onto the northerly flank, always very steep and often extremely exposed as well. Usually to gain the flank of the cornice meant negotiating a tricky corner, often at the same time bridging a waiting crevasse. Bill's step cutting and route finding were excellent.

I was taking my share of leading on our rope and, in doing so on tricky pitches, was able to note how the concentration required would, for the time, banish fatigue. The natural reaction was that, at the completion of the pitch, there would be several moments hold up while I recovered breath. It was reassuring that the sky was perfectly cloudless, which meant, as far as time was concerned, that we would not be robbed of any daylight hours. And, admirably, Hugh never once showed impatience.

When at last we seemed to be mounting the final summit cornice, the San Juan produced a most exacting sting in its tail. The true summit – yet another steep cornice – was divided from the one on which we stood by an impassable gash in the ridge. Bill and Myrtle had reached this first snow peak nearly half an hour ahead of Hugh and me and we met them, returning from the main summit, on a narrow crest just to our side of the gash. They reported the loss of much time casting about for a route, and indeed, they told us, the crux of the climb was the final pitch yet to come.

One side of the narrow crest on which we stood was undercut, the other offered a very steep 10m descent in ice and snow whose condition could only be described as rotten. The extreme heat from the sun at this altitude had been working away at this crest reducing it to the condition of a pile of sugar through which water has percolated. Portions were solidified into a skeleton of ice, but the whole was held together by soft, crumbly snow.

A thin, exposed ledge of ice made possible a traverse below the gash and to the final wall. This, although of hard snow and ice of a more reliable texture, remained exposed and extremely steep. On this last obstacle Bill had cut excellent steps but, leading this pitch and recalling their report of difficulty in reversing it, I cut for us a short series of handholds that were soon to prove valuable on our return. The last few metres as the angle suddenly eased off, brought us to the summit (5843m).

Spending only a few minutes on photography and for admiring the splendid Huantsan massif now visible to the south, plus the still awe-inspiring Nevado Chinchey to the north, we turned for the descent. It was already 2.00 p.m. The others were well on their way down. Nor did we wish to give the scorching sun any more time to worsen the condition of that delicate traverse back to the first summit. Reaching the latter safely but with no time to loose, we continued the descent. But as the more difficult sections were gradually placed behind and above us, intense concentration gave way to fatigue and our progress became less rapid.

The others were now a long way below and by about 3.30 p.m we could see them threading their way down to our high camp. Then, later, two specks were moving off from the tent; they were going to make base camp and hot food and drink that night.

It would be high camp for us, and in fact I was so much slowed by the altitude that it was 6.45 p.m. and quite dark when at last we reached the tent. Too much in need of liquid to eat, we sucked snow with glucose sweets and Kendal mint cake. We did this seemingly for hours, in fact at intervals during the whole night, between bouts of sleep. It was well after the warmth of the sun had reached the tent that we made a move the next morning. Laboriously striking camp, we donned crampons and rope once more, shouldered our packs and began the descent to base. Once unroped, Hugh almost sprinted ahead to a lunch that consisted of several gallons of hot soup.

An afternoon of rest quickly brought new life and fresh determination; plans were made to move base camp round into the Quebrada Tulparaju. From there we would attempt the Nevado Chinchey. The highlight of the afternoon came when Bill, stirring himself from his sunbathing to open a tin of butter, was reminded forcefully that the tin had been sealed at sea level. A stream of liquid butter spurted out and artistically spattered his torso.

The Nevado Chinchey (6223m):
Not a race of distance but usually a race against time, weather and altitude deterioration, is the climbing of a six thousand metre peak. In the Peruvian Andes, during the months of June to August, the weather is perhaps the least of these adversaries since it can generally be relied upon to provide stable periods for climbing. The Cordillera Blanca contains over thirty peaks whose summits rise to more than 6000m. All, with one possible exception, had in the late 1950s already been climbed at least once. The ascent of a 6000m summit is a milestone that represents a challenge to most mountaineers, although often more difficult technical climbing can be found on lower peaks. The most rewarding accomplishment is surely when the summit is also virgin; if this was not possible in the Cordillera Blanca in 1958, there was still much exploration to be done and many new routes to be found on these majestic giants carved from snow and ice.

It was Friday 16 August, at base camp the day after our climb of the Nevado San Juan. Following a leisurely breakfast we spent the morning ferrying loads to a delightful site at the head of the gentle Quebrada Tulparaju, a distance of about 4km. In the afternoon Bill and I packed medium loads up about 700m to the foot of the glacier, so lightening burdens for the following day. We intended to put an assault camp on the col at the foot of the west ridge, at an elevation of some 5500m. Whether we could reach this west col in one day, or should need an intermediate camp, remained to be seen. It depended on the glacial terrain at the head of the valley, a section of the route to the col that had not been visible from the San Juan. We set off at first light and in 2½ hours had reached the point where Bill and I had dumped our loads the afternoon before.

The route took us through some very pleasant scrubland, past primitive Indian dwellings and out onto moraines that skirted a large glacial lake. Into this lake spilled a huge glacier, fed from a cirque of peaks that formed an impressive, unbroken wall of ice and snow. At its lower end a large rock dam had been constructed, presumably as a precaution against a disaster similar to that which occurred to the city of Huaras in 1941, when a huge glacial lake above in the Yuanchanucco valley had – as the result of the masses of ice from the glacier that floats and then jams at the lake's outflow – burst its banks and swept away part of the city and its inhabitants.

Roping for our glacier, we had first to tackle a minor ice fall; a route into a northerly running glacial cwm, where a long 3km snow plod to the head of the cwm brought us to the steep slopes below the west col. We were ready for a long rest and second breakfast before tackling the crevassed slopes to this col. It began to look as though we would reach our designated spot for high camp that same day and in fact it was shortly after 4.00 p.m. when a platform for the tent was being cut in a sheltered spot just below the col.

From this camp we could now examine the profile of the south ridge of the Nevado Chinchey which had run out towards us in our view from the San Juan; it could readily be gained by a straightforward traverse from camp. However, although the angle there was considerably easier, an unbroken series of unattractive cornices made us decide on the steeper west ridge. Accordingly we retired to the tent to prepare a hot meal. It is probable, had a count been made, that at least four boxes of matches would have been found among the party that evening.

We were slow to get moving next morning. Our altimeter was reading 5550m and a certain amount of lassitude could be attributed to soroche (Andean altitude sickness). This was augmented, however, by the effects of some minor carbon monoxide poisoning the night before. An occasional failing of primus stoves at high altitude is that, when a cold surface is placed in the flame – such as a pan full of melting snow – the fuel, already burning in an insufficient supply of oxygen, is caused to burn incompletely and carbon monoxide results. It took a little while for our heads to clear of the effects and it was past 7.00 a.m. before we were on the move.

Myrtle and I led off on one rope and kicked steps in the snow, hardened overnight, up the remaining 50m or so to the col. Here the others quickly overtook us and as we started up the west ridge sun beams began to appear over the corniced summit above; for a few minutes we were treated to a most beautiful trick of lighting, with the other roped pair silhouetted against a reddish glow that was reflected and distorted a thousand times by the tiny pinnacles of ice on the crest, and with the sun itself appearing to be between us and the summit ridge! The effect vanished after a few minutes, as suddenly as it had come, and we received then the full and comforting warmth of the sun.

Our route proved as much a face climb as a ridge climb, for the latter, in its upper portions, forced us to work out onto the north-west face. It again fell to Bill, on the leading rope, to do all the step cutting. The final traverse out across the face to reach a flank leading to the summit cornice, was a fine piece of cutting and at this altitude a very exacting one. Heavy clouds had been building all day and clear indications that a break was coming in our spell of fine weather added to the mounting tension.

A last tricky corner and we had gained the final broad but corniced ridge to the summit. There remained only a gap in the final cornice, similar to that on the San Juan, but which this time had been visible and was supplied with a convenient snow bridge. The tiny window in the cornice thus formed had, we realised, caused the pin-hole camera effect that had produced an image of the sun – as it rose from behind – to our side of the summit ridge as we were climbing the slope above our tent in the early hours of that morning. To confirm, we could just make out, through the hole formed by the snow bridge, our green Meade, 700m below. The bridge proved safe and the peak became ours. It was 2.00 p.m.!

No time was to be lost if we were to reach camp again before dark. The first part of the descent would demand full concentration. Then gradually, as our tent – that green speck in the massive expanse of whiteness below – grew more distinct, the technical difficulties grew less. But snow that had been hard and firm that morning had since been reduced to a knee-deep mush. Ploughing down through this mush, it was a tired party that reached camp amid the glory of an 'Alpenglo' mountain sunset. The tent that night formed a haven for four weary but complacent mountaineers. For each of us it had been a first six-thousand metre summit!

For Bill, Hugh and Myrtle it proved a prelude to their ascent of The Huascarán (6770m), the highest in Peru; for me it was back to work in La Oroya but the prelude too, with Janet, to a handful of lesser ascents, some of them virgin like Tunshu (5709m) and Tullahuto (5750m), in the environs of Cerro de Pasco and La Oroya, and later in the Cordillera Vilcabamba on our way south from Huancayo along the 600km of dirt road that – crossing the grain of the country to the east of the Andean chain – winds its way over no fewer than four 4000m passes and then down each time to a bridge, at elevations as low as 1000m, over one of the many mountain rivers that flow out some 5000km eventually to the Amazon basin; a road that was originally built in the time of the Incas and on which we reached in our Land Rover their hidden and now-famous incredible Lost City of Machu Picchu.

NEW CLIMBS SECTION

OUTER ISLES

LEWIS, Bearasaigh (NB 122 424):
The following routes are taken from a mini-guide by K.Archer & P.Headland.
Access is by boat.

Upper Hadrian's Wall:
Hadrian's Wall extends, on more than one level, from the NW corner of the island back southwards. From a ruined building at the NNW end of the island, walk north for a few yards to a small grassy depression from which a right-trending ramp and small corner give access to a huge boulder-covered platform. Follow this westwards to arrive at the non-tidal Upper Hadrian's Wall. The first route starts by the first two obvious crack-lines with an undercut start and a striking 'snake' pattern in the rock.

Long Time Coming 15m Severe 4b. K.Archer, P.Headland. 11th June 2007.
Start by the snake pattern, enter and follow the left crack.

Finger Ripping Good 15m VS 4c *. K.Archer, P.Headland. 11th June 2007.
From the same starting point as the previous route, follow the rightwards trending right-hand crack-line. At the second small triangular niche step left onto the face and follow it to the top.

My First 1000 Words 15m VS 5a. P.Headland, K.Archer. 11th June 2007.
Start 5m right of the snake pattern in the centre of a small face and climb directly up the wall.

Eight metres further right is a very obvious small steep slab, 'The Coal Face', with a central break and a 'handrail' across its top leading into a corner on the left.

The Whale & the Snail 18m Severe 4b. P.Headland, K.Archer. 11th June 2007.
Start at the right end of The Coal Face. Move right after 2.5m to a steep ramp and crack and follow this to the top.

Red Hot Chilli Pipers 18m VS 5a. K.Archer, P.Headland. 11th June 2007.
Start as for the previous route but follow the upper traverse leftwards across the top of the slab, then up through a niche just right of the corner.

Back on Your Heads 18m E1 5b *. P.Headland, K.Archer. 14th June 2007.
Climb directly up the centre of the face, move left to a small overhung corner and climb through this to the top.

At the far right end of Upper Hadrian's is a fantastically featured arete with a very undercut lower section sloping down into a huge tidal cave.

Christina Mackay & the Grana 26m E1 5b **. K.Archer, P.Headland. 13th June 2007.
Start 3m left of the arete and climb through the undercut to gain a downwards and rightwards-trending sloping ledge. Follow this right, then climb a layback to the base of a corner. Follow the slabby corner before stepping left and climbing a short wall to finish.

Lower Hadrian's Wall, St Bees Sector:
Access to this area is by a scramble down a north-facing cracked black slab facing out to sea, opposite the base of Christina Mackay. This leads to a non-tidal sloping platform from which the following routes start.

In my Dreams 10m Severe 4b. K.Archer, P.Headland. 13th June 2007.
From the base of the access route start at large rounded flakes in a short overhung corner. Climb through an overlap and continue to the top.

Dubh Ron Ron 18m Severe. K.Archer, P.Headland. 15th June 2007.
Six metres further left. Follow the right side of the left-trending black ramp line left of the overhanging wall adjacent to the access route.

Birthday Route 25m Severe. P.Headland, K.Archer. 15th June 2007.
Follow the banded fault left of the black rock.

Priam Raiders 16m VS 5a *. P.Headland, K.Archer. 13th June 2007.
From the base of the access route walk 6m right to the arete (this is above a black overhung slab). Start at the right arete and climb the initial overhung arete to a shallow scoop, then follow the edge of the upper slab.

Treasure Island 20m Hard Severe 4b *. P.Headland, K.Archer. 15th June 2007.
From the same start as the previous route, climb the initial overhung arete and move right to follow a rightwards-rising ledge and wall, then a short corner to finish.

Abseil down the black slab below the previous routes to take a stance on ledges just above sea-level to gain the start of:

Cool & Smooth & Curious 18m HVS 5b *. K.Archer, P.Headland. 15th June 2007.
Traverse right and climb a short wall on to a slab to the bottom of a black overhung corner beneath the big roof. Follow the strenuous corner to finish at the base of the previous two routes.

Lower Hadrian's Wall, North Sector:
Access can be gained either by traversing at sea-level from the St Bees Sector (tidal) or by a 28m abseil from a large rectangular block located at the head of a gully to the NW corner of the boulder-covered ledge leading to Upper Hadrian's Wall. This gains barnacle-covered ledges (tidal).

That Harry Potter Thing   25m   Severe 4a *. P.Headland, K.Archer. 13th June 2007.
From 2m left of the abseil line, climb the slabby wall to a left-rising crack-line. Follow this to and then through a notch to the top.

Polly Wise & Wonderful   28m   Severe 4a *. K.Archer, P.Headland. 13th June 2007.
Start 3.5m left of the abseil, then traverse left to the centre of a black slab. Climb this trending left to climb through a broken overlap, then trend up and left to finish.

Mop Route   25m   Severe *. P.Headland, K.Archer. 13th June 2007.
From the base of the abseil, traverse right to a mussel-covered ledge. Start from the left end of the ledge, climbing a left-trending fault line, to pull over right onto a short slab. Go right to a wonderful finishing corner.

Weatherman's Geodha:
The big geodha in the centre of the eastern side of the island. Access is by abseil (from boulders and back rope) down the big vegetated slabby southern corner. Traverse around the geodha to the base of the big northern ridge with a slabby southern face.

September Ends   65m   Severe. P.Headland, K.Archer. 14th June 2007.
Start from a huge platform at the centre of the broad eastern arete. Climb the centre to take a stance by a huge block (35m). Continue up the narrowing arete to a notch, then move out onto the left face to finish (30m).

Pictland:
This is the area on the northern end of the island. From the base of the corner used to access the big boulder covered platform (leading to Hadrian's Wall areas), go northwards to a point roughly opposite the centre of Seana Chnoc and identify a clean corner above a ledge and below this barnacle-covered sea-level ledges (non-tidal starts but will be wet in a big swell). Abseil down the corner.

The Best Man's Speech   18m   VS 5a *. K.Archer, P.Headland. 14th June 2007.
Climb directly up the main corner.

Picksley's Pickles   18m   VS 5a *. P.Headland, K.Archer. 14th June 2007.
From the same start, climb steeply left of the abseil line to a ledge, then up the wonderfully featured wall.

Olive Oil Overdose   18m   Severe 4b. P.Headland, K.Archer. 14th June 2007.
Climb steeply up and right of the abseil line to a left-facing corner.

False Sense of Senility   19m   VS 5a. K.Archer, P.Headland. 14th June 2007.
Move right, then climb awkwardly to the second corner right of the abseil line and follow it to the top.

Stac an Tuill (The Bell Tower):
This 50m stack lies off the south-western corner of the island, separated by a channel containing a second stack of about 20m with two summits and a distinct flat central platform.

Approach: From close by the remains of old buildings in the south-western corner of the island, take a 58m abseil down to ledges at the tide line, then traverse northwards until opposite a large rock with a non-tidal summit, between the second stack and the island. Set up the following Tyrolean traverses (swimmer required). Firstly from the island to the large rock mentioned above, secondly to the top of a chimney on the southern end of the central stack's platform, then traverse around and down to a platform on the south-western corner of the central stack. The third tyrolean goes from here to a large niche just right of a big ledge on the south-eastern corner of Stac an Tuill. 98m of static rope was used. Start from the left end of the ledge.

Ask not for whom the Bell Tuills   35m   E1 4c. K.Archer, P.Headland. June 2007. Climb up to a ramp at 4m, then follow this leftwards and up to a right-facing corner. Traverse up and left to a runner before dropping down into the long slabby right-facing corner. Follow this to exit through a short cracked wall. Grass remains to the summit. Abseil directly to the ledge from the stance.

Campaigh, Geodh' an Tuill Area:
Friggin' Direct   12m   HVS 5b. A.Norton, K.Archer. 31st May 2005.
Start as for Friggin' in the Riggin' but climb direct, trend right to finish.

Campaigh, Wheeling Gull Wall Area:
Black Heart of McLeod   17m   HVS 5b *. K.Archer, A.Norton. 31st May 2005.
Start at sea-level ledges 4m left of Wee Restorative. Traverse 2m right and up then climb the stepped corner until forced to make difficult moves rightwards into the corner of Wee Restorative 3m from the top.

Campaigh, Landing Geodha Area:
This lies on the south-western corner of the island and can be identified by a small buttress with strangely weathered gargoyles.

Dun Carloway Sheep Police   15m   Hard Severe **. A.Norton, K.Archer. 31st May 2005.
Start at the right side of the small buttress at the back of the small geo. Climb direct until possible to move out right onto the fantastically shaped gargoyles.

Sgeir Rebrie:
Absence Makes the Heart...   40m   HVS. K.Archer, A.Norton. 30th May 2005.
From the overhung slabs left of Bosta'in, traverse in to the corner where it abuts the main face. Climb it until possible to hand-traverse a small ledge, then continue up a corner to reach the stance of Bosta'in (20m 5a). Finish up pitch 2 of Bosta'in (20m 4b).

Sgeir Rebrie, The Narrow Box Geo:
This is the big square-cut geo lying immediately south of Sgeir Rebrie (Bostadh Groove and To the Max lie on its NW arete).

Out of the Box 20m E1 5c *. K.Archer, A.Norton. 30th May 2005.
Abseil to a sloping ledge that rises from left to right. Start at its right end. Climb a short overhanging wall via a hard mantelshelf, then continue up before moving right to finish up a short corner.

NORTH UIST, Madadh Gruamach (NF 955 667):
The island of Madadh Gruamach is situated to the south of Madadh Mor Island on the entrance to Loch Maddy. The rock is basalt and is about 30-35m high at its highest. The west facing crag receives plenty of sunshine. Access, as with other islands, is by boat or sea kayak, the latter being easily landed on the back of the island which slopes towards the sea. The crag itself comprises many corners, aretes, cracks and a number of roof systems. It is possible to belay well back from the top and so another rope may be useful for this. The routes are close to the north end of the island and described from left to right.

Northern Chimney 5m Very Difficult. D.Brown. August 2007.
Short chimney pitch, with some thrutching to be done.

Niall's Surprise 25m VS 4c. D.Brown. August 2007.
Easy ground leads into a corner system, beneath an obvious small roof to the left with an arete to its right above halfway. Step around this small feature and continue upwards to finish up a small diedre.

Sea Fury 15m Very Difficult. D.Brown. August 2007.
The obvious southern corner system that cuts from the water to the top. Good holds throughout.

MINGULAY, Geirum Walls:
Junior Keel E4 6b. E.Brown (unsec). 29th June 2007.
Breaches the prominent 45-degree roofs forming the left side of the Main Walls. Climb the deceptively steep juggy wall to the left of Seriously Twitching to below the right-hand of the two cracks breaching the roof. Place good protection in the crack and make wild moves out to and over the lip of the roof.

Wee Geo, Ryan's Wall (NL 553 845) NW facing:
Squeeze Out Another One 20m E1 5b/5c. A.Fulton, R.Barnes. August 2007.
Positioned between Turd Compressor and Tigger's Don't Like Honey. Climb straight up the slab to the roof, climb steeply up the roof, trending slightly right and finish up a short capped corner forming the right side of the roof.

Wee Geo, Tarmacadam Wall (NL 553 845) NE facing:
Don't Look Back in Anger 45m HVS *. M.Airey, A.Goodridge. August 2007.
1. 5a Follow Ron the Seals Quick Drying Wall Climb to the large flat ledge splitting the face at half-height.

2. 5a Walk left to the end of the ledge and climb an overhanging flakey crack which leads to the right end of a right-curving groove. Pull through the bulge with difficulty.

Guarsay Mor, South Pillar (NL 549 840)   NW facing:
A square-shaped stone sits 50m back from the cliff-top, near a series of tiny weed-filled lochans. A 100m abseil from the cliff-top on a bearing of 300 degrees magnetic from this stone gains a small circle-shaped ledge 15m above the sea (50m of spare rope required for rigging). These routes are to the north of the established South Pillar routes.

Wake up and Smell the Guano   110m   HVS. P.Cunningham, A.Goodridge. August 2007.
Despite a revolting first pitch, good climbing is to be had above that. Abseiling to the platform at the bottom of pitch 2 is recommended!
1. 25m 4a From the ledge, climb a left-facing cracked ramp on the right up to a large guano infested ledge. Traverse the ledge left for 15m until you can climb onto a large clean platform with a right-slanting corner/groove system above.
2. 20m 5b Climb the groove until it is possible to climb directly up a huge flake to a roof. Step right with difficulty to gain a small sloping ledge.
3. 25m 4c Continue right for 6m until a groove leads directly up. Boldly climb up to reach good holds. Continue up to a second guano ledge, and step right to under a chimney.
4. 40m 4b Climb direct up the chimney, step left to climb a dark left-facing corner and continue direct to the top on easier ground.

Guantastic 100m E1 *. R.Barnes, A.Fulton. August 2007.
A good route spoiled by guano and a poor final pitch; well worth the effort for the exposure.
1. 15m 4b From the right edge of the belay ledge, ascend the left-facing corner and easy-angled wall until the first guano-covered ledge is reached. Belay below the steep black wall.
2. 35m 5b Ascend the black wall via interesting layback flakes (technical crux). After 8m traverse left via prominent jutting blocks onto the frontal face of the crag. Gain another guano covered ledge and move left until under a blocky overhang. Ascend this and follow stepped corners and cracks to below an overhanging right-facing corner-crack.
3. 25m 5a Ascend the steep corner and step left onto a small ledge. Make a rightward rising traverse onto a slightly overhanging juggy wall, climbed straight up to a ledge.
4. 40m 4a Follow the line of least resistance to the top of the crag.

Shooting Star 100m E1 **. M.Airey, J.McCulloch. August 2007.
Takes the big long soaring groove up and right from the small ledge, extending nearly the full height of the crag.
1. 15m 4a   Follow the same left-facing corner as the above routes to a small jutting spike on the guano ledge at its top.

2. 10m 5b Climb the layback flakes on the wall above and pull right with difficulty at the top onto a narrow ledge.

3. 30m 5a Climb the big corner/groove system issuing from the right of the ledge, weaving left into a small cave, then back right at 20m, to a big 3m ledge at its top.

4. 25m 5b At the back of the ledge is a big right-facing corner. Climb it to exit left via some detached blocks at its top on to a ledge.

5. 20m 4a Easy vegetated steps lead rightwards to the top.

Geo an Droma:
Right of the corner of Fluorescent Jellyfish (Little Corner) there is an obvious triangular-topped slab with two crack-lines. Access to the base is best via a juggy sea-level traverse from the end of the point.

Lithoded's Crawl 8m Very Difficult. P.Snow, A.Morris. 8th August 2007.
The left-hand crack-line.

Pleasure in a Jug 8m Difficult *. A.Morris, P.Snow. 8th August 2007.
The right-hand crack-line. Fantastic holds.

Jellyfish Geo:
From the spur forming the top of the south-facing walls of Geo an Droma, a north-facing cliff forms the north side of the spur. Access is by scrambling down near the seaward end of the point and then doubling back landwards. The cliff is non-tidal and there is a large rockpool with a large guano-covered rock under the left-hand side of the continuous section.

The Chap 22m Very Difficult. P.Snow, A.Morris. 8th August 2007.
From the guano-covered rock in the rockpool, climb the crack/groove in the lower wall, before continuing in the same line to finish up the corner left of Desperately Clinging On.
Note: A line between these, starting up the tiny inset groove and finishing up the face left of Desperately Clinging On, was climbed on the 9th August 2007 at VS 4c by others in the party.

Desperately Clinging On 25m VS 5a *. P.Snow, A.Morris. 8th August 2007.
The obvious central corner-line above the right-hand side of the rockpool. Climb the corner with increasing difficulty to a crux at the top.

The Piano 25m Hard Severe 4b *. A.Morris, P.Snow. 8th August 2007.
There is an obvious pink bulge/nose towards the right-hand side of the cliff. This route follows the groove bounding this on its left to finish up the prominent pair of flakes near the top.

Whisky Drinkers' Destiny 24m Hard Severe 4b **. A.Morris, P.Snow. 8th August 2007.
Climbs the bulbous pink nose at the right of the cliff. Start at the groove of The Piano, and traverse right a few feet before a step up into a small groove allows

access to the base of the bulge. Heave over on glorious holds and amble up the pleasant flake-crack to the top.

PABBAY, Grey Wall Recess:
U-th   30m   E3 5c ***. T.Fryer, I.Taylor. 12th June 2007.
Left of pitch 2 of U-Ei is a soaring crack-line, trending slightly rightwards. Gain the crack from the right and follow it through roofs and bulges to join U-Ei below its final pitch. Well protected and low in the grade.

Banded Geo:
Redemption Ark   85m   E6. N.McNair, D.McManus. June 2007.
The first route to breach the impressive gothic cave of Banded Geo. The first pitch is three-star climbing but the next and last pitches deserve XS due to looseness and wetness.
1. 25m 6b Start on top of the innermost boulder at the bottom of the geo, the size of a small car. Step hard left for 3m into a wildly overhanging groove/corner system and follow this to a wall and an obvious bow-shaped crack. Take the crack rightwards and up to step out right under the overhang. Hanging belay.
2. 30m 5b Traverse left for 4m to a prominent spike, then climb up and over a bulge to reach an obvious but wet and loose traverse leftwards across pink and orange rock. Continue past a detached block for 6m, step down and belay in a black corner.
3. 30m 5c Step left and climb the middle and slimmest of the three corner-crack systems. Continue up this terrifyingly until better rock is reached in a bay. Take the middle groove to grass.

Jonny Scuttlebutt   45m   E5 6a. N.McNair, A.Robb. June 2007.
Climbs the wall right of Ship of Fools. Start as for that route to the roof. At the rib on the lowest point of the roof, gain the wall above. Climb slightly left, then follow the line of least resistance to an obvious crack in steep brown rock near the top. Finish up this.

Banded Wall, South Face:
Partial Bastard   40m   E3 6a *. A.Fulton. August 2007.
The obvious challenge of the crag, taking the roof on the prow between the west and south faces of Banded Wall (just to the left of Silver Fox). Climb easily up to a fist-sized crack splitting the roof at its widest point. Make technical and powerful moves to surmount the roof. Continue up the easy wall above, via an S-shaped flake-crack.

Bay Area:
It's not the Size that Matters   10m   VS 4c. P.Cunningham, M.Airey. August 2007.
Scramble round the corner at the right (north-east) end of the bay area (low tide) to a large sloping platform 4m above the sea. In the centre of a short steep 10m wall above, this route takes the obvious crack/groove up the centre of the wall, finishing up a small niche on the left. Sustained and pleasant despite size.

Pink Wall:
What! More Puffin 80m E6 6b, 5a ***. S.Crowe, K.Magog. 9th June 2007.
With a new independent finish. The grooved arete on the right edge of the wall (right of The Ancient Mariners). The initial arete has a crack on both sides. Start by climbing either crack to gain the ledge, then move up to the Y-shaped crack. Move up then left to finger lock powerfully through a steep bulge (just right of The Ancient Mariners) and gain a good break and awkward kneebar rest. Tip toe rightwards on good crimps to regain the arete and move up steeply to a huge flake. Teeter right to reach easy ground and a superbly exposed position on the very edge.
Notes: *The Ancient Mariners* was considered E4 5c; *The Herbrudean* E4 5c and *Big Chief Turning Bull* E5 6a.

RUM, Kilmory (NG 353 042):
Kilmory is about 2hrs walk from Kinloch. North-west of Kilmory is a stony beach with a non-tidal stack and a larger rectangular stack on a partly tidal rock platform. Two routes were climbed on the crag to the east of the larger stack and facing it. Both are tidal. There is potential for a number of Reiff type routes on several small sandstone crags on this coast.

Left-Hand Crack 20m Very Difficult *. C.Moody, C.Grindley. 31st March 2007.
The left of two cracks at the left side of the face.

The Indirect 25m Severe. C.Moody, C.Grindley. 31st March 2007.
Climb the crack that leads into the recess in the middle of the face. Step right and continue to the top. The direct finish would probably be a better route.

MULL, Mink Wall:
Unnamed 15m VS 4b. C.Moody. 24th July 2007.
The crack right of Helga.

Ben More:
The following routes were climbed by C.Wells at Easter 2008.

Professor Falls 30m II/III (NM 52277 33878; 704m).
At the right-hand (north) end of the outcrop lies a higher, more broken area of ground. A noticeable broken cascade flows down this in a series of steps. Climb this to where the angle eases off.

Cascade Karen 30m III (NM 52220 33925; 625m).
About two-thirds along the cliff going south an icy ramp cuts through the steeper ground. Follow the ramp to an awkward bulge which leads onto less steep mixed ground.

Vertige Vivienne 30m II/III (NM 52277 33878; 625m)
About 15m left of Cascade Karen, towards the south end of the outcrop, lies a slightly easier angled break in the cliff down which flows an icy cascade. Climb

the cascade, steepest in the first 10m before the angle eases and becomes more mixed.

Cioch Cleft 50m I.
On the north side of the interconnecting ridge between A' Cioch and Ben More is a prominent well-defined narrow gully line splitting a buttress on the Ben More side just upslope from the lowest part of the ridge. Straightforward snow leads to the lower part of the NE ridge to Ben More.

TIREE, Ceann a' Mhara, Selkie Wall (NL 933 403):
From Flaking Wall work north round the massive abutting block on large boulders. Once round the corner scramble up an upwardly slanting ramp to a slightly rising (left to right) ledge about 15m above the sea, about 25m long, backed by a wall decreasing from about 20m at the south end to 10m at the north. The easy descent route is down a gentle diagonal fault from north to south. The situation is spectacular with crashing waves right below, and no signs of bird nesting, although the occasional fulmar flies past.

Fishing for Mackerel 7m Difficult. H.Carus, J.Hawkins. 7th September 2007.
The second significant chimney from the left. Go up the right-hand arete of the broken chimney.

Way Too Many Spiders 15m Severe. H.Carus, J.Hawkins. 7th September 2007.
Mid-way along the wall there is an obvious left-facing S-shaped corner. Start from a raised area of bedrock. This gives a great satisfying climb that on an accessible crag would be polished in no time. Not for arachnophobics!

Shortbread or Crackers? 14m Mild VS. H.Carus, J.Hawkins. 7th September 2007.
A well-defined right-slanting crack 2m left of a block. Squeeze between this block and the wall to reach the start from the right. At the top of the climb there is a large block sitting on the edge immediately to the right. The crack is narrow with a very narrow outward-sloping ramp on its right which in places gives some opportunity for laybacks.

SKYE

SGÙRR A' BHASTEIR:
Hillary's Wake 380m II *. M.Francis, R.Lawson. 11th January 2008.
Start at a shallow gully just right (west) of the obvious huge gully that splits the North-East Ridge. Follow the gully to a fork. Take the right-hand branch to an exit onto a large snowfield (120m). Continue easily up the snowfield in a direct line toward the summit. Above the snowfield a series of rock steps and ribs lead to the North-East Ridge about 100m below the top. Much variation is possible.

COIRE A' GHREADAIDH, An Dorus Buttress:
Baptist 140m Severe 4a. I.McCabe, J.Shanks, J.Dyble. July 2006.

Start at the centre of the slabs on the left of the buttress to the right of Trapist, at a vertical trap dyke that is crossed by the obvious low diagonal trap dyke at a height of 2m.

1. 20m Climb diagonally leftward along an obvious line, scant protection, to belay below an overhang.

2. 30m Move right round the overhang and easily up slabs and short walls heading for the ragged notch above. Belay on the grassy terrace above.

3. 45m 4a Initially follow the trap line over the bulge, then move left towards the skyline, then back right to climb a steep cracked wall to a hanging slab. Belay below a triangular overlap.

4. 45m 4a Move left round triangular overlap, then climb easily in the groove line, surmounting a steep little wall by a prominent crack on the way to the top.

SGÙRR MHIC CHOINNICH, Bealach Buttress:

Rainman 70m E5 ***. P.Benson, G.Robertson. 18th June 2007.

A tremendous route up the smooth right side of the big vertical wall. Start immediately left of a grassy recess below the prominent overlap on the bottom right of the wall (this point can be reached by abseil, or by starting up Thunderbolt Shelf).

1. 20m 5b Climb up left to enter and climb the obvious groove at the left end of the overlap, then continue directly for a few metres to a semi-hanging belay at a small sloping ledge.

2. 30m 6a Step left, then climb directly up (bold) passing just left of a large niche to gain an obvious sloping ledge. Continue up, then trend right to follow a vague crack-line over a small overhang to a good rest. Continue up the crack to below a bigger overhang, then traverse horizontally left below this and pull up through its left-hand end. Make some thin moves up and leftwards to gain a line of flakes leading back right and up to a ledge below a short crack.

3. 20m 5a Climb the crack, then escape out right to avoid a loose finish.

SGÙRR MHIC CHOINNICH, Coireachan Ruadha Face:

Dawn Grooves VIII,8 ***. G.Robertson, M.Garthwaite. 11th January 2008.

The summer route was followed for four pitches until below the 'steep 15m wall'. From here a short pitch traversed right to the rib, then up to below the split overhanging nose. A long final pitch (in the dark) approximated the Direct Finish to Crack of Dawn, trending right up a right-facing groove with a wide crack in the back. A superb, sustained and well-protected winter adventure in a magnificent setting – every pitch apart from pitch 5 has considerable difficulty (tech 7 at least). The first pitch is probably the crux of the route. There was some useful ice on the first ascent.

COIR' A' GHRUNNDA, Thearlaich–Dubh Cliff:

Grand Deirdre VI,6. G.Briffet, M.Lates, P.Macpherson. 11th January 2008.

A winter ascent of the direct line. The second pitch was steep and very sustained but on great tool placements. The crag was plastered in very icy rime which was more helpful than east coast rime.

Eilidh's Ceilidh 50m V,7. P.Macpherson, M.Lates. 11th March 2008.

A route beside Bower's Climb. Start about 20m up T–D Gully at the first continuous fault.

1. 35m Climb the fault past an awkward groove and continue up a steep wall via cracks to a ledge with a roof above on the right. Climb strenuously through a roof pulling right into a hanging groove (crux). Continue up the groove on tiny footholds until above a chockstone.

2. 15m Climb direct up an easier left-facing corner to easy ground level with the top of the T–D Gap.

CORUISK, Sgùrr a' Mhadaidh, Coir'-uisg Buttress:

Skye Wall   105m   E7/8. D.Birkett, A.Steele. May 2007.

The obvious blank wall on the right side of the buttress. Start 10m right of the obvious left-facing corner at a vertical white seam.

1. 20m 6b Follow finger cracks and small poor wires to a good ledge.

2. 35m 6b/c Move up and right to a small ledge. Thin moves up the wall gain a sloping hold and loose flaky sidepulls. Bold climbing leads to a crack, followed to a ledge.

3. 50m 5b Move up and left, then go straight up to easy ground.

CORUISK, Coire an Uaigneis, Unknown Buttress (NG 453 229):

It is a possibility that this buttress is the same as the one above.

Paradise Found   200m   E2 *. P.Benson, G.Robertson. 17th June 2007.

A fine route with good rock and an outstanding outlook, taking the most obvious line up the centre of the larger, but slabbier, left side of the buttress. The main difficulties are concentrated in the first half of the route; thereafter the angle eases. Start well up and left from a tongue of easy-angled rock in the centre-left of the buttress (left of the huge dirty groove).

1. 45m 5a Climb up onto a tiny shoulder of rock, pull over onto a slab, then trend up slightly rightwards aiming for a prominent crack-line cutting through overhangs. Belay in a small alcove left of the crack-line itself.

2. 40m 5c Traverse delicately right into the crack, then follow this with sustained interest to a ledge.

3. 45m 5a Continue directly up, then trend right across an unprotected slab to gain a stepped right-trending groove.

4. and 5. 70m 4c Follow the groove line to the top.

Coruisk Slabs (NG 484 210):

The route currently mentioned in the guidebook appears to have been destroyed by the large and obvious rockfall of the mid to late nineties. This route lies to the left taking the cleanest section of slabs. To descend, continue by scrambling to the top of the buttress escaping right on grass ledges to reach the Druim nan Ramh ridge.

Swamp Donkey   265m   Severe 4a *. R.McMurray, C.McGregor. 10th June 2007.

Start on the clean sweep of slabs, to the left of the rockfall at a crack lying roughly 20m to the right of a dark roof. This point is roughly halfway between the lowest area of slabs and the large area of rockfall. The route takes a direct line up the slabs aiming for an obvious corner forming a way through the overlapping roofs above. The rock is generally excellent and provides very enjoyable slab climbing.

1. 45m Climb the crack and slabs to the right of two detached looking dinner-plate slabs to a steeper left-facing corner on the right which is exited on the left via some dubious blocks to reach a corner.

2. 50m Continue up the corner with some blank slab sections to a grass ledge. Continue up the easier slabs to reach a terrace below some steeper slabs.

3. 45m Climb directly up the bold slab above to find a way through the blank section via a welcome flake (crux). This leads to a ledge and overlap and continuation above on bold slabs to the corner.

4. 45m Continue up the easier slabs trending right to reach a grass terrace and the first tree at the base of the obvious corner.

5. 45m Climb the slab left of the corner trending left to climb the arete where it steepens. Move back right to blocks at the top of the corner.

6. 35m Move out left to climb the final slabs directly to where the angle lessens.

BLA BHEINN:
Note from G.Robertson: On the crux pitch of *Stairway to Heaven,* the route traverses down and right from the top of the flake-crack onto the obvious handrail, then follows this horizontally right for about 8m before climbing straight up to the prominent short crack.

Main Wall:
The Invisible Crack Adventure   60m   E2 **. M.Lates, M.Beeston. 22nd June 2007.
An obvious ramp runs up the left side of Main Wall. A crack-line splits the wall above. The route zig-zags across the crack through some very steep terrain.

1. 20m 4c Gain the ramp easily at the lowest point. The second steep section leads to a small belay ledge with an obvious break onto the right wall.

2. 20m 5c Traverse right, crossing the crack-line, then surmount a large pillar. Make a rising traverse left across the steep wall on positive holds (crux) to reach an overhung ledge. Two huge flakes sit on this ledge. Traverse these (with fingers crossed) and continue rightward to a cramped corner stance with a good thread on the pillar above.

3. 20m 5a Hand-traverse 6m further right to easier ground. Step onto the slabby wall above the basalt break. Reach more large flakes which lead left to a loose finish onto the exit slab above.

Scramble easily up the slab to finish.

North Face:
North Face Route   II (route length unknown). A.Matthewson, L.Tidmarsh. February 2000.
In winter the extensive and complicated North Face has a remote feel, but continuous lines are lacking. This long mountaineering route connects a succession of features up the full height of the face, finishing directly on the

summit. A gully leads to a short section of ridge on the left. From the top of the ridge bear left up a shallow gully to the summit.

South Buttress:
Maclaren's Lament   60m   V,6 *. M.Lates, M.Francis. 23rd November 2007.
A short and very entertaining route some 70m up the gully from Scorpion. Finishes on the huge terrace which gives an easy walk off.
1. 15m Take an obvious leftward rising break to a large flake. This is directly below a large deep chimney.
2. 25m An awkward step off the belay flake gives entry to the deep chimney. Fun moves lead behind two massive blocks to a confined ledge below the final impasse. Excellent gear protects some ridiculous contortions in a battle to the top.
3. 20m Break out of the cleft. Finish easily up to a broad terrace.

ELGOL, Schoolhouse Buttress:
Beekeeper's Bother (Left-Hand Start)   8m   HVS 5b. A.Matthewson. 26th July 2007.
Start 2m left of the normal start. Climb a left-trending corner until overhangs necessitate a long stride rightwards across to the ledge of the normal route.

NEIST, LOWER WALLS, Poverty Point:
Slot Machine   18m   E2 5b *. B.Davison, A.Nisbet, C.Grindley, C.Moody. 16th June 2007.
The corner left of Any Spare Change?. Step right at the top of the corner, then continue up.

Stonewall   50m   E4 ***. G.Robertson, A.Crofton. July 2007.
A superb route up the steep wall on the landward side of the non-tidal inlet. At the right end of the wall are two short crack-lines in black rock. Start up the obvious flake-crack immediately left of this.
1. 25m 6a Climb the crack, and from its top pull left onto a ledge. Traverse this to its left end, then step precariously round left and pull up to a good slot (protection). Use a sharp undercut to step back right, then make a sequence of technical moves up to gain a shallow groove with a good finger crack. Follow this to a ledge.
2. 25m 4b Climb a short rib above, then scramble more easily to the top.

Crossfire   25m   E3 5b. G.Robertson, A.Crofton. July 2007.
Round right from The Man From Ankle is a steep wall scored by numerous grooves. This route takes grooves immediately left of a prominent left-curving crack in the lower left half of the wall. It is very loose and definitely not recommended!

Rhubarb Crumble   30m   HVS 5a. A.Nisbet, B.Davison. 16th June 2007.
This route climbs a shallow corner on the left side of the wall to the right of Golden Shower, the easiest looking line on the wall. Start just round to the right of Golden Shower. Gain and follow the corner to a ledge. Step left and climb

good holds to a final crack in deteriorating rock. Step right into another crack for the final moves.

Lower Walls:
The following route lies on the sea-walls below the Wall Street area, where there is a prominent little grassy headland, immediately left of a large birded inlet (looking out). This is thought to be below the bigger headland north of Shoals o' Herrin' area. The rock is generally excellent, but a little care is required near the top, where sea grass is also significant; cleaning on abseil would certainly add a star. From the little headland, a long abseil was made to non-tidal ledges from a large block just below the cliff top, down the left-hand (looking down) of two deep chimney grooves. A short tricky traverse right gains the base of a steep clean wall which is capped by huge overhangs, and defined on each side by slots. This route takes the right-hand slot.

Burnout 40m E2 5b **. G.Robertson, A.Crofton. July 2007.
Climb the steep and sustained crack system directly up into the slot, pull out right, then follow the equally sustained continuation directly to the top.

Euro Zone:
Unnamed VS 4c *. C.Moody, C.Grindley. 12th May 2007.
Start below the left side of the rib between Summer Time Blues and Spindrift. Move up to a short corner, step right and climb the crack on the right side of the rib. Finish up Spindrift.

Dogs Head Wall:
Dog Violet 25m VS 4b *. C.Moody, C.Grindley. 13th May 2007.
Left of Dry Escape is a 12m high buttress. Climb the corner-crack left of the buttress, good easy climbing with one harder move.

Dog House 25m Severe. C.Moody, C.Grindley. 13th May 2007.
Climb the chimney on the left side of the 12m high buttress, then the poor crack above.

Dogleg 20m Very Difficult *. C.Moody, C.Grindley. 13th May 2007.
Climb the open chimney on the right side of the 12m high buttress, step left, then climb the crack up and slightly right.

Dry Escape 20m Very Difficult *. C.Moody, C.Grindley. 18th August 2006.
Round left of Dogs Head Wall is a crack which gives good climbing.

Dog Rose 20m HVS 5a *. C.Grindley, C.Moody. 13th May 2007.
The corner on the right-hand side of Dogs Head Wall. Climb up to a bulge, step right, then back left above the bulge. Continue up the corner with a difficult top section.

Citronella Wall:
Short Rib HVS 5a *. C.Moody, C.Grindley. 12th May 2007.
Start left of Short but Sweet and climb the right side of the rib.

Cumhann Geodha:
Bagpipe Deadline, Left-Hand Finish   15m   Severe. S.Kennedy, R.Hamilton. 17th June 2007.
Climb Bagpipe Deadline till above the bulge, then continue up left to finish.

Silent Witness   15m   HVS 5a *. S.Kennedy, R.Hamilton. 17th June 2007.
Well right of Clam Dredger are diverging cracks. Right of this is an obvious steep crack. Abseil to a tidal start.

Gardyloo Wall:
The wall below the approach to Conductor Cove. These three routes are approached by abseil, but it is possible to scramble between the starts at low tide.

Gloom   14m   HVS 5a *. C.Grindley, C.Moody. 17th June 2007.
The left-facing corner crack left of the dark central wall. Climb up to the bulge, go over this and continue up the right-hand crack.

Black Death   16m   VS 4c **. C.Moody, C.Grindley. 17th June 2007.
The obvious fine crack in the dark central wall, tidal start. Possibly HVS 5a; the start is hard.

Bob's First Whale   14m   Severe *. C.Moody, C.Grindley. 17th June 2007.
Climb the left-facing corner chimney right of the dark central wall; tidal start.

FLODIGARRY:
The Angry Pirate   40m   Severe. I.Armstrong, S.Macdonnell. 5th May 2007.
Climbs the wall to the left of Newspaper Taxis. Start as for Newspaper Taxis. Traverse immediately right for 3m then go directly up the face. At the very top traverse back into Newspaper Taxis as a direct finish requires some cleaning.

BORNESKETAIG:
Skull and Jawbone   20m   HVS 5a. C.Moody, C.Grindley, M.MacLeod. 3rd November 2007.
Go down the 'easy descent' and head east towards the Mitre. The first feature of any size is a west-facing wall with two crack-lines leading to a neck between two fingers of rock. A long sling was placed round the southern finger before climbing for a belay. Climb the right-hand crack. A step left was made at the bulge high up but climbing direct would probably be the same grade. Descend down to the grassy slope on the right (facing the cliff).

The next four routes are west of the 'easy descent'. A pillar forms an impressive arch just west of the descent.

It's a Shame   22m   VS 4b *. C.Moody, C.Grindley. 6th October 2007.
Recessed twin cracks give fine climbing spoilt by a loose finish above. Fence belay 30m back.

Thorn and Verucca 22m Severe. C.Moody, C.Grindley. 6th October 2007.
Right of the previous route is a wide crack then twin cracks then an open chimney. Climb the chimney (15m left-east of the arch facing it) then a loose finish. Fence belay 30m back.

Earth Shower 22m VS 4b *. C.Moody, C.Grindley. 7th October 2007.
Climb the obvious crack round left of the arch then short twin cracks. At the top of the twin cracks move right to finish above the arch. Belay on twin stakes.

Power to Believe 22m E1 5b ***. C.Moody, C.Grindley, R.Hamilton. 7th October 2007.
Climb the very fine crack right of the arch, higher up it is possible to also use the crack on the side of the pillar. Pull left onto the top of the arch and finish above. Belay on twin stakes.

GRESHORNISH:
The Vibrator, West Ridge 15m Severe. G.Reid, S.Kennedy, A.Nelson. 20th October 2007.
The west ridge was climbed on reasonably solid rock.
Note: The original route (*The Vibrator* – SMCJ 2001 p620) was repeated by the above party when significant quantities of loose rock were removed in a futile attempt to improve the solidity of the route. However, the work undertaken has resulted in a reduction of the grade from VSL (Very Severely Loose) to SL (Severely Loose). The height of the stack is unaltered.

NORTHERN HIGHLANDS NORTH

BEINN DEARG, Glensquaib Cliffs:
First Tooth Buttress 200m V,5. J.Edwards, J.Gordon. 12th January 2008.
A good line on turf up the buttress between Centre Party and Wee Freeze Gully. Several pitches could be run together.
1. 30m Go up to the base of a right-trending ramp.
2. 30m Climb the ramp and easier ground to below a very open bay capped by a large jutting roof.
3. 30m Climb up passing the roof on its right.
4. 40m Easier ground leads to a belay below a short steep wall.
5. 20m Climb the wall for 5m before easier ground is reached. Traverse left to the base of a gully.
6. 50m Easier ground leads to the top.

Salsa Saga 250m VI,6. M.Hind, G.Hughes. 12th January 2008.
Climbs the steep section of cliff between Tower of Babel and War of Attrition. Start on a large ledge at the bottom left of the lower tier of the cliff. Climb up turfy ledges on the left edge of the icy groove to reach the top of an easy snow terrace. Traverse up and left across slabs, then climb a short corner breaking the overhangs above and move up the easy terrace. Climb the obvious corner on the upper tier then quickly break left climbing a series of awkward turf ledges on the

left wall of the corner, to belay on the upper left edge. Move up and right to climb a difficult crack above the corner onto a pedestal, then descend the left side onto a ledge and traverse boldly leftwards to finish up the last two pitches of Tower of Babel.

KEANCHULISH SEA-CLIFFS, The Otter's Holt, South-East Wall:
This short wall serves up a number of short but exciting deep water solos, due to the off vertical nature of the wall. At high tide there is just enough water to fall into, but experience may pay dividends. Access the wall by an easy traverse from the bay on the right. Routes described from right to left.

Kelpie 8m DWS 5b ** S2. J.Lines. 12th May 2007.
The first line on the wall above deep water, take the fine dog-legged seam to a rounded finish.

Fachan 8m DWS 6b ** S2. J.Lines. 13th May 2007.
The feint sickle feature gained via a mantelshelf and a pebble, finish up some flakes. Thin and Gritstonesque!

Hydra 8m DWS 6a ** S2. J.Lines. 13th May 2007.
The sustained wall just left on micro edges is rather thought provoking.

Barracuda 8m DWS 5b/c * S2. J.Lines. 12th May 2007.
A couple of good flakes just left lead to some technical climbing, before easing.

Note: *Jaws* (2002) can be graded DWS 4c * S2.

Hammerhead 6m DWS 4b S1. J.Lines. 13th May 2007.
Climb the short overhang about 3m right of the arete.

Shark Fin Soup 6m DWS 5a/b * S1. J.Lines. 13th May 2007.
The right side of the arete is short but fun.

The Traverse 6m (25m) DWS 4b * S2. J.Lines. 12th May 2007.
The full traverse of the wall, then shuffle left along the break where the crag changes direction (rock underneath), to gain the south-west arete, climb this utilising the jam crack to the left.

Nessie 12m (30m) DWS 5b * S1. J.Lines. 12th May 2007.
As for the traverse, but bridge across to the next buttress and climb the right side of the hanging prow via a roof and sloping finish, all above a deep well.

COIGACH, Red Slab:
(NC 129 082) Alt 80m South-West facing
This is a pair of slabs right by the roadside at the foot of Cul Beag. They are composed of top quality Torridonian sandstone.

Tadpole 15m HVS 5a. A.Nisbet, J.R.Mackenzie. 20th July 2007.
A steep wall with good holds which forms left of the left slab. Climb up right of large blocks topped by heather to a ledge. Step left and finish equally steeply.

Help ma Boab 20m E2 5b *. A.Nisbet, J.R.Mackenzie. 20th July 2007.
Climbs the left side of the front face. Start where the cliff base slants up left. Climb easily up slabby ground to where it steepens. Move up left to hollow blocks (good runners above). Move up, then reach left to the arete bounding the edge of the face. Return immediately right and move up (bold) to gain the easier upper slab. Go straight up this to finish.

Note: *Pebbledash* and *Pink Panther* (the existing routes on p114) are effectively the same route although starting either side of the crack (but this is easy). Pink Panther uses a runner on the right whereas Pebbledash doesn't.

Toad Rock 20m HVS 5a *. J.R.Mackenzie, A.Nisbet. 20th July 2007.
Climbs the right side of the front face below and left of the projecting block (The Toad – use your imagination), starting up a narrow crack and climbing past a heather ledge to step left across the top of a large flake to below a shallow scoop; climb the bold wall to step left into the scoop and straight up the great slab to the top.

Bel's Crag:
(NC 089 101) Alt 130m South facing
A sandstone crag with a distinctive curving crack partially seen from the road. Park in a large layby to the west of the crag and surmount the fence, keeping to the left of the wood to reach the rocks, some bushwacking involved but a delightful spot once there; 15mins. Quick drying but potentially midgy!
The crag reaches 20m in height, is very steep but has good flakes and cracks, usually well protected and more amenable that they look. The crag has a large cave up and left of Cave Crack, waterproof and capable of holding a large gathering. The Cave Crack area is the central mass with two smaller buttresses up left and a series of other steep buttresses to the right. The rock is sound with the odd block or flakey section.
The two smaller buttresses are separated by an easy gully. The left-hand buttress has a distinctive overhang at the start and at two-thirds height whilst the right-hand one has two crack-lines.

Pensioner's Profit 12m VS 4c *. R.Brown, J.R.Mackenzie, A.Nisbet. 18th June 2007.
A nice clean line on the left-hand buttress. Surmount the lower overhang via the two cracks and climb centrally to and over an overhang.

Peasant's Revolt 10m HVS 5a. A.Nisbet, J.R.Mackenzie, R.Brown. 18th June 2007.
The left-hand line of flakes on the right-hand buttress which lead to a strenuous finish.

Revolting Peasants   10m   VS 4c. J.R.Mackenzie, A.Nisbet, R.Brown. 18th
June 2007.
The shallow corner to the right of the flakes on the right-hand buttress.

The square-cut main crag has the eponymous Cave Crack as the most obvious
feature slanting up and right with the cave reached by a scramble leftwards up a
groove.

Cave Crack   20m   HVS 5a or 5b **. A.Nisbet, J.R.Mackenzie. 18th June 2007.
Scramble up towards the cave but take the vertical short crack to below the roof.
Either chimney (facing out!) between overhang and roof before revolving like a
dervish or more conventionally by hand jamming strenuously to follow the
slanting crack to the final bulge taken on huge jugs. Highly unusual but well
protected by cams.

Bel's Route   20m   HVS 5a **. A.Nisbet, J.R.Mackenzie. 30th April 2007.
To the right of Cave Crack is a corner and disjointed cracks higher up. An
excellent route, well protected. Climb the corner to the tree; climb the crack on
the left to a ledge and then climb a top crack to finish over a juggy bulge on the
left in a fine position.

The Splitter   15m   HVS 5b *. J.R.Mackenzie, R.Brown, A.Nisbet. 18th June
2007.
Well to the right of Bel's Route is a buttress split by a strikingly obvious thin
crack. Climb the well protected crack to the top; easier than it looks.

Lugainn's Lurgy   12m   Hard Severe 4b. A.Nisbet, J.R.Mackenzie. 18th June
2007.
The buttress at the far east end of the crag has a pleasant shallow corner on the
south face.

Stac Pollaidh notes (Des Rubens):
Vlad the Impaler – 4c for the first pitch (rather than 5a), so VS overall.
Summer Isles Arete Direct – last pitch 5a (rather than 4c), worth 2*.

Meall na Saille:
(NC 055 135)   Alt 30m   South-West facing
This rocky hillside of gneiss, clearly seen from the Achiltibuie road, has a left-
curving (bow shaped) line of continuous rock roughly in the centre. This gave a
pleasant 60m Difficult, taking the easiest line (A.Nisbet, 4th July 2007).

BEN MOR COIGACH, Cona' Mheall:
Achininver Pinnacle is described more clearly as follows:
Achininver Pinnacle   150m   Very Difficult *
A pleasant ramble improving with height. Start at the square block at the base
and follow the best line to below a wide crack at about half-height. Either climb
this 10m pitch direct or turn it on the right and up a groove to a level blocky
section. At the end of this follow a series of short grooves with an assortment of

cracks to near the top where a groove right of an easy chimney and left of a harder groove leads direct to a final good pitch up a steep cracked groove.
Variation: Penultimate Crack 25m E1 5b *. J.R.Mackenzie (unsec). 4th June 2007.
The fine harder right-hand groove is in fact an off-width chimney recessed into a corner above a cosy nook. Climb up to reach the nook via a turfy crack, 10m. Start up on the right by a crack right of the chimney, then transfer left to the crack on its left, 15m.
Note: The left-hand groove was also climbed just left of the normal central one but was very dirty and awkward and not recommended.

RUBHA DUNAN SEA-CLIFFS (NC 02091 06768):

A 250m long stretch of sandstone cliffs reaching up to 15m in height of clean-cut corners and knobbly walls; the rock is red, smoother textured than Reiff and mostly solid despite some interesting convolutions in the rock. They face south, are a sun-trap and dry very quickly and have fabulous views over to Ben Mor Coigach, Horse Island and An Teallach southwards. The climbing is sustained, usually adequately protected and often easier than it looks, accessible at all states of the tide unless very high.
Approach: From a large parking bay near the Woolshed beyond Achiltibuie. Follow the signposted track (past a broch) down to the peninsula and the crags will be seen after 15mins walk following the coast. The highest section of cliff, Tumbledown Wall, is reached first from the east, bordered by a corner, Old Nest Corner, with an arch, smaller corners and walls to its right. At Tumbledown Wall's west end is the best area of cliff containing four corners, two little ones and two deep chimneys, the second (western) of which is used for descent, Descent Chimney. All this area, called Wake Wall, is hit by the Stornoway ferry's wake several times a day.
　Beyond Wake Wall the cliffs turn west towards a wide geo with shorter walls above a platform, Scalloped Wall, that has a slot chimney and on the other side of the geo more walls above the sea before lessening in height. Bouldering is also possible here and above another platform on the landward side of this geo.
　Routes are described from left to right. At low tide it is possible to gain access to the entire frontage of cliff, otherwise use Descent Chimney. 100m west of Scalloped Wall is an area of short walls and aretes, giving highball bouldering or short routes. There is a higher wall at this area's western end.

Ping 7m VS 4b. J.R.Mackenzie, A.Nisbet. 6th October 2007.
This is the shallow flakes and corner on the left (tidal) end of the wall, only very marginally protected.

Scalloped Wall:

This is reached at low tide via a crack or by ledges further west, and is very short (4 to 7m) but has some short routes or bouldering. A geo cuts off this cliff from Wake Wall or from the mainland continuation cliffs except at low tide. Just to the right of an overhung corner are two broken cracks with a slot chimney between them.

No Scallops Tonight   5m   Difficult   J.R.Mackenzie. 19th August 2007.
The left-hand crack.

A Slot Above the Rest   5m   Very Difficult. J.R.Mackenzie, C.White. 19th
August 2007.
The jolly slot.

Splodge   5m   Difficult. J.R.Mackenzie. 9th August 2007.
The right-hand crack.

Razor Clams For You   5m   VS 5a *. C.White, J.R.Mackenzie. 19th August
2007.
The sharp little wall with the thin crack to the right.

Wake Wall:
Non-tidal save at the far west end with a good platform at its base, most easily
reached by descending Descent Chimney, the second deep chimney-gully
reached from the east. A fine vertical wall cut by four pronounced corners and
two short ones to the left with more dubious rock left of the Descent Chimney.
At low tide access is possible from the beach boulders.

Don't Wake the Stone   12m   HVS 5a. J.R.Mackenzie, C.White. 19th August
2007.
The corrugated face at the left end of the wall has an alcove. Climb past this to a
ledge, pull up via the beak step right then back left and finish next to a left-
slanting break which has a hole near the top. Take care with the rock.

Don't Wake For Me   13m   Hard Severe 4b *. J.R.Mackenzie, E.Austin. 8th
August 2007.
Start right of Don't Wake the Stone near the right end of the vertical wall. Climb
the wall then continue up and left up stepped corners and a fine mantel near the
top; good jug pulling lower down but the mantel is the thing!

Descent Chimney   15m   Moderate.
The second (western) wide chimney; initially down on the right then step right
into the chimney; continue down two short grooves to the platform.

Descent Chimney Arete   15m   Difficult. J.R.Mackenzie, E.Austin. 8th August
2007.
To the right of the descent is an arete. Climb it starting from the right, passing a
large thread en route and finishing up the crest and arete in an exposed position.

Splashdown   13m   VS 4c *. C.White, J.R.Mackenzie. 19th August 2007.
The wall to the right of the arete has a particularly fetid pool at its foot; start
above the pool, gain the jug and climb the centre of the fine wall to the top; good
climbing but the pool awaits.

Fetid Pool Crack   13m   VS 4c *. J.R.Mackenzie, C.White. 19th August 2007.

The thin crack to the right of the pool is tricky but good, followed by the easier left-slanting ramp; perhaps a little harder than Splashdown.

It's got to be a Diff 13m Difficult *. J.R.Mackenzie, C.White. 19th August 2007.
The easterly companion chimney to the Descent Chimney; rather pleasant and with a chockstone too.

Waking and Watching 13m Very Difficult. J.R.Mackenzie, E.Austin. 8th August 2007.
The wall now turns south again with the two short corners reached first. Start up the west-facing plaques of rock before moving into the top right short corner finishing via a crack.

Crossover 14m VS 4b *. C.White, J.R.Mackenzie. 19th August 2007.
The south wall has a thin layback crack near its left edge; climb this (no protection) to the halfway ledge, move left into the leftmost of the short corners and finish up this.

Time and Tide 12m VS 4c **. J.R.Mackenzie, C.White. 19th August 2007.
The first of the four main corners. Start direct and finish by the layback crack.

Spinal Tap 13m VS 4b *. JR Mackenzie (unsec). 9th August 2007.
The next shallow corner to the right of Time and Tide. Climb direct to the 'vertebrae' and climb these to gain a small ledge and the final corner, very entertaining.

Kicking Horse 13m E1 5b *. A.Nisbet, J.R.Mackenzie. 6th October 2007.
The wall to the left of Wake Up! has a shallow groove high up; start on the right side of the wall and climb to below a bulging section. Step left and climb steeply to a good horizontal break near the top, then a final tricky move. High in the grade.

Wake Up! 13m VS 5a **. J.R.Mackenzie (unsec). 9th August 2007.
The deep right-angled corner gives possibly the best climb here. Good rock, climbing and position all the way to the top.

Wake Wall 13m HVS 5b *. A.Nisbet, J.R.Mackenzie. 5th October 2007.
The thin crack between Wake Up! and Lateral Thinking is not as hard as it looks.

Lateral Thinking 13m HVS 5a *. C.White, J.R.Mackenzie. 19th August 2007.
The hanging cracks on the wall to the right of Wake Up! are reached by a ledge; climb the crack to good flake holds higher up and the top; fine climbing, quite tricky but the name is a clue.

Foreboding Pleasures 13m E1 5b **. J.R.Mackenzie (unsec). 19th August 2007.
The fourth and final corner, unlikely looking for the grade, is as good as Wake

Up! A boldish start right of the corner leads to the edge and a step back left towards the corner. Climb the right-hand wall direct to the corner and finish up it.

Tumbledown Wall starts just right of Foreboding Pleasures and extends to the obvious right-facing corner. It is largely non-tidal save at its west end. This is the highest and smoothest section of cliff but also the most suspect. On-sighting would not be clever on the main face.

Tumbledown Wall   20m   E1 5a/b *. J.R.Mackenzie, A.Nisbet. 6th October 2007.
Potentially very good given a little traffic and a bold approach. The top overhanging block is exciting and solid fortunately. On the left of the wall is a cracked corner leading to the overhang; start well right of this below a shallow corner. Boulder the lower overhang or easily traverse in from the right to the corner. Traverse horizontally left to reach the cracked corner, climb this and the bulge above to the crux block and a final mantel to finish.

Old Nest Corner   12m   VS 4c. J.R.Mackenzie, E.Austin. 9th August 2007.
The right-facing corner is dusty but will improve, giving traditional climbing all the way.

OLD DORNIE, MEALL DEARG, Dome Crag:
(NB 98555 10480) Alt 110m   South facing
A slabby dome of good rock giving short but pleasant routes.

Totally Calmed Out   15m   Difficult. J.R.Mackenzie, E.Austin. 14th September 2007.
The groove on the left with a finish up right.

Orange-ade   15m   Very Difficult *. A.Nisbet, J.R.Mackenzie. 5th October 2007.
Start below an orange block, climb up to it, mantel it then go up a smooth slab on the right to the top; very pleasant.

Nervous Twack   12m   Hard Severe 4b *. I.Cattanach, B.McDougall. 28th May 2006.
The obvious crack with delicate climbing, the best route here.

Cool for Cats   12m   Hard Severe 4c *. A.Nisbet, J.R.Mackenzie. 5th October 2007.
Another good route up the parallel crack right of Nervous Twack, close to it but with independent climbing.

Fill in the Blank Space   12m   Severe *. J.R.Mackenzie, A.Nisbet. 5th October 2007.
The seemingly blank slab between routes 4 and 6; not what it seems and better for it.

Crazy Takes Big Any Day 10m Severe. B.McDougall, I.Cattanach. 28th May 2006.
The crack on the right of the slab that peters out but leads to good holds to the top.

April Fool Crags (NB 986 111):
When looking up from the large layby at the head of the bay, there is an obvious, large hanging slab on the left side of an upper bowl. Scrappy Doo starts below and 25m to the left of this, and leads to Crimp and Chimp and subsequently Cattching!

Scrappy Doo 8m Difficult. I.Cattanach, B.McDougall. 28th May 2006.
A scrappy pitch up a small corner following a crack system. Start 5m left of a larger corner.

April Fool Crag – Lower:
A strikingly pink crag facing south-west, routes a maximum of 10m.

Crimp and Chimp Hard Severe 4b *. B.McDougall, I.Cattanach. 28th May 2006.
Start just right of an obvious triangular niche, delicate climbing up spidery finger cracks to finish on good crimps.

Avoiding the Issue Difficult.
The left edge of the face to some loose blocks then move left to an easy finishing slab.

Fooled Again HVS 5a *. J.R.Mackenzie, E.Austin. 30th April 2007.
Climb up a slanting ramp to an overhang and climb directly over this via a crack to a surprise finish.

The Perfect Fool E2 5c *. J.R.Mackenzie. 30th April 2007.
Takes the thin cracks between Fooled Again and April Fool. Some quite serious climbing on very small gear. Go straight up by a narrow left-facing edge to a good break and cams. Finish straight up the headwall. A bold feel to the climb.

April Fool Severe *. J.R.Mackenzie. 1st April 2007.
The straight wide crack gives a nice route.

Sudden Impulse 1 Hard Severe 4b. J.R.Mackenzie. 1st April 2007.
The left-hand and easier looking of the twin cracks.

Sudden Impulse 2 Severe. J.R.Mackenzie. 1st April 2007.
The harder looking but easier right-hand crack.

Fools Paradise VS 4b/c **. J.R.Mackenzie. 1st April 2007.
Climb the middle of the wall just left of a curving crack starting left of a little corner at the base.

Straight Crack   Severe. J.R.Mackenzie. 1st April 2007.
The pleasant crack to the right.

Finishing Touches   Severe. J.R.Mackenzie. 1st April 2007.
The short wall to the right.

April Fool Crag – Top:
Centreline   10m   Severe. J.R.Mackenzie. 1st April 2007.
Climb the centre of the wall.

Cattching!   9m   Hard Severe 4a. I.Cattanach, B.McDougall. 28th May 2006.
On the upper tier gained from Crimp and Chimp. The obvious rib come arete sprouting from the left-hand side of a small niche. Nice moves up the rib lead onto the arete (easier on the right) with some thin climbing and protection for the grade. Confidence can be gained from the soft boggy landing.

Cattatonic   8m   Severe *. B.McDougall, I.Cattanach. 28th May 2006.
Walk rightwards for 300m from the previous routes to reach this route, located on the right-hand end of the large upper tier basin above old peat cuttings. Delicate climbing up the main crack and breaks on the slab. Starts off steeply but eases off towards the top.

REIFF, Stone Pig Cliffs:
Taking the Abyss   15m   E3 6a **. I.Taylor, T.Fryer. 1st April 2007.
Start right of Sonique in the jaws of the deep chimney. Climb steeply on good holds to the start of a thin crack. When the hand holds run out 'fall' across the chimney, then bridge to the top.

To the left of Daunts Arete at the far end of the Stone Pig Cliff is an undercut slab bounded on the left by Slabby Corner Crack (which is Easy not Moderate).

Dauntless   20m   HVS 5b *. J.R.Mackenzie, B.Wright. 12th June 2007.
Near the right edge of the slab the overhang is cut by an alcove. Climb through this to a difficult landing on the easier slab which is climbed direct to the top. Well protected but tricky.

Hidden Geo:
This narrow geo is situated just beyond Slabby Corner Crack at the far end of the Stone Pig Cliffs. Either abseil in to non-tidal platforms or descend Slabby Corner Crack and make an easy tidal traverse around the headland into the geo and platforms below the south wall. The south wall is of steep immaculate black sandstone whilst the easier angled north wall is of sound pink sandstone.

Hidden Geo, South Wall:
Above the platform is a black recess between the headland section and the rest of the crag.

The Glorious 12th   15m   Severe *. J.R.Mackenzie, B.Wright. 12th June 2007.

Left of the recess is a shallow corner. Climb the corner to a headwall; step up left onto a ramp to finish. The original route (J.R.Mackenzie 11th June 2007) moves right from the headwall to finish up a groove at overall V.Diff standard. Both ways enjoyable.

The Stoater   20m   HVS 4c **. J.R.Mackenzie, B.Wright. 12th June 2007.
Climbs the buttress with a capping hood-like roof to the left. Thinly protected and thus serious. Start at the lowest ledge and take an open corner to a leftwards mantel onto a ledge which is the second break. Traverse up and right to below the hood and climb its right edge via thin moves, crux, and more easily to finish. A very good route.

The Stonker   22m   E1 5b ***. J.R.Mackenzie, B.Wright. 12th June 2007.
Takes the semi-hidden corner to the left of The Stoater. Climb the Stoater to the mantelshelf ledge and traverse left into the corner. Climb the excellent corner with adequate protection over two cruxes to the top.

The Stonker Direct   20m   E3 5c/6a ***. J.R.Mackenzie, A.Nisbet. 4th July 2007.
A low tide alternative starting off the pointed boulder. Move up from the boulder then step left and go up the corner. This gives a sustained and excellent route; the lower third significantly harder than the rest.

Hidden Geo, North Wall:
The north wall of Hidden Geo is part of a peninsula. To reach it descend a groove on the seaward end and make a step left (facing out) onto slabs to avoid the lower groove; it is now easy to descend to sea-level. There is an overhung alcove just beyond the step left and an overhanging headwall above the slabs split by two corners further on. Descend the slabs to a ledge above the sea. Appearances are deceptive from below.

Puzzle Me Quick   20m   VS 5a *. J.R.Mackenzie, J.M.E.Austin. 19th June 2007.
The easy slabs lead to an unusual overhanging corner.

Start, Stop   20m   VS 5a. J.R.Mackenzie, R.Brown, J.M.E.Austin. 19th June 2007.
Between the two corners the headwall has a small overhang. Climb the slabs and surmount the overhang centrally. Good climbing.

Chimera Groove   20m   Mild VS 4b/c *. J.R.Mackenzie, R.Brown, J.M.E.Austin. 19th June 2007.
Climb the right-trending groove in the easy slab to the rightmost corner which curves back left giving pleasant delicate climbing. The best of the three.

Recess Slabs   25m   Moderate to Difficult *. J.R.Mackenzie. 22nd June 2007.
The back wall slabs. Climb direct via the back wall, a good Difficult or if taken by the easiest possible line, an equally good Moderate.

Long Geo, South Wall:
This is the long geo just north of Hidden Geo, with a small beach at the north-east end. To reach the south wall descend the groove as for Hidden Geo North Wall but traverse easy ledges around the headland to platforms on the south side of Long Geo. At the far left-hand end of this wall (looking in) is a chimney.

Sea Pink Arete   25m   Difficult. J.R.Mackenzie. 12th June 2007.
Climb the left arete of the chimney to a grass ledge. Climb the avoidable steep wall above (Very Difficult).

Flowery Buttress   25m   Very Difficult. J.R.Mackenzie. 22nd June 2007.
At low tide walk in from the beach to an obvious arete bordering a deep slot and cave. Climb the broad buttress on good rock to a final groove, crux, and a flowery finish on less stable rock; good in parts.

Long Geo, North Wall:
Most easily reached by traversing along ledges at one-third height from the beach. The seaward half has an area of sound black rock with a prominent left-facing shallow corner and a slighter one to its left.

Black Groove   15m   Difficult to Very Difficult. J.R.Mackenzie. 22nd June 2007.
The more prominent right-hand corner is climbed to near the top where a step right into a slender groove (Very Difficult) or wall to its right, finishes the route.

Mechanics Geo:
Spare Tyre   10m   E3 5c *. T.Fryer, I.Taylor. 1st April 2007.
On the far right of the crag is a straight narrow groove. Starting from a rounded ledge, climb the groove. Slow to dry.

Seal Song Area:
Aoxomoxoa   15m   Severe *. D.Preston, M.Volume. May 2007.
This left-trending crack-line is surprisingly obvious. Start left of Guttersnipe beneath a short open corner. Climb the corner and follow the crack-line, finishing right on good holds.

Minch Wall:
A near Minch Occurrence   10m   HVS 5b. A.Cashman, F.Murray. 17th August 2007.
Start at a small corner 1m right of Clam Jam (Clam Jam was thought undergraded). Climb up and slightly right to a sloping shelf, then up to a break. Finish straight up.

Rubha Coigeach, Golden Walls:
Wild Blue Rock   E2 5c. V.Scott, E.Tressider. 10th September 2007.
Takes the capped overhanging groove up the arete left of the corner of Milkshake. Start at the bottom of Goldie Horn, move up and right into the overhanging groove to below the roof. Using an obvious sidepull on the right,

pull through onto the wall above (crux) and continue up the easier arete to the top. Pumpy and well protected (small cams).

Slab Inlet:
The Font Sporran   6m   VS 4c. F.Murray, A.Cashman. 19th August 2007.
Start to the right of The Slab. Rock up onto a foothold on the lip of the undercut slab. Finish straight up.

Achmelvich, Red Wall (NC 056 256):
A pleasant, south facing, partially tidal, short crag just visible from the west side of Achmelvich Bay. The crag is seamed with cracks and plastered with positive, angular holds.
Approach: Follow sheep paths northwards from Achmelvich Bay past the smaller sandy beach and then round the headland. Chewitt's Chimney is the obvious gash on the wall ahead. Cross the small stile above the tidal slot and continue to the top of the crag ahead. 20 mins.
Descent: At either end of the crag, easier at the west end.
An obvious shattered red gneiss wall tapering toward the west end. Described from right to left.

In Remote Part   12m   Severe. J.Dyble, K.Hewitt. 19th October 2007.
To the right of the obvious chimney is the highest part of the crag. Start in the recess below the chimney and climb rightwards up the side of the flakes aiming for a short crack at top.

Scottish Fiction   12m   Severe. J.Dyble, K.Hewitt. 16th October 2007.
Climb the arete and slab to the right of the chimney. Looks steeper and harder than Severe from the ground.

Chewitt's Chimney   10m   Difficult. J.Dyble, K.Hewitt. 19th October 2007.
Obvious, finish direct. Entering the chimney is size-dependent!

Breabach   10m   Difficult. J.Dyble, K.Hewitt. 16th October 2007.
Climb the wall and arete to the left of the chimney.

Tsunami   9m   Difficult. J.Dyble, K.Hewitt. 16th October 2007.
Two metres left of the previous route. Follow the angular flake in its entirety.

Woombling Around   9m   Very Difficult. J.Dyble, K.Hewitt. 19th October 2007.
Left again is a broken crack running from bottom to top. Climb it.

Twilight Sad   9m   Difficult. J.Dyble, K.Hewitt. 19th October 2007.
One metre left again is a bigger crack. Follow it direct.

Sula   8m   Difficult. J.Dyble. 19th October 2007.
To the right of the grey rock patch is a short wall. Climb it on positive holds.

Bassana   8m   Very Difficult. J.Dyble. 19th October 2007.

To the left of the grey rock is a right-slanting crack. Follow this then head straight up.

OLD MAN OF STOER:

Note: D.Cronshaw & D.Ryden had previously climbed *Diamond Face Route* on 26th September 1982, graded it E2 5b and named *Ròs Dearg* (only reported in a climbing magazine).

CONIVAL:

Note: A.Brook made an ascent of the South Ridge of Conival in the winter of 1968, along with D.Brook, D.Leonard & D.Weston. The route is mentioned on page 229 of Northern Highlands North (called South-East Ridge) but is worthy of a full description.

BEINN AN FHURAIN, Traligill Crag (NC 295 211):

Approach: Follow the path up the side of Traligill River to Conival and Ben More Assynt, heading up for the bealach between Conival and Beinn an Fhurain. The crag is visible on the left, 1hr 30mins.

The crag is a Quartzite escarpment, with the right side showing 40m groove lines and a steep right side wall with a descent gully at the far right. The central section is made of a steep initial wall with a slab in the centre and broken walls above. The crag breaks away left into 10m walls.

Father's Day Disaster 45m Severe. G.Jones, M.Collins. 17th June 2007.
Start at the left end of the central section on the left edge of a heather ledge. Climb a wall 5m right of a crack and move up left under an overhang. Gain the crack and climb to top walls, moving right.

Justified and Ancient 30m Hard Severe. M.Collins, G.Jones. 17th June 2007.
Start at the toe of the buttress before the descent gully. Make for an obvious groove line above passing a large leaning pillar on the left.

Smooth Coated Milligan 20m VS 4b. G.Jones, M.Collins. 17th June 2007.
An obvious striking crack on the descent gully wall. Climb the crack and move left at the top.

BEINN AN FHURAIN, Summit Crag:
(NC 304 215) Alt 800m South facing

From the Beinn an Fhurain to Conival col, approach to within a few metres of the summit of Beinn an Fhurain. The crag is just below the summit. Drop down a quartz boulder filled gully, crossing the remains of a wall, to access the crag. Excellent quartzite climbing.

Chopping Block Corner 40m Difficult **. D.Broadhead, D.Rubens. 14th April 2007.
The huge corner near the upper end of the crag, Bear left higher up to maintain interest.

Sunblock Slab 40m Very Difficult. D.Broadhead, D.Rubens. 14th April 2007.
About 10m below Chopping Block Corner is a corner. Start in the line of the corner, then avoid loose overhangs above by bearing right. Scrappy.

Blockbuster 40m HVS 5a **. D.Broadhead, D.Rubens. 14th April 2007.
About 40m below the Curving Corner, start at another corner. Climb the corner until it trends into a slight ramp, terminating at a small spike. Go up right for 2m via an undercut hold, then up to a crack-line (slightly suspect) to finish.

New Kids on the Block 40m VS 4c **. D.Broadhead, D.Rubens. 14th April 2007.
The cleanest part of the crag terminates 50m below the Curving Corner. Beyond the arete forming the right end of the crag, the rock becomes more shattered. The route follows the line of a small corner on the arete formed by the right edge of the clean area of rock. Start 1m left of the right end of the crag. Climb a thin crack to a ledge (5m) then follow line of the shallow corner and the arete.

TARBET SEA-CLIFFS, Geo an Amair (SMCJ 2006):
Note from S.Charlton: This is the same crag as The Grey Slabs (p244 in Northern Highlands North). The Upper Tier of the Red Wall is the same as Dog Crag. The route *Loan Shark* is the same as *Midsummer Madness. The Long Road to Nowhere* appears to be a combination of *Prawn Stars, Prawnography* and *Creelman*. The route *Sundance Kid* is the same as *Ben Boy*.

Dolphin Crag:
Out of the Blue 27m HVS 5a *. S.Kennedy, R.Hamilton. 9th June 2007.
The back wall of the geo comprises a steep lower wall, a slabby central section and a steep upper wall containing a right-facing corner. Abseil approach down the corner right (east) of Inshallah, then traverse right onto the wall. Start in a groove just left of the leftmost of two prominent fins of rock. Climb the groove and a vague line of ramps out leftwards in an exposed position. Move right under a bulge onto a slab, then directly up to the central slabs. Finish up the right-facing corner.

Black and Tan 30m VS 4c **. R.Hamilton, S.Kennedy. 9th June 2007.
Takes a line between Meal for a Seal and Sneak Preview. Start up the slab just left of the foot of Meal for a Seal and negotiate the lower overlap a metre or so from its right end. Move up leftwards to a thin left-slanting seam running up a black slab. Climb the seam and upper slab fairly directly to the top.

Misty Arete 25m Very Difficult. S.Kennedy, R.Hamilton. 9th June 2007.
The rounded arete at the left end of the slab left of Solitary Man.

SHEIGRA, First Geo, South Side Inner Wall:
Frigging the Flake 25m E3/4 6a. T.Fryer, I.Taylor. 11th August 2007.
Climbs the hanging corner right of Daylight at Midnight, using a suspect-looking flake. Finish leftwards up slabs and a short steep corner.

Treasure Island Wall:
X 40m   E5 6a. S.Crowe, K.Magog (both led). 17th June 2007.
Left of Designed by the Flawed. Climb the prominent groove to a small overlap
and good protection. Pull slightly left and climb boldly to the top. Care needed
with some of the holds as this area is often damp.

CAPE WRATH CRAGS:
Note: F.Cannings climbed the stacks of A' Chailleach and Am Bodach solo in
August 1973 (Northern Highlands North has them as 1989).

WHITEN HEAD, Mainland Cliff:
Note: The bottom section of *Mosscheeper* has fallen down since the first ascent.
It was climbed again by R.I.Jones & N.Wilson. The grade and description
remain unchanged.

Shuffle Finish to Eskimo Shuffle   HVS 5a. R.I.Jones, N.Wilson. 31st March
2007.
After the overlap traverse out leftwards and climb the wall to the left direct.

WHITEN HEAD NORTH COAST STACKS:
Approach: Park at Achininver and follow the track west through a farmyard
and up a hill until it ends and continue across moorland to the headland just east
of Geodha Brat (40mins) for the descent to Geodha Brat – East Stack (40mins).
A burn is a further 5mins to the west (access for Geodha Brat – West Stack) and
Rubha Thormaid is a further 10mins to the west where another burn cascades
into the sea.

Geodha Brat Stacks, West Stack:
(NC 550 676)   Tidal
This prominent 30m stack is easily seen to the north of the bay. Access is gained
by scrabbling down the gully 50m to the north of the burn and then 400m along
the coast from mid to low tide. The stacks passed on the way are in a dangerous
state of collapse. Abseil descent from an in-situ stake.

A' Bòcan   35m   HVS 4c *. R.I.Jones, N.Wilson, S.Nadin. 1st April 2007.
Climbs the south-east face. Start at the right of a small overhang. Pull through
this on the right and traverse up and left onto the arete. Climb the final short wall
by a steep right-slanting groove to the top.

East Stack (NC 554 671):
The 25m stack can be seen from the headland east of Geodha Brat. Access is
gained by a 100m abseil down the cliff above the stack from a rock thread and
stakes (not in-situ) followed by a further 60m abseil from blocks. The stack is
gained by a 15m swim to a large platform on the south-west side. Descent is
from a thread below the summit.

A' Càmhal   28m   HVS. R.I.Jones, J.H.Stocks. 18th September 2006.
1. 12m 3b. From the platform climb cracks to a sloping platform. Traverse this
to below the east wall of the stack.

2. 10m 5a Climb the hanging exfoliated wall, pulling through on to a ledge on the left.
3. 6m 3b Climb the easy ramp to the top.

Stac Thormaid (NC 548 678) Tidal:
This is a fine looking 35m stack that deserves more ascents based on its easy access, situation and climbing. The stack has remained unreported. M.Tighe made an ascent with a party on 20th May 1993 by the landward arete (Original Route). This was assumed to be a second ascent as halfway up, a wooden wedge with a small hemp rope tie was found.
Approach: Park at Achininver and follow a track west through a farmyard and up the hill until it ends. Continue across moor to where the burn cascades into the sea at Rubha Thormaid (1hr). The stack can be seen to the east. Access is gained up an easy scramble to the bay and wading across ledges 1.5 hours either side of low tide.

Original Route 40m Hard Severe 4b **.
A fine route that takes the landward arete. From the base climb to a ledge and then up to a steep wall. Step left around the arete and climb a wall for 2m, then the arete to the top.

Rùn-dìomhair 40m HVS 4c. R.I.Jones, R.Reginski. 22nd April 2006.
Start at the chimney to the left of the seaward face. Climb the wall above for 3m before making bold moves right and upwards to sidestep an overhanging wall. Pull through blocks to a large ledge and an easy scramble to the summit.

MELVICH, Lady Bighouse Rock (NC 909 657):
This is a fine 25m stack that is precariously perched on the edge of a sloping ramp.
Approach: Park at the farmhouse (NC 894 649) east of Bighouse from where it is a 20 to 25mins walk. A 20m abseil from a large block overlooking the stack into the sea followed by a 15m swim. Return by tyrolean or swim.

When the Big Lady Sings 20m HVS 4c. R.I.Jones, M.Dent. 6th May 2006.
Climb the corner on the east face before traversing up and leftward to pull through onto a large ledge on the landward (south) face and then easy to the top.

Unnamed Stack Severe. S.Sustad, M.Fowler. 30th June 2006.
Walk out to the coast via a track which starts between the main road signs indicating the Sutherland/Caithness border. This is a couple of miles east of Melvich. On reaching the coast the stack is soon apparent. It is about 1km east of Little Bighouse Stack. Abseil and swim to the stack. The climb takes the easiest route just to the right of a deep green corner on the seaward end of the north face.
1. 10m Climb up easily to beneath a large overhang.
2. 12m Traverse left and up to finish just right of the green corner.

RED POINT:
See Northern Highlands North p345. The routes are described from left to right.

Fast Reactor   10m   Very Difficult. M.Dent, R.I.Jones. 7th May 2006.
Abseil to a platform below an overhang at the left end of the wall and which looks over a narrow slot. Climb the wall, then up and right of the overhang to the top.

£2 Million Fine   10m   Hard Severe 4b. R.I.Jones, M.Dent. 7th May 2006.
The prominent V-groove accessible at low tide from the platform beneath the north wall.

A crack-line up the middle of the wall was assumed to have been climbed before (10m Severe).

Second Day Resolution   10m   VS 4c. R.I.Jones, M.Dent. 2 January 2006.
Start from the bottom of the right-facing groove and pull onto the wall on the left and climb direct.

The right-facing groove/corner was assumed to have been climbed before (10m Severe *).

The next routes are on a small headland immediately right which is separated by a deep narrow slot. Routes on the east wall can be accessed by abseil or stepping across the slot towards the right end from the platform.

The Cornered Yorkshireman   15m   Severe. M.Dent, R.I.Jones. 7th May 2006.
From the left end of the ledge, climb the corner and groove above.

Orphan   15m   HVS 5a * (1999) – Grade and quality confirmed.

Spikey   15m   Hard Severe 4b *. J.Sanders, R.I.Jones. 29th October 2006.
Climb the wall 3m right of the corner to a break. Step left and pull up onto the hanging wall and take the groove above.

Illegal Dumping   15m   HVS 4c. R.I.Jones, J.Sanders. 29th October 2006.
Climb the wall 2m right of Spikey, just left of the niche and left of the blunt arete to the left of the black wall. Sparse gear.

Cornwall Crack   15m   HVS 5a ** (1999) was thought to be VS 4c, no stars.

Chain Reaction   15m   E1 5a *. R.I.Jones, J.Sanders. 29th October 2006.
Climbs the right side of the black concave wall direct. After bold moves up the slightly overhanging wall, pull through onto the wall which is climbed directly.

Fusion   15m   HVS 5a **. R.I.Jones, M.Dent. 7th May 2006.
From the right end of the wall traverse around the arete and belay beneath the wall of the arete. Climb the wall to mid-height, then the wall left of the arete stepping back on the arete in the final moves.

The next existing routes are accessible by abseiling down the west-facing wall.

Chiabop 15m HVS 5a * (1999) – Grade and quality confirmed.
Chiasmus 15m VS 4c * (1999) – This route is worth a star.

Right of Chiasmus is an easy ramp. The next two routes take the north-facing undercut wall to the right.

£140,000 Fine 15m Severe. J.Sanders, R.I.Jones. 13th July 2007.
Start at the bottom of the ramp and climb the corner groove.

Corporate Negligence 20m E2 5c **. R.I.Jones, J.Sanders. 13th July 2007.
Climb up 3m and traverse out across the bottom of the wall for 4m. Climb the crack to a ledge. Step right and climb the wall above, pulling up and left to a break, then direct to the top.

CAITHNESS, SARCLET, Big Buttress:
The Flow 25m E2 5b *. R.I.Jones, C.Las Heras. 19th August 2007.
Climb the wall on small cracks immediately right of Groove Armada direct and left of centre. Climb the wall direct to a small lip at 10m. Balance through this to a pocket jug and continue up to finish as for Groove Armada as it exits right. Moving out onto the centre of the wall below the lip provides easier climbing and reduces the grade.

Notes: R.I.Jones also thinks *Sarclet Pimpernel* deserves 4 stars (see SMCJ 2006) but only HVS 5a (A.Nisbet agrees with E1 5a). *Groove Armada* at VS 4c seems unanimous.

Second Bay:
Let them Eat Jelly Beans 20m Severe. J.Sanders, R.I.Jones. 13th July 2007.
Start up the left-facing corner 4m left of Rinse and Repeat. Climb the corner and the wall and corner above.
Note: *Rinse and Repeat* (VS 4c) was good. Definitely 2 stars, not necessarily 3.

Cave Bay Area:
Roof and Ready 20m VS 4c. J.Lyall, A.Nisbet. 19th September 2007.
Right of Occum's Razor is a recessed corner, then another steep buttress. Right of this, on the seaward face is the next recess, with a wide crack on its left side leading to a roof. Climb the crack, step left to pass the roof and back right above to finish steeply.

Sparklet 15m Very Difficult. A.Nisbet. 19th September 2007.
The next recess to the right forms this corner.

Ruff Arete 15m Severe 4a. J.Lyall. 19th September 2007.
The right arete of the above corner.

MID CLYTH, Mid Clyth Stack:
Pulsating Toe Climb 18m E2 5c. S.Sustad, M.Fowler (alt). 1st July 2006.
Takes the obvious crack on the north side of the stack. The shortest climb in the world with three pitches? Start at the platform at the north end.

1. 6m 4a Climb to a ledge.
2. 6m 5b Trend right up through shale overhangs to gain a projecting ledge on the north face.
3. 6m 5c Go up a crack to the top.

OCCUMSTER, Occumster Stack (ND 263 352):
Park at Occumster (ND 265 354), as for the Occumster sea-cliffs, and head west across the field to the bay. Access to this stack can be gained at low tide. A scramble takes you to the summit of this rib of rock.

Roy Geo West Stacks:
Approach: Park by the houses at Clyth (ND 273 362). Roy Geo is a 500m walk to the south-south-west. There are five stacks west of Roy Geo, three on a platform accessible by abseil and a boulder hop at mid to low tide. Island Stack, a steep sided island permanently surrounded by the sea and South Stack, a finger of rock to the south of Island Stack require a swim or boat. Descent by simultaneous abseil unless stated.

West Stack:
Flame on the Horizon 25m VS 4c. R.I.Jones, A.Porter. 24th March 2007.
Climb the up the centre to the south face into a wide groove. Pull out right onto a terrace and easier ground.

Centre Stack:
Uncertain Entertainment 15m HVS 4c. A.Porter, R.I.Jones. 24th March 2007.
Climbs the wall below the central groove on the south face. The cracked groove is somewhat precarious. Layback this and pull on to a ledge on the right and the safety of the summit.

The North-West face/arete (very loose) was climbed and descended by S.Sutherland & H.Miller in the early 70s.

East Stack:
In the Company of Rigs 15m VS 4b. R.I.Jones, A.Porter. 24th March 2007.
Climb the wall and a difficult pull into the left of two groove/corners to the top.

The west arete (loose) was climbed and descended by S.Sutherland and H.Miller in the early 70s.

Roy Geo East Stack (ND 276 355):
This was previously referred to as Occumster Stack. An amended name and grid reference; the route description in Scottish Rock Climbs remains unchanged.

ORKNEY, YESNABY, False Stack Area:
Benton 747 20m E2 5c *. R.I.Jones, M.R.Porter, M.J.Porter. 22nd June 2007.
Climb the open book corner left of Variety Show and pull into the hanging groove above. Finish by traversing into the final moves of Variety Show to avoid the loose direct finish.

Double Act 20m HVS 5a. R.I.Jones, R.Benton. 21st June 2007.
Climb the overhang and wall above right of Variety Show.

HOY, Broughs of the Berry (ND 245 895), North Brough:
Dislocation Crack 15m HVS 5a *. R.I.Jones, M.R.Porter. 23rd June 2007.
The overhanging crack on the north wall of the small inlet on the seaward side.

South Brough:
Little Pinky 15m VS 4b. M.R.Porter, R.I.Jones. 23rd June 2007.
Poor climbing up the central wall of the landward face.

The Berry:
Walk north for 100m from the top of Beriberi to a deep parallel sided gully that
goes down to sea-level – the Goody Gash. The crack starts at about half-height
and is unmistakeable on the right wall. Abseil a step and then descend the gully
to a ledge line on the right-hand side (looking out), 50m above sea level.

Black Crack 170m XS. M.Fowler, S.Sustad (alt). 27th June 2006.
1. 30m Traverse the ledge easily to belay at the foot of obvious loose corners.
2. 25m 4b Climb the two loose corners and move left to belay on a large ledge.
3. 25m 5c Climb a greasy overhanging wall (2PR) to a horizontal break.
Traverse left until a right-trending line leads up right to a fine stance.
4. 10m 5a Continue up the groove to a good ledge at the start of the crack.
5. 20m 5b Up the crack passing an interestingly poised block with care.
6. 35m 5b Continue up the crack to where it widens into a chimney.
7. 25m 5b Climb the back wall of the chimney passing the capping overhang on
the right.

EAST HOY, Scapa Flow:
Marked on the OS Map as such, this looks like a possible sea-stack when viewed
from the road south of Moeness. In fact it is a grass-topped pinnacle standing
above a beach. The summit is easily reached from the landward side. This route
takes the arete facing Moeness. Start at the toe of the buttress reached by
descending a gully on the north side of the candle.

Candle of the Sale 30m E2 5c. S.Sustad, M.Fowler (alt). 28th June 2006.
1. 20m 5c Deceptively difficult grooves lead to an unhelpful crack and a stance
where the rock becomes lighter.
2. 10m 5a Climb the wall above via cracks, first slightly right, then slightly left.

SHETLAND, ESHANESS:
Abbing A Fence 40m HVS 5a. R.I.Jones, P.Sawford. 30th May 2007.
The often damp chimney between Anguiral and Not Necessarily Stoned. Start
from ledges by the sea. Pull out of the chimney early to avoid a horrible thrutch.

Hanging Arete 20m VS 4c *. P.Whitworth, R.I.Jones. 31st May 2007.
The hanging arete left of Solan.

Angrist   40m   E1 5a. R.I.Jones, P.Whitworth. 31st May 2007.
From the belay for Achilles Last Stand, pull out left and climb the wall direct.

Right of Achilles Last Stand is a wall with two lines. Belay on a small ledge at the bottom right of the wall.

Narsil   40m   E2 5b **. R.I.Jones, P.Whitworth. 1st June 2007.
Traverse out left and climb the left-hand wall direct. Fine, bold climbing with good rock but limited gear.

Gurthang   40m   E3 5b. R.I.Jones, P.Whitworth. 31st May 2007.
From the belay climb direct for 4m and pull up onto a ledge just right of the arete. Pull out left onto the wall and climb direct to the top. Good rock at the bottom with minimal gear. Rock deteriorates towards the top.

Further south:
Not so Perfect Arete   45m   E1 5a. R.I.Jones, P.Whitworth. 31st May 2007.
From the belay for Perfect Groove climb the wall just right of the arete.

Sirens of Calder   45m   E2 5b **. R.I.Jones, P.Whitworth. 1st June 2007.
The wall right of Perfect Groove. Bold climbing on superb rock.

Imperfect Crack   45m   VS 4c *. R.I.Jones, P.Whitworth. 31st May 2007.
Belay on the large ledge to the right of the wall. Climb the crack up the centre of the wall right of Sirens. Fine climbing spoilt by deteriorating rock for the last 8m.

Framgord   45m   E1 5a *. R.I.Jones, P.Whitworth. 31st May 2007.
The wall left of Near Perfect Arete and right of Imperfect Crack.

The Darkness of my Mind   40m   HVS 4c. R.I.Jones, P.Whitworth. 2nd June 2007.
Right of Bubblebox is rib beneath a hanging corner. Climb the rib to the overhang and pull out left onto wall right of Bubblebox and climb to the top.

Shetland Girls   35m   HVS 4c. D.Rayner, A.Cheetham. 17th August 2007.
Climb the arete below and left of Tirricks, traverse left under a roof at half-height and climb a crack to the top.

Mustn't Crumble   20m   VS 4a. R.I.Jones, P.Whitworth. 2nd June 2007.
A shockingly poor route on poor rock and rubbish protection up the arete to the right of Watching Whales.

Note: *Perfect Groove* thought high in the grade VS 4c not HVS 5a.

THE FAITHER, North Wall:
A black north-facing wall lies 100m to the north of the Arch Wall. A good

alternative when the sun hasn't come around onto the other walls. Abseil down the corner on the right side of the wall to a ledge 10m above the sea.

The Harbinger 30m VS 4c *. A.Whitworth, P.Whitworth, R.I.Jones. 27th May 2007.
The crack-line and corner above the ledge.

The Necromancer 30m E1 5b **. R.I.Jones, A.Whitworth, P.Whitworth. 27th May 2007.
Pull up left from the ledge onto the wall and climb straight up. Crux is the final smooth section of wall near the top.

Prophecy Wall:
The Augurist 40m E1 5a ***. R.I.Jones, P.Whitworth. 27th May 2007
Follow the Faither Prophecy until the pull right into the slanting crack-line. Instead climb the wall direct for 3m and pull up left and climb the wall above into a left-facing corner. At the roof pull out right onto an arete and a fine finish.

Note: *The Faither Prophecy* was repeated by R.I.Jones and A.Whitworth and regraded E1 5a (not 5b). The first pitch is 30m and total length 50m. *The Oracle* is 45m not 50m.

FOGLA TAING:
(HU 415 169) Non-tidal South and East facing
This crag offers great climbing on hard and solid sandstone.
Approach: Park at Troswickness (HU 409 172) and head 600m south-west to the crag. Abseil to ledges.

Fogla Taing, Main Wall Area:
Left of the main wall is a left-facing corner and a smaller wall.

Kalessin 25m HVS 5a **. R.I.Jones, P.Whitworth. 26th May 2007.
A fine climb up the corner and layback crack above.

At the right side of the main wall corner capped by an overhang.

Ancalagon of Morgoth 30m E3 *. R.I.Jones, P.Whitworth. 28th May 2007.
The grade is for the top pitch.
1. 15m 5c Climb the corner to the hanging roof and traverse left 3m and pull out onto a ledge.
2. 15m 5b From the left end of the ledge step up and leftwards. Bold and unprotected climbing gains a hanging crack/corner. Climb this and the corner above.

Yevaud 30m E2 5c *. R.I.Jones, A.Whitworth, P.Whitworth. 26th May 2007.
Climb the centre of the right wall just left of an incut groove/chimney to a break. Climb the crack above pulling onto a small ledge (crux). Step right and climb up to a shelf. Climb the short wall above and the corner, pulling left to finish. A

Camelot 5 or 6 is essential to use in the break otherwise the grade will be E3. South of the main wall is a small geo, then an undercut hanging wall. The next route is the corner-groove 5m south of the hanging wall. Abseil to a ledge just right of the corner-groove.

Glaurung   25m   E2 5b **. R.I.Jones, P.Whitworth. 28th May 2007.
Make a poorly protected 3m traverse left from the ledge to the bottom of the groove. Climb the fine groove to a ledge at half height and a layback crack to the top.

Puff The...   30m   VS 4c. P.Sawford, J.Maguire. 28th May 2007.
Climb the left of two shallow corners 10m further south. Good rock at the bottom which deteriorates with height.

South of this corner is a large tidal ledge and east facing wall before the bay of Fogla Taing.

UNST, Skaw Point:
All of the routes in this area are bird free. The venue has a good number of low grade climbs with plenty of gear, though not as many as the guide suggests.

The Pinnacle, East Face:
Croft My Ride   15m   E2 5c **. R.I.Jones, P.Sawford. 29th May 2007.
Climbs the thin crack-line right of slanting crack-line of Half Face (1996) to a sloping crimp (crux) just below the top.

Full Fare   15m   Hard Severe 4b **. R.I.Jones (solo) 29th May 2007.
The crack-line up the centre of the face.

The Conductor   15m   Severe 4a. R.I.Jones (solo) 29th May 2007.
The crack-line to the right

The Inspector   12m   Severe 4a. R.I.Jones (solo) 29th May 2007.
The right trending crack-line from the bottom of The Conductor.

The Pinnacle, West Face:
First Stop   20m   Difficult. R.I.Jones. 29th May 2007.
Just left of the arete of Back Seat. Crux at the top.

Main Wall:
Skaw Crack   16m   Hard Severe. P.Sawford, S.Broadhurst. 21st April 2006.
The crack between Mr Bounce and Park and Ride.

Note: *Top Deck* is Very Difficult not Severe.
Back Seat and *Last Stop* are both worth a star.

Crofter Slab:
80m north of the main wall is a clean 5m wide undercut north facing black slab and provides three good routes.

Dreaming of Cold Pigs 12m E1 5b. R.I.Jones, P.Sawford. 29th May 2007.
Start at a notch and climb the left side if the wall and left thin crack-line above.

Rufus 12m E1 5b. P.Sawford, R.I.Jones. 29th May 2007.
From the notch climb the right side of the wall and the right thin crack-line above.

The Crofter 12m Hard Severe 4a. R.I.Jones, P.Sawford. 29th May 2007.
Pull onto the arete from the right and climb this to the top.

GRIND OF THE NAVIR, Crystalocean Wall:
The Scientist 10m Severe **. A.Ratter, P.Whitworth. 2003.
The fine crack on the wall to the south of the tidal pool.

Whittslab 12m HVS 5a *. P.Whitworth, P.Sawford. 2005.
Left-trending tracks and the slab above left of Pea Groove.

Pea Groove 10m VS 4c. P.Sawford, P.Whitworth. 2005.
The short groove and arete left of Spray.

Squibs 10m Very Difficult. P.Whitworth. 2003.
The easy angled slab and corner right of the niche of Grindstone.

North Wall:
The Subterranean 15m Severe. P.Sawford, P.Whitworth. 2006.
The large crack above the cave.

North Nose:
Little Secret 15m Hard Severe 4b **. P.Whitworth, P.Sawford. 2006.
Start from the left of the ledge and climb the slabby corner which is right of The Subterranean.

Back Burner 15m VS 4c. A.Whitworth, P.Whitworth. 8th June 2007.
Start left of Barnicle Bill up the blocky corner, crossing the route at two-thirds height and continuing up the headwall above.

Gully Slab Crack 15m HVS 5a *. P.Sawford, J.Posnett. 2004.
The thin crack on the slab right of Piltock.

South Nose:
Minus Lab 6m HVS 5a. P.Whitworth. 2006.
The delicate slab left of Darklands.

Lark Sands 10m VS 4c *. P.Whitworth, A.Whitworth. 2004.
Start as for Darklands but instead of stepping into the niche continue up the headwall.

Two Tone   15m   HVS 5a *. P.Whitworth, A.Whitworth. 8th June 2007.
The delicate crack-line up the centre of the wall left of Ponder.

Ponder   15m   E3 6a *. A.Whitworth, P.Whitworth. May 2007.
The narrow crack-line opposite Streams of Whiskey. Fiddly protection on crux.

Sumsuch   20m   Severe. P.Whitworth. 2005.
Right of the descent scramble and left of Briggistanes. The short corner-crack and stepped wall to the top.

Note from A.Whitworth: *Pockets of Excellence* is well protected with cams, hence regraded VS 4b from HVS.

South Wing:
Pocket Chimney   10m   Severe *. P.Whitworth, A.Whitworth. 2006.
The chimney between Crabbie Crabbie and Rib Tickler. Pull round the arete to finish.

NORTHERN HIGHLANDS CENTRAL

BONAIDH DHONN:
Anvil Buttress   140m   V,6. S.M.Richardson, R.G.Webb. 2nd February 2008.
To the right of Route 1 and Route 2 is a vegetated square-cut gully. This route takes the rounded, but well-defined buttress to its right, and is defined by a prominent anvil-shaped block visible on the skyline from the approach ledge.
1. 50m Climb vegetated grooves up the crest of the buttress to an easing.
2. 50m Continue up a slabby wall on good holds, then trend up and left to below the steep upper section of the buttress.
3. 40m Climb steep cracks on the left side of the headwall on excellent holds and continue to belay just above the 'anvil'.

LOCH TOLLAIDH Notes:
Six routes have been climbed on a wall named Appendix Wall, two more routes on Grass Crag, one on Lobster Crag and one on Red Walls.

RUBHA MOR, Opinan Slabs:
Ramalina Dingdong   15m   Severe. J.Dyble, C.Hewitt. 18th February 2007.
Climb the cracked slab in the gap between A Good First and A Poor Second.

Mellon Udrigle, Deep Geo, Sron an Dun-Chairn:
The following route is situated on the promontory on the west side of the geo mentioned in the guide (p154).

Breach of Contract   10m   VS 4c *. S.Kennedy, R.Hamilton. 28th April 2007.
Based on the left arete. Two deep clefts are situated left of The Contract. Start up the leftmost cleft and move up and left to the edge. Step left around the arete then up and back right to rejoin the arete to finish.

One of the towers forming Bab n' Ali, Jbel Sarhro, Morocco. Photo: Hamish Bown.

NEW CLIMBS

BEINN LAIR:
Tower Ridge III. A.Nisbet. 22nd March 2008.
A line as near the crest as possible was taken. The final tower was summited but without a rope, a line on the west was taken to gain the summit plateau.
Note: *Geodha Ban* climbs the main gully left of North Summit Buttress, with *Tower Ridge* the ridge on its left, so the guide has the routes in the wrong order, plus Geodha Ban is wrongly placed on the diagram. But Geodha Ban is easy to find from the description and looks good.

Breaking into Heaven 400m II/III. A.Dye, S.Drummond, M.Griffin. 23rd March 2008.
The buttress left of Tower Ridge is climbed by a prominent central runnel of weakness. Start at the bottom left-hand corner of the buttress where an easy ramp leads right out onto the face. Follow the ramp until below an obvious runnel that splits the buttress. Climb the runnel line for two pitches before following a shallow gully leftwards until below a steep chimney. Go up the chimney (crux) and the easy gully above, bearing left where the gully forks below a tower. Traverse airily out along a ramp on to the front face of the tower before climbing to its summit. An exposed easy ridge leads to the top.

Marathon Gully 500m III. A.Nisbet. 19th April 2008.
A deep narrow twisting gully close on the right of Marathon Ridge. It held snow well in the late season. Low down, a short waterfall pitch of clean rock about Difficult was climbed in crampons because of an exit on to ice. Thereafter followed 400m of Grade II, mostly snow with three short ice pitches. At a fork near the top, the left of two possible gully finishes was taken.

Note: The winter ascent of *Right Wing, Butterfly Buttress,* as described in the new guide, was an ascent of North Summit Buttress.

A' MHAIGHDEAN, Pillar Buttress:
The Great Game 190m VII,7. R.G.Webb, S.M.Richardson. 19-20th January 2008.
An outstanding route in an immaculate position taking the prominent series of corners and chimneys cutting the left side of the buttress. The first pitch is probably common with Bell's summer route on the buttress, but the relationship with the other summer routes on the buttress is uncertain.
1. 30m Start left of a deep cleft (in line with the corners above) and climb up and right to join the series of chimneys.
2. 35m Follow the chimney-line over a couple of steep steps to an easing below an overhanging slot.
3. 30m Climb the slot to a good ledge below steep cracked wall.
4. 20m Ascend twin cracks (crux) and exit left to a good ledge.
5. 35m Continue up a grassy corner for 10m, step left onto the wall and climb turf to gain a short hanging chimney. Climb this, then move up and right to easier ground.
6. 40m Move and right to join the final buttress crest that leads to the summit cairn.

*Andrew Wielochowski climbing Casablanca, HVS 5a, in Tizgut Gorge, Anti-Atlas, Morocco.
Photo: Noel Williams*

GRUINARD CRAGS, Car Park Area:

Note from I.Thow: *5 Minute Crack* is harder than the other routes on Very Difficult Slab, worth Severe (although it spoils the name!). Starting up *Gneiss* and following the obvious crack system up left is pleasant and worth a mention (*Still Gneiss*, Very Difficult). The layback flake right of *Black Wall Special* and the groove above is Very Difficult too (*Black Wall Right-Hand*?). All the above soloed 28th May 2007.

Road Crag:

Weapons of Mass Distraction   20m   E2 5b *. K.Kelly, P.Ebert. March 2007.
A natural line following the lower diagonal fault in its entirety. Start as for Mongo. Follow the diagonal fault past the steep groove. Where the crack peters out, continue in the same line up and left, crossing Raglan Road, bold. Gain the now large diagonal break once more and follow this to its end.

Blame Canada   18m   E1 5b **. P.Ebert, K.Kelly. March 2007.
Start on the far right as for Ataka. Climb the obvious left-slanting crack beneath the roof. Follow this prominent crack traversing past Trojan and gaining the crack of Raglan Road. Step up and continue leftwards following the diagonal crack. Enjoyable climbing with the crux at the end.

BEINN DEARG MOR:

Big Wednesday   210m   VI,6 **. R.Webb, P.Macpherson, G.Briffett. 26th March 2008.
Superb situations and enjoyable climbing, poorly protected in places. Start about 25m up Trident Gully (to the right of Central Buttress) at an obvious left-trending turfy fault line which is 10m right of another turfy ramp.
1. 30m Climb the turfy fault boldly past a steepening to a turf ledge. Continue up the fault passing a niche to a large ledge.
2. 25m Climb an awkward off-width turfy crack on the right to a ledge below a steep corner. Traverse/crawl left over a slab to join the main fault line again and climb direct with great moves up a left-facing corner to the crest of buttress.
3. 30m Climb fairly direct up the crest of the buttress at first trending slightly right via a groove and step, then take a left-hand steep groove with a steep pull on turf to a ledge.
4. 50m Climb up trending right and continue up a ramp. Pass a large slot with a chockstone and continue more easily.
5. and 6. 75m Continue easily up the buttress, finishing by a fine arete connecting it to the hill.

AN TEALLACH, Corrie Hallie Crag:

Dispatch   18m   VS 4c. A.Nisbet, J.Preston. 11th June 2007.
A direct line right of Patch, passing through the white patch between two heather clumps at half-height and which is mentioned in the description of Piff Shlapps.

Pensive   20m   E1 5a. J.Preston, A.Nisbet. 11th June 2007.
Climbs close to a white (when dry) water streak which runs parallel and right of

Stylus. Start 3m left of Ullapool Fish Week and slant slightly right up the streak to pass through a small round depression near the top.

Two Scoops 18m VS 4c. A.Nisbet, J.Preston. 11th June 2007.
A parallel line right of Escoop and finishing just left of a crack feature which runs from half-height to the top.
Note: *Escoop* was thought to be HVS 5a and this route only slightly easier.

Eave Ho 20m HVS 5a. J.Preston, A.Nisbet. 11th June 2007.
A direct line right of the crack feature and passing through a deep horizontal crack between two large grass tufts (at half-height on the cliff). Start by a pointed boulder.

Take the Biscuit 15m VS 4c. A.Nisbet, J.Preston. 28th September 2007.
Climb the centre of the fractured rock right of Tiffin (not loose) past two slightly recessed horizontal cracks one foot apart at 10m.

The next two routes are in the blockier section right of Inception.

Exception 15m VS 4c. A.Nisbet, J.Preston. 28th September 2007.
Start 2m right of Inception, just left of a grass ledge at 1m. Climb straight up the wall keeping midway between Inception and some heather tufts to the right. Trend slightly right near the top.

Going Green 15m HVS 4c. J.Preston, A.Nisbet. 28th September 2007.
A clean band between the heather tufts and a green streak which emanates from a recess. Start just right of the 1m ledge. Trend right to climb just left of a green streak. Finish above the green streak.

Silicon Daze 18m E2 5b. J.Preston, A.Nisbet. 28th September 2007.
The wall right of the green streak. Start 4m right of the streak. Climb up to a small spike on the left. Move right with difficulty across a smooth section to better holds and a tiny left-facing corner. Go up trending slightly right and keeping left of a fainter green streak to the top.

Moss Killer 15m VS 4b. A.Nisbet, J.Preston. 28th September 2007.
The right end of the wall with Blankety Blank. Take a fairly direct line, passing 2m right of the mossy hole.

Podiatry 15m VS 4b. A.Nisbet, J.Preston. 30th September 2007.
Left of the crack of Pick the Lock and just over half-height is a shallow right-slanting pod. Take a line up to it and finish up a faint crack from its top.

Running Deep 20m E1 5b. J.Preston, A.Nisbet. 30th September 2007.
Start below the left end of the arch, whose centre is taken by Shallow Waters. Climb to this, then move left to a pink patch. Go back right and climb up a crack left of two overlaps. Continue direct to the top.

Cameo   18m   HVS 5a. A.Nisbet, J.Preston. 30th September 2007.
A line through the middle of the overlap between Try Me and Ron Move Wonder. Climb straight up to a grass ledge, then the left end of a smaller rock ledge. Climb through the overlap where there are three small right-angle steps. Finish easily.

Oakum   15m   Hard Severe 4b. J.Preston. 30th September 2007.
Climb the left end of the wall, just right of the oak in a heathery chimney.

Blink   15m   Severe 4a. A.Nisbet, J.Preston. 30th September 2007.
A crack-line right of centre on the wall with Tricam, finishing up a short left-facing corner on the right.

Next right is a twin vegetated break, then another with a small holly at 3m.

Holly Tree Wall   12m   HVS 4c. J.Preston, A.Nisbet. 30th September 2007.
Climb the wall just right of the holly.

Break Even   12m   Hard Severe 4b. J.Preston, A.Nisbet. 24th October 2007.
The narrow heavily-fractured buttress right of Row yer Boat gives a good pitch on solid rock.

Starboard   18m   VS 4c *. J.Preston, A.Nisbet. 24th October 2007.
A direct line up the right side of the wall leads to a finish up the right crack. The left start and direct finish remains as a separate and more logical line (Port E2 5c).

The following routes are on the section 50m downhill to the right. The routes either abseiled off or finished easily on a ledge which led right (not in the length).

Untouched   18m   VS 4c. A.Nisbet, J.Preston. 24th October 2007.
Climb the wall just right of Sleazy.

Pineless   20m   VS 4b *. J.Preston, A.Nisbet. 24th October 2007.
The left side of the main face. Climb past the right end of a long grass ledge at 4m. Continue up past a small overlap at two-thirds height.

Primal   20m   VS 4c *. A.Nisbet, J.Preston. 24th October 2007.
The first crack-line on the main face of rock. Primera is the second crack-line.

Trimera   20m   VS 4c *. J.Preston, A.Nisbet. 24th October 2007.
A third but less distinct crack-line.

Badrallach Crag:
Fat at Fifty   20m   Very Difficult. J.Lyall, J.Preston. 13th April 2007.
Climbs cracks in the wall right of Fresh at Forty, finishing up the open corner.

Note from I.Thow: Starting up the groove on the right makes the route Moderate (28th May 2007).

Wisecrack 25m Hard Severe 4b. J.Lyall, J.Preston. 13th April 2007.
Climb the crack in the wall left of Fresh at Forty. At the steepening, step up and left to climb the fine flake-crack to the top

Note: *Nimue* was thought Severe (not VS 4b). I Thow agreed, but still 4b.

Gatecrasher 35m Hard Severe 4b. J.Lyall, J.Preston. 13th April 2007.
Bridge steeply up the obvious corner (between Nimue and Garden Party), then climb the crack in the slab above to cross Garden Party and finish up the steep crack above.

Spurning the Invitation 35m Difficult *. I.Thow. 28th May 2007.
Climb the clean rib left of Garden Party, cross this at its narrows, then go up right to finish up the rib right of the slab. From the narrows one can go up left to join the top part of Lapsang Souchong, making it a good Severe.

Pebble Dash 35m VS 4b. J.Lyall, J.Preston. 13th April 2007.
Start up the hanging corner left of Garden Party and follow cracks to a small roof. Step left and climb a crack through the roof, then the pebbly wall above. Step right and climb the obvious crack right of the Lapsong Suchong corner to the top.

Pillar of Anxiety 35m VS 4b. J.Lyall, J.Preston. 13th April 2007.
The rib 30m left of Harvest Moon. Stay on the crest and finish up the right-hand rib. Eliminate but good.

Crack 'n' Rib 35m HVS 5a. J.Lyall, J.Preston. 13th April 2007.
Ten metres to the left is a steep crack up a wall which leads to a rib just left of the above route.

THE FANNAICHS, Sgùrr Breac, North-East Nose:
The Slot 100m II. J.R.Mackenzie, A.Nisbet. 8th April 2008.
The right end of this crag holds a deep gully which is mostly easy except for a very short final step (technical 4 on the day).

Sgùrr Breac, North Face:
Sgùrr Breac has a large but often broken north face.

Chill Out Chestnut 100m II. J.R.Mackenzie, A.Nisbet. 8th April 2008.
Low down in the centre of the face are two buttresses separated by a gully. The right buttress is short and steep; the left is climbed by this route (NH 15631 71351; alt 723m). Difficulties are turned on the left otherwise climb the crest to open slopes.

Cool Down Coconut 150m II *. J.R.Mackenzie, A.Nisbet. 8th April 2008.

A left traverse from the top of Chill Out Chestnut leads to another two buttresses, the right with a roofed base. This gully between them is well defined and had two ice pitches. Above the gully, long open slopes lead to a point about halfway between the two summits of Sgùrr Breac.

Misty Mountain High   300m   II/III **. E.Austin, J.R.Mackenzie. 11th April 2008.
Near the right side of the face is a narrow straight gully well seen from the main road (NH 15425 71325, alt 720m). Grade III on this occasion but will vary. The gully base lies at 720m and is in condition quite often. A short introductory ice pitch, then snow to an exit of 20-25m ice. Mixed ground was followed up left to a steep headwall and cornice.

STRATHCONON, Creag Ghlas:
Ugly Sisters   45m   E3 5c. M.Hind, D.Moy. 5th May 2007.
An intricate and delicate wander up the slab left of Glass Slipper.
1. 10m Climb the first pitch of Glass Slipper but belay at a big block on the left.
2. 35m Step off the block into a crack. Move right and up to another thin crack left of Glass Slipper's overlapped corner. Continue up and left to the left side of two small overlaps. Traverse right below the overlap and up some thin moves to flake holds and runners. Continue up and left to a poor RP 4, then climb boldly up blind cracks and slopey holds on the right to reach the top of the slab just below the wide crack of Glass Slipper (abseil tat above).

Allt Gleadhraich:
Klingon Wall   40m   IV,V. M.Hind, R.McHardy, P.Mayhew. 11th January 1997.
A steep ice wall left of Allt Gleadhraich at NH 274 511. It shows up well on the Explorer Map. The party continued up a the side tributary and climbed another Grade II pitch.

STRATHFARRAR, Sgùrr na Fearstaig, South Top, East Face:
White Wizard   100m   Severe. J.R.Mackenzie, A.Nisbet. 15th July 2006.
Takes the right edge of the big slabby wall right of The Sorcerer. Start at the foot of Rising Damp and climb left over the blocky edge, then follow it to reach the base of the slabby wall (40m). Continue left of the edge over a bulge, taking the cleanest rock up the slabs to a recess (45m). Continue up on the right to the top (15m).

Winter: 100m   V,5 **. D.McGimpsey, A.Nisbet, J.R.Mackenzie, N.Wilson. 19th January 2008.
A fine intricate route with an excellent second pitch, loosely based on the summer line.
1. 40m The blocky left edge was traversed in from the right. In lean conditions a 20m ice chute can form below giving an extra pitch. Climb the blocky edge to reach the base of the slabby wall.
2. 40m A short difficult wall leads to a groove on the right. Climb this moving left to reach two 'ears' well seen from the stance. Move left below these to reach and climb a narrow turf groove leading to overhangs. Traverse right below these

to step up to another groove and up this for a short distance before moving right to a recessed wide crack.
3. 20m Step right and climb a funnel to the cornice.

CREAG GHORM A' BHEALAICH:
Sentinel Ridge 85m III. M.Hartree, B.Shackleton. 16th March 2008.
The ridge between the two gullies described in Northern Highlands Central p349. It gives an interesting excursion from the toe of the lower buttress to gain the slender ridge above. From 15m up a ramp overlooking the right-hand gully, gain the alcove in the buttress above by a steep step (or reach more directly, from lower down the ramp if well iced). Traverse left across the alcove to reach a fine belay overlooking the left-hand gully at the foot of the slender ridge (35m). Follow the fine ridge as directly as possible to finish at the summit cairn (50m).

SGÙRR NA LAPAICH, Creag na Lapaich:
Dire Straits 150m IV,5 **. J.R.Mackenzie, N.Wilson. 21st December 2007.
The slot chimney to the right of Cool Runnings lying roughly centrally in the crags. Probably impossible for large climbers or rucksacs! In late season it forms ice thickly due to a spring but can be climbed when lean as more rock protection is available.
1. 25m Steepening ice leads to rock belays on the left; the pitch length will vary with the amount of ice.
2. 20m The chimney slot gives steep ice and narrows further to a sideways squeeze under a chockstone and a tight exit further on from a dead-end. Continue up a short run of ice.
3. etc. 105m More ice leads to steepening snow and a cornice, outflankable on the left.

CANNICH:
Note: *Plodda Falls* (Grade V), *Corriemony Falls* (Grade III), and *Guisichan Falls* (Grade III) were climbed on 18th January 2001 by M.Hind, P.Mayhew, G.Lowe. *Falls of Divach* (Drumnadrochit) was climbed on 20th January 2001 by the same team at IV/V.

BEN WYVIS, Coire Mor:
Interrupted Buttress 165m III,4 *. N.Wilson, J.R.Mackenzie. 30th December 2007.
To the right of Interrupted Gully's recessed start is a broad rambling buttress that lies right of the existing routes. It freezes more readily and holds snow well, a good choice in less than perfect conditions. The climbing is much better then appearances suggest. A dark cave lies right of centre in the lower section of crag, reached by steepening slopes.
1. 50m The roofed cave is climbed by a traditional struggle, crux, to a ramp which is followed rightwards then up to a point where steep moves up left lead up to a recess.
2. 40m Step left from the stance to cross Interrupted Gully's right branch and head up the centre of the buttress to a zigzag line that ends below a steeper section of grooves.

3. 50m Climb out steeply to climb the first groove on the left and exit onto easier slopes.

4. 25m   Follow the ridge which borders the right-hand side of Interrupted Gully's exit to the plateau.

Interrupted Gully Right Branch   200m   II. N.Wilson, J.R.Mackenzie. 16th March 2008.

A reasonable route when the turf is unfrozen and plenty of snow cover. Start up Interrupted Gully and follow this   past its turn-off left to head up a hidden leftwards ramp further on. Climb this narrow ramp past a cave and a steepening to move left and either climb a short overhanging corner or avoid it on the left. Finish up a steep snow fan and probable cornice.

MOY ROCK:

There are now six sport routes. There is a nesting restriction from the beginning of February to the end of July. The routes are left to right on the Big Flat Wall area:

1. 20m 6c+. *The Dark Side* (20m)
2. 20m 6c. *Little Teaser* (20m)
3. 20m 7b. *Pulling on Pebbles* (20m)
4. 25m 7a+. *The Ticks Ate All the Midges* (25m)
5. 20m 7a. *Cloak and Dagger* (20m)

About 10m further down and right is

6. 12m 7b+. *The Seer* (12m)

NORTHERN HIGHLANDS SOUTH

SOUTH GLEN SHIEL, Sgùrr an Lochain:

Horseplay   120m   IV,5 **. A.Nisbet, J.Preston. 19th March 2008.

Based on the ridge between Flying Gully and Right Gully. The name will become obvious on a sensational finish. Start about halfway up Right Gully where a gully leads up its left bounding wall.

1. 40m Climb the gully to gain access to a ramp which leads right overlooking Right Gully. Follow the ramp to near its top.

2. 40m The only line of weakness above is a left traverse across a wall using small turf ledges. From its end on the crest of the ridge, climb a moss groove to below a final tower.

3. 40m Move right on to the very crest, initially overlooking a vertical wall, and climb the crest using flakes to a finish which should be less corniced than the gullies.

KYLE OF LOCHALSH, White Dyke:

Silver Sixpence   12m   HVS 5a **. J Dyble, J.Shanks. 12th July 2007.

The obvious left-facing corner to the right of Shilling Corner gives a surprisingly tricky climb. Move leftwards under the bulge at the top to finish up the reddish flake. Probably climbed before.

Merlin's Groove 10m E1 5a **. J.Dyble, B.Hay, D.Currie. 12th July 2007.
A holly tree sits to the right of Slab Climb. Above is a bulbous overhang. Start directly below the overhang and climb through broken horizontal bands to arrive directly at a right-facing corner on the right of the overhang. Step right under a smaller upper overlap to finish at a small aspen tree. Thinly protected but quite good really!

Spin the Black Circle 10m HVS 5a. D.Currie, J.Dyble, B.Hay. 12th July 2007.
Rises between Anthrax and Crack Climb, sharing some of the early moves of the former. Step rightwards at half-height and continue directly through a bold upper slab. Sustained climbing throughout with some great moves on the pleasing upper section.

FUAR THOLL, North-West Face:
Summit Rib 150m II. A.Nisbet. 4th March 2008.
The route named Summit Rib in Northern Highlands South is not the same as the route named Summit Rib in Northern Highlands Scrambles. The route in the climbing guide should be renamed South Rib. This route starts lower and left and with a well defined Grade I gully on its left. Follow the crest closely, taking in all the difficulties and ignoring escapes.

SGORR RUADH, Central Couloir:
East End 220m IV,4. A.Nisbet, J.Preston. 25th March 2008.
The rib right of Post Box Gully. Climb an icefall some 10m right of Post Box Gully (40m), then another icefall above and left (40m) to reach an easier section. Follow this to below a steep prow (55m). Go diagonally right under the prow to a crest overlooking the final gully of Gravesend (55m), then finish up a line of weakness just right of the crest (30m).

Mayfair 80m V,5. A.Nisbet, J.Preston. 25th March 2008.
A shallow groove on the south wall well up the couloir, beyond High Gully. A short smooth slab-ramp leads left into its base. Start below the groove and climb a grassy trough leading up right (25m). Continue up to steep walls, then step left and climb a short tricky wall to below the slab-ramp. Traverse delicately left under this and return to its top and the base of the main groove, iced on this occasion. Climb the groove to easy ground (55m).

BEINN BHAN, Coire na Feola:
Suspense Wall 175m VII,7 **. T.Blakemore, M.Moran. 2nd February 2008.
This fine route climbs the steep cliff on the right side of Suspense Gully by a sustained and sometimes bold line. The line trends left up breaks in the precipitous upper wall. Start on the terrace 10m right of the fork between the branches of Suspense Gully at a right-facing corner.
1. 30m Climb the corner, moving to its left arete after 10m, where thin moves gain the big terrace above.
2. 30m Follow a right-slanting turfy fault (poorly protected), then swing up left on perched blocks to stance by a rock spillikin.
3. 55m Climb straight up for 6m (bold) to a break and traverse this left for 8m

to a chockstoned chimney which gives entertaining moves to a large block (possible belay). Drop down the left side of the block and climb leftwards up vague grooves to an easier chimney (bold, sketchy climbing – crux). Reach a terrace, then go up a final short corner to gain easy ground.
4. 60m Easy mixed ground and steep snow to the top.

Coire nan Fhamair:
Outrage 200m VII,7 **. G.Robertson, D.MacLeod. 26th March 2008.
A very worthwhile route providing a more sustained alternative finish to Gully of the Gods, taking the obvious fault line in the right edge of the right wall of the easier upper gully.
1. and 2. 100m Climb the first two pitches of Gully of the Gods, breaking up right at the end of the difficulties to below a prominent chimney left of a huge block.
3. 40m Climb the chimney and continue up into an overhung bay with a wide crack slanting up left. Pull left over an overhang to gain and follow the strenuous crack. At its top step right and continue up to below the upper fault.
4. 60m Climb the excellent upper fault with sustained interest to a spectacular sting in the tail. This pitch would be better split to avoid rope drag.

Green Giant 150m VI,8 *. M.Moran, A.Nisbet. 5th February 2008.
The wall right of Great Overhanging Gully gives a good option for a shorter day, and bypasses the improbable lower wall by starting up The Chimney (Girdle Traverse).
1. 45m Gain the rising traverse line by a turfy open gully, and follow it left until just before a pyramid of moss which issues from a big groove which forms the only break in the steep tier above.
2. 35m Climb the moss and groove above, which is hard but well-protected, then continue to belay above the next terrace.
3. 45m Climb the next wall on the left where it is formed into two steps. Continue up a long left-slanting ramp to below the final band.
4. 25m Move right behind a large block which sits below an arete which formed a break in the cornice.

BEINN NA-H-EAGLAISE, East Face:
Summit Gully 250m II. P.J.Biggar. 8th April 2008.
This is the long curving gully (NG 912 523) which borders on the right the steeper more compact rocks of the east face of Beinn na-h-Eaglaise; well seen from near the stepping stones on the Annat to Coulags path. It appears on the OS map as a stream and brings one out at a small col just below the summit of the hill.

SEANA MHEALLAN WEST, Pink Walls:
Salt and Vinegar 15m E2 5b. D.King, N.Carter. 7th June 2007.
The rib between Fish and Chips and Unmasked, climbed with gear in the steep thin crack to the left. Continue up the wall above to the small overhang and pull over this to finish.

LIATHACH CRAGS, Path Crag, Lower Tier:

Jampot 15m VS 4b. J.Lyall, A.Nisbet. 29th September 2007.
Towards the left end of the crag is a left-facing corner bounding a more prominent rounded buttress. Gain and climb the corner.

Panorama 15m HVS 5a. A.Nisbet, J.Lyall. 29th September 2007.
The rounded buttress has a central crack-line with another to its left. Start on the left side of a lower plaque of rock. Either climb straight up this (5b), or climb its left side to reach the crack-line which is followed to the top. Well protected.

Goldmine 15m HVS 5a. J.Lyall, A.Nisbet. 29th September 2007.
Start at the lowest point of the plaque of rock. Climb a right-slanting crack to a chimney on the right edge of the rounded buttress. Climb the chimney and move left to finish up a crack on the right side of the rounded buttress.

Cheese and Chalk 15m HVS 5a. A.Nisbet, J.Lyall. 29th September 2007.
Climb a vegetated chimney 5m to the right. Step right and climb a fine overhanging crack slanting right.

Digitalis 15m HVS 5a. A.Nisbet, J.Lyall. 29th September 2007.
Ten metres left of Foxglove Crack (which is actually near the right end of the crag) is another right-slanting flake-crack. Climb this, step right and follow its continuation rightwards.

Odds 15m Severe. J.Lyall, A.Nisbet. 29th September 2007.
A short undercut crack leads to stacked flakes, climbed out left. A direct finish is vegetated so traverse a ledge left to finish up a short wall.

DIABAIG, Upper Diabaig Crag:
(NG 811 593) Alt 160m North-East to North-West facing
A small crag seen across Loch Diabaigas Airde and shaped like the prow of a ship. The left face has smooth rough rock like Diabaig but the steeper right face is of poorer rock. 20mins walk.

Crazy Maise 20m HVS 5a . A.Nisbet, R.I.Jones. 25th June 2007.
A central crack-line in the left face passes through three small niches.

Changing Times 20m E3 5c *. R.I.Jones, A.Nisbet. 25th June 2007.
Cracks on the right side of the face give some sustained thin climbing with protection which is hard to place. Climb a well defined crack until it thins at 4m. Make hard moves right into another thin crack and climb this until moves left along a horizontal crack lead to a finish straight up.

The Prow 20m Very Difficult. A.Nisbet, R.I.Jones. 25th June 2007.
Starting on its right, climb the crest between the two faces. Limited protection.

Barking 15m HVS 5a. R.I.Jones, A.Nisbet. 25th June 2007.

The first well defined line right of the prow, on the right face. Gain and climb a steep flake-crack. Step left and finish up a narrow groove.

DIABAIG, Charlie's Dome:
The following route lies on the same wall as Terrier Trauma.
Dire Wolf 25m E1 5c *. M Barnard. 17th February 2008.
This route climbs the left side of the wall (left of the obvious central corner) to gain a crack starting at mid-height. To the right of the tree-filled corner bounding the left side of the wall lies a smaller corner. Start by climbing the blunt arete in between (watching out for the occasional loose hold) until the corner on the right ends, before moving up and right on small holds to the foot of the crack. Climb this (easily at first, then with strenuous jamming when it bulges, crux) to the top.

DIABAIG PENINSULA, Loch a' Bhealaich Crag:
Whimbrel Wall 40m HVS 5a *. J.Lyall, S.Aisthorpe. 25th October 2007.
Lies right of the overhanging wall. Start at the base of a slab and climb up left to a roof; turn it on the right to climb a groove for 3m. Pull steeply left to reach a crack which is followed to easier rocks and some heather.

LIATHACH, Coire na Caime, Northern Pinnacles:
Slighe Annaig 120m V,5. A.Nisbet, W.R.Robertson, D.Tunstall. 30th March 2008.
Climbs the steeper face right of Holy Trinity. Start about 20m right of Holy Trinity at the next break.
1. 40m Climb a turfy groove up and then slightly left (left of a bigger icy groove capped by a roof with icicles). Go up to a ledge and move right to an arete.
2. 30m Climb a groove just round the arete. It curves left to a ledge (possible alternative belay). Go up a short corner and move left to below a shallow chimney. Step down left to a small ledge.
3. 50m Climb the chimney and easy ground to the crest of the Northern Pinnacles (100m to the top).

BEINN EIGHE, Far East Wall:
Morning Wall VII,8. M.Bass, S.Yearsley. 14th March 2008.
A great little route, which, given its lack of turf, should be climbable in lots of conditions. It packs a lot into its relatively short length. The crux second pitch gave very technical and precarious wall climbing, only protected with real thought and effort. The moves up to and through the mantelshelf were the definite (and quite exciting!) crux.

Sundance VIII,8 ****. G.Robertson, I.Parnell. 10th January 2008.
The summer route was followed throughout. Pitch 3 was extended to take in both the overhangs, leaving a 20m fourth pitch to finish. Both the overhangs on pitch 3 had significant quantities of ice (useful), the second one sporting a 20ft Damoclean ice fang. The climbing is superb, generally well protected and exceptionally sustained, with spectacular exposure high up. The final short pitch is bold.

Eastern Ramparts:
Pinkyponk Route 90m IV,5. N.Carter, P.Macpherson. 15th January 2008.
Gain a chimney about 50m left of Cornice Groove via broken ground.
1. 40m Climb the chimney, pull through a bulge and continue up the fault to easy ground. Carry on up a snow band to belay about 15m up and slightly left at a cracked boulder.
2. 50m Climb up to a rib above and slightly right. Climb at first on the left, then move right and continue up a vague groove.

West Central Wall:
Maelstrom, Direct Start and Right-Hand Finish VII,7 ***. P.Davies, T.Marsh. 4th March 2008.
Started at an ice filled groove, the last groove below the steep section of West Central Gully. Climb the ice to the lower of the Upper Girdle ledges. Traverse 3m right to a 10m vertical corner, climbed to the upper ledge and another short traverse right to beneath the main corner. The original route was then followed up the corner but instead of traversing left, the party moved right and followed a right-trending groove system to the top, perhaps joining Blood, Sweat and Frozen Tears?

Fuselage Wall:
Note: On the second ascent of *Fight or Flight*, P.Macpherson & W.Wilkinson on 4th March 2008 climbed direct at the start of pitch 2, so didn't go left to the big flake.

Sail Mhor:
Vista 220m V,5. A.Nisbet, C.Wells. 27th March 2008.
The left flank of the ridge right of Morrison's Gully holds a prominent icefall which is the main feature of the route. The grade might be IV,5 with thicker ice. Start just below the entrance to Morrison's Gully. Climb a groove to snowy terraces and continue in roughly the same line to the base of the icefall. Climb the icefall in three main steps (50m). Move left and climb a slabby corner to the crest of the ridge (50m).

CAIRNGORMS

COIRE AN T-SNEACHDA, Mess of Pottage:
Just a Spot o' Sightseeing 90m IV,5. F.Hughes, E.Olivarius. 23rd November 2007.
A winter ascent of the summer line, except on pitch 3 (passing the small overhang), a direct line was taken up the buttress on the right of Hidden Chimney.
Note: While much or all of this has been climbed before in sections, it was thought to be a logical direct line.

Fluted Buttress:
Lambda 130m IV,5. J.Lyall, A.Nisbet, J.Preston. 11th December 2007.
A direct line through Wavelength. Start 10m left of Fluted Buttress Direct (the

alternative and original start to Wavelength). Climb up the fault to join Wavelength and follow it to where it traverses right into the left-hand fault (40m). Instead, go straight up three steps to an easier section which is followed parallel to Wavelength to the base of a groove (30m). Climb the groove (15m). Continue to the crest overlooking Spiral Gully and follow this to join and finish up Wavelength (45m).

Fiacaill Buttress:
The following routes are on the small buttress containing Halibut Habit and White Dwarf.

Tiny Dancer　30m　V,6. J.Lyall, A.Nisbet. 25th February 2008.
The furthest left of the grooves has two steep sections. Climb the first, then step left on to a platform and return right above the second to finish direct.

Groovelet　30m　II. A.Nisbet, J.Lyall. 25th February 2008.
The next groove to the right finishes below a hanging wide crack. Move right to finish on steep snow. The next groove right often contains an icefall and has been climbed by J.Lyall at Grade III.

Shortlist　45m　II/III. J.Lyall, A.Nisbet. 25th February 2008.
The rightmost groove on the buttress, finishing at the same place as White Dwarf.

COIRE AN LOCHAIN, No. 1 Buttress:
Circumvent　60m　V,7. J.Preston, M.Moran, A.Nisbet. 26th November 2007.
A steep groove between the big corner of Inventive and the grooves of Adventure. Start at the top of the chokestones of The Vent, as for Inventive.
1. 25m Follow this route to below its big corner.
2. 20m Make a awkward traverse right to gain the groove in the rib. Follow this over two strenuous bulges to a ledge.
3. 15m Climb up to and underneath a huge flat block to gain easy ground.

Note:　As an alternative last pitch of *Coronary Bypass*, J.Edwards & O.Metherell climbed the following on 25th November 2007. Although it was 35m to the plateau, lengths are traditionally given to easy ground here (as for the previous route):
5. From the left side of the big ledge where it overlooks the gully, go up and into a deep cave. Squeeze out of the back and exit rightwards. Enter another body width slot above and shuffle along for a few metres until it widens and easy ground now leads to the summit.

Note:　J.Preston & A.Nisbet made a left-hand finish to *The Vent* on 20th November 2007. Start just as the gully of The Vent opens out. This is just below a level arete on the right where Ventilator joins. Take a groove leading out left, steepest after 30m, then easy to the top (50m III). It has been climbed before.

No. 2 Buttress:

Cyberian Cave Route   100m   V,7 *. J.Lyall, J.Preston. 15th March 2008.
A wild direct start to Ventilator.
1. 40m Start just right of the Vent Rib and climb the fault line direct through two caves, with the second giving the crux. Continue over a tricky bulge to enter a slim groove which leads to a belay in the left-hand corner variation to Ventilator. Follow this to the top.

Cyber Space   100m   V,6. J.Lyall, A.Nisbet. 30th January 2008.
The rib between Ventilator and Chute Route, although with a tricky independent start left of Ventilator. Start below the middle of the wall between Vent Rib and Chute Route.
1. 35m Gain and climb a steep turfy groove (just left of a better defined rock groove) to join Ventilator.
2. 40m Move immediately right to cross Ventilator on to the rib on its right. Climb turf just left of the crest to gain and follow it, finishing over a small roof on its right.
3. 25m Climb a groove on the right to regain the crest. Follow this over a pinnacle and a sharp snow arete to the top.

Note: Variation finishes to *Snow Bunting*:
1. Follow the wide stepped crack all the way to an overhanging wall, then climb over a large block on the right to regain the original line.
2. Direct Finish IV/V,6 *. P.MacPherson, J.Lyall. 20th December 2007.
Climb the overhanging groove directly out of the easy snow bay.

No. 3 Buttress:
Note: A.Clark & R.Bentley made a variation to pitch 3 of *The Vagrant* in 2004, climbing the corner and cracks up on the left (VI,7). Being good and slightly easier, this might become popular (there was in-situ gear). N.Carter & A.Sharpe also climbed this line in 2007.

No. 4 Buttress:
Swallow-tail Pillar   VII,7/8. M.Walker, A.Gilmore, R.Rosedale. 2nd March 2008.
By the summer route. The split grade is uncertainty, as it was both bold and hard on pitch 2.

Note: I.Parnell & J.Winter made an independent start to *Prore* through the roofs 3m right of Savage Slit. Very steep, interesting technically and a bit more committing than the original. Top end VII,8 on the assumption that the original is VII,7.

CARN ETCHACHAN, Upper Tier:
Python Alternative Start   30m   V,6. M.Cook, A.Nisbet. 16th March 2008.
Adds some extra climbing. Start at the base of the Guillotine fault but move right and climb a crack-line and ledges to a big ledge (15m). Walk to its right end, step round the corner overlooking the Nom-de Plume fault and return left up two big steps to a ledge. Make exciting moves up right to join Python after its initial pitch (15m).

Note: *Python* is very good and worth two stars.

Gully Face:
Cobra 110m II/III *. R.Hamilton, S.Kennedy, A.MacDonald. 17th February 2008.
Follows a line a short distance left of Attic Rib. Climb an obvious snow shelf running out left below the start of Attic Rib (described in the guide as an alternative start to Castle Gully) and climb a short groove to below the headwall (50m). Climb a short groove on the right then continue rightwards via a ledge system to join Attic Rib above the snow arete. Finish up Attic Rib (60m).

HELL'S LUM CRAG:
The Seventh Circle 50m E6 ***. I.Small, G.Latter. 10th August 2007.
The stunning slim groove and hanging crack in the wall just below the main pitch in the Hell's Lum. Gain the base by a 60m abseil from 8m left of the Chariots of Fire abseil point (starting down the front face).
1. 22m 6b Climb the groove, moving out left then back into the groove, past a PR. Pull over a small overlap, stepping left to a good rest. Return and make difficult moves up and right to get established in the crack, which leads with difficulty to a good ledge.
2. 28m 6b Traverse left into a good flake-crack and follow this past a projecting block to a rest on the wall on the right. Step left and pull over a roof with difficulty leading to better holds above. Continue more easily up a crack to a good ledge above. Scramble out rightwards to finish.

STAG ROCKS:
Bambi 70m Difficult *. J.Lyall, A.Nisbet. 12th October 2007.
A pleasant climb by the winter route.

Big Alec 70m VS 4c. J.Lyall, A.Nisbet. 12th October 2007.
Climbs the wall overlooking the start of Apex Gully. Start at the lowest point of the wall and gain a recess of reddish rock. Climb awkwardly out of the recess to a ledge above, then go left and back right to a hidden chimney. Climb this and a jam crack to join Alb (45m). Follow Alb to a gully immediately right of its steep wall. Climb its steep right wall on poor rock (25m).

Wee Timorous Beastie 150m Hard Severe 4b *. J.Lyall, A.Nisbet. 12th October 2007.
The winter description should say to start 20m up Deception Inlet, since the first roof is 70m up. The winter route was followed on clean but slightly gritty rock. The second roof and slab above was the crux and best climbing.

Staggering 60m E1 **. J.Lyall, A.Nisbet. 19th October 2007.
A series of corners on the very edge of Longbow Crag and overlooking Amphitheatre Gully. Start at the same belay as for Relay Climb's crux pitch (which is 4c and probably just VS, 'one of the hardest free pitches in the Cairngorms', to quote Mac Smith). Approach by traversing across Amphitheatre Gully from the left or by the start of Relay Climb.

Lurcher's Crag South, (NH 968 029) Alt 860m West facing. Photodiagram: Andy Nisbet.

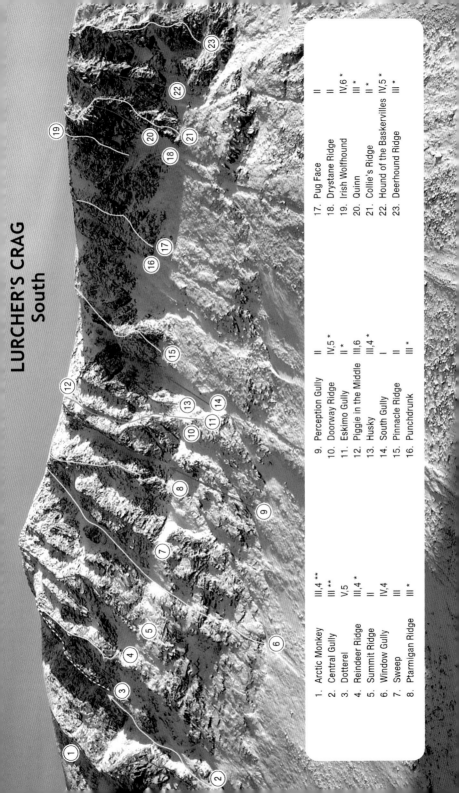

LURCHER'S CRAG
South

1. Arctic Monkey — III,4 **
2. Central Gully — III **
3. Dotterel — V,5
4. Reindeer Ridge — III,4 *
5. Summit Ridge — II
6. Window Gully — IV,4
7. Sweep — III
8. Ptarmigan Ridge — III *
9. Perception Gully — II
10. Doorway Ridge — IV,5 *
11. Eskimo Gully — II *
12. Piggie in the Middle — III,6
13. Husky — III,4 *
14. South Gully — I
15. Pinnacle Ridge — II
16. Punchdrunk — III *
17. Pug Face — II
18. Drystane Ridge — II
19. Irish Wolfhound — IV,6 *
20. Quinn — III *
21. Collie's Ridge — II *
22. Hound of the Baskervilles — IV,5 *
23. Deerhound Ridge — III *

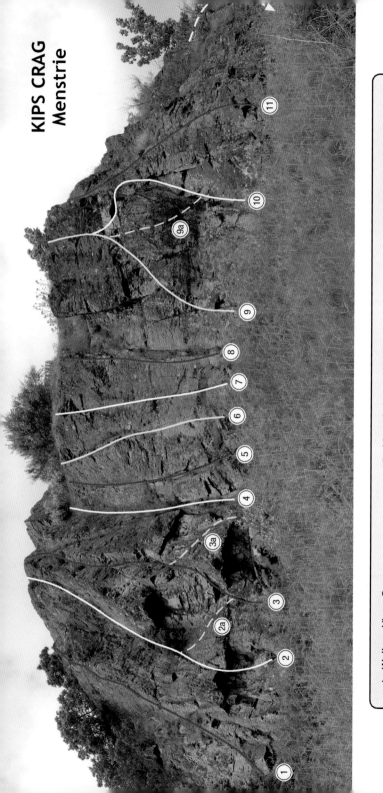

KIPS CRAG
Menstrie

1. Wallace View S
2. Left Edge VS (2a S)
3. Rancho Rib VS,5b (3a S)
4. Grassy Corner Diff

5. Lhasa's Leap V.Diff
6. Waterwork Wall S
7. The Man from Menstrie S
8. Right Edge S

9. Beinn's Buttress VS,4c
9a. BB Direct VS,5a
10. Creag's Arete S
11. Staircase Route Mod

1. 25m 5a Climb two consecutive corners.
2. 10m 5b A strenuous jam crack.
3. 30m 4b A vegetated corner right of another jam crack with vegetation. This leads to a steep mossy corner but the pleasant groove on the right was climbed to the easier upper section of Relay Climb. This pleasant groove is shown as Relay Climb on the photodiagram in the new Cairngorms guide, but the original route went further right, as for the winter route. The upper section of Relay Climb could then have been climbed, but it is more interesting to move into the amphitheatre and climb the following route.

Maranatha Very Difficult. J.Lyall, A.Nisbet. 19th October 2007.
By the winter line. Clean rock but a few hollow blocks.

LURCHER'S CRAG:
Credibility Crunch 105m V,7 *. S.Allan, A.Nisbet. 10th April 2008.
A line up the front face of the steep central section of the ridge on the left of Central Gully. Start as for Arctic Monkey or traverse in from Central Gully to reach the base of the steep section.
1. 30m Take a prominent slabby traverse line of weakness up leftwards (the higher of two lines).
2. 10m Return right over a short wall and slab to the base of a big corner slanting left.
3. 15m Climb the corner over two main steps, the second with a wide crack, to a large block.
4. 50m Step left from the block and climb straight up over a bulge, then trend left on slabby ground to join Arctic Monkey in its easier upper section.
5. Take the easiest line to the top (not included in length).

Arctic Monkey 300m III,4 **. S.Allan, A.Nisbet. 6th January 2008.
The ridge on the left of Central Gully. Start left of Central Gully's lower icefall and climb easily to where the ground steepens. A line on the right of this steep section was taken, climbing rightwards up a line of weakness and passing a smooth groove which heads left to reach a recess below a prominent jutting block. Pull out left through a small cave (crux) and go left up a less well defined groove to reach the crest (50m). Follow the crest which becomes progressively easier until just scrambling to the top.

Dotterel 130m V,5. S.Allan, A.Nisbet. 6th January 2008.
The ridge immediately right of Central Gully, gained by descending the easy upper section of Central Gully, then heading left (facing down) down a ramp above its big ice pitch (but could also be reached by heading north from South Gully beyond the following routes). Start below the easiest looking groove.
1. 50m Climb a ramp and a short groove to reach a deceptively steep shallow corner. Go up this and step left before returning right to an easier section which leads to a short narrow chimney. Climb this to blockier ground.
2. 50m Climb the blocks to the crest and follow this to easier ground.
3. 30m Finish pleasantly up this.

Kips Crag, Menstrie (NS 84763 97230) Alt 80m   South facing. Photodiagram: Ken Crocket.

The following routes are ridges described heading north from South Gully. Approach by descending South Gully to where it opens out, then traversing a ledge northwards to below the ridges.

Husky   150m   III,4 *. A.Nisbet. 3rd December 2007.
The nearest ridge on the north side of South Gully has many fine torquing moves and jammed flakes, best when well frozen and not too dry. Much of the climbing is escapable but still entertaining. Easier and harder lines are possible, but this seemed fairly direct while still natural. Start at the lowest rocks and climb a groove in the initial crest. A short walk leads to a steeper section. Start this by a right-slanting ramp, then make a tricky step left on to the crest. Climb a narrow chimney just left of the crest. Climb the next steep section by a groove just left of the crest. This leads to the sharp but very artificial upper ridge, still fun over every block.

Piggie in the Middle   120m   III,6. J.Lyall, A.Nisbet. 10th December 2007.
A subsidiary ridge which lies between Husky and Doorway Ridge, but starts 60m up the depression between the two. Either gain the start up this depression or traverse from South Gully across Husky. Climb on to a flake just right of its crest, step right and make difficult moves up a shallow groove (or climb the crack above the flake). Continue leftwards on to the crest and follow this much more easily to finish over a well defined raised section to upper snow slopes.

Perception Gully   180m   II. J.Lyall, D.Fanning. 22nd March 2008.
Gain the amphitheatre right of Doorway Ridge and climb an icy mixed pitch on the left, then follow the gully above, between Doorway and Piggie in the Middle.

Doorway Ridge   200m   IV,5 *. J.Lyall, A.Nisbet. 8th December 2007.
The second ridge on the north side of South Gully. Start on its right side and climb a subsidiary buttress to reach a steep corner which leads up to the crest, followed to a slight col (45m). Continue just right of the crest, then over a slight pinnacle and a steep section to reach easier ground (45m). Finish up this easier blocky crest over the doorway. The last two steps are definitely optional.

Eskimo Gully   240m   II *. J.Lyall, B.Cook, J.& K.Penrose. 12th March 2008.
The gully line left of Doorway Ridge. A shallow icy fault up the lower slabs leads to a steeper ice pitch, which is followed by an easy gully.

Ptarmigan Ridge   200m   III *. S.Allan, A.Nisbet. 9th December 2007.
The third ridge is tackled via a groove in the centre of its steep lower section. Start by going up towards the groove, then right and back left to its base. Climb the groove to a barrier wall. Traverse right to break through the wall at its right end and climb blocky ground right of the crest until the crest is reached. Follow the crest as closely as possible, including a narrow section with a pinnacle and a steeper upper wall climbed by a narrow chimney. Low in the grade.

Sweep   200m   III. J.Lyall, A.Nisbet. 10th December 2007.

The fourth ridge has a wider base undercut by a smooth overhanging wall. Start left of this, which is just right of the crest. Pick a line up slabby ground, with the difficulty dependent on conditions, but generally trending right to gain an easier crest which is most of the length. Follow this crest, fun but somewhat contrived, until it joins the steeper upper wall of Ptarmigan Ridge. Climb this by a groove well left of the narrow chimney of Ptarmigan Ridge (technical 4).

Summit Ridge 250m II. A.Nisbet. 8th December 2008.
A long but scrappy route with many of the difficulties optional. Traverse from South Gully to beyond the upper gully of Window Gully. Continue for about 60m until steep rocky ground above ends at a slight ridge. Climb just right of this slight ridge (the easy ground on the left is not visible), with one short section on the left, until the ridge curves left. The upper section, which is much better, then heads direct to the summit.

Reindeer Ridge 150m III,4 *. A.Nisbet. 10th January 2008.
The next ridge north is the first ridge right of Dotterel. Its base is well defined with a line of prominent flakes leading left from its right side to below a groove. Start along the flakes and pull through a bulge (crux) into the groove. Go up this for a few metres, then step out left on to slabs (straight up also looks possible). Climb the slabs leftwards to another groove with an awkward block near its top. Climb this to easier ground. Continue up the crest, artificial but with some fine moves, to a blocky upper section.

Pinnacle Ridge 150m II. A.Nisbet. 9th November 2007.
The ridge right (south) of South Gully. Climb a right-slanting turfy fault, then move left to the crest. Follow this over the pinnacle, which is avoidable but the best climbing, to a col. Finish easily by a right-slanting fault.

A broad buttress just left of Drystane Ridge is both harder and better than it looks and provides the following two routes. Its base starts higher on the left and slopes down to the right.

Punchdrunk 130m III *. A.Nisbet. 8th December 2008.
Start at the higher left corner of the base. Break steeply out right on to the face. Take a line slanting slightly left to the base of a big right-facing corner. Traverse 8m right and climb a line of weakness up to join the left crest high up (the corner looks climbable too). Follow this to the top.

Pug Face 130m II. A.Nisbet. 3rd December 2007.
Start left of the lowest rocks and climb through a steep fault to easier angled ground. A line on the right side of the broad section was taken, moving right on to the right crest higher up. High in the grade. Follow the crest which eases in angle as it narrows to a sharp but escapable crest.

Hound of the Baskervilles 150m IV,5 *. A.Nisbet, J.Preston. 9th November 2007.
A prominent ridge between Collie's and Deerhound Ridges gives good climbing

but easy ground lies close on the left. Start up a groove in the lowest rocks and climb this to a steep wall. Move left and up a small groove, then a short chimney with a capstone before a blocky corner on the right leads to a level section (40m). A vertical wall lies ahead. Climb a right-facing corner on its left side, then more easily up the crest to a slabby wall and short arete (50m). Go left and back right up the final blocky section to a finishing chimney (60m).

SRON NA LÀIRIGE:

Kasbah 160m V,5. D.McGimpsey, A.Nisbet, S.Wood. 12th January 2008.
The left of the three groove systems on the right face of Lairig Ridge. Start just left of Sinclair's Last Stand. Move left into the base of the groove system and climb it in three pitches to gain and finish up the crest of Lairig Ridge. The third pitch is much harder than the rest, but would be a grade easier with consolidated snow.

Pupster 130m III. D.McGimpsey, S.Wood. 22nd January 2008.
Climbs the rightmost of the three main groove lines sharing some ground with Gormless in the middle section. Start 10m left of Gormless at a turfy groove.
1. 50m Climb the groove for 20m into the left side of a wide snowy bay. Follow this to its top to belay as for Gormless.
2. 40m Continue up and right on easy ground to a large fin of rock. Gormless climbs the groove on the right of this fin, instead pull into the groove on the left below the main upper groove.
3. 40m Follow the fine groove to its top.

Idiot Proof 140m IV,6 *. J.Lyall, A.Nisbet. 2nd April 2008.
First pitch by J.Lyall, 18th March 2008.
A line of grooves up the right wall of Gormless (left wall of Braer Rabbit ridge). Start just right of Gormless and climb a groove tucked in against the wall. A steep step at the top can be climbed or passed on the left (50m). Climb another groove in the wall, including a short overhanging section (crux) until near the crest of Braer Rabbit ridge (40m). Continue diagonally left under the crest until it is joined just beyond its difficulties. Follow the crest easily to join the top of Lairig Ridge (50m).

April Fool 80m III. J.Lyall, A.Nisbet. 2nd April 2008.
A turfy ramp (lower of two) high on the right wall of Braer Rabbit ridge. It finishes as for Idiot Proof.

Ghruve 220m II. J.Lyall, A.Nisbet. 2nd April 2008.
A long well defined groove between some more broken ridges and the bigger ridge with the following route. It heads for two pinnacles near the top of the ridge and gives sustained climbing at the grade.

Ghrusome 200m V,6. J.Lyall, A.Nisbet. 14th January 2008.
The left-hand of two ridges separated by a big gully which lies on a sector of cliff north of the Lairig Ridge area. Climb the lower crest, well defined but not very prominent, to reach a steeper section. Climb the central of three grooves to

reach a steep upper tower. Climb cracks just right of a smooth right-slanting ramp which bounds the steepest section on the right. Gain a ramp which spirals round the right side of the tower to reach its top and an easy upper ridge.

Ghruling Gully 220m III. J.Lyall. 18th March 2008.
A less obvious left-hand gully. The gully just right of the lower crest of Ghrusome becomes less pronounced as height is gained and has a short mixed crux, followed by easy upper slopes.

White Hunter 220m IV,5.* H.Burns, J.Lyall. 8th January 2008.
The slim pillar between the two gullies. The easy angled lower crest leads to a steeper section after 90m. Gain and climb the left-hand groove, then a cracked wall to pass left of prominent roof (45m). Easier buttress and snow slopes to the top.

Ghruvy Gully 220m III **. J.Lyall. 18th March 2008.
A choice of two starts lead into the main gully line between White Hunter and Polar Bear. A classic winter gully with the final ice pitch giving the crux. This was climbed on cruddy ice on the first ascent, making it feel quite serious – perhaps IV,3!

Polar Bear 200m IV,5. J.Lyall, A.Nisbet. 7th January 2008.
The right-hand of the two ridges. The route follows a turfy groove system on its crest. The crux is a smooth section which was climbed near its right arete.

SGÒRAN DUBH MÒR, No. 2 Buttress:
Central Gully and Rib 275m III. J.C.Higham, S.Cormack. 11th February 1979.
In the centre of No.2 Buttress (NH 912 004) a prominent icefall develops over steep rocks and is formed by melt from a snow gully lying above. The icefall was climbed for 75m. Rather than continuing up the snow gully the broken buttress on its left was climbed to the top of the mountain over enjoyable but gradually easing ground (200m).

SGÒRAN DUBH MÒR, Fan Corrie:
Noggin the Nog 100m III,4. B.Davison, A.Nisbet. 13th November 2007.
Immediately right of Diamond Buttress but left of the main gully which forms its right side, is a narrow buttress, initially shallow but forms a more distinct tower at the top. The lower part may bank up a lot under heavy snow. Start just on the left of its base and follow the crest as closely as possible to where it merges with the finish of Diamond Buttress. This is easy and not included in the length.

Sparkler 200m III ***. D.McGimpsey, A.Nisbet, S.Wood. 11th January 2008.
Roughly based on Bell's original line on Diamond Buttress, it was thought excellent with the 1986 route at least as good. Start higher up the right bounding gully, roughly level with the top of the easy lower section of the buttress. Here is a rib, probably the line of Bell's first route, which goes up to join the main crest.

1. 50m Move left under a steep wall to gain a bay. Climb a turfy groove out of its top left corner to a smaller bay.
2. 40m Go right and climb another turfy groove to the crest of the rib. Follow this to just below the main crest.
3. etc. Go up almost to the crest and climb a short turfy corner to gain it. Continue up the crest to the top (the highlight).

Clangers 100m II. B.Davison, A.Nisbet. 13th November 2007.
A high buttress directly above the main gully which forms the left side of Diamond Buttress, but actually left of its continuation. Very blocky and with short technical moves above ledges.

Silver Rib 250m II. A.Nisbet. 15th January 2008.
The long rib left of Diamond Buttress, climbed in January 1956 by T.W.Patey & G.McLeod and described as 'steep scrambling only'. It seems unlikely to have been in winter condition as it would certainly have been worth writing up. It was climbed in December 2007 by Nisbet & J.Preston when frozen but without snow and thought Moderate. The start is easy leading to the crux, a steep but very helpful right-facing corner. Continue up the crest direct and over a set of pinnacles which lead to easier ground. Finish up an intermittent rib.

No.4 Buttress:
Note: The best approach from the top to the upper ribs is to descend the north bounding ridge of the buttress to the first flattening, then descend the gully from here into the main gully (Grade I). This approach gully does not cornice, unlike other possibilities. One is now too low for the upper ribs. Climb the main gully for Gooey Rib or find a way through various minor ridges for Einich Rib. A long descending traverse finds the following route.

Four Ribs 400m I/II. A.Nisbet. 6th February 2008.
This is the ridge on the left of the large deep gully which is formed in the lower part of the buttress. A scrappy route, more scrambling than climbing, but with good scenery. The crest was climbed, but all the difficulties are avoidable.

GLEANN EINICH:
Note: C.Wells made an ascent of the burn into Coire Dhondail at Grade II on 23rd November 2007 and was surprised not to find a recorded ascent (it does bank out).

EINICH CAIRN, Coire nan Clach:
Schoolmaster's Gully 100m I. S.M.Richardson, R.S.D.Smith. 16th February 2008.
The prominent right-slanting gully in the centre of the crag.

Hey Teacher, Leave Those Kids Alone 50m II. S.M.Richardson, R.S.D.Smith. 16th February 2008.
Left of Schoolmaster's Gully is a crescent-shaped gully (Grade I in descent) that is cut by a chimney-groove on its left side. Climb the chimney to an easing below a steep headwall and finish left up an easy ramp.

BRAERIACH, Garbh Choire Mor:
Note: A.Watson points out that snow did survive the summer in 2004 and 2005, but not 2003 and 2006. So the new Cairngorms guide is not correct. Snow has survived in 2007 in several places from Braeriach to Ben Nevis.

Unwanted Birthday Present   150m   III. J.Higham, A.Higham. 15th February 2003.
This route is located on the left-hand side of the lower corrie (NN 945 977) and climbs the buttress to the left of a prominent isolated pinnacle that occurs about 100m below the plateau rim (also left of Col Gully). Ascend the right flank of the buttress by the easiest line. No significant cornice at the time of the ascent but normally the cornice is very large and could be problematical.

West Buttress Left Edge   200m   II. A.Nisbet. 2nd December 2007.
The buttress forms a vague crest close to Col Gully. Start just right of the undercut base of this crest and follow a groove before moving left. Follow various grooves in the crest to a final steepening which provides the only Grade II section. The original ascent of this buttress started up a gully on the right side of the buttress but moved left to avoid the cornice, probably finishing just right of this route.

Note: R.G.Webb and S.M.Richardson climbed the well-defined gully defining the left edge of Crown Buttress (150m Grade I) on 2 December 2007. An obvious weakness and almost certainly climbed before, but normally defended by a huge cornice.

Bunting's Gully, Far Left Branch   100m   III or VI,6. S.M.Richardson, R.G.Webb. 16th December 2007.
The furthest left fork of Bunting's Gully runs into a deep overhanging cleft tucked into the right side of the Tiara Buttress. This feature was one of the last unclimbed gullies in the Cairngorms and for good reason. It is either choked by powder, or is banked out but has an impossible cornice. The first ascensionists climbed the route in lean conditions and found thin ice running down the right wall that gave a steep pitch reminiscent of Minus One Gully on Ben Nevis. J.Lyall climbing solo in exceptional conditions in February 2008, found the pitch to be well banked out with thick ice on the right wall (Grade III). Incredibly he encountered no cornice difficulties.
1. 30m Climb Bunting's Gully to the central depression where Snow Bunting forks right.
2. 30m Move left and climb the far-left branch over a couple of steep steps to a good stance below the overhanging cleft.
3. 40m Climb the gully using thin ice on the right wall to enter the easier upper gully and the cornice.

Little Black Feet   65m   IV,4 *. J.Lyall. 19th February 2008.
Another line up the headwall between the branches of Bunting's Gully. Start at the foot of the right branch and follow a system of right-facing corners. The initial corner gave mixed climbing to a roof, which was passed on the right, then thinly-iced corners and slabs led to the cornice.

Garbh Choire Dhaidh:
Sorbet 250m III. N.Carter, A.Nisbet, J.Preston. 19th December 2007.
Icy grooves on the left side of the largest buttress (between Pea Soup and Chewing' the Fat). Each person took a different line. A start was made up three parallel ice lines left of Pea Soup before moving right to the base of the buttress. An iced corner then led to a snow ramp which forms the left side of the buttress, and a finish either left or right. An alternative was a right-slanting fault with a V-groove continuation which led to the crest of the buttress. The V-groove was thinly iced and passed on the left, followed by a traverse back right to finish up snow grooves on the crest.

Crystal 250m III. A.Nisbet. 17th December 2007.
About 15m left of the icy fault of Pea Soup (i.e. on the left of the two steeper buttresses) is a stepped narrow groove which holds ice. A start was made between Pea Soup and Chewing' the Fat, mostly up snow but with a couple of short icy steps to reach the lower groove. Climb this V-groove (approx 50m, the ice is hidden until close under), then move left to climb the upper groove and finish on the left above the crest of the buttress (approx 50m). There was no cornice in the lean icy conditions.

COIRE SPUTAN DEARG, Snake Ridge Area:
To a Mouse 100m I. W.Munro, I.Munro. 16th February 2008.
Starting 60m up Narrow Gully climb steeply up the shallow gully on the left to a narrowing. Above the narrows climb open snow slopes finishing to the left of Narrow Buttress. Under heavy snow the steep lower section probably banks out.

Central Buttresses:
Blackmail 80m HVS. J.Lyall, A.Nisbet. 2nd October 2007.
Ramp lines on the right side of the Black Tower. Start at the base of the buttress, below and right of the slime on the normal start.
1. 45m 4c Climb a grassy ramp rightwards, then step left to a right-slanting crack which leads to a terrace. The normal route could be gained by moving left.
2. 35m 5a Go up flakes on the right to a ramp. Go up this and over a bulge, then step right and climb the sidewall to a ledge. Climb an awkward wall to the short arete of the normal route and easy ground.

Penguin 35m VS 4c. J.Lyall, A.Nisbet. 2nd October 2007.
A line of flake-cracks on the right side of Flake Buttress, overlooking Precocious Gully. Star at the base of the gully and move out left on a grass ledge. Climb two grass-topped corners to reach the base of the main flake-line. Climb this to easy ground and abseil descent.

Terminal Buttress:
October Wall 45m HVS 4c. J.Lyall, A.Nisbet. 2nd October 2007.
Climbs near aretes between Wee Heavy and April Wall. The rock is poor. Start in a small bay just left of April Wall. Climb a rib to the base of a prominent cracked wall (15m). Climb a groove at the right end of the wall to reach its right arete. Climb this to where a line of weakness leads left above the wall to the left arete (overlooking the final gully of Wee Heavy). Climb this to the top (30m).

BEINN A' BHUIRD, Coire na Ciche:
The Grinder   VII,8. P.Benson, R.Hewitt. 2nd December 2007.
A winter ascent by the summer line. Despite being short the first corner packs a punch. Climbed with icy cracks causing difficult gear.

Coire an Dubh Lochain:
Screwless   175m   V,5. S.M.Richardson, D.Tunstall., 24th February 2008.
The isolated buttress situated just above the lochan low down on the left side of the corrie has a distinct hanging icefall in its centre. Start below the centre of the buttress.
1. 45m Climb a short wall to reach the central snow slope that runs up to the rock wall containing the hanging icefall.
2. 30m Traverse right below the icefall and climb its right side for 20m.
3. 50m Climb the icefall and continue delicately up the rock buttress above trending right to reach a right-facing groove-line on the right edge of the buttress. Belay by a steep bulging corner cutting into the crest on the left.
4. 50m Climb the corner to easy ground and a snowfield.

Coire nan Clach:
Renticulata   120m   III,4. S.M.Richardson, D.Tunstall. 10th February 2008.
The icy right-tending ramp to the right of the depression of Snowdrop.
1. 60m Start as for Snowdrop and move right onto the ramp. Follow this past a steepening to broken blocks.
2. 40m Continue up the easy crest above, surmount a short wall to below the cornice.
3. 20m Move up and right to the top of the buttress of Jack Frost, and follow this to the top.

Jack Frost   80m   III. S.M.Richardson, D.Tunstall. 11th November 2007.
The small buttress to the right of Nipped in the Bud is the highest feature on the south wall of the corrie. Start below the steep crest and surmount a short 3m wall and trend right along a turfy ramp. Move up and left to a steep wall and climb this to the blocky crest of the buttress and the plateau.

Garbh Choire:
Slochd Wall   IX,8 ***. G.Robertson, P.Benson. 21st January 2008.
A high quality but serious and intimidating undertaking in a very remote location. The summer route (right-hand variant) was followed in three hard pitches to the terrace below the headwall, then the final pitch scurried right to escape up the obvious fault. Pitch 1 was split into two, with a belay below the crux overhang. Pitch one was tenuous but well-protected, pitch 2 more strenuous and very runout, and pitch 3 was bold to start (though not technically quite as hard as the previous pitch). On the first ascent conditions were lean but very unhelpful; little rime, but lots of snow and verglas/ice. One rest was taken on the crux to excavate a reasonable runner above the overhang, then the leader (Benson) lowered down and lead the pitch clean (there were no runners for the crux 7m up to the belay).

Commando Direct   125m   VI,6. P.Benson, R.Hewitt. 11th December 2007.
A direct line based on the existing line of Commando Route; start to its left.
1. 45m Climb directly to the traverse line of that route (old peg in situ) step left (free) and pull into the easy gully. Climb the left side of the gully to the foot of the buttress where Commando route goes right.
2. 20m Start on its left-hand side and climb the buttress direct to a large ledge. The route now joins West Side Story.
3. 20m Climb up to a wide crack above and belay a cheval on Mitre Ridge.
4. 40m An easy trot along Mitre Ridge.

Stob an t-Sluichd:
Token Rib   100m   III. A.Nisbet. 26th February 2008.
The crest right of Token Groove, which is the right-hand crest of the buttress left of M and B Buttress. Start at the base and climb a groove just right of the true crest. Near the top of this, break out left on to the crest (crux), and follow the crest to the top.

M and B Buttress   200m   II. A.Nisbet. 26th February 2008.
The best winter line is a ramp left of the vague crest on the left. Follow this to its top, then break out right on to the crest which is followed to the top

LOCHNAGAR, Southern Sector:
The following two routes are on the rightmost of several small buttresses just right of the col, the first reached when entering the corrie. The crag is 50m high and finishes about 35m below the rim of the plateau.

Sonshine Corner   40m   III. A.Porter, W.Wilkinson. 12th January 2008.
An obvious right-facing corner in the centre of the buttress.

Fluffy Face   50m   IV,4. W.Wilkinson, A.Porter. 12th January 2008.
This takes the inset face left of the rib that defines the right edge of the buttress. Climb the centre of the clean slabby face past the odd turf patch via helpful cracks to underneath an obvious split roof. Turn the roof on the left through some steep ground (crux). Step right to gain the arete and continue to the top.

The Sentinel:
Sentinel Gully   70m   I. M.Fowler, S.M.Richardson, D.Tunstall. 25th November 2007.
The shallow well defined gully right of The Sentinel. In cold early season conditions it gives a continuous run of easy low-angled ice and is a pleasant way of reaching the plateau.

Sunset Buttress:
Aramis   70m   III. M.Fowler, S.M.Richardson, D.Tunstall. 25th November 2007.
The shallow buttress between Ham Butty and Iffy. Climb a short icy groove just right of Ham Butty to gain a small snowfield, and follow this to its top left

corner. Continue up a steep right-trending fault to enter a V-chimney that leads to the top.

Sunset Buttress Direct   100m   IV,7. A.Porter, W.Wilkinson. 16th December 2006.
Climb direct up the nose of the buttress to the prominent crack, which itself was climbed. On pitch 2, finish direct up the steep wall.

Notes: J.Workman thought *Sunset Buttress* was IV,6. There have been suggestions that *Quick Dash Crack* is IV,7 in lean conditions.

Sunset Boulevard   100m   IV,5. S.M.Richardson, R.G.Webb. 6th January 2008.
The steep narrow rib to the right of Sunset Buttress.
1. 40m Surmount the steep lower wall via a deep crack on the right edge and continue up the narrow crest to below a steep barrier wall.
2. 20m Break through the wall via a left-trending slot.
3. 40m Trend left up easier ground to the crest of Sunset Buttress, and finish up this to the top.

Triangle Buttress:
Pelican Groove   80m   II/III. I.Munro, S.BenBrahim. 15th March 2008.
Climb a series of grooves up the left side of Triangle Buttress overlooking the obvious wide gully. Entry to the groove was gained by climbing steep snow up the centre of the buttress and following a left-trending ramp.

Porthos   70m   III. S.M.Richardson, M.Fowler, D.Tunstall. 25th November 2007.
The square-cut groove on the left flank of the buttress starting 20m up and left of Once Upon a Time in the East. Climb the groove, easy at first, until forced left into a short and steep impending groove. Step left again to reach the crest of a blocky ridge that leads to the top.

Perseverance Wall:
Booby Prize   80m, III *. B.Duthie, F.Templeton. 16th December 2007.
Start in the same place as The Gift. Where this begins to move right, continue straight up into a small snow basin moving left near the top to a steepish finish.

Tenacity   80m   V,6. P.Benson, S.M.Richardson. 9th December 2007.
A good short technical route based on the summer line. Start as for summer below the alcove.
1. 30m Climb the groove up to the roof, then step left onto a ledge and move on to the left arete. Climb the wall above and move easily up to a stance on the right on top of a small tower.
2. 50m Step left and climb the steep groove just left of the arete to the plateau (this lies between the chokestoned groove of The Vice and the crest of the arete taken by the summer line).

Athos   80m   III. M.Fowler, D.Tunstall, S.M.Richardson. 25th November 2007.

The groove line between Temptress and Windfall.

1. 30m Climb the groove past a steepening and head for a V-slot on the skyline.

2. 40m Continue in the same line and climb a right-facing ramp overlooking the steep retaining wall of Windfall. Belay just above the Windfall chimney.

3. 10m Easy slopes lead to the top.

Athos, Right-Hand Start 50m IV,6. P.Benson, S.M.Richardson. 9th December 2007.

1. 20m Start as for Windfall and move up easy ground to the foot of a right-facing corner to the left of the ramp of Windfall. Climb mixed ground into the corner and belay by a large ledge on the left.

2. 30m Continue up the corner to where it steepens into a smooth clean-cut groove. Step right and climb a steep crack just right of a steep arete and exit on well-spaced turf. Continue up easier ground to the junction with Athos. Follow this to the top (30m).

Central Buttress:

Central Buttress Superdirect 90m VI,6. S.M.Richardson, R.G.Webb. 2nd March 2008.

A direct version of Central Buttress Direct taking the triangular section of crag to the right of Mantichore. Start 20m left of Central Buttress Direct.

1. 35m Climb a slab and shallow groove above to a steepening. Move right 3m to a second groove system and follow this past a steep bulge to just left of Central Buttress Direct.

2. 15m Climb the bulging corner above and continue up mixed ground to join Central Buttress Direct.

3. 40m Continue up Central Buttress Direct to exit on the crest of Central Buttress.

Parallel Buttress:

Note: B.Duthie & F.Tempelton took the following line in March 2008. Above the shallow 3m groove, instead of moving left at the jammed spike, move 2m right under bulging blocks above onto a mini arete, then up left through a V-notch in the ridge to join the original line.

THE STUIC:

Reboot 80m IV,5. B.Davison, A.Nisbet. 12th November 2007.

The rib which forms the right side of The Stooee Chimney. Scramble up to the base of the chimney and start at its right wall. Traverse out on to the rib and climb up to a huge block. Gain a ledge above and move right into a narrow ramp. Pull out left from its top to another ledge and a large flake-crack. Climb this rightwards and gain easier ground above (40m). Finish more easily up the rib which peters out into broken ground (50m).

Finesse 60m III. B.Davison, A.Nisbet. 12th November 2007.

Between the buttresses with Big Block Groove and House of Cards is a slightly recessed area with two parallel faults. This is the left fault, which starts up a chimney leading to blocky ground.

Trump 60m III. B.Davison, A.Nisbet. 12th November 2007.
This is the right fault which becomes a left-facing corner high up.

Unblocked 50m I. B.Davison, A.Nisbet. 12th November 2007.
Right of House of Cards is a gully capped by a huge block. There is a through route in early season which would soon fill and the finish might become harder.

Glottal Slot 40m III,5. B.Davison, A.Nisbet. 12th November 2007.
Right of Slot Buttress is a wide gully with a steep finish, taken by a corner forming its right wall.

Coire Loch nan Eun - Coire Lochan na Feadaige (near The Stuic):
Plover 100m II. G.J.Lynn. 24th February 2008.
On the larger, most westerly buttress in the corrie (NO 221 856), to the right of Goldie. Start at the right-hand toe of the buttress, climb broken grooves, following the easiest line to reach the upper snowfields and a junction with Goldie. Follow the left-slanting ramp on the upper rocks as for Goldie.

BROAD CAIRN BLUFFS:
Tombstone Blues 40m HVS 5b. B.S.Findlay, G.S.Strange. 8th September 2007.
This climb lies on the wall of red slabs left of Coffin Chimney. Start from a terrace and climb the right-hand crack before veering left and up to a grass-floored recess (20m). Continue up another crack and climb a V-slot in an overhang (crux). Traverse hard left to beyond a perched block then finish straight up (20m).

CREAG AN DUBH LOCH, South-East Buttress:
Dark Souls 160m IV,4 *. A.Main, M.Jarvie. 20th January 2008.
A nice winter line up mixed grooves and chimneys. Start just below and right of Dogleg, below a left-facing groove, next to a small tree.
1. 50m Climb the groove to a snow platform, follow the chimney and exit right, to belay where the route crosses Souls on Fire.
2. 50m Continue rightwards to the next chimney and follow this with increasing difficulty to a bulge (crux). Surmount this and belay in an obvious cave above.
3. and 4. 60m Join South-East Buttress and follow easy ground to the top.

EAGLES ROCK, Plateau Buttress:
Cumulus 150m Severe. A.Nisbet. 13th September 2007.
Climbs the full height of the buttress taken by Flanker's Route. Start near the left end of its horizontal base, well below and right of the watherfall. Take a line slanting slightly left, keeping between very smooth rock on the left and more vegetation on the right. It probably crossed Flanker's Route high up. The upper section is slow to dry.

GLEN CALLATER, Coire Kander:
Talus Buttress 300m II. J.Higham, M.Allen, M.Higham. 9th February 2006.
There are two buttresses that descend close to Loch Kander. The route started on

the left (higher) of the two buttresses at its lowest point (NO 189 808). Climb for 150m directly up open icy grooves in the lower part and an exposed ridge in the upper. It is possible to descend easily from here but better to continue on up the buttress lying directly above. Follow a steep gully (50m) and then break out left onto the buttress edge and follow this directly to the summit (100m).

Consolation Buttress   200m   II. J.Higham. 9th March 2002.
A buttress (NO 185 807) located in the centre of the back corrie wall of Coire Kander just to the left of a prominent snow gully (with steep ice pitch in the middle, possibly Wee Gem). Start at the foot of the buttress and follow to the summit. A steep and awkward wall halfway up is best tackled on the right. The route may bank out in snowy winters.

GLEN CALLATER, Unnamed Crag:
Flu Sunday   80m   II. J.Higham. 23rd January 2005.
The route is located on a small buttress high on the west slopes of Glen Callater at NO 190 817. The cliff is characterised by a prominent ridge on the left-hand side of an easy gully which splits the right-hand side of the cliff. The route follows this ridge for 80m.

LITTLE GLAS MAOL, North Facing Buttress:
Slanting Ramp   150m   II. J.C.Higham. 20th March 1999.
On the left-hand side of the North Facing Buttress below Little Glas Maol is a right-slanting runnel in the upper part of the face (NO 176 762). Ascend directly to the start of this feature over mixed ground and then follow the easy runnel to the summit plateau.

GLEN CLOVA, Coire Wirral:
Central Buttress   175m   III. J.Higham, R.Higham. 30th December 2000.
Two prominent buttresses are present in the corrie overlooking Loch Wirral. This route follows the right-hand buttress (NO 360 747) which has a steep rocky start that gives way in the upper part to a broad snowy ridge. Start at the lowest point of the buttress and spiral up to the right for 50m until at the top of a prominent rib. Continue directly up the grooves above and onto the crest of the buttress. This is then followed more easily to the plateau.

Corrie Bonhard:
Bonhard Buttress   IV,4. S.Cameron, A.Thomson. 1992?
Climb to base of a groove. Go up the groove to a dark overhang and traverse out left to and follow a snow line to the crest of the buttress. Climb this to easy snow. Photo provided.

Corrie Fee:
The Comb   IV,6. A.Thomson, S.Cameron. January 1986.
Also G.Gatherer, S.Elliot, G.Connor. 8th December 2007.
By the summer line, good in lean conditions, with difficulties mainly on rock. The described line needs more snow on pitch 1 and misses the highlight, the steep upper comb and arete.

Nits on the Comb 60m? IV,5. A.Thomson, S.Cameron, G.Rodgers. February 1988.
The obvious corner between the slabby left wall of the Comb and the steep wall on the left. Climb easy snow to reach its base, then climb the corner direct to reach the plateau.

GLEN ESK:
Hunt Hill Falls 110m IV,5 *. D.Tunstall, J.Irvin. 21st December 2007.
The first stream crossed above the Falls of Unich descends from a cliff on the right bank (NO 383 797). The second pitch provides the meat of the route. In better conditions a direct pure icefall line just to the right should be possible.
1. 40m Climb the stream easily for 40m.
2. 35m There is a short steep section after 10m which has not yet been seen fully frozen, so climb a short ramp 3m to the left which has a steep exit that leads to a big ledge with trees. Traverse right to regain the main falls which are climbed in the centre using a series of iced grooves on the left.
3. 35m A short steep wall leads to a narrow gully which is followed for 10m before widening and the angle easing. This is followed for another 20m to a tree. There is a good descent path off to the left.

NORTH-EAST OUTCROPS

GIRDLE NESS POINT (NJ 972 055):
A small inlet just down from Girdleness Lighthouse.
Ness Girdle 50m Severe. G.J.Lynn. 25th August 2007.
A traverse of the north facing wall. Start at the landward end and traverse around to a small bridge on the headland, climbing generally above the high-tide mark.

EARNSHEUGH:
Grimly Fiendish Direct Start 20m E5 6a **. G.Lennox, E.Barber. 8th July 2007.
Step onto the wall from the block as per the normal start, then traverse right to the arete (PR). Make hard moves up to the break and traverse right to good friend placements at the undercut arete. Pull over the bulge at jugs and continue boldly up to join the original route.

JOHNS HEUGH:
Note: *Hunchback Direct* (SMCJ 2007) is at Johns Heugh, not Boltsheugh Lower South.

DOONIE POINT, Castle Rock of Muchalls:
A Slice Short 30m E1 5a. R.I.Jones, C.Las Heras. 19th May 2007.
Start at the bottom of the right-rising ramp on the north face. Climb the centre of the wall and take the overhang on the left. Climb the groove on the right of the arete on the wall above.

LONG HAVEN QUARRIES, Scimitar Ridge, South Wall:

The Trial   12m   E8 6c ***. G.Lennox. 3rd November 2007.
Start as for Comfortably Numb, but where this route breaks out right, continue up the crack with a very hard move, then a devious excursion out left to gain the final section of crack, above the Niche. Hard, sustained and technical, but with good gear if you can place it.

ROSEHEARTY:

Shapeshifters Direct   12m   E5 6a *. G.Lennox, E.Barber, A.Coull. 2nd July 2007.
An eliminate with good climbing up the centre of the wall. Climb directly to the flake at the junction of Coming up Roses and Shapeshifters. Follow these routes to the first break, then continue up the centre of the wall (crossing Shapeshifters as it escapes right), aiming for a right-facing flake below the final block. Exit by the right notch.

LOGIE HEAD, The Pinnacle:

The following routes are on the east face. The rock is not as good but still reasonable.

Kerfuffle   15m   E1 5b. A.Nisbet, J.Preston. 22nd September 2007.
The steepest part of the face has this crack-line right of centre and which leads through a bulge into a distinct niche. Reach up from its top, then step right to an arete. Follow this left to the top.

Greybeard   15m   E1 5a. A.Nisbet, J.Preston. 23rd October 2007.
Climb up to the left end of a long down-pointing flake. Use this to pull right into a hollow and finish straight up.

Krakatoa   15m   VS 4c. J.Preston, A.Nisbet. 22nd September 2007.
On the left side of the face are two parallel faults. This is the right one.

Fit for Porpoise   15m   VS 4c. J.Preston, A.Nisbet. 22nd September 2007.
The left fault line.

Podcast   10m   Very Difficult. J.Preston, A.Nisbet. 22nd September 2007.
A shallow chimney line left again, which leads to a square-cut niche at the top. The niche can be gained by starting further right and climbing short walls and ledges at Very Difficult.

Flipside   8m   Severe. J.Preston, A.Nisbet. 22nd September 2007.
A shallow chimney with a pinnacle formed between twin chimney-cracks. This is the more continuous right crack.

Delphinius   8m   Very Difficult. J.Preston, A.Nisbet. 22nd September 2007.
This is the left crack.

Flipper 6m 4c. J.Preston, A.Nisbet. 22nd September 2007.
A bulging fault line at the entrance to a deep slot.
Flip Flop 6m Very Difficult. J.Preston. 22nd September 2007.
Up between two chokestones at the seaward end of a gully which lies near the inland end of the face.

Blackadder 10m Hard Severe 4b. J.Preston, A.Nisbet. 23rd October 2007.
West of this pinnacle is a smaller squat pinnacle. This route climbs its seaward face. Start up the left arete and move into the middle of the face at half-height. Finish on the left arete.

HEAD OF GARNESS:
Taken to the Cleaners 45m E1. J.Preston, A.Nisbet. 18th May 2007.
A sea-cliff adventure. The east leg of the Head of Garness is formed below an impressive prow which finishes at the height of the fields behind. The right side of the prow is a steep wall formed above a sea cave. From the crest of the east leg, an undercut slab slopes down into the cave. Start down from the crest at a flake-ledge which is the only place where the wall can be gained.
1. 35m 5a Step up on to a small sloping ledge, then make a sensational rising traverse right to a good flake. Step down right onto a ledge then climb up rightwards to a green crack. Now climb up and slightly left using incut holds and a flake. Above this point the climbing eases but the rock is dirtier. Continue straight up on small ledges and cracks to a big ledge (possible escape).
2. 10m 5b Step down and right from the belay, then make steep moves up the right side of the arete. Continue up the corner above. Old stake belay. Plenty of loose rock was removed on abseil but the underlying rock seemed reasonable and the protection was also reasonable.

The following routes are on the lower cliff described in SMCJ 2005.

Guttersnipe 8m Hard Severe. J. & D.Preston. 11th April 2007.
From a boulder platform in a hole halfway up Drainpipe Gully, climb the grey corner on the left.

Squiggly 15m VS 4b. J. & D.Preston. 11th April 2007.
Start as for The Garnest. Step up and then immediately left to a ledge. Climb the steep left wall (crux) and follow the crest of the ridge more easily to the top.
The next four routes all lie on the wall left of the ridge of Squiggly. Approach by 20m abseil (slightly diagonally leftwards facing out) from a large block on the crest of the headland running out to sea. Belay on a convenient small square-cut ledge just above the high water mark.

Wiggly 18m Severe. J. & D.Preston. 11th April 2007.
Step right from the belay ledge and follow a deep crack to a sentry box. Bridge steeply out of this and continue in the same line to the top (passing right of a small yellow pinnacle near the top).

Going Ga Ga   18m   Very Difficult *. J. & D.Preston. 11th April 2007.
Climb cracks above the belay ledge to an overlap. Climb through this on the left
and finish more easily (passing left of the yellow pinnacle).
Garfish   18m   Difficult. J. & D.Preston. 11th April 2007.
Angle (spot the deliberate pun!) up left from the belay to start then climb
straight to the top.

Gargoyle   18m   Very Difficult. J. & D.Preston. 11th April 2007.
Traverse 2m left from the belay ledge, then climb up to a ledge and continue up
a green crack to finish on fine rough rock.

The next three routes lie further left (north) on the same slabby wall but are
approached by abseiling to a left-rising ramp 10m left of the square-cut ledge.

Garland   18m   Hard Severe 4b *. A.Nisbet, J.Preston. 18th May 2007.
Start from the lower right end of the ramp just above high tide level. Step right
on to the wall and climb straight up to a long ledge. Continue up a steeper
headwall and climb its right side by a left diagonal crack.

Black Garter   16m   Hard Severe 4b. J.Preston, A.Nisbet. 18th May 2007.
Start 2m right of a chokestone which forms the left end of the ramp. Climb
straight up to finish up the left side of the headwall, moving right and back left
at the base of the headwall.

Garlic   16m   Very Difficult. J.Preston, A.Nisbet. 18th May 2007.
Start at the chokestone. Climb up the wall to a right-facing corner. Go up this to
finish up steep but more broken ground left of the headwall.

REDHYTHE POINT, The Gully Buttress (SMCJ 2005/2006), South-East Face:
Traverse right (facing in) from the base of the Bird Poo Wall descent past the
slab of Wibble and step down to a ledge below a short overhanging wall.

Wobble   10m   Very Difficult. J.Preston. 22nd April 2007.
Climb the short overhanging wall and continue straight to the top.

Cardinal Biggles   10m   Difficult. J.Preston. 22nd April 2007.
The grooves between the overhanging wall and Cardinal Fang.

North-East Face:
It is unclear where the SE face becomes the NE face; possibly the dividing line
is the arete of Cardinal Fang. The SE Face is then nearer east-facing.

Break Point   10m   Hard Severe *. J. & D.Preston. 15th April 2007.
Independent climbing between Break Out and Clean Break. Directly above the
foot of Ramage a good undercling and cracks lead to the overlap which is
climbed at its widest point on good holds to the top.

Crackers 10m Very Difficult. J. & D.Preston. 15th April 2007.
The crack immediately left of Rampage is followed rightwards under the overhang.

Direct 10m VS 4c. J. & D.Preston. 15th April 2007.
Climb straight through the overhang at its widest point.

And Now For Something Completely Different 35m Hard Severe 4b **. J. & D.Preston. 15th April 2007.
Ministry of Silly Walks (SMCJ 2006) is essentially the same as the High Tide Traverse (SMCJ 2005) with the option to continue right. A right-to-left (facing in, north-to-south) traverse avoids the unpleasant jump at the north end. Start at the base of the Gully Wall below The Deep, as for Flying Circus. Make the first move as for this route and then continue left with feet just above the high water mark all the way round to Bird Poo Wall. Great fun, ideal at high tide or just before.

The following routes lie on the section of cliff south of the easy Bird Poo Wall scrambling descent. A deep narrow gully cuts into the cliff at one point. Most of the routes, in fact all but three described here are between the BP wall descent and this Deep Gully. All routes can be accessed at low tide or by a 15m abseil from huge blocks on a ledge south of the BP wall descent. From the very base of the BP wall scrambling descent, traverse left (facing in) at low tide for 5m on a barnacle and mussel encrusted ledge.

The Poop Deck 14m Severe. J.Preston, P.Amphlett, T.Sharp. 22nd April 2007.
This route follows the first obvious break, belay on a good spike above the high tide mark. Move up right on a brown slab to a small green ledge. Then climb straight up (left of BP wall) and up to the top through an overlap.

Pooped 14m VS 4c. J.Preston, P.Amphlett, T.Sharp. 22nd April 2007.
From the same spike belay (low tide) climb straight up to a constriction. Step up and right onto a sloping green ledge. Continue up right and surmount the overhanging wall to finish more easily on green slabs. At high tide, approached from a belay further left on the edge.

At low tide the traverse left can be continued past an awkward step to belay for the next two routes on a ledge above the high tide mark. This is on an edge where the cliff swings round and starts cutting in towards the Deep Gully. Alternatively abseil in to this small ledge.
Up and Under 14m Hard Severe. J.Preston, P.Amphlett, T.Sharp. 22nd April 2007.
Above the belay is a tapering ramp-line. Climb this rightwards to a thread runner and where it narrows step up right. Climb the overlap and finish up slabs.

The next two routes are separated by a narrow white ledge, the only sign of bird activity observed on this section of the cliff.

Boil Your Bottom   14m   VS 4c *. J.Preston, P.Amphlett, T.Sharp. 22nd April 2007.
From the same belay as Up and Under climb up left to the large overhang. Layback smoothly into the niche above. Bridge up out of this and pull through leftwards on good holds to a slabby finish.

Nailed to the Perch   14m   VS 4c. J.Preston, P.Amphlett, T.Sharp. 22nd April 2007.
From a spike belay 5m further left, climb easily to the large overhang. Climb this strenuously up a crack on good holds. Make another steep move up left from the ledge and continue straight to the top.

The following four routes are further left again and start from the base of the Deep Gully. The easiest approach is to abseil to the very foot of the gully to a point below several chockstones by some red rock. This is above the high water mark.

Pythonesque   14m   VS 4c *. J. & D.Preston. 15th April 2007.
Climb easily up right from the base of the gully on ledges to squirm effortlessly through the slot at the steepening.

Green Fingers   14m   HVS 5a. J. & D.Preston. 15th April 2007.
The green wall above the base of the gully is climbed direct. Good steep climbing although escapable at half-height.

Rampart 14m   Severe. J. & D.Preston. 15th April 2007.
From a point level with the chockstones in the gully, climb the narrow ramp on the right.

The Holy Hand Grenade   16m   Hard Severe 4b. J. & D.Preston. 15th April 2007.
Climb up the bed of the gully over several chockstones to a steep wall. Step up right and follow a narrow ramp rightwards. Finishing direct is also possible but belaying at the top is then problematical.

Conk City 14m   HVS 5a *. J. & D.Preston. 15th April 2007.
The overhanging wall on the south side of the gully. From a spike belay above the chockstones, climb the wall direct on good holds to finish on a yellow pinnacle.

Big Nose 14m   Very Difficult *. J. & D.Preston. 15th April 2007.
Left of Conk City, climb twin diagonal cracks leftwards to a large green and yellow block. Step off this and climb to the top.

A large ledge (still above the high water mark) leads around left from the south of Big Nose to The Tea Cleft. The next route starts where this ledge runs out.

Greenland Odyssey 16m Severe. J.Preston. 15th April 2007.
From the far end of the ledge south of Deep Gully, make an awkward step left around a rib onto a sloping green ledge. Climb a wall on the right then slabs to the top. Well situated, overlooking the Tea Cleft.
Further left the ledges peter out completely and the cliff drops abruptly into the sea.

HIGHLAND OUTCROPS

POLLDUBH, Tricouni Buttress:
Stag Day Afternoon 25m HVS 4c. E.Grindley, R.McHardy. 31st March 2007.
The overhanging wall between Black Slab Edge and Black Slab. Unprotected.

Pandora's Buttress:
Over and Out 25m E5 6a ***. E Grindley, R.McHardy. 27th May 2007.
Exposed and technical crack climbing above the big roof to the right of Phantom Slab. Start at the tree belay at the start of Phantom Slab. Climb the corner of Pandora until it is possible to step left to gain the thin crack which runs leftwards above the lip of the roof. Follow this to reach a groove which finishes at the top of Lucy Lime.

Parallelojam 30m E2 5c **. E.Grindley, J.Macleod. 26th March 2007.
From the top of the corner on Pandora Direct, climb a shallow right-facing corner to a good hold part-way along a slanting crack. Move right along this crack and finish up the right-hand of the two wide parallel cracks.

Repton Buttress:
Ripley Holden 30m E4 6a **. E.Grindley, J.French, S.Abbott, J.Macleod. 9th May 2006.
Climb the first few feet of Tyke's Climb, then step right to the foot of a steep groove. Go up this with poor protection initially to gain the slab below Sprauchle's groove. Finish up this.

Blackpool 35m E3 5b/c *. E.Grindley, J.French, S.Abbott, J.Macleod. 6th May 2006.
Climb the very shallow open niche just left of Sprauchle to gain a thin crack, then step up left to gain good holds on the slab. Climb the slabs and go straight up the bulge on sideholds to gain a tiny spike. Continue up the unprotected slab to the top.

Scimitar Buttress:
The Great Beast 25m HVS 5a *. E.Grindley, J.French. 6th June 2006.
Start 2m left of Nutcracker and climb up to steeper rock. Climb the rib via an obvious block to a slab. Finish up through the right-hand side of the niche above.

Floatin with Roo   35m   E1 5b **. E.Grindley, J.French, R.Mackintosh. 7th June 2006.
Start just up and right from the right edge of the front face and climb a slab to an oblong roof. Move over this using vertical cracks and continue up the pleasant slab.

Gorge Crag:
Brief Candle   35m   E2 **. E.Grindley R.Grindley. 30th September 2007.
Varied climbing up the rib to the left of Pupil Power. Start 5m to the left of Pupil Power, just left of a heathery groove.
1. 15m 5b Climb the steep wall stepping left to exit via a left-facing corner to a ledge on the left of the rib.
2. 30m 5c Climb up easily until the rib steepens, then go up a thin crack just right of the rib and continue to a ledge. Climb the slab above, stepping right before finishing direct to a clump of trees.

GLENFINNAN, Dome Buttress:
Clementine   25m   E5 6a ***. E.Grindley, C.Mackintosh, P.Brian. 25th August 1998.
The central rib. Rather bold, but good. Start 2m left of Manic Laughter and climb slightly rightwards to the rib on the left of that route. Step up left and climb the steep wall to a ledge on the rib. Step high left onto the face and go slightly rightwards to the rib. Step left again and continue to easy ground. There are good peg belays in the slab near the top of the cliff above Clementine.

STRATHSPEY, Farletter Crag:
Firelighter   13m   Severe. J.Lyall. 1983.
Start directly below a slot in the roofs left of Farrlake. Go straight up through this to finish out left.
Spark to a Flame   30m   HVS/E1 5a. J.Lyall. 20th April 2007.
Start at the right end of the crag, just right of some rock shelves going out left. Go up through a low overlap and move left to good runners at the foot of a slanting groove. Continue up the edge right of the groove to a ledge. Big holds lead boldly up the right edge of the wall to a niche (runners); pull out left to another ledge. Finish by the tree and final wall of Strike One.

DUNTELCHAIG, Dracula Buttress:
Monster's Edge   10m   E4 6b. R.Betts, N.Carter. 22nd April 2008.
Takes the hanging arete to the left of Frankenstein. Start up the crux corner of Frankenstein (often wet), then move left up the arete with a long reach off a painful finger jam for the crux.

Note: *Mummy* (SMCJ 2007) was climbed by Robert & Ruairidh Mackenzie; D.Moy made the second ascent.

Seventy Foot Wall:
Insomnia   15m   E3 5c. J.Murray (unsec). 9th April 2008.
Climb the initial crack of Anne Boleyn's Crack until its end. Gain the arete

directly above via thin awkward moves until a better hold is reached (possible groundfall?). Step slightly left and finish (a dubious Cam in a pocket protects).

ASHIE FORT:
Note: N.Carter repeated *Whipper Snapper* (SMCJ 1999) and thought E3 5c, well enough protected.

INVERFARIGAIG, Monster Buttress:
Notes: A.Tibbs & C.Eatock climbed a second pitch to *Monster Magic* on 19th May 2006. Climb diagonally up leftwards through steep bulges on good holds to a tree (15m 5a).

A.Tibbs & D.Moy climbed a route, probably *Dances With Blondes* on 24th June 2006. Scramble up a mossy slab 10m left of Farigaig Corner and move left through some small trees to a short rib of rock; start here. Climb the rib of rock and the crack above it (30m E1).

TYNRICH SLABS:
Angels Wings 15m HVS 5a. A.Tibbs, J.Biggar, L.Biggar. 18th May 2007.
Start 5m left of Scorpion. Climb a short wall to gain a right-trending line which leads to a crack immediately left of Scorpion. Climb this crack to join Scorpion to finish.

CRAIG A' BARNS, Polney Crag:
Twilight Direct Start E4 6a *. A.D.Robertson, C.Jordi. 28th July 2007.
Starting at the base of the Twilight / Wriggle Direct corner, make strenuous moves out left into the bottomless groove just left of the arete with no protection then continue up to join and finish up the normal route. Inspected on abseil prior to ascent.

CREAG NA H-EIGHE:
Raindodgers Wall 8m Very Difficult *. S.Holmes. 27th May 2007.
On the far right of the crag on the left of the final slab. Start just to the left of the obvious boulders. Climb the slab and wall passing just to the right of the mid-height overhang. Well protected. Fine quality rock on the upper half of the climb.

BEN NEVIS, AONACHS, CREAG MEAGAIDH

BEN NEVIS, Little Brenva Face:
Steam Train VI,7. D.MacLeod, A.Hudelson. 20th March 2007.
By the summer line.

Minus Face:
Subtraction VIII,8 *. V.Scott, G.Robertson. 15th April 2008.
This winter ascent gives hard, varied and committing mixed climbing following the summer line into Minus Two Gully, then finishing up that route (the upper groove was bare). There was some ice present but it was of limited use; on pitch

2 it was good enough to hold crampons in places. More ice would undoubtedly help on the first pitch (crux), but the second pitch will probably always be hard.

Note: G.Robertson thinks that *Minus Two Buttress* (1974) goes up iced slabs left of the lower part of the initial groove, then breaks right to gain and follow the upper continuation. *Subtraction* climbs the lower part, then goes on to the rib on the right.

Observatory Ridge, West Face:
The Frozen Chosin   80m   VI,6. S.M.Richardson, R.G.Webb. 16th March 2008.
The buttress between Abacus and Maelstrom. Start just left of Maelstrom below a right-facing corner that cuts up the right edge of the buttress.
1. 20m Climb the corner, step left to a second right-facing corner, and climb this to icy slabs. Belay in the shallow cave above.
2. 40m Traverse left for 3m then move up icy slabs to join the right-trending line of weakness that cuts through the barrier wall above. Follow this and continue up the shallow icy depression overlooking Abacus to below a short wall.
3. 20m Continue easily up the buttress to the crest of Observatory Ridge.

Indicator Wall:
Stormy Petrel Variation   60m   VII,6. B.Fyffe, I.Small. 24th March 2007.
3. 30m As the corner was ice-free, climb the rightmost of two parallel grooves right of the corner to exit onto the big slab above. Belay on the left side of the slab to the right of large roofs.
4. 30m Climb the large corner above, on its left wall on thin ice (this is left of the original route's corner) to belay on the traverse line of Flight of the Condor. Finish by the original chimney.

Douglas Boulder:
Walking Through Fire   VII,7. R.Bentley, M.Davies. 14th March 2008.
Follow the summer line throughout but climb the overhang direct at the start of pitch 3 and also climb the final chimneys at the top of the V-groove direct before trending right to the south-west ridge. Pitch 2 is by far the crux with poorly protected moves on snowed up slabs to gain the belay below the inverted V-overhang.

Goodeve's Buttress:
Techno Wall   140m   V,6. S.M.Richardson, A.Cave. 20th April 2008.
A direct line up the centre of the front triangular face of the buttress between Goodytwoshoes and The Borg Collective.
1. 40m Start as for Goodytwoshoes and move up and right through a steep section to gain the steep blunt rib bounding the groove and chimney system of The Borg Collective. Climb this to a large pinnacle block beneath the headwall.
2. 30m Pull through steep cracks to reach a steep wide niche. Step right and climb a steep crack to reach the short hanging chimney-groove that runs parallel to the upper chimney of The Borg Collective. An excellent pitch.
3. and 4. 70m Continue up easier ground to reach the plateau as for Hale Bopp Groove.

The Comb:
Don't Die of Ignorance 275m XI,11. D.MacLeod, J.French. 16th March 2008.
A free ascent based on the 1987 aided route, taking a more direct line at the crux.
Climbed ground up, onsight, 6th attempt. Start on the left side of the Comb at
the start of the huge diagonal shelf/crack system.
1. 30m Follow the easy snow and ice ramps to a belay before the ledge runs out.
2. 30m Step down into the wide undercut crack and tin opener tenuously to the
arete (cams, bulldog). A foot-off tin opener move gains access to the rib on the
right (peg). The aid route continues along the crack. Quit the crack and climb
leftwards on the tenuous wall above to gain a ledge. Go right beneath a steep
groove and move round its base to gain a thin crack in an open slab. Climb this
to below a chimney.
3. 55m Step up and right to gain the huge open groove of Don't Die and follow
this with sustained interest to a hanging belay on the right at a large block.
4. 25m Step left and follow the crest, moving left again across a fault to a ledge
and good belay at a flake.
5. 20m Mantel the flake and step right to regain the crest which is followed to
the snow crest on the apex of the buttress (good spike belay).
6. 60m Climb the easy snow crest to a steepening.
7. 40m Climb snow grooves in the buttress crest to a flat knife edge leading to
the plateau.
8. 15m The knife edge leads easily to the plateau.

Number Three Gully Buttress:
Last Tango 140m VII,8. I.Small, S.M.Richardson. 13th April 2008.
A steep icy mixed route based on the huge left-facing corner to the right of the
icy slab of Quickstep. The route climbs the corner then breaks out right through
the retaining wall to finish up the crest of the rib.
1. and 2. 65m Climb the first two pitches of Quickstep and belay below the
corner.
3. 40m Climb the corner for 20m, then pull out right onto the impending right
wall to reach a small ledge. Climb a small inset left-facing corner for 10m then
traverse delicately back left into the main corner line. Step left and climb thin ice
over a steep bulge to a good stance. Junction with Quickstep.
4. 15m Traverse 5m right to a turfy niche and climb the fault above to reach the
crest of the rib.
5. 20m Climb the rib to the cornice. (On this ascent, the cornice was impassable,
so it was bypassed by a long traverse right to exit as for Two Step Corner).

The Survivor 90m VII,8. S.M.Richardson, I.Small. 9th March 2008.
A difficult mixed climb based on the prominent corner-niche on the left side of
the front face of Number Three Gully Buttress.
1. 40m Start directly below the niche and climb snow and ice trending left
across a shallow depression to a short wall. Surmount this, move right, and
climb a second wall to enter the niche. Belay on the right wall.
2. 20m Climb the corner at the back of the niche to a small triangular ledge.
Traverse left along a hidden horizontal break to a good stance.
3. 30m Surmount a steep bulge and continue up the diagonal fault line to reach

a narrow ledge after 20m. Climb the steep icy groove above to join the platform on Number Three Gully Buttress.

Snuff Wall   55m   VIII,8. I.Parnell (unsec). 19th March 2008.
This takes a line between Babylon and Winter Chimney, starting out technical and tenuous, then with an extremely bold but less technical central section on thin ice (ground fall possibilities) before a steep gymnastic finish. Climb 6m up Winter Chimney until it is possible to pull left and climb the left side of a wide shallow recess. This is climbed for 6m until it is possible to traverse right past steep thin cracks to a short ramp/arete. Climb up this, then make a super thin traverse right to gain an obvious long curving ice ramp (one of the main features of this wall). This is followed with almost no gear (the first ascent had poor half inch ice, exceptional conditions will make the route easier) until a huge chockstone (good gear) is reached. Climb steeply straight up past this and another pointed chockstone to a crack-line leading to the top.

Notes: B.Fyffe climbed a variation finish to *Chinook* on 30th December 2007, traversing hard left after the groove and climbing an exposed crack overlooking Two Step.
T.Stone thought *Babylon* VI,7 although VII,7 is a more common opinion.

Creag Coire na Ciste:
The Secret   70m   VIII,9. A.Turner, S.Ashworth, V.Scott. 10th December 2007.
The often eyed but rarely tried crack on the right wall of No.3 Gully. The main pitch involved a mind-boggling array of axe techniques. A sustained 35m crack pitch ranged from fist to finger width. The route was led on-sight and in perfect style.
Note: The second ascent opinions varied from VIII,8 to IX,9 ***.

Stormtrooper   VIII, 8. S.Ashworth, A.Turner. 8th January 2008.
Climb a steep and rather bold groove just right of Darth Vader to access a belay niche in the middle of the wall. The second pitch takes a hanging and tapering ramp with the steep Darth Vader wall dropping away below. The crux of this pitch is at the narrows before an easing and arrival at the large ledge.

Unnamed   110m   VIII,8. I.Small, S.M.Richardson. 6th April 2008.
A sustained and challenging mixed climb taking the prominent rib on the left side of Creag Coire na Ciste between Archangel and South Sea Bubble.
1. 20m Start as for South Gully and climb easily up steep snow to belay at the foot of a deep groove that cuts up and left just right of the rib crest.
2. 30m Climb the groove (passing a prominent tower-flake on the left after 15m) to where the groove steepens and opens up to offwidth. Climb the offwidth to a steep bulge split by a Y-shaped crack. Step on to the exposed left edge and a good block.
3. 20m Return back right into the groove and climb the through the bulge and Y-shaped crack (crux). Step left and move up a shallow slot to a good ledge that cuts across the crest of the rib. This banks up with snow and is a prominent feature on the route.

4. 20m From the right end of the ledge, climb the left-trending fault line that leads to an exposed position on the left edge of the rib. Pull through the overhanging wall on the right to a tiny ledge on the crest of the rib and finish up the impending crack in the wall above to reach easy ground.

5. 20m Continue up easy snow to the cornice.

The Sorcerer 140m VII,8. S.Ashworth, N.Nielsen. 1st March 2007.
The name is an attempt at capturing some of the White Magic. Start just left of Central Gully and Lost the Place below a steep corner.

1. 40m Climb over ledges to gain the corner. Climb the corner exiting via its right wall. Trend left over ledges to belay directly below the crack splitting the wall above.

2. 50m The magic crack pitch! A couple of thin poorly-protected moves off a ledge gain the crack-line This is very similar to Magic Crack, a bit harder and twice as long. Easy ground above the wall leads to a belay shared with Lost the Place.

3. 50m Pull round the corner as for Lost the Place and immediately take a right-trending ramp-line which takes a diagonal across the steep upper buttress.

South Trident Buttress:
Note: R.Jarvis & M.Moran climbed *Strident Edge* in December 2007 by the second and main pitch direct all the way up the crack and considered it VII,7.

Under Fire 85m VII,7 *. D.MacLeod, M.Tweedley. 6th February 2008.
Start left of The Minge, below a roofed chimney. Climb the chimney with hard moves through the roof and the continuation corner above, to exit left onto a ledge underneath an overhanging wall. Traverse left for 5m and round to the base of a large slanting corner (common to 1944 route). Climb the corner and crawl right along a thin ledge to another corner which leads to the top.

MAMORES, Am Bodach
Rufty-Turfty 180m III *. M.J.Munro, G.A.McIntosh. 5th January 2008.
On the north face of the Am Bodach's eastern satellite. A continuous right-trending turf line 5m parallel left of Solo Gully. Rock protection is limited so turf protection is recommended. Start as Solo Gully and follow the turf fault line to a horizontal terrace belaying next to a large block (40m). Continue on the diagonal turf line passing a small tree with 4m vertical section leading to easier ground (120m).

Stob Ban, South Buttress:
Groove Rider 160m IV,4 *. A.Nisbet, C.Wells. 18th March 2008.
Start as for North Groove by traversing out right but then climb a smaller but well defined groove straight up (a direct start had insufficient ice) – 50m, 35m. Gain and climb the ridge to the summit (75m).

Summit Groove 140m IV,4 *. A.Nisbet, C.Wells. 18th March 2008.
Start about halfway up South Gully and climb a big groove, almost a gully, which leads close to the summit. Continous soft ice, would be Grade III in better conditions.

CARN DEARG MEADHONACH:

The north-west face comprises a lower tapering buttress, and an upper pyramid-shaped buttress. The existing routes are located on the lower buttress (p249 of guide).

Chevron   60m   IV,5 *. L.Harrop, A.Nelson. 9th March 2008.
Takes a line close to the upper right edge of the lower buttress. At this point the buttress is made up of two clearly-defined steps. Start left of the buttress edge and climb a short groove rightwards to gain a left-trending upper groove. Climb the groove to the top of the first step (40m). A sharp arete leads to the East Ridge (20m).

Perilous Journey   70m   IV,5 **. S.Kennedy, R.Hamilton. 9th March 2008.
The upper buttress is defined by a prominent right-facing corner. A short pitch leads directly to the foot of the corner (20m). Climb the corner for 10m then move out onto the slabby right face. Thin moves lead across the face via small ledges until close to the right edge. Continue up interesting mixed ground just left of the edge to finish on slopes right of the East Ridge (50m).

Like Father, Like Son   60m   IV,4 *. L.Harrop, A.Nelson. 9th March 2008.
Start in a snow bay well left of the corner of Picket Line. Climb a short ice pitch to gain a right-sloping shelf which leads to a short chimney. Climb the chimney (crux) and finish up mixed ground.

AONACH MOR, Coire an Lochain, Web Buttress

History Won't Mind   90m   IV,5 *. M.Dowsett, C.Randall. 23rd March 2008.
The buttress immediately left of Easy Gully contains Spider Rib and The Web. This route takes the mixed line up the steep chimney/groove immediately left of Easy Gully. Follow a snow ramp up into the foot of the groove and then mantel and bridge steeply upwards with spaced and sketchy protection until it is possible to pull over and onto the upper snowfield directly overlooking Easy Gully. Easy to finish and normally no cornice.

Ribbed Walls:

Jet Lag   70m   III. S.Allan, A.Dennis, K.Grindrod, A.Nisbet. 29th January 2008.
An icy groove right of Castaway (SMCJ 2007) and capped by a roof high up. Like all the routes in this area, sections will have been climbed before. Climb the lower continuation of the groove and move right into the main groove. Follow this to a steepening. Move left, then traverse back right above it and below the roof on to a rib on the right. Follow this to the upper snow slopes. Best after a big thaw when the cornice has collapsed.

Shark Walls:

Unnamed   70m   V,6. S.M.Richardson, I.Small. 23rd December 2007.
The upper section of the tower right of Hidden Pinnacle Gully is cut by a shallow chimney-fault on its right side. Start 20m right of Hidden Pinnacle Gully below a shallow gully line.
1. 30m   Climb the gully passing a steep V-chimney to reach the central depression of Aquafresh.

2. 30m Continue in the line of the chimney-fault to reach the hanging gully. Climb this and exit left at the top (or harder, climb the capping roof). An excellent pitch in a fine position.
3. 10m Finish up easy snow to the top.

Wise Goat 110m IV,5. S.Allan, A.Dennis, K.Grindrod, A.Nisbet. 29th January 2008.
An ice line which forms right of Hammerhead Pillar, issuing from the final section of Gondola with the Wind. Start up Tunnel Vision until just above its narrows (40m). Move left on to a curving ramp and follow this to the ice line. Climb the ice through a mixed but helpful section and a short bulging slot to the point where Gondola from the Wind joins from the left (50m). Finish on snow as for this route (20m).

Central Buttress note: An obvious turfy line right of Morwind, joining Morwind higher up, has been climbed several times at Grade IV,5.

Twins Area:
White Noise Direct 100m V,5. A.Nisbet, D.Tunstall. 7th April 2008.
A direct and better line based on White Noise (SMCJ 2007). The barrier wall was climbed direct on thin ice and an icy groove parallel to Lost Boys was climbed to finish (the original route tended right).

White Light 100m IV,5. A.Nisbet, D.Tunstall. 7th April 2008.
A parallel line of ice right of White Noise formed a bulging ice column level with its barrier wall.
1. 20m Start as for White Noise (or White Bait) to below the ice column.
2. 30m Climb up under the column and pass it by an iced groove just on the right to rejoin the line, followed to a snow bay.
3. 50m Continue up icy grooves directly above, joining White Noise original.

White Horses 120m V,6. A.Nisbet, I.Parnell. 29th December 2007.
The rib on the right side of the face right of Right Twin, right of White Bait and left of the icefall of The Slever.
1. 20m Climb easily up to a large sentry box.
2. 20m Step left and climb a groove before moving right on to the rib.
3. 40m Climb the rib to a bulging section. Climb this on its right side to reach the large snowy bay. Move right to a rib formed between White Bait and the upper gully of The Slever.
4. 40m Start up a steep groove at the very base and continue up the crest to the top.

North Buttress:
The left end of North Buttress is formed by two narrow ribs, the right of which is Grooved Arete. Between this and the left rib is a wide easy angled slot with a distinctive overhanging top. The following route is based on this but avoids the overhanging section well to the right.

Slipstream   140m   IV,5. A.Nisbet, J.Preston. 23rd December 2007.
1. 50m   Climb the easy angled section of the slot until immediately under the overhanging section.
2. 20m   Gain a ledge on the right and follow it to the end of a vertical wall above.
3. 20m   Climb two short vertical walls rightwards, then move up left to a ledge with a big spike.
4. 45m   Climb a short chimney to easier grooves. Move left to the continuation above the overhanging section and follow it to a blocky arete under the cornice.
5. 5m   Finish over this.

The corrie south of Coire an Lochain has a series of narrow buttresses at its northern end. These lie just left of the dividing ridge with Coire an Lochain. There are two main buttresses, split by an icy gully.

Monkey Business   70m   V,6. S.M.Richardson, R.G.Webb. 30th December 2007.
The left-hand buttress is split by a prominent narrow right-facing groove in its upper half.
1. 20m   Climb easily up a depression that narrows towards the upper groove.
2. 50m   Continue up ice in the lower part of the depression to reach the groove. Climb this with increasing interest to a steep exit. A short snow slope leads to the cornice.

Drunken Monkey   70m   III. R.G.Webb, S.M.Richardson. 30th December 2007.
The central gully line splits into two branches in its lower third. Climb the right branch to reach the main gully. Climb this over a steepening to exit left onto the upper snow slope.

Monkey Puzzle   70m   III. R.G.Webb, S.M.Richardson. 30th December 2007.
The right-hand buttress is cut by a fault running up its length. Climb easy snow to where the fault line steepens. A dogleg right, then left, avoids this section (or climb it direct at III,4) and continue up the easier upper section to the final snow slope.

AONACH BEAG, North Face:
Away from the Crows   300m   II. M.J.Munro, P.Baillie. 16th February 2007.
Start as for Queen's View until the snow basin. Climb left over broken ground and head for an open gully left of The Black Prince. Once the gully ends, veer right then left into a large open gully that runs until a snow arete finish.

An Aghaidh Garbh:
Note: *Inducement Groove* is left of *Braxton Hicks*. The Grade III gully line done by I.Small is on the left side of the buttress.

West Face, Raw Egg Buttress:
Blackbeard   70m   VII,8. S.M.Richardson, I.Small. 4th January 2008.
A spectacularly steep mixed climb up the right arete of the Chandelle Wall.
1. 25m   Start just let of Ruadh Eigg Chimney and directly below the arete below two stepped corners. Climb the first corner with difficulty to a narrow ledge,

step right and climb the cracked right edge to a good ledge on the right. This is level with the horizontal break at the start of pitch 2 of Pirates.

2. 45m   Pull through the overhang above (on the right side of the arete overlooking Ruadh Eigg Chimney) then trend left up a steep wall to the regain the arete (crux – bold and serious). Continue up steep cracks on the very edge of the buttress to reach a left-trending ramp that leads to the top.

STOB COIRE AN LAOIGH:
Note: On an ascent of *Centrepoint* on 10th December 2007, R.Cross & A.Benson climbed straight up the wider crack instead of the right traverse. This led to an easy finish up the top of New Labour.

Note: *Loupie Louie*: After the col, R.Bentley took the ridge direct and climbed the steep wall on the right halfway up (rather than step left) – IV,6.

BEN ALDER, Garbh Coire Beag:
Pedal Power   170m   II. C.Marden, F.Marden. 17th February 2008.
The route climbs the snow face and open gully left of the steep mixed ground which merges with the top of the Short Leachas, finishing to the right of a small but distinctive downward pointing buttress. Approach by a rising traverse across snow terraces from the flank of the Short Leachas. Reach the toe of the downward pointing buttress in three long pitches, from where a rising traverse leads right to a steep cornice finish.

CENTRAL HIGHLANDS, GEAL CHARN, Creag Dhubh:
Colscot Adventure   125m   III,4 *. J.Foden, G.Buckingham. December 2007.
An ice line north-east of the existing routes. GPS reading for the start of the route: NN 595 799 (474m alt, end at 575m alt). Two pitches of 45m up a gully, followed by a 35m pitch including the 10m crux and a finish left of the gully.

GLEN COE

BUACHAILLE ETIVE MOR:
Note: J.Craig on 21st January 2008 climbed a Grade III gully just left of Lagangarbh Buttress, then went left of a higher buttress. Start on the path where it crosses a large area of stone debris. Ascend a burn over heather ramps, ignoring crags on left and right. The burn becomes a gully line. On the left is a small waterfall (not frozen), so a 4m icy ramp on the left was climbed. After 30m a large waterfall was bypassed by a turf corner on the right. After a steeper 35m another watherfall was passed by a 4m ramp on the left. Finish by 50m of steep snow.

BEINN FHADA, Summit Buttress:
West Rib   210m   II. S.Kennedy. 22nd March 2008.
The buttress forming the right edge of The Ramp. Start either directly or by a short chimney on the right (slightly harder). Join The Ramp at its top to finish up the crest.

STOB COIRE NAN LOCHAIN:
Note: *East Face Route* is now established at VI,7.

Wandering Wombat   400m   II. S.Swalling, N.Jordan, M.Drain. 14th March 2008.
The ridge and snow slopes left of Boomerang Gully. Start at a small scoop in the lowest rocks. Move up through this and keep trending slightly left to a face with a shallow chimney and with a boulder off to the left. Break left from the boulder and stay close to the rocks through a small chimney to a ridge running left of Boomerang Gully. Follow the ridge to a ledge. Go up a large snow slope to rocks and a prominent spike. Follow snow and rocks to a small gully, from which the main ridge line from Gearr Aonach to the summit of Stob Coire nan Lochan was reached.

DIAMOND BUTTRESS:
Diamond Diretissima   205m   HVS 4c *. R.Hamilton, S.Kennedy. 5th May 2007.
A more direct line than Bell's 1931 Direct Route, taking a line up the central slabs. A long dry spell is desirable. Starts almost at the lowest point of the buttress below a clean right-trending slabby ramp. The route has a serious feel to it. 60m ropes used.
1. 50m 4c Climb the ramp, following the right edge in the upper part, to a large block under a steep wall below the central slabs. Direct Route crosses here from the right.
2. 55m 4c Move up left passing some large flakes, then pull left into a slabby corner. Move up the corner then step right and climb cracked walls left of a prominent right-facing wall/corner (containing some loose blocks). A steep groove leads to the mid girdling ledge.
3. 55m 4b Traverse left for 5m along the ledge then climb slabs above to enter a deep recessed area. From the top of the recess pull out left by a large block and continue up steep slabs on the left to reach easier ground.
4. 45m Scramble up broken ground to reach the left edge of the buttress a short distance from the top.

SGORR DHONUILL (above Glenachulish):
Peekaboo   70m   VIII,8. D.King, M.Pescod. 10th January 2008.
Climbs the obvious undercut flat wall on the granite crag at NN 033 555.
1. 30m Pull through the overhang and climb the wall on good cracks. Trend right to a sloping ledge. Pull back onto the vertical wall and head left on tenuous hooks to a big spike around to the left. Another few moves gain a big ledge.
2. 40m Traverse horizontally right under the obvious corner to the rightmost (bottomless) chimney. Climb this with an overhang at the top.

CREACH BHEINN (Morvern), Coire Dubh, East Face (NM 874 582):
The following routes are situated on a prominent wedge shaped buttress on the right (west) side of the upper corrie beyond the sprawling north-east face. The buttress is bounded on the left by a prominent gully and is only fully seen from the upper part of the coire. A further buttress with an area of steep slabs lies left

of the gully. Approach from a large parking area in Glen Tarbert (NM 874 605) in about 50mins.

The Black Prawn 100m III,4 *. S.Kennedy, A.MacDonald. 12th January 2008.
A delightful route. Takes a line fairly close to the left edge of the buttress with some deviations right. Start almost at the lowest point of the buttress at the foot of Voodoo Gully. Easy ground leads to a slot near the left edge which is climbed to a cracked wall. Follow ramps leading up rightwards then straight up to belay (50m). Short walls lead to a narrow arete which provides a nice finish (50m).

Excavator 85m IV,5 *. R.Hamilton, L.Harrop. 12th January 2008.
Starts up a steep right-facing corner in the first break in the right wall of Voodoo Gully about 15m above the start of The Black Prawn. An easier groove lies just to the right of the corner. Climb the corner (crux), moving right near the top, to reach the buttress edge (35m). Finish up The Black Prawn (50m).

Voodoo Gully 110m I. R.Hamilton, L.Harrop, S.Kennedy, A.MacDonald. 12th January 2008.
The gully bounding the left side of the above buttress. Used in descent.

The Rover 130m II/III. A.MacDonald. 21st January 2008.
This route is located on the sprawling north-east face and follows the most prominent leftward-trending gully/corner line on the left side of the face. The crux is a narrowing in the lower section. Move out left near the top below a steeping to finish up a shallow gully.

SOUTHERN HIGHLANDS

MEALL BUIDHE:
Note: D.Stewart thought *Echo Edge* was III,4 **. A very good line and quite safe in unconsolidated conditions once on the edge proper. The current guidebook description is a bit sparse. Also found *The Scoop* in reasonably icy conditions to be III,4 and worth a star.

BEINN AN DOTHAIDH, North-East Corrie:
Stairway to Heaven, Direct Start 60m IV,5. I.Small, S.Jensen. 11th March 2006.
Traverse out right from the start of West Gully on a large ledge. From the centre of the buttress take a right-slanting turfy ramp to its end. Climb a steep corner, then move left to gain a slim groove which leads to a large ledge. Climb the bulging turfy fault above to easier ground and junction with Stairway to Heaven.

Note: On an ascent of *The Screaming*, T.Stone climbed the main pitch direct up the crack-line. The description to start says 'Gain a niche from the right' but this possibly means the same line, but if so, he thinks it misleading.

Creag Coire an Dothaidh:
Note: N.Stevenson & J.Telling in December 1996 finished *Lucifer Rising* straight up from the end of pitch 3, rather than traversing into the Professorial Seat/The Flasher as shown in the 1997 guide.

BEN LUI, Stob Garbh, North Face:
Garbh Couloir 180m II. J.Hageman. 18th March 2008.
A straight gully starting at 620m and finishing at 800m on the crest of the Stob Garbh ridge. Short steep sections. A headwall was avoided by a rising traverse right.

CREAG THARSUINN:
The Tingler 60m V,6. A.Clark, I.Dempster. 10th February 2007.
Climbed in three pitches of good cracks following the summer route to the top of the huge flake on pitch 3. Here a traverse left was made in a very exposed position to the top.

LOCH SLOY CRAGS:
In the FA list (Arrochar guide p361), the first five routes were climbed around 1985 not 1995.

THE ANVIL, LOCH GOIL:
Metalcore 20m 8c+. D.MacLeod. 2nd March 2007.
Start up Bodyswerve, but follow the faint crack-line all the way to the peak of the Anvil roof, joining Body Blow for its redpoint crux.

GLEN CROE:
Boulder Dash VS 4c. S.Burns P.Greene. 1999.
Start up a wide crack left of The Sharp Kiss. Move right at a patch of quartz to gain a handrail. Follow this to the centre and finish direct up the slab.

COILESSAN CRAG (NN 241 001):
Ajare 30m E6/7 6b. N.McNair. 2007.
The obvious jutting prow high up the hillside east of Cnoc Coinnich (the west flank of Loch Long). The route takes the obvious arete on the southern edge of the main crag. Mostly bold and technical wall climbing on the left side of the arete in stunning positions.

LOWLAND OUTCROPS

AYRSHIRE, The Quadrocks:
Atonement 8m E5 6b. K.Shields. 26th May 2007.
Climb the face to the left of Green Corner, boost for the obvious pinch in the middle of the face, then move right and finish up thin moves. Probably a backbreaker if you fall.

Time 4 Tennents 12m E4 6b. K.Shields. 28th May 2007.
Climb the blank wall to the left of Lichen Angel, thin moves and no pro until the last few metres.

Turning the Corner 10m E1 5a. K.Shields. 11th April 2008.
Basically the direct finish of Slab and Corner. Climb the slabs direct then directly up the face between Slab and Corner Route and Sunburst Red.

Loudon Hill:
Troll Wall 10m E2. G.Tyldesley, C.Moreau. July 2007.
Climb Cave Crack to two-thirds height. Step right under the blank nose. Hug up the nose direct to finishing jugs.
Note: *Mur* was thought E4 6a without a side runner.

AUCHINSTARRY QUARRY, Trundle Area:
A Stroll with Marigold E1 5b. G.Duncan, P.Mosley. 25th June 2007.
A right-slanting line crossing several routes. Start at the boulder start for Replicant. Traverse right and up aiming for 1m below the underside of the block at the top of Midas Touch. Continue the diagonal line round and over Gold Rush to finish at the top of After the Gold Rush (picture provided).

GALLOWAY HILLS, Craigdews, Ramp Slabs:
Toga Confusion 55m Severe *. J.Biggar, I.Brown. 27th September 2007.
Climbs the left-hand side of the slab taken by Dirty Old Raingoat, passing a good lug runner at 10m to heather ledges. Good runners (large cams) can be found here. Continue up on good clean rock by a small left-facing overlap. Much better than Dirty Old....

Craigdews, White Slab:
The Banana Goat 12m VS 4c. I.Brown, J.Biggar. 27th September 2007.
Start on the ledge on the left. Climb a blank slab, step 1m left, then climb a short vertical crack and easier cracks to finish.

Just One More Goat 15m Very Difficult. I.Brown, J.Biggar. 27th September 2007.
From the lowest point climb the slab, then the short crack right of the black chimney, finishing by the overlapping block. This may be a mixed up with One Man One Goat, but there are definitely two lines hereabouts.

The Merrick:
Monsieur Marmalade 150m III,4. J.Biggar, J.Kinnaird. 19th February 2008.
Start about 100m left of the Black Gutter and slightly lower at a narrow dark slot in the lower tier of rock. Directly above is an ice stream that takes a dog-leg to the left. Climb the slot with a steep exit left (30m). Cross snow or grass for 30m. Climb easy steps and ice to the leftwards dogleg in the ice stream above (30m). Climb the upper ice stream to below a steep 5m wall (50m). Climb the steep wall, then scramble to the top (25m).

THE BORDERS AND DUMFRIES, Clifton Crag, The Slab:

Frictional Belief 12m E1 5b **.J.Biggar, I.Brown, K.Brown. 25th September 2007.
Gives good independent climbing. Start about 3m right of the central crack. Climb the reddish slab to the horizontal break, then the blankest section of slab above, about 2m left of the corner.

GALLOWAY SEA-CLIFFS, Meikle Ross, Crab Slab:

Crab Slab is just to the east of Limehouse Blues Cliff. The best access is down the grassy ramp (as described for the west end of Fox Craig). Crab Slab is directly ahead from the ramp, accessible at all but the very highest tides.

The Arete 18m Moderate *. I.Brown, J.Biggar. 6th September 2007.
The obvious arête on the left.

Crab Eyes 12m Severe 4a *. J.Biggar, L.Biggar, D.McNicol. 23rd July 2007
The diagonal crack to the right. Crux at top.

Tropic of Cancer 12m Very Difficult. J.Biggar, I.Brown. 6th September 2007.
The next diagonal crack, easier than it looks.

Mutant Slater 12m Hard Severe *. A.Slater, I.Brown, J.Biggar. 6th September 2007.
The next diagonal crack, harder than it looks.

Dave's Route 12m Severe 4a *. D.McNicol, J.Biggar, L.Biggar. 23rd July 2007.
The next diagonal crack.

Arthropomorphic 12m VS 4b **. J.Biggar, I.Brown. 6th September 2007.
The slabby wall, very nice but poorly protected.

Linda's Route 12m Very Difficult. L.Biggar, D.McNicol, J.Biggar. 23rd July 2007.
The next big crack.

Winkle Up 14m Very Difficult. I.Brown, J.Biggar. 6th September 2007.
Start as for Linda's but go diagonally right

Landsickness 15m VS 4c *. J.Biggar, I.Brown. 6th September 2007.
About 3m to the right. Climbs through the overlap by the little triangular niche, then on to the top.

Laggantalluch:

Flying Arete 12m Very Difficult **. J.Biggar, L.Biggar, J.Kinnaird, I.Brown. 4th June 2007.
An excellent route on the northern of the two Island Walls, with a dramatic finish. Climbs the broad rib at the south end of the north wall, accessed from

either the right (descent gully) or the left. The rib is easy at first, but don't miss the dramatic finish, stepping left into a corner and hanging off the flying arete.

Crammag Head, Lighthouse Walls:
Note: J.Biggar climbed *Little Flasher* (1999) in summer 1996. It was named *Marine Boy*, Hard Severe.

Lighthouse Walls, Seaward Wall & Hourglass Slab:
This fine slab lies west of the lighthouse and is best reached by an easy scramble down the wall opposite it. The first routes lie on the seaward face.

Reach for the Moon   15m   Difficult **. S.Baxendale, S.Reid, J.Biggar. 14th February 2008.
The obvious groove is juggier than it looks and gives a fine pitch through bulges on huge holds.

Ascents of Porpoise   15m   Difficult *. S.Reid, J.Biggar, S.Baxendale. 14th February 2008.
The broken arete to the right of the groove, stepping left onto the jutting prow at the top.

Grooved Arete   12m   Severe **. J.Biggar, S.Reid, S.Baxendale. 14th February 2008.
Start just right of the arete at the right end of the Seaward Wall and climb a crack to a ledge, then the slim groove in the arete above.

Heart of the Matter   10m   Hard Severe *. S.Reid, J.Biggar, S.Baxendale. 14th February 2008.
Climb a short grey wall on jugs to a large ledge and junction with Santa's Little Helper. Climb the groove on the right, to a junction with Hourglass Slab then traverse delicately left above the roof.

The next routes start from the gully, under a hanging shield of rock above the left-leaning groove/roof of Bully Beef.

Brief Encounter   7m   Mild Severe. S.Reid, J.Biggar, S.Baxendale. 14th February 2008.
The fault up the left side of the shield.

Short Affair   7m   Very Difficult. J.Biggar, S.Baxendale, S.Reid. 14th February 2008.
The fault up the right side of the shield.

STIRLING AREA:
Kips Crag, Menstrie (NS 84763 97230)   Alt 80m   South facing
5 mins from road, fast drying, sound rock, max. height 8m.
Approach: From the A91 go up Park Road and turn left on Ochil Road to park near the Scout Hall and just before old bridge. Walk across bridge and turn right

up concrete path to gain hill. A few minutes leads to crag on left. Most routes were soloed by K.V. Crocket excepting Left Edge (KVC), Rancho Rib and Beinn's Buttress (R. Anderson) and BB Direct (T. Prentice). Some slabby rock further left provides a few more climbs. Grades are approximate. Do not use fence for belays as this may incur some Water Board's wrath.

For details of routes see photodiagram opposite page 145.

ROSYTH QUARRY:
Briggy Pop   8m   HVS 5b. G.Seggie, S.Burns. 11th September 2007.
Start at the 'Briggy' graffiti between If Pigs Could Fly and The Stinking Swordsman.
Climb the obvious flake-crack to pop rightwards to a juggy finish.
Note: *Pogo Groove* has been removed from the new guide due to rockfall. It's actually still there; the rockfall was further left.

FIFE, The Hawkcraig:
Five o'clock Shadow Arete   11m   HVS 5a. J.Dyble, B.Hay, S.Macfarlane. June 2007.
Start in the alcove at the bottom of Shadow Corner and climb directly up the arete on the right side of the variation of Flake and Wall. Don't step onto the top of the flake to the left or use the crack of Flake and Wall variation. Udge upwards using the deep crack on the right wall of the arete then follow a series of great but blind moves on the right.

BERWICKSHIRE, The Brander:
Note: N.Harris notes that the numbers on the diagram on Lowland Outcrops p425 have been reversed (the key and text are correct).

STOP PRESS

BEN NEVIS,   East aspect of Tower Ridge, about 1100m alt.:
Echo Wall ****   100m 'Harder than Rhapsody' D. MacLeod. 28th July 2008.
A spectacular route taking the huge sharp arête of Echo Wall, well seen from Tower Ridge or when ascending Observatory Gully. Poorly protected in general with groundfall potential at 20m near the end of the crux section.

1. 30m Climb easy slabs to a belay at the foot of the grossly overhanging arête of the buttress.
2. 70m Pull into an overhung groove and exit this with immediate difficulty. A hard and poorly protected boulder problem leads to the roof and an upside down rest. (wires, poor camalot 6). Pull leftwards over the roof with desperate climbing up the wall just right of the arête to a shakeout (RP & Skyhook in suspect rock). Move left to the arête and make very serious moves up this to a good spike and reasonable gear. Continue with more ease up the arête (runout) to a small ledge (drop your left hand rope to relieve drag). Continue up steep flakes in a great position to gain easy ground and a short solo to reach Tower Ridge.

MISCELLANEOUS NOTES

The W.H. Murray Literary Prize

As a tribute to the late Bill Murray, whose mountain and environment writings have been an inspiration to many a budding mountaineer, the SMC have set up a modest writing prize, to be run through the pages of the Journal. The basic rules are set out below, and will be reprinted each year. The prize is run with a deadline, as is normal, of the end of January each year. So, assuming you are reading this in July, you have, for the next issue, six months in which to set the pencil, pen or word processor on fire.

The Rules:

1. There shall be a competition for the best entry on Scottish Mountaineering published in the *Scottish Mountaineering Club Journal*. The competition shall be called the 'W.H. Murray Literary Prize', hereafter called the 'Prize'.

2. The judging panel shall consist of, in the first instance, the following: The current Editor of the *SMC Journal*; The current President of the SMC; and two or three lay members, who may be drawn from the membership of the SMC. The lay members of the panel will sit for three years after which they will be replaced.

3. If, in the view of the panel, there is in any year no entry suitable for the Prize, then there shall be no award that year.

4. Entries shall be writing on the general theme of 'Scottish Mountaineering', and may be prose articles of up to approximately 5000 words in length, or shorter verse. Entries may be fictional.

5. Panel members may not enter for the competition during the period of their membership.

6. Entries must be of original, previously unpublished material. Entries should be submitted to the Editor of the *SMC Journal* before the end of January for consideration that year. Contributions should preferably be word-processed and submitted via e-mail, although double-spaced typewritten hard copies will also be accepted. (See Office Bearers page at end of this Journal for address etc.) Any contributor to the SMC Journal is entitled to exclude their material from consideration for the Prize and should so notify the Editor of this wish in advance.

7. The prize will be a cheque for the amount £250.

8. Contributors may make different submissions in different years.

9. The decision of the panel is final.

10. Any winning entry will be announced in the *SMC Journal,* and will be published in the *SMC Journal* and on the SMC Web Site. Thereafter, authors retain copyright.

THE W.H. MURRAY LITERARY PRIZE 2008

The winner of this year's W.H. Murray Prize for his article *A Tale of Dangerous Obsession* is first-time contributor Gordon Smith.

One of the stipulations of the W.H. Murray prize is that entries shall be writing on the general theme of 'Scottish Mountaineering'. The judges were happy to interpret this requirement in its broadest sense, for Gordon is a Scot even though his story is set in the French Alps. The tale of his dangerous obsession thirty years ago is also rather a long one, but it is extremely well told and holds the attention throughout. It proved an easy first choice. 'A racy, gripping, entertaining and very well written narrative of a clearly significant ascent.'

President Paul Brian said 'Smith's writing is just right – no hint of self-aggrandisement or hubris. There is something especially endearing about a writer who can describe such epic events in a light-hearted, almost humourless vein.' His style reminded the judges of his illustrious namesake: ...'drolly reminiscent of the Robin Smith classics, but ... tacitly acknowledging this heritage without aping it.' 'I like his "stream of consciousness" style (why am I reminded of that other Smith?) ...'

Also highly commended was Guy Robertson for his story *For Our Eyes Only*. Guy is a previous winner as well as a top-notch climber, and he gives here a thrilling account of an ascent of Centurion in extraordinary winter conditions. Paul Brian was present on that dark and wild February afternoon, sheltering in the lee of the CIC Hut: 'I clearly remember peering up through the clouds of wind-driven sleet at two figures high on the crag and thinking, "What on earth can it be like up there?" Now I know – and I'm greatly impressed! I particularly enjoyed the debacle with the headtorch and absent compass. It shows that even the hotshots get it wrong sometimes.'

One of the mysteries surrounding the WHM Prize is how is it that in its ten year history it has not been awarded to Iain Smart? Iain's stories are always interesting and extremely well written and few in recent years have produced writing of such consistently high standard. He delights us again with his tale *By the Way*. 'An imaginative and charming fantasy, slightly reminiscent of Eric Linklater's much more scary short story *Sealskin Trousers* ... in its handling of its supernatural element.'

Also a favourite with the judges was *A Ghost of Christmas Past* by first-time contributor Graeme Morrison, '...clearly the work of a fine writer.' His turning away of a couple from the Club's haven on Ben Nevis results in a troubled dream that weaves together snippets of past and future events on the mountain.

Special mention must also be made of Mike Jacob's scholarly and well crafted account of *Harold Raeburn – the Final Journey*. This is a fascinating piece of research into the sad circumstances surrounding the final illness of one of the Club's most accomplished climbers.

Fatal Error by John Burns also struck a chord with our youngest judge – clearly in tune with the electronic age. Space precludes us mentioning some of the other worthy efforts.

In conclusion we extend our congratulations to Gordon Smith, and our commiserations and thanks to the other contributors. As ever the winning article can be read in full on the SMC Web Site as well as in the pages of this Journal.

SCOTTISH WINTER NOTES 2007/8

By Simon Richardson

THE IRREPRESSIBLE Andy Nisbet, our esteemed New Routes Editor, reckons that good winters come around every seven years. The 2007/8 season was the next one in his seven-year sequence and early indications were that it was going to be a good one. The season started as early as 18 September when an autumn snowfall gave the Cairngorms a fleeting taste of winter. Predictably, Nisbet was the man on the spot, and snatched a quick ascent of *Pygmy Ridge* (IV,5) on Coire an t-Sneachda with Jonathan Preston – possibly a record for one of the earliest winter ascents ever. Inevitably, conditions were very short-lived. The route thawed in the afternoon and was soloed in training shoes the day after.

Last summer, several leading winter activists predicted that this winter season would be something special. There is now so much interest in mixed routes and Scottish winter climbing in particular they argued, that standards would be driven higher as a greater number of people climb the top end routes. This prediction has proved to be exactly correct. Although the weather was rarely settled, and February had disappointing levels of snow cover, January and March were superb months for Scottish winter climbing with many teams pushing the boundaries and pioneering some excellent new routes.

It is a little unfair to single out a star performer, but Guy Robertson's two new Grade VIIIs and a Grade IX in the space of eleven days (*Sundance*, *Dawn Grooves* and *Slochd Wall*) was nothing short of breathtaking. Five years ago these three routes climbed over a lifetime would put you firmly in the top division of Scottish winter climbers, but for the current generation this level of activity is becoming commonplace. Scottish winter climbing is on a roll, so watch out next season for the likes of Parnell, Benson, Garthwaite, Ashworth, MacLeod, Turner and Small who I have no doubt will once again ascend a series of sensational climbs that will once again take our breath away.

Although there was considerable focus on climbing new routes, there were some noteworthy second ascents and early repeats too. Notable examples include *Enigma* (VII,7) on Mainreachan Buttress by Malcolm Bass and Andy Brown, *Sioux Wall* (VIII,8) on Ben Nevis by Steve Ashworth and Tim Blakemore, *Genesis* (VII,7) on Beinn Bhan by Martin Moran, Alex Moran and Nick Carter), *Haystack* (VI,7) on An Teallach by Moran and Carter and *Centurion* (VIII,8) on Ben Nevis by Guy Robertson and Pete Benson.

BEN NEVIS:

The most intense activity took place on Ben Nevis, which had one of its most significant seasons in its history. The first big news was in early December when Andy Turner, Steve Ashworth and Viv Scott made the first ascent of *The Secret*. This steep crack-line slicing the right wall of Number Three Gully had been stared at by Nevis mixed climbers for a number of years, but its unremitting steepness and apparent lack of footholds meant that most looked at it in disbelief. Turner's three-hour lead of the 40m crux pitch was a Scottish winter climber's dream – an on-sight first ascent of a cutting edge winter-only line at the first attempt.

Situated high up in Coire na Ciste, The Secret is fully exposed to the blast of northerly winds and quickly becomes rimed and coated white with hoar frost and snow. In contrast to many other top Scottish winter routes that require specific conditions and several seasons patient waiting, The Secret comes into condition fast and was a clear target for a quick repeat. So it was no surprise the next time the wall was hoared later that month, it was attempted by another very strong team in the shape of Ian Parnell, Guy Robertson and Mark Garthwaite. Their ascent went without a glitch with Garthwaite quickly despatching the difficult entry pitch and Parnell taking the honours with a smooth lead of the long crux crack.

Inevitably, the relative ease of the second ascent led to some discussion about the grade. After some deliberation, based on their experience of many top-rated Scottish ascents, the first ascent party decided on X,10 for their climb, but the second ascensionists thought that the route was somewhat easier. The second ascent trio are all known to be tough graders, but they also have a vast amount of experience climbing routes at the upper spectrum of the Scottish game, and the route has now settled down at VIII,9. The team was full of praise for Andy's lead stating that The Secret is one of the finest winter pitches they have ever climbed. Undoubtedly The Secret's quality and readiness to come into condition means that it will become established as one of the Scotland's most sought after mixed test-pieces.

In January, Ashworth and Turner were pushing the envelope once again with the very impressive line of *Storm Trooper*, which takes the wall and narrow tapering ramp right of Darth Vader on Creag Coire na Ciste. They spotted the line the day they climbed The Secret in December, attempted it the very next day, and returned at the next opportunity on 8 January. This time Turner took a more direct line up a shallow groove to gain the ramp, which turned out to be harder and less well protected than the original way. Following the intense grading debate after their ascent of The Secret, they rather conservatively rated the climb VIII,8, but there is no question that the route is at the upper end of its grade.

Later in the month, Dave MacLeod and Michael Tweedley visited Ben Nevis with their eyes set on a steep unclimbed chimney-line to the left of The Minge on South Trident Buttress. A large icicle-fringed roof barred progress, and after bombarding Tweedley with several huge icicles, MacLeod pulled over this only to be stopped by an overhanging wall above. Fortunately, an exposed traverse led left into the upper corner of 1944 Route that made an excellent finish to the appropriately named *Under Fire* (VII,7).

Unfortunately the promise of a superb February was short-lived. There was a superb spell of dry and windless weather through the middle two weeks of the month, but a deep thaw had stripped the cliffs a couple of days before the settled weather arrived, so only the highest corries were in condition. Most of the activity centred on Ben Nevis, where it was the classic lines such as *Good Friday Climb*, *Glover's Chimney*, *White Line*, *Central Gully Right-Hand* and *The Cascade* that saw most of the traffic. The enterprising, and talented French team of Julien Desecures and Arnaud Guillaume were the only climbers who consistently ventured onto the harder routes, and they made efficient ascents of *Satanic Verses*, *Psychedelic Wall* and *Albatross* on Indicator Wall in very thin conditions. Several other parties climbed Satanic Verses, but all drew the line at climbing Albatross, that was in difficult mixed condition and probably two grades harder than last season, when it was draped in thick ice.

Fortunately in early March the weather turned wintery again. Heavy early snowfalls brought several of the lower routes on the Ben into condition, and the classic Grade III *South-West Ridge* of the Douglas Boulder saw well over a dozen ascents. This easily accessible mixed climb is a good choice in poor conditions although the grade is a little sporting and IV,5 may be a more realistic rating. Just to its left, Rich Bentley and Mark Davies made a winter ascent of the summer VS *Walking Through Fire* to give a tricky VII,7. An excellent long pitch up a groove defines the route, but the tricky part is reaching it. There was 'one iffy move away from a tiny RP under a flake, that would have probably ripped, to get established in the groove,' Rich reported, 'and if you come off you're going for a big swing!'

A few days later, Iain Small and I climbed *The Survivor* (VII,8), the groove system on the left side of Number Three Gully Buttress. This prominent line had escaped the recent intense development elsewhere on the buttress, and is characterised by a large niche. This is so overhung that it rarely catches much snow, but the continuous bad weather in early March meant it was well hoared. Staring up at the niche after the first pitch I was not sure that the line was going to go, because the capping roofs looked blank and the vertical back corner of the niche itself was lined with a thin and unstable flake. Iain made a virtuoso lead, climbing protectionless up the flake to avoid disturbing it, before pulling left across the blank wall along a hidden horizontal crack. The pitch above provided more steep and sustained climbing that was greatly assisted by hard névé on every ledge and flat hold to give sinker placements.

A week later I was back with Roger Webb to take advantage of more hard snow conditions. We set our sights on the unclimbed buttress between Abacus and Maelstrom on the West Face of Observatory Ridge, but unfortunately a short thaw had lifted the snow-ice from the rock resulting in a very tenuous expedition. In more amenable conditions *The Frozen Chosin* will provide a good VI,6 icy mixed outing.

The climb of the day however, was the first free ascent of *Don't Die of Ignorance* by Dave MacLeod and Joe French on the front face of The Comb. Andy Cave and Simon Yates first climbed this route in February 1987, which is based on the great hanging groove to the right of the crest of the buttress. A huge overhanging wall prevents direct access to the groove, so they used aid to traverse right along a wide break from the foot of Tower Face of the Comb. Their ascent was graded VI,6 and A2 and has not been climbed since, although in 2001 Andy Nisbet and Chris Dale repeated the traverse pitch to reach a second corner-line further right. They named their route The Flying Groove (VI,6) after Nisbet took a big fall from the main corner. Dave MacLeod is clearly inspired by this part of the mountain. In 2005 he added the difficult summer climb Anubis (E8) to the crest of The Comb, and the next project on his agenda was a free ascent of the original line of Don't Die of Ignorance.

MacLeod had failed to free the route for the fifth time just two days earlier, so this was his sixth attempt: 'I was back once again, staring at that grim undercut crack disappearing round the prow into no man's land,' he recounted on his blog.

'I desperately struggled to seat my axe in the crux tin opener. I screamed to Joe to expect a fall and released my left axe, cutting loose onto one arm. The axe slid and jerked a centimetre. My heart missed a beat and the jolt nearly made me fall, my hand sliding down the upside down axe to the head and rolling onto three fingers. A dynamic match and kung fu [move] allowed one foot to swing onto the wall to the right and up to the peg I got in on Friday. The vertical wall above was climbed in an utterly 'go for broke' style, axes ripping, dropping onto one hand and gasping with pump and shrieking for slack.'

With the crux in the bag, the rest of the route should have been a formality, but French took over two hours to second the traverse, and by the time he reached the belay MacLeod was suffering severely from the cold. Two pitches of rapid climbing up the hanging groove and then easier climbing up the upper crest of The Comb saw the pair reach the plateau well into the night with the hardest technical winter climbing ever done on Ben Nevis below them. MacLeod graded their free version of the route XI,11, the same grade he gave to his winter ascent of The Hurting in Coire an Lochain in the Cairngorms, which he climbed last season.

The final new addition in March was by Ian Parnell on the left wall of Winter Chimney on Number Three Gully Buttress. Several teams had probed this short, but very difficult line, so it was no surprise that it was a technical and tenuous climb. There was 'an extremely bold central section with lots of ground fall possibilities and almost no gear before a steep gymnastic finish,' Ian told me later. 'It turned out to be a very intense three-hour lead, and the boldest winter route I've done so far.' Parnell graded the ominous sounding *Snuff Wall* a rather conservative VIII,8 commenting that better ice on the central section may make it a little less serious.

Cool northerly winds persisted through most of April and headline news was a winter ascent of *Subtraction* on the Minus Face by Guy Robertson and Viv Scott. This summer E1 climbs grooves on the right side of Minus Two Buttress, before crossing Minus One Gully, to finish up a steep impending 5b groove on the left flank of Minus One Buttress. As the most difficult climb on the Minus Face, the route has a certain cachet as a rock climb, and a winter ascent has been discussed for over twenty years. Since the lower section of the climb approximately coincides with the Grade V winter route Minus Two Buttress, the main challenge in winter was thought to centre on the difficulty of the final groove.

It has been several years since Minus Two buttress has been fully iced, and Robertson and Scott found this section to be in challenging mixed condition. Scott made a bold lead of the first pitch, which was technically sustained and only marginally protected. The second pitch was also technically hard, and a little steeper, although the gear was at least adequate. Unfortunately, by the time they had climbed these two pitches, the upper groove had stripped in the morning sun, so they finished up Minus Two Gully. Their climb provided sustained VIII,8 climbing, but I'm sure that Guy and Viv will be the first to admit that a full winter ascent of Subtraction is still on the cards.

Iain Small and I were lucky enough to realise that the late March north-westerly storms had lined some of the mountain's north-facing grooves with good ice. This crucial information allowed us to make the first ascent of the pronounced rib between Archangel and South Sea Bubble on Coire na Ciste. Only a centimetre-thick trickle of ice had formed on the left wall of the impending lower groove, but this was enough for Iain to place his picks sideway in the ice. Above, a steep overhanging Y-shaped crack led to the very exposed upper rib with another overhanging crack to finish, resulting in a fine VIII,8. The following weekend, Iain made another thin ice lead up *Last Tango* (VII,8), the deep corner and hanging groove right of the icy slab of Quickstep on Number Three Gully Buttress. This looked like the end of the season, but incredibly the cool weather held on for another week, prompting Andy Cave and I to climb *Techno Wall* (V,6), a direct line between Goodytwoshoes and The Borg Collective on the front face of Goodeve's Buttress.

Elsewhere in the Central Highlands, the pace was less frantic, although there were some good additions on Aonach Mor spearheaded by Andy Nisbet and friends. Mike Pescod and Donald King paid a visit to cliffs at the head of Gleann a'Chaolais in the Ballachulish Horseshoe at the west end of Glen Coe where they found *Peekabo*, a two-pitch VIII,8, and Iain Small and I climbed *Blackbeard* (VII,8), the steep right arête of the Chandelle Wall on Raw Egg Buttress on Aonach Beag.

SKYE

A sure fire sign of a good winter is when new routes are climbed on Skye. Local expert Mike Lates was the most active with ascents of *MacLaren's Lament* (V,6) with M. Francis on Blaven, and *Eilidh's Ceilidh* (V,7) and *Grand Diedre* (VI,6) in Coir' a' Ghrunnda with Pete MacPherson and Graham Briffett. Grand Diedre is a daunting summer VS, but was in superb winter climbing condition in January. 'I headed up the first pitch expecting it to be the crux,' Pete told me, 'but found great hooks in the crack at the back of the corner all the way. On the right wall of the corner there was very helpful icy rime, which took a mono[point] just nicely. If there wasn't any icy rime on that wall the pitch would have been a lot harder!'

But it was Guy Robertson and Mark Garthwaite who stole the show with their first winter ascent of *Dawn Grooves* (VIII,8) on Sgurr Mhic Choinnich. 'We thought a summer VS would maybe give us a VI or VII,' Guy recalled afterwards, 'so we were slapped in the face a bit! It was a very sustained route, with superb climbing all the way. I was pretty chuffed with our ascent – we didn't hang about. There was a pitch of 6, three of 7 and two of 8, all of them were very sustained, so eight hours was rapid enough. That's the great thing about climbing in January – it puts a spring in your step!'

Several teams enjoyed a traverse of the *Cuillin Ridge* over the Easter period. This great prize normally involves at least one bivouac, although a couple of teams managed it in a day. Most impressive was Steve Ashworth who made a solo traverse in 9 hours 7 minutes. This is almost certainly a winter record, and now Steve has stated a precise time, it throws down the gauntlet for other teams to attempt the traverse, and perhaps complete it in even faster times.

NORTHERN HIGHLANDS

In early January, Guy Robertson and Ian Parnell made a winter ascent of *Sundance* (VIII,8), a summer E2 that takes a steep corner-crack in the centre of the Far East Wall of Coire Mhic Fearchair on Beinn Eighe. 'Sundance is a contender for best mixed route in Scotland,' Guy told me afterwards. 'It's on a par with the likes of Vertigo Wall and Fhidhleir's Nose. Truly outstanding climbing – thin and delicate, then pumpy and intimidating on pitch two (probably the crux), then super-sustained and utterly sensational on pitch three. This was one of the most 'out there' pitches I've done in Scotland in winter – there was a ten-metre Damoclean fang hanging over the final lip which proved vital for the feet pulling round and up to the belay.' The matter-of-fact nature of Robertson and Parnell's ascent was breathtaking. Sundance was a well-known winter objective by Beinn Eighe winter devotees, but its unremitting steepness had deterred any previous attempts.

A quick thaw towards the end of the third week in January stripped many of the buttress routes in the Cairngorms and Central Highlands, but fortunately the warm air did not penetrate much further north than Inverness and the North-West escaped more or less unscathed. The forecast was cool and cloudy for the weekend, which prompted Roger Webb and I to attempt a winter ascent on Pillar Buttress of A' Mhaidghean in the Fisherfield Forest, considered by many to be Scotland's remotest Munro. Tactics were all important for this venture because the route faces south-west and strips in the sun, so a cloudy day with snow showers was ideal. The buttress is not only situated a long way from the road, but it is also tricky to get to from below, and the approach over the summit followed by an abseil down an adjacent gully took over nine hours. The effort was worth it because the six-pitch route up the crest of the buttress was one of the finest either of us had ever done. We topped out at 1 a.m. in the morning and it wasn't until midday that we made it back to the car after a 30-hour round trip. *The Great Game* (VII,7) will probably only ever be repeated by the most fanatical connoisseurs of Scottish winter climbing, but we were not the only people climbing on the remote Letterewe Estate that day. Alex Runciman and partner made a rare ascent of *North Summit Buttress* (III) on the wild and lonely North Face of Beinn Lair.

Two weeks it was cold in the North-West once again, and Martin Moran and Tim Blakemore visited Coire na Feola on Beinn Bhan and scored a notable coup with the first ascent of *Suspense Wall* (VII,7), the impending cliff to the right of Suspense Gully. This large section of cliff was free of routes and highlights the vast potential for technical exploratory climbing in the North-West away from the prominent lines. Moran returned to Beinn Bhan a couple of days later with Andy Nisbet, and climbed the wall right of Great Overhanging Gully. *The Green Giant* (VI,8) starts up the lower section of The Chimney to bypass the steep lower wall, before following the turfy open gully topped by a difficult, but well protected wall. A few weeks later, Guy Robertson and Dave MacLeod found the spectacular *Outrage* (VII,7) that breaks right from half way up Gully of the Gods and takes the obvious fault line in the right edge of the right wall of the easier upper gully.

In early March, Malcolm Bass and Simon Yearsley added to their collection of superb new routes in the North-West with the first winter ascent of *Morning Wall* (VII,8) on the Far East Wall in Coire Mhic Fhearchair on Beinn Eighe. Although innocuously graded VS in summer, the route had seen off at least one attempt from a strong team. Just to the south, Pete MacPherson, Roger Webb and Graham Briffett made a five-hour approach into the remote Beinn Dearg

Mor where they climbed a turfy fault-line on the left side of Central Buttress. The expedition entailed an 18hr round trip to the car, and the 200m-high route was appropriately named *Long Wednesday* (VI,6). More long approaches were made in to the lonely North Face of Beinn Lair where Andy Nisbet soloed the first winter ascent of the 400m-long *Tower Ridge* (III) and Adrian Dye, Sonya Drummond and Matt Griffin climbed *Breaking into Heaven* (III) which takes the buttress to the left. Nisbet made an opportunistic late season visit on 19 April and climbed *Marathon Gully* (III), the deep and narrow twisting feature tucked into the right side of Marathon Ridge.

CAIRNGORMS:

Incredibly, the ever-popular Northern Corries continue to provide new routes. In November, Andy Nisbet and Jonathan Preston teamed up with Martin Moran to climb *Circumvent* (V,7), the steep attractive-looking groove between the big corner of Inventive and the grooves of Adventure on No. 1 Buttress in Coire an Lochain. Later in the season, Andy Nisbet and John Lyall found *Cyber Space* (V,6) up the rib between Ventilator and Chute Route, and M. Walker, A. Gilmore and R. Rosedale made a winter ascent of *Swallow-tail Pillar* (VII,8) on No. 4 Buttress. Andy Nisbet also continued to develop the crags lining the northern end of the Lairig Ghru with John Lyall, Sandy Allan and others, and added a string of routes on Lurcher's Crag and Sròn na Lairig. This area is already becoming known as a worthwhile middle-grade alternative to the Northern Corries, and *Credibility Crunch* (V,7) and *Arctic Monkey* (III,4) look to be amongst the pick of this year's crop.

Roger Webb and I hit it lucky in Garbh Choire Mor on Braeriach. The far left branch of *Bunting's Gully* was probably one of the last remaining unclimbed gullies in the Cairngorms, but an overhanging cave defends its base. The secret to success was a dribble of ice down the right wall that gave 15m of one-notch placements in perfect squeaky ice before gaining the sanctuary of the upper gully above. This pitch felt like a harder version of the crux of Minus One Gully on the Ben, and we graded the route VI,6.

Pete Benson and Ross Hewitt made a couple of good early season additions to Beinn a'Bhuird on the eastern side of the Cairngorms. In Coire na Ciche they made a winter ascent of *The Grinder* (VII,8) on the left end of the crag. This summer E1 put up a strong fight despite having only one main pitch. 'The cracks were very iced which required a lot of clearing to get some dubious pro, which otherwise would have been bomber,' Pete told me. 'I felt trashed five days after the ascent, largely I think due to hanging in stress positions to clear snow.' Their second route, *Commando Direct* (VI,6), was in the more remote Garbh Coire Mor, and was based on a direct line up Commando Route finishing up the buttress taken by West Side Story.

The big event in the Cairngorms was the first winter ascent of *Slochd Wall* (IX,8) on the West Face of Mitre Ridge on Beinn a'Bhuird by Guy Robertson and Pete Benson in January. A winter ascent of this summer HVS had been the subject of considerable speculation over the years, and was clearly going to provide a very technical climb on the most remote of the great Cairngorms crags. 'It was quite a route, and quite a day,' Robertson enthused afterwards. 'The track was heavily iced, and it took us four and [a] half hours to walk in. The climbing was brilliant, but hard; not super-strenuous, but very sustained, technical, tenuous and runout in places. Conditions probably weren't optimal – there wasn't much hoaring, but it was very snowy, icy and verglassed. Pete resorted to a rest on the second pitch, primarily to excavate a decent runner, then he lowered down and led it clean. Having finally got established above the overhang, he couldn't find anything more than an old bolt stub, which he promptly threaded! It turned out that the nut he dug out was the only decent runner between the overhang and the belay. Scary stuff, and a rather gripping lead.'

Equally impressive was John Lyall's lightning visit to Garbh Choire Mor on Braeriach in February. He soloed eleven routes including the classic *Vulcan* (V,4), a new line to the right of Daddy's Gone-a-Hunting, and second ascents of *Liaisons Dangereuses* (V,6), *Comanche* (V,5) and *Custer Corner* (IV,4) and newly-added *Far Left Branch* to Bunting's Gully. Incredibly, he was back at the car, having notched up a season's worth of routes on one of Scotland's remotest cliffs, after a mere eight hours!

Checking the plans for the new extension at the CIC Hut, June 2008.
L to R: George Bruce (Health and Safety), Brian McDermott (Stonemason), Paul Brian (The Club President). Photo: Noel Williams.

MOUNTAIN RESCUE COMMITTEE OF SCOTLAND
INCIDENT REPORT 2007

This report is only an interim one as details of some incidents have still to be submitted by teams. Please note also that some of the past year's figures have changed due to late reporting and corrections of previous inaccuracies.

Table 1: Mountaineering incidents

Year	Incidents	Fatalities	Injured	No Trace	Persons Assisted
2007	317	19	140	3	496
2006	315	29	155	1	469
2005	319	27	168	5	449
2004	311	18	160	1	424
2003	289	19	151	3	394

Table 2: Non-mountaineering incidents

Year	Incidents	Fatalities	Injured	No Trace	Persons Assisted
2007	125	29	29	12	125
2006	106	21	31	3	117
2005	118	16	28	12	124
2004	84	17	14	3	79
2003	99	15	24	14	100

Mountaineering 2007
I am still awaiting a few incidents from one of the major teams for 2007. Despite this mountaineering fatalities are down by 33%. Reasons for this could be the extremely mild winter and wet summer keeping people off the mountains. Teams are now reporting standbys and 'talk downs' off the hill; this is happening a lot more often as mobile phone coverage improves. It seems expected that casualties can now 'phone a friend', the local Mountain Rescue Team Leader, and get talked to safety. The Data Protection Act has made it extremely difficult to gain information on casualties; names cannot be released without permission.

Non-Mountaineering 2007
Teams are now involved more in non-mountain searches for vulnerable persons. These are mainly searches for the elderly, many with dementia, and vulnerable persons who go missing from home or nursing homes.

IT Update
There is now an updated version of the software programme used to collate details of incidents. This system was designed by Ged Feeney the Statistician for Mountain Rescue in England. It has been used by the MRC of S for recording Scottish incidents since 2002. This is a bespoke programme that Ged has given at no cost! He has now incorporated the SMC Areas into the reporting system. This still has a few problems before we can implement it with the annual reports.

Kinlochewe Hotel, SMC Easter Meet 1899. Photo: SMC Archives
The same venue, SMC Easter Meet 2008. : Photo A. Staddon.

MRC of S Archives at the Scottish Library
The Statistics from 1964-2005 are now held in the Scottish Library in Edinburgh with all the other Mountaineering Archives. This means that Stats will be available for future generations. Anyone seeking access to these documents will have to gain permission through the MRC of S.

Doctor Bob Sharp has compiled a report on the Accident Statistics from 1964–2006, which is very interesting reading. A great deal of information is available from this. It can be viewed on the MRC of S website: www.mrcofs.org

The Future
My plan is to complete the database of all incidents, going back as far as the records began, making use of the SMC archives. At present I am processing from 1900–1945. This will be a huge undertaking, but with time it may be possible. This would give unique information on Mountain Rescue and mountain accidents for future generations. Imagine the possibility in a major search, with the Search Manager, of being able to see where casualties have been found since the Statistics started? Some of the 'old and bold' are retiring and we must try to benefit from their experience and log information before it vanishes. It has taken nearly two years, with help from IT specialist Mike Walker and the Rescue Teams, trying to catch up with the lost incidents from the past. We are nearly there.

Please note
The MRC of S Statistics are copyright the MRC of S. The information may be reproduced free of charge, in any format or medium, for research, private study, or for internal circulation within an organisation. This is subject to it being reproduced accurately, and not used in a misleading manner. The material must be acknowledged as Mountain Rescue Committee of Scotland copyright, and the title of the publication specified.

D. 'Heavy' Whalley
MRC of S Statistician

100 YEARS AGO: THE CLUB IN 1908

THE 19TH Annual Meeting and Dinner took place on Friday 6 December 1907 in the Central Station Hotel, Glasgow, with John Rennie presiding. Treasurer Nelson announced a balance of £196 11s. 1d. which together with the Life Membership Fund brought the Club's total funds to £484 6s. 9d. Journal costs were 48% of total expenditure. Secretary Clark announced 9 new members, and Librarian Goggs reported that catalogues of the Library had been distributed and that four copies of the Slide Collection catalogue were available. At the Dinner, a silver tea-service was presented to William Douglas as a token of appreciation for his 'long-continued and heavy labours' on the *Journal*, and to prepare for his imminent marriage, brought about, as President Rennie indelicately put it, 'by an accident that happened in the cosy recesses of a balcony.'

The New Year Meet was held at the Alexandra Hotel, Fort William, and was attended by 27 members and 6 guests. The first arrivals, Charles Inglis Clark, Thomas Goodeve and John McIntyre, embarked on an ascent of Tower Ridge on Saturday 28th which went badly wrong, and culminated in a night of toil on what is now known as Raeburn's Wall, escaping to the summit by Hale Bopp route, or thereby, and then taking a tumble in Five Finger corrie. This ruined the sleep of the later arrivals who wandered the mountain looking for the 'lost sheep'. Raeburn eventually rounded them up and shepherded them down. This escapade is described at length by Clark in 'Thirty Hours on Ben Nevis' (*J*, 10, 73-81), and by McIntyre in his report of the Meet (*J*, 10, 112-119). Raeburn had a busy Meet, climbing the Castle on the 30th with Ling and Harry Walker, a new route on the North Wall of Castle Ridge (alone) on the 31st, and a wintry ascent of the Great Ridge of Garbh Bheinn and descent of its North-East Buttress with Bell, Ling and Walker, accomplished with the use of the foot-ferry and bicycles, on New Year's Day. On the same day, a second ascent of the Castle was achieved by MacRobert, McDougall, Morrison and Macalister, who completed the route in darkness under the watchful eye of Naismith, waiting anxiously above.

Late January saw Nettleton and Naismith attempting ski-mountaineering in the Wildstrubel area, the Clark family visiting the Black Forest runs, and Wm. Douglas, perhaps on honeymoon, sampling Norwegian ski-ing near Bergen – marking the start of a persistent aberration amongst our members.

The Easter Meet of 36 members and 15 guests (probably the largest Meet of the Club until the 1997 Yacht Meet) was held at the Fife Arms, Braemar, with a subsidiary Meet of 10 members and 8 guests at Tyndrum. Secretary Clark had laid on extraordinary facilities: a breakfast car on the Aberdeen-Ballater train on Friday 17th; shooting brakes at Ballater to Alltnaguibhsaich and Glassalt; daily carriages to and from Callater and Derry Lodge, and the use of the latter; a Grand Dinner to which all local factors were invited, etc. Weather conditions, however, were very wintry, with deep snow, bitter frosts and blizzards, and little was accomplished beyond lengthy traverses of the tops, apart from the ascent of Black Spout Buttress by Goodeve, Ling and Raeburn – strangely counted as a summer ascent in guidebooks. At Tyndrum, a large party climbed the Couloirs of Stob Gabhar, finding old steps made by Raeburn's mixed party (Mr and Mrs J. Bell, Ruth Raeburn and Ling) a few weeks before. While all this was going on, idle hands Jane and Mabel Inglis Clark together with Lucy Smith, met at a boulder near Lix on Saturday 18th, and founded the Ladies Scottish Climbing Club.

On 8 June, Leslie Shadbolt and Alastair McLaren (not yet members) climbed the long chimney left of Ossian's Cave which bears Shadbolt's name. In mid-June Francis Greig travelled to Glen Brittle along with P.C. Morris, W. Boyd and A. Gibson, by steamer from Oban to Struan, and thence by chartered lugsail to Carbost. They stayed at Ewen Campbell's house where they were joined by S. Cumming, T. Crombie and H.C. Boyd. On the Cioch, Greig's party of three climbed the Cioch Nose, presumably the first ascent. The group enjoyed such good weather for two weeks that little else was done beyond indolent bathing and loafing. However, after a while, and with the dubious assistance of an ass, they set up a high camp in Coire na Creiche from which several good days' climbing was enjoyed. Their only other new climb, however, was Hidden Gully on Sgurr a' Ghreadaidh. Hugh Munro was also in Skye that month, and experienced the same frustrations as in 1906. Since John Mackenzie was engaged at Camasunary, and Robertson had employed young Rory Mackenzie at Sligachan, Munro – staying with Colin Phillip at Glenbrittle Lodge (who chose to paint) – had to make do once again with the Misses Prothero, nieces of Phillip, for guides. They managed Sgurr Mhic Coinnich, but his object of the Inaccessible Pinnacle was once again not attained. His bad luck continued in July, when he and William Garden, attempting a midnight ascent of the Carn an Fhidleir group from Blair, ran out of light sources on the top of An Sgarsoch, and had to give up Carn an Fhidleir. There were several other Club parties on Skye during the summer, but the only new route achieved was W.W. King's acrobatic ascent of the North Chimney of Bruach na Frithe, climbed in August with William and Mabel Inglis Clark. King overcame the crucial chockstone pitches by elaborate rope maneouvres. It is open to doubt whether this startling climb has ever been repeated (see *J*, 10, 225-6).

In the summer, members struggled with bad weather in Norway and the Alps, a repetition of 1907. Goodeve and Walker made the season's first traverse of the Grepon on 10 July. They then tackled Mont Blanc from the Tête Rousse cabane, where they were snowbound for two days. They had a deal of trouble with guides, losing one of their own to injury, and almost losing the other, who wandered over a cornice. Then they found three porters lost below the Vallot. Descent guided by SMC compasses brought the whole lot to safety. A week or so later, Ling and Raeburn traversed the Dent Blanche from the Mountet by the Viereselsgrat. Moving west, they made a complete east-west traverse of the Chardonnet before walking round to Montenvert and up to the Charpoua for a reverse traverse of the Drus, with a forced bivouac in a snowstorm on the descent of the Petit Dru – 'Thanks to double Shetlands, helmets and wool gloves, we were none the worse.' Edward Backhouse enjoyed the best weather of the season in the Paradiso group in September, climbing the north-west ridge of the Grivola and several other peaks in the group.

In September, Raeburn, Harry Macrobert (who was camping near the site of the present Hut), and David Arthur climbed the North Buttress of Carn Dearg (now 'Raeburn's Buttress'). After some exciting boulder-trundling on the finishing arête, – 'one block, over half a ton in weight . . caused a perceptible tremor to shake the whole of the great buttress' – Raeburn surmounted a final *mauvais pas* with considerable difficulty. Macrobert, allegedly quoting Kipling, described the vertical slabs on the right as falling 'as straight as a beggar can spit' into South Castle Gully. Macphee, in his 1936 Guide, described a method of avoiding this *mauvais pas* by traversing the steep slabs to a corner. However, modern guides since Marshall make no mention of this obstacle. Perhaps it has fallen off.

The Journals for the year featured Guide Book entries for all the Islands other than Skye. The entry for Arran is the most extensive, but perhaps the most interesting is Raeburn's description of the Shetlands, which contains information about local climbing traditions, sea-stack ascents, and so forth. Apparently Raeburn climbed a sea-stack himself, and reported the ascent in the *Zoologist* for April 1891, five years before he joined our Club. Apart from 'Thirty Hours on Ben Nevis', the more interesting articles 'A Cairngorm Climb' (Raeburn) and 'The Eastern Buttress of Coire Mhic Fhearchair' (Backhouse) dealt with events of 1907. Gilbert Thomson's dry piece 'Some Mechanics of the Rope and Axe' dealt impressively with rope problems such as crevasse rescue and holding falls, but his discussion of axe techniques provoked a long letter from Raeburn – an ambivalent mixture of endorsement and qualification.

Robin N. Campbell

SCOTTISH EAST GREENLAND EXPEDITION 1958

THIS IS the half centenary of Scottish East Greenland Expedition 1958, the first of the many to the Stauning Alps from Scotland and specifically from the SMC.

Greenland was just beginning to become affordable for summer expeditions. In the period of post-war development a mine had opened up at Mestersvig in Scoresby Land, two days walk from the mighty Staunings. The mine was serviced by an airstrip big enough to accept a mighty four-engined DC6.

Life was more casual fifty years ago. We landed at Reykjavik from Glasgow. The airport was completely open and unguarded. We slept and cooked in an open hangar beside a rudimentary terminal without let or hindrance. The next evening we boarded the venerable DC6. Icelandair had only the one aircraft. It was ex-American and had been rescued from a glacier where it had crash landed. During the day this rehabilitated plane flew passengers to Glasgow, London and/or Copenhagen, perhaps even Boston, Massachusetts. At night as many seats as necessary were taken out and it went on freight/passenger charter to East or West Greenland. We shared our charter to Mestersvig with Northmine, the international company extracting lead and zinc from below a hillside about 10 miles from the airstrip. The plane was loaded with whatever was necessary: equipment and personnel for the mine and us. As long as the door could close, loading criteria were met.

The plane lumbered off, eased itself off the runway just before the sea and flew sedately north, not very high up. I think it was struggling. For me it was a magic flight: the first site of pack ice, big mountains and unknown glaciers. We were young and romantic. Not many people got to Greenland in those days; it was all new and the bloom was still on the grapes of adventure. I know there was at least one air hostess, because I saw her sitting on the pilot's knee when the cabin door swung open. Ah, these were the days. We landed sedately at Mestersvig.

The Expedition was in two parts. While waiting for the fjord ice to clear, we relayed food over the Gefion Pass and made our first camp in the Skel Valley. Somehow we had carried over a big army bell tent. An unnecessary burden. We were inexperienced. From there we climbed some peaks. One morning Malcolm and I with difficulty forded the Skel River. In early July the water was high and the crossing dodgy. Having proven it was possible we all relayed food, tents and equipment to the upper Berserkerbrae, to a site we called Sun Valley. We climbed a few quite presentable mountains.

The next and main part was to travel to the head of Alpe Fjord which we reached in a small pram dinghy driven by a 5HP 'British Seagull' outboard.

We put in our major effort on the peaks of the Seftstroms glacier and, in the other direction, cross the Southern Staunings to the Inuit summer settlement at Syd Kap on Inner Scoresby Sound and finally to cross the central Staunings by the Col Major back to Mestersvig. These objectives were achieved

Malcolm Slesser was of course the leader and overall planner of the enterprise. Donald Bennet was the major organiser. The other members were Ken Bryan, Roddie Cameron, Len Lovat, Stan Paterson, Charlie Rose, Douglas Scott and Iain Smart.

Iain Smart

WINTER MOUNTAINEERING IN THE FALKLAND ISLANDS

As a MEMBER of the RAF you occasionally get detached to out of the way places. The Falklands Islands are one of these. It is a wonderful place and though the mountains are small, the highest just under 2500ft, they do have a great appeal for the climber. All the outcrops are of quartzite; almost everywhere the bedding is steeply inclined so almost all the outcrops in the Stanley area are slabby, Tumbledown being the exception. The first climbs were done in 1946 by members of the Falkland Islands Dependencies Survey, who were waiting at Stanley on their journey South. The Royal Marines based at Moody Brook until 1982 did a lot of exploration, and since the conflict many service climbers have enjoyed the Falkland experience – climbing on near virgin rock.

Many routes have been left unrecorded. Individuals have enjoyed discovering crags, and finding out for themselves what is climbable. Previous to my visit, only two routes were known to been have climbed in winter. One of these was by Stephen Venables en route to South Georgia in 1989 although little is known about it.

Most of the popular peaks under 1000ft were the scene of bloody battles during the 1982 conflict and are still littered with the remnants of those awful days. Minefields abound, too many to clear, giving a new meaning to the word, objective dangers! However they are well marked and fenced off. The military have built a road from the camp to the capital Stanley. This has a deep monsoon ditch on both sides of it which makes it an interesting drive in winter. It is often closed for the military due to blizzard conditions.

The Falklands has a unique weather system. It can contain all four seasons in one day and one must expect the unexpected, especially when walking or climbing alone. The weather, which originates in the Polar Regions can give exceptional climbing conditions very quickly. It can be fairly difficult finding a climbing partner though, because when winter comes few venture out of the Military complex in search of excitement.

When I was first detached to the Falklands in late March 1996, the 'Adastral winter' was just starting – my second winter that year. Most of my friends who had been out before were very vague about the possibilities of the 'winter experience' and they were of the general opinion that conditions never came in and any attempt at winter climbing was a complete waste of time. Therefore I took minimum kit and was prepared for the 'mother of all winters' with high winds, tons of snow and no ice. I should have known better.

I arrived and went down to the gymnasium, asking the usual questions about the hills and the potential for climbing on the Island and asking if I could borrow some kit. Unfortunately there was none available as there was no need for such specialised equipment and there was never any ice or snow worth climbing. In typical mountaineering tradition I decided to go out 'for a look' after all 'time spent in reconnaissance is seldom wasted'. Just outside the camp is Pleasant Peak which although only 700ft high gave an excellent but short scramble. The vegetated quartzite, full of cracks would be ideal for winter climbing, even for me! As luck would have it on the next aircraft came my good friend Graham Stamp. His climbing CV was extremely impressive; The North Face of the

Eiger, 8000m on the West Ridge of Everest and the Troll Wall in Norway. Unfortunately he was a very keen rock man who needed 'to develop' his winter skills. All we needed was some kit and one month later it arrived courtesy of the RAF Priority airfreight marked 'rescue equipment'.

The boys and I had been round the usual hills and the potential was incredible. Mount Harriet, which overlooks the Stanley road, is a magic wee hill. It has everything including a scramble up to the Memorial cairn on the summit. It was named after a sailing clipper in the 18th century. One line stood out on Mount Harriet a slab with a crack running down it, full of vegetation including big sponge-like plants – 'Balsam Bog'. These grow very well on the steep cliffs and when frozen give magnificent placements to the ice climber. The crack, though only 120ft high, would give excellent sport. By June winter was with us and I convinced Stampy and a new recruit, an Army Physical Training Instructor, to have a look. Stampy was not convinced that it would be worth the 20-minute walk in and the one-hour drive to Mount Harriet. Our main problem was that we only had one pair of crampons between us, one set of ice tools and my pair of size 9 plastic boots. It was really cold and the temperature was very low -15°C. As they were my boots it was my lead! Our friendly army chap was shown how to belay and Stampy laughed! The turf and Balsam Bog, growing in the crack was brilliant and 'bomb proof'. A steep corner led after 30ft to the main crack and a steep wall. I tried to get up the wall for over an hour but as usual it was well beyond me. Back on the ledge I was frozen and exhausted but saw a thin crack, which would just take axes, and I tried again – failure; I'd had enough and was lowered back to the belay.

Trying to change over boots and crampons in a blizzard and a gale is not easy; eventually we swapped kit and the great man Stampy set off. He was soon at the high point and blasted up the steep wall torquing on his axes – a few more delicate moves and some scrabbling about and he was up the crack. The weather had broken; it was wild, Stampy was laughing in the face of the gale, and the final chimney and wee chockstone were dealt with easily; he was up. The boots were lowered down along with the crampons and I set off up. The gear was taken out and on my usual tight rope, the route was superb. Stampy was belaying with no boots on and his feet were frozen solid. Old frostbite injuries were acting up and we bailed out. Tony our belayer was frozen solid as he had been belaying now for nearly 3 hours and never got to try any ice climbing! By now the gale was in full force and blowing from Patagonia. We ran back to our landrover for a nightmare drive back to camp on an ice-rink called a road. The road had been closed all day and we had some explaining to do and got the usual looks from everyone. What a great day – loads of fun – but my feet still suffer from the swapping of boots.

A few days later I got hold of a guidebook, which listed five winter routes including our line on Harriet. The guidebook stated Grotto 120ft IV *** an excellent, sustained and technically demanding route with magnificent hooking and torquing. Graded Very Severe in summer, it is a superb line. I returned again and completed the climb and managed to get a few photos on a brilliant day out.

I was detached again to the Falklands in winter 2000 and had my eye on a few more climbs. As usual transport was very difficult to obtain; nevertheless, I managed to get an old military vehicle, borrowed some snow chains and set off at first light for some fun. I had no partner but one of my friends on one of the satellite radar sites had promised to be my safety cover. If the worst occurred, 78 Sqn Seakings were friendly due to my mountain rescue background and promised they would come and look for me if I did not return by next morning.

The epic drive took over 2 hours, some of it done with no lights as the road was officially closed! By way of a wee bribe I managed to convince the police checkpoint that all was well. I had spotted some good lines on a mountain called Two Sisters; it was a long 5km walk in over rough ground. The cliff is over 200ft high, which is big for the Falklands, and set in splendid isolation. By now it was daylight and the views in the unpolluted air were magnificent, similar to the West Coast of Scotland – the mountains and the sea a superb combination.

Conditions were thin but the crack line had lots of vegetation and was frozen solid – perfect placements, a good grade III. This had been my first winter route since I had lost two great friends ice climbing on Lochnagar. I had even had a short break from the rescue team, the first for 27 years, as I sorted out my head and my feelings on mountaineering. Days like this are very rare; you have to grasp such opportunities when they arise. Every placement was perfect and I soon climbed the route and onto the ridge to the summit. Each summit in the Falklands has a memorial to those who died in the war; a reminder to all and a time to reflect. I had a quick break; it was only midday. I had plenty of time left so I moved on to Tumbledown. It meant a longer day but the weather was so special, I had to make the most of it.

All these small mountains where the battles were fought are so impressive. As I walked along the main ridge, it was hard to believe what had happened here, in such a peaceful and tranquil place. Many of the intricate bunkers and Sangars were built into the rocks and are still clearly evident, especially to a mountaineer's eye. There was to be no retreat from Tumbledown. I had read at great length various accounts of the battle and had a deep understanding of what had happened on this small hill. Having been a mountain rescue team leader at Lockerbie and numerous other horrific incidents, death and carnage are all too familiar to me. The Scots Guards had fought a long and bloody battle for Tumbledown and one could not fail to experience evocative thoughts in a situation such as this. The ground I was walking on was awful, broken by gullies, cliffs and peat hags. It would have been difficult enough to search for someone but to fight for each few feet; it is impossible to appreciate. The snow was falling again and drifting around the rocks but the weather was holding and I felt that there was some time left to fit in another climb.

I climbed an excellent line on the North Face. Again it was a short route, 150ft grade II/III. As I climbed to the summit the winter sun had dropped and I could see Stanley in the distance. The sunset was amazing and as a mark of respect and a thank you, I made time to clean the memorial plaque to those who had fallen on the cross on the summit. It was very hard to move away from this place and I spent considerable time here. I kept my crampons on for the descent; there was no need for a headtorch as the moon was sparkling. As the ground levelled I came across the remains of a field kitchen and lots of equipment left from the war. It was hard to imagine how the troops had lived and died in this place and how they felt as they waited in the waterfilled scrapes for a counter attack that never came. There was also a little cave built up into a shelter where the troops had eaten, again still strewn with kit. Feeling very alone on that cold winter night, I thought of those that had fought and died for this place and the futility of war. I had a long 2-hour walk across the moor; time to think on what had been an eventful day in those marvellous little mountains. Safely back at my wagon I was pleased that it started first time, the usual epic drive back to base and to the real world.

The Falklands in winter is a special place.

D. 'Heavy' Whalley

ARTHUR WALKER RUSSELL 1873–1967

ARTHUR Russell was the subject of very short obituary in our Journal,[1] for such is the common lot of those who live to great age. In view of his family's very generous donation of his Walking Diaries to our Archives in 2006,[2] it seems appropriate to give a more detailed account of his life, so far as it bears on our history, and to draw attention to the remarkable nature of his diaries. He was an important figure in the history of the Club, joining in 1896 and serving as Custodian of the Slide Collection and then Librarian in the early stages of these institutions. He also spent two periods on the Committee, the latter as Vice-President (1923–5). As his obituarist Bob MacLennan pointed out, he was the longest-surviving member of those who joined in the nineteenth century. He also made two important mountaineering contributions, described in his diaries, which I will come to later. Finally, he used his position as Law Agent for the National Trust for Scotland to see to it that important mountain groups such as the Glen Coe peaks were preserved for public use.[3]

Russell was the second child of Arthur Russell (1821–91) and Margaret Reid (1835–86). He had two sisters, Madeline and Margaret (who died in her early twenties), and a brother Robert (b. 1876). Russell Snr was a solicitor and Bank Agent based in Cupar, Fife. After school at Cupar and in Blackheath, London, young Arthur went to Edinburgh University to study law in 1890 and began his mountaineering career with an ascent of Ben Wyvis. In the years that followed, apart from the summer of 1892 which was spent in Italy, Russell kept mountaineering diaries. These were initially full of detail, and give a full picture of the infrastructure of nineteenth century mountaineering here – the carriages, trains, hotels, ferries and so forth, together with meticulously-recorded timings and expenses associated with each of these. Russell's mother died in 1886 and his father in 1891, so the orphaned children moved to live with their aunt Madeline Reid at Alburne Knowe, Markinch, and the early expeditions recorded in his diaries begin from there, usually with a train journey to Perth.

The diaries for 1891, 1893 and 1894 record walking tours. The 1891 tour – with David Reid, presumably a relative of his mother, and brother Robert (j. 1898) – left the train on 30 July at Dunkeld and proceeded on foot to Fort William via Loch Laggan, with stops at Blair, Dalwhinnie and Moy. After climbing Ben Nevis (one shilling for use of the Path) they walked on to Stronachlachar, with stops at Ballachulish and Inveroran. The tour ended in public transport: the steamer down Loch Katrine, the coach to Callander, and trains home. Hotel costs for the 8 nights came to £2 12s. 2d, and 162 miles were walked in 7 days (Sunday kept at Moy). The same party toured again in 1893. Leaving the train at Dunkeld again on 26 July, they walked to Dalwhinnie via Loch Rannoch and Loch Garry (Loch Ericht had not yet become the obstacle it

---

[1] *J* (1968) 24, 88–9. The obituary gives his birth year wrongly as 1864, crediting him with an outstanding 103 years. In a second mistake, an editorial note identifies a photograph of William Naismith as being Russell.

[2] See *J* (2007) 39, 629–30 for an inventory of these diaries.

[3] The story of these acquisitions is a long and complex one, and I will not attempt it here. My entry for Percy Unna in the *Oxford Dictionary of National Biography* (2004) gives the bare bones of the story, and offers references to other better sources.

is today) with a stop at the Bunrannoch Hotel and an ascent of Schiehallion. After walking on to Lynwilg, where they spent the Sunday, they traversed the Lairig Ghru (32 miles) to the Fife Arms in Braemar 'a comfortable and very good hotel, but of course decidedly expensive'. Next they climbed Lochnagar by way of Glen Callater, then down to the Dubh Loch and over the Mount road to Milton of Clova. On the following day after walking to Kirriemuir, they took the train back to Markinch. Hotel costs for 7 nights were £2 6s. 3d., and 145 miles were walked in 6 days. In 1894 he toured with Andrew Robertson Wilson (j. 1895), a medical student friend. Leaving the train at Comrie on 17 April, they traversed Ben Vorlich and Stuc a' Chroin to the Kingshouse Hotel. On the 18th they sent their luggage on to Tyndrum by train and traversed Stobinian and Ben More to Crianlarich, continuing to Tyndrum by train. The pair enjoyed a game of board-free chess on the summit of Stobinian, a pastime to which both were addicted. The tour continued with a traverse of Ben Lui to the Dalmally Hotel, a traverse of the Cruachan Range to Taynuilt Hotel, and a long cross-country walk through Benderloch to the Clachaig Inn, where Sunday was kept as usual with the exception of sinful chess, and the carving of mountain names on their walking sticks. They were 'immensely taken with' the Inn, 'splendid food, very comfortable and very moderate – board = 6s. per day.' Monday was occupied by an ascent of Bidean, and an attempt on Clachaig Gully. In deteriorating weather they walked to Dalmally with a stop at Inveroran, before returning to Edinburgh by train. Hotel costs for 9 nights were £3 1s 9d., and around 130 miles and 7 Munros were walked in 8 days.

From 1895 onwards, Russell's diaries record ordinary mountaineering expeditions, mostly day trips, or weekend, as well as longer holidays. These are too numerous to describe in any detail. His usual companions were Robert, Madeline, Andrew Wilson, Aleck Fraser (an actuary, j. 1895) and in later years our well-known member Frank Goggs. Goggs and Russell were both prodigious walkers, and it is no surprise that they enjoyed each other's company. His best-known mountaineering exploit is his first traverse of the Aonach Eagach ridge in 1895. He, Fraser and Wilson stayed at the Clachaig Inn from 1 to 14 August along with Madeline, and Annie Wilson (probably Wilson's sister). There is no published account of this traverse apart from a short confusing note by Fraser[4], so it is worth including Russell's account in full here. The exact dates of the ascents are indefinite, but must have been around the midpoint of the holiday.

Aonach Eagach was our next ascent, we three. We left the road about halfway between hotel and loch and slanted away up, took some time finding a crossing of a deep narrow gully; from here AF's photo of the ridge was taken, the summit and previous drops looking good. For our last several hundred feet we were in thick mist but on other side of ridge it was quite clear away north to Ben Nevis and the Mamore hills. The glimpses too across or through the mist to Bidean, Ossian's Cave and out to Rannoch Moor were very fine. The peculiar whiteness of the Mamore hills struck us. Played some chess and took some lunch on ridge before proceeding. We must have gained the ridge just a little beyond the west side of my photo of ridge as seen from Coire nam Beagh. An ascent to an intermediate summit and then a steepish descent with fairly precipitous sides on

---

[4] *J* (Jan. 1896) 4, 64. Fraser's later Guide Book entry in *J* (May 1902), 7, 108–9 is even more confusing, since it mis-identifies the Munro tops.

the south. Then we had to scramble up the big square looking block as seen on AF's photo above mentioned. Then came an abrupt descent. The eastmost side of this block is sheer, so also the south but there is a fair route though loose on its north side ending with a jump for a few feet on to a patch of grass a few feet square, the connecting point between two very steep and narrow stone shoots. Thence an ascent leads on to another descent or drop of 10 or 12ft fully; this is the second drop as seen in the photo. Then the final ascent, easier by keeping well towards the left. We built a small cairn on top. The descent from here to the 'Spooks' is pretty abrupt. ARW went down by keeping round to the north side of the ridge; we went straight down by a cleft using the rope for a handhold as the latter were not very visible. The 'Spooks' seemed too shaky and the descent was made by the big stone shoot, the west arm of which begins at the 'Spooks'. A distinctly rough stone shoot, ending in a smooth waterfall of almost 40ft. This was skirted by going round to our right, as the descent was steep and rocks very loose we roped up and got down all right, rope here was not essential but safe. Thence a series of windings back and forward at last brought us down to the road. We saw an eagle and 3 peregrine hawks while on ridge.

AF and I made another ascent of ridge before leaving. We left hotel at 9.23. Ascended by side of a narrow and steep gully, at places very bad, gained the ridge by 11.45 just to the east of its lowest point, just to the left of the 'Eagle'.Thence straight to the top by 12.15 and on to the 'Spooks' taking the north side route. The first 'Spook' is divided into 2 by a cleft SW-NE, rather too narrow to squeeze through; one half is slightly loose. AF went up so far. We then passed round its south side and up to the ridge connecting it with the second one. We each ascended it and then on without any check at all. What appears to be a very steep pitch in the photos being quite simple, we passed up its south side. It is then just a walk away on to the highest point on the ridge, the extreme right hand big lump in my photo from Corrie [Beagh?], which we gained at 1.40. There is here a good cairn, Meall Dearg 3118ft. A sheep fence runs along here so far for proceeding east we came to a perpendicular drop which neither we nor sheep fence could negotiate. There is no difficulty in getting round on the north side. From the Col which we then reached the ascent is difficult of this last summit. It is steep and chiefly ledges of heather and grass and rocks which cannot be too much trusted. This summit, also above 3000 we reached at 2.40 and had no difficulty in descending to the road; where we met Madeline and Miss Wilson whom we had seen for some time.

The references to the 'Eagle' and 'Spooks' – the latter name clearly applied to the rickety pinnacles west of Meall Dearg – suggest that these features of the ridge were familiar to other climbers, but I have been unable to find these terms used before or since. Our Journal[5] contains an interesting note which records a second traverse of the ridge 'from end to end' by 'an English climber, who is not (yet) a member of the S.M.C., but who is well known at Wastdale'. Examination of editor Wm. Douglas's correspondence shows that this is George Bennett Gibbs, and that his traverse was made on 22 July 1896 in company with Alexander W. Peacock, his brother T.R. Peacock, and Thomas J. Crombie, a Hawick businessman who joined the Club in 1919. Gibbs refers to the Meall Dearg pinnacles as the 'Manikins'.[6]

---

5 *J* (Sep. 1896) 4, 178.
6 Letter dated 26 July from Gibbs to Douglas, in NLS Acc. 11538 Item 41.

Russell was particularly fond of the Cairngorms, which offered ample scope for long and taxing expeditions, and he frequently rented rooms at Guislich, a farm just north of Coylumbridge. The most impressive of the many lengthy traverses he made is acknowledged as the first circuit of the four 4,000 Munros.[7] This was done by Russell and Fraser on 20 May 1897 in a round trip from Edinburgh – the pedestrian section beginning and ending at Aviemore station. While there is a brief note of the traverse in the Journal by Fraser,[8] and a greatly belated short account by Russell,[9] it is worth giving Russell's diary account. It does not seem that either Russell or Fraser appreciated the possibility that theirs may have been the first traverse of the Cairngorm giants.

The short climb of Good Friday made me turn my way again to the Cairngorms especially as the weather was very settled, clear and bright with a moderate east wind, so being fortunate to get Alec Fraser we left on Wednesday night at 9.5 for Perth, carriage to ourselves, good game of chess, I lost but should have made it a draw. At Perth Station we put in fully 1½ miles on the platform ere we left at 12.40, the guard getting us a carriage to ourselves. It was a fine night, from about Struan the view back over Ben y Vrackie very fine in the yellow light; up by Dalwhinnie the white clouds were quite low, slept very little; Aviemore at 3.50, went to Waiting Room and soon had cocoa ready and having arranged rucksacks etc. left by 4.35; the sun just scattering the clouds on Cairngorm. A steady swing brought us up past near Coylum Bridge and on to near the Bothy in Einich at 6.40 where we halted for breakfast of brown bread and Melton Mowbray pie. Even the lower slopes of Braeriach were scarcely visible owing to the heavy cloud still hanging over the hill and all up Glen Einich. By 7.10 we were away and, crossing the Allt na Beinne Bige, held up the first slope in the direction of Choire an Lochain and on reaching the plateau at about 2000 we found the mist almost off and the sun bright and strong. Holding on up the slope in front, some little distance to the right of the course of the burn, then a long snow gully we had a very hot walk over boulders till we reached the Loch at 8.50. The loch hard frozen over, probably solid, big cracks at the side, several feet deep, and snow over all, all round the back a splendid corrie, of about 500 ft; steep snow slopes a good deal of rock on the left and also on the right what appeared one or two good ridges, one especially; we settled on a route up the centre, free of rock and with a less formidable cornice. The ridge on the left between it and Corrie Ruadh is only a walk and by it the ascent could be made in 4½ hrs from station. Passing round the loch we attacked the slope, the snow in fine condition but very icy here and there in the track of falling cornice. Before long however we roped and continued kicking and cutting, Alec leading; the angle got steep by some rocks in the middle, up what was probably the course of the burn. Crossing a couple of small but actual crevasses I took the lead for a bit and then gave it over again to Alec and ere long we reached the cornice; the snow beneath was very steep and hard; the cornice overhung a bit, with a ledge beneath, the slopes being both hard and steep above the cornice we did not attempt to break our way up it as the time was going on rather fast. Our only plan then seemed to be to crawl along this ledge and up round the side, a distinctly interesting climb. After photos had been taken at the top we had a

---

[7] See Chapter 3 of Ronald Turnbull's *Life and Times of the Black Pig* (Millrace Books, 2007).

[8] *J* (Sep. 1897) 4, 343.

[9] 'Some Memories of Braeriach', *J* (Nov. 1928) 18, 214–19.

considerable bit to go over softish snow slopes to get to where the Cairn should have been – but no sign at all – buried in the snow, we prodded with axes but could not find any sign. The top was reached at 11.15 and driving in our axes we sat thereon for lunch. We remained on the top for an hour, taking photos of cornices and changing plates. An eagle soaring round aloft was transplanted to the Pocket Kodak. The view was hazy but fairly good. Nevis and Alder visible I think. Earlier in the day a heavy bank of clouds in the north showed up the white-topped Torridon hills and probably Ben Wyvis, just appearing over it. After settling upon a route down Cairn Toul and up Muich Dhui we left at 12.15 for Cairn Toul; making pretty straight for Einich Cairn over wide fields of snow almost the whole way; rather heavy walking as the snow gave considerably beneath the foot; the cliffs and corries all along were very fine. Following pretty well the edge of the Corrie we soon thereafter reached the site of March Cairn which like the Einich Cairn was not visible, all snow. The March Cairn top had especially fine cornices into the big corrie. Passing round the back of Sgor an Lochain Uaine, we got off the snow a good deal and struck the edge of the cliffs again at the other side for the final scramble of 400ft or so up the boulders of Cairn Toul, the Cairn on which was reached at 1.55 and gladly so for it had been a heavy walk round, the sun being very strong and the snow rather soft. It would be nearly as quick to come down from Braeriach by the edge of Coire Bhrochain and up by Sgor an Lochain Uaine. The views from summit were rather finer than from Braeriach, the latter's corrie looking very well so also the Larig itself. After some gingerbread on the top we left at 2.20 and made tracks for the Larig at the junction of the Dee and the Larig water at about 2000 [feet]. The snow was rather steep and ended badly for glissades into Coire Lochan Uaine, the loch being also frozen; so we held a pretty straight course for our point of crossing the water; the descent over boulders and scree was very steep but frequent patches of snow gave a helpful glissade and took us across the water by 3.10; it was pretty much a case of walking through the Dee, the stepping stones being well covered with water. We waited by the waterside for 25 minutes, I changing another dark slide, and left for Muich Dhui at 3.35. Thinking the Allt a' Choire Mhoir would take too long being full of snow we held straight up the hillside, skirting the left side of a small corrie well up Muich Dhui. The first several hundred feet was over grass and heather etc. but after that it was pure boulders of all sizes and stability, which, through rough scrambling, takes one up very quickly. Much amused by the ptarmigan on the hillside which always seemed to be taking Pocket Kodak photos, their cry was so similar to the noise of changing the film after exposure. The last 100ft or so was over snow or gravel and the Cairn was reached at 5.15; we found tracks in the snow but they seemed at least a day old. We waited here quarter of an hour for photos, rest and "lunch" and then made for Cairngorm, holding round to the left of the 4244 summit, the snow being of fair consistency. The descent of Muich Dhui to the Larig would have given splendid glissades at many a place; we passed over the snow which was very deep in places as we saw when crossing the Garbh Uisge Beag, where there was one big hole away down to the water. We kept on till we came to the rocks over which the Feith Buidhe flows and then keeping to our left we crossed the Coire Domhain fairly high up and then made for the edge of the cliffs overhanging Coire an t-Sneachda. Taking the top several hundred feet of Cairngorm very easily we reached the Cairn comfortably by 7.7 and would gladly have lain and basked in sun were it not for the walk before us to Guislich. Leaving the summit therefore at 7.25, our fourth 4000 top, we got a fair glissade down into Coire Chais and then a good swing down the glen and round the hillside brought us to the Cairngorm path and very soon thereafter to the bridge and on to Glen More Lodge, passing again numberless deer. After passing the lodge a little we halted for a drink and some chocolate and then on in the growing twilight and reached Guislich by 10.15, i.e. 17 hours and 40 minutes from station.

We were then most glad of a wash and tea and left again about 11.30 for a slow steady walk to the station. One must confess that after leaving one felt the fences rather a nuisance, but otherwise felt almost quite fresh. Pretty dark down through the forest and then a wait at the station and up came our train; same guard as we had going up so he promptly put us into a first and there for my own part I slept right on to Stanley Junction with a single break at Struan. Walking up from Haymarket I was at 76 [Thirlestane Road] before 9 and at office soon after 10. Felt sleepy during afternoon but that was all. Several days till my face recovered, the whole skin nearly peeling off with the sun. Cairngorm had disappointingly little snow and small glissade. The whole walking distance was probably a little over 30 miles and adding the walk at Perth station and down to Aviemore station at night, the total must have been about 35 including four 4000 hills; it must be one of the finest walks we have had, granted good conditions as we had almost to perfection, barring the heat and a slight haze over more distant hills. Such as Lochnagar and Ben y Gloe however were quite clear.

These two expeditions were perhaps the high points of Russell's mountaineering career, but study of the diaries shows that he was a genuine enthusiast, interested in all aspects of mountaineering, and perfectly competent on difficult ground as his diaries for Skye in 1898 and 1900 reveal, as does his rapid traverse of Gnifetti – Lyskamm – Zumsteinspitze – Dufourspitze –Silbersattel – Betemps with George Sang in 1910. As well as his own long service to the Club and to the interests of Scottish mountaineering, he encouraged three of his sons Colin, George and Victor to share his enthusiasms. All three became members of the Club. It is unfortunate that since Colin's death a few years ago, we have had no descendant of Arthur Russell among our membership.

Robin N Campbell

Arthur W. Russell

THE SAGA OF THE MIDNIGHT COWBOYS

(Scottish Winter Climbing Down-Under)

THERE WE were, nine o'clock on a cold moonless June night, trying to find our way across to the approach gully to the Homer Saddle. Just a wee miscalculation. I suppose it was all my fault really, it was me who had persuaded the boys that Winter climbing was fun, it was me who suggested the line we'd been on, and, more to the point, it was me who'd left his glasses and torch at the bottom of the route with the bags!

So, nine o'clock one cold and not very promising June morning, Steve Skelton and I were puffing our way in the general direction of the Homer Tunnel, looking for Warren Biggs, who'd been abandoned at the tunnel car park. Conditions looked pretty abysmal, but we wandered on up to the lower cliffs in McPherson Cirque. It looked as if there was some ice from a distance, but on getting there, while there was ice, it wasn't the sort you'd really want to climb on unless there was no alternative. Just to our left though, was a nice looking easyish buttress, snow, rock steps, and TURF. We could just cruise up that no trouble.

After a relaxed break for a munch (we'd been on the go for a whole hour), we deposited the bags at a convenient boulder (we were just going to cruise this remember), and started soloing off up a snowy ramp heading towards the crest of the buttress. There was a wee diversion up an overhung groove which reminded me of a pitch on a route Ken Crocket and I did on The Brack years ago, but I couldn't get up this one either.

On the crest of the buttress, we roped up and climbed five full rope-lengths up rocky steps, reasonable firmish snow, and some deceptively steep turf. Nice enjoyable climbing, long run-outs, and the boys found out what the Warthogs were for. The late start and the casual approach took its toll though, and before we knew it, the time was after four o'clock, and it was starting to get dark. Some of us started muttering about roping off down into the gully on our right, but The Mighty Steve would have none of it and powered off up through the next wee rock band into the gloom, climbing fast to escape the whining from below. One more snow pitch after the rock brought us to a wee saddle below a steeper headwall leading to Talbot's Ladder. By now it was almost dark, and my rapidly diminishing vision suggested that finding our way down across the snowed up slabs might be prudent. Also, Warren was expected home in the early evening, but we'll go there later.

It was a beautiful night, cold, clear, windless. We got to see a lot of it as we spent five hours working our way over, up and down steepish but straightforward ground. The biggest problem we had was my lack of a torch and poor night vision without the glasses, but the boys looked after me very well. We'd send Steve away down to run out a rope length, then Warren and I would follow, very close together, so I could get the benefit of his torch. Just when we thought we might be getting close to escaping into the Homer Saddle approach gully, we ran into some more complex ground. At this point frustration took over, I mugged Warren and took his torch, and disappeared off on the end of the rope. One big downclimb into a dead end, one big upclimb, a wander through

The Darren Mountains, New Zealand. Photo: Alastair Walker.

some wiggly grooves, and we were on a belay from which we knew we would get into the gully in one more rope-length.

Though there was never any gear between belays, and sometimes no belays, we were never in any doubt as to our getting off. The snow on the slabs was very thin, but was also very squeaky. After a stumble off down to the bags to stuff ourselves full of food and water, we plodded off back to the hut to wake up the new arrivals, pick up our gear and head off home. Sometime just before midnight.

The trip back to Te Anau was fun too. Someone had got a bit concerned that we weren't back at the appointed time and had called the police. The police in turn called the Southland Cliff Rescue who were close by on one of their "training" exercises. We're friends with some of those guys, and they were so concerned that they laughed down the phone, told the police not to worry, and went back to the serious business of having a wee nip or two of something tasty. The police got bored after chucking out time in town, and came for a drive up to see what was going on, meeting us half-way down the road. Warnings that Warren was in trouble were passed, and we continued on our respective ways. Steve and I left Warren to explain on his own and slunk off into the night quietly. Such big brave he-men.

That's only half the story, and the other half is almost as comical. August, and the sense of the unfinished pulled us back up to McPherson Cirque again. There was a fair bit more snow around by now, even a big avo track down the valley. No trouble in keeping high on the valley side though, and well clear of any trouble. Although there was more snow, conditions were – as they had been for most of the Winter – not brilliant.

Four of us this time, apart from Steve and myself, we had a fresh-faced Martin Gennet out in Winter for the first time, and a slightly wrinkly Hamish McDonald who had started climbing with us earlier on in the Winter. As usual, all good plans to get up early and away while it was still dark went out the window. Well, we had to wait for Hamish, he's had to get up at two o'clock in the morning, feed out on the farm, then drive over from The Key. After his obligatory two cups of coffee, we got away at – yep, you guessed it – nine o'clock. There was a bit more soft snow around in the Cirque this time, but we also had Hamish the machine to break the trail for us. Steve and I could never keep up with him even following in his tracks. Another leisurely break at the usual spot, and off we went.

This time Martin and I were on one rope, Steve and Hamish on the other. We like to have fun on a route, and much abuse and Eiger Effects flew around. Martin was a bit quiet, but the other three of were just plain horrid. I tried to teach them all how to sing Barnacle Bill the Sailor , but no-one appreciated my fine voice.

Conditions weren't too bad, snow was a bit softer and deeper than it was the first time, so we had to dig for the turf. One wee technical point here, although the turf in the Darrans is pretty fair stuff for climbing on, it has a bit more vegetation than it's Scottish counterpart, and just doesn't have the same orgasm inducing qualities. However, it's good material for all that. We cruised up to the wee saddle, and actually got there still with a few hours of daylight to go. Steve and Hamish had taken all the wee rock steps directly, I went looking for some gear which had got jammed on the previous trip. Well, I do come from the Land of Rain and Midgies........

Above the saddle, we had a couple of choices. Hamish and Steve put dibs on the short rocky step directly above, Martin and I took a nice looking steep icy runnel to the left.

The boys had lots of fun on the rock step, only about ten metres, but Steve reckoned grade 18 (E1) in crampons. Good rock gear for all that. There was much squawking when Hamish followed, until he found out that crampons actually bit into the sloping holds. They then had a couple of very long snow pitches to the top of The Ladder. Fun was obviously the order of the day, with much screaming, and finding out about the ever expanding pitch length which means you never have just quite enough rope to get where you want to go.

Our groove was technically quite straightforward, about thirty metres of steep hollow ice with bulgy bits, but no gear. However, it did end in the most amazing belay, with stunning views over to Moir and down the Hollyford. Martin finished off with a nice elegant traverse over onto Talbots Ladder, and still enough daylight to let us get down able see where we were going. And even better, Warren was nursing bruised ribs, but had decided to come up to the hut to talk rubbish with us, and arrived at the car park to get us. What a friend, he even brought up extra beer.

Not so straightforward for the Gruesome Twosome. We knew they'd made it out by the increased volume of noise, but they decided to stop and have a wee moment and admire the view. Then it got dark. Then they had trouble finding anchors to get them off the top of The Ladder. Blows were almost exchanged, but then an anchor was eventually dug out, and the descent was completed without further incident. In the dark. Again. Two happy boys piled into the truck at the tunnel, and we got them back to the hut sometime after ten o'clock. Again.

Hamish's day wasn't over yet, he still had to drive back home to The Key that night, so he could be up an some unearthly hour in the morning to feed the stock again. We stuffed a load of dead Dexter into him, a beer, some chippies, and sent him on his way sometime around midnight with Martin to keep him awake until Te Anau. As I said, the man was just a machine.

So there the Saga ends. The route is around 800m long, straightforward, but pleasant and not too serious. A good starter route if you want to get into real Winter climbing. I give it a Scottish Grade III, because I can still remember how to grade accurately with that system but am still trying to get my head around the new system used in the Darrans Guide.

As you might guess, the Winter climbing in The Darrans is very similar to Scotland, only much bigger, and more serious. It is real avalanche territory at times, but if you use your head you can usually find some place with a lower risk. Conditions can change very quickly too, but no more so than Scotland. The climbing is similar to The Ben, but normally with more turf on the scratchy routes. Protection has to be looked for, but is no worse than on the big routes on The Ben. The big ice routes don't form up so well these days, but later on in the season are simply stunning. There are very few established Winter routes, and the possibilities are endless, especially for mixed climbs.

Despite all this, apart from our own wee group, there is virtually no-one climbing here these days. Some may pop over once every other Winter, but not many. The reality is that in New Zealand there are very few people active in the mountains in Winter at all. Most climbers tend to go for short waterfalls and bolted M routes, and there's a growing number of quality venues for those, along with a fairly active scene. But for us, there's nowhere quite like The Darrans, we've got big, high quality routes to explore, and peace and quiet to do it in our own way.

Alastair Walker

THE ASCENT OF RUM DOODLESBJERGE

With profound apologies to W.E. Bowman. Please note that any
similarity to true life characters or events is entirely coincidental

The team:
Glorious leader – A Greenland veteran combined with an in depth first aid manual made him an ideal choice for both expedition leader and medical officer.
The quiet man – a wealth of Greenland knowledge is to be acquired from this experienced fellow, but only if you can get him to talk about it
The technical meister – much experienced in just about everything which arose in conversation, this is the chap you need to tell you how to do things
Das 'Boer' – This mysterious, yet likeable and jolly fellow is still adapting to the British way of life, all with a second tongue!
The Irish boys – renowned throughout Christendom as the finest singers in the whole of East Greenland. Sponsored by dolphin friendly tuna.
Twin cheeks – The feisty female in the team. Who during the trip suffered from both exposure to her cheeks and exposure to a bunch of wussy males.
The author – modesty prevents further comment on this fine fellow.

Day 1
Monday 30th April 2007 and the motley crew are all assembled at 72 degrees north, in Constable Point, East Greenland for the short hop into the heart of the Staunings Alps aboard the trusty Twin Otter. The captain looks like a reliable chap but his young assistant (who could do with a haircut) seems unduly flappable – something about the 50 litres of fuel slopping about on the floor of the cabin perhaps? Anyways the SMC East Greenland Staunings Alps expedition in association with Dolphin friendly Tuna – hereafter referred to for simplicity as the SMCEGSAEAWDFT – is presently airborne and before anyone can utter 'Crikey, they don't look like the Cairngorms,' we disembark onto the Lang Glacier. [*Linguistic note: Lang means long in Danish. This prosaic nomenclature captures the wild imagination of those early Danish explorers.*]

The excessively Scottish weather made for soft snow resulting in a rather unfortunate nosedive for the Twin Otter. Surprisingly, some of the team are blessed with healthy 'pre-expedition' physiques for digging out the nose ski and later the extra weight of 8 people in 'the boot' bumps the nose up and the plane sits horizontal again. And so with a hearty 'Cheerio' the plane motors off down the glacier, and keeps motoring, and motoring until it disappears! After an embarrassed silence, with no sign of the flying machine, Glorious leader is starting to fret somewhat. Very professionally he opens the Boys Own First Aid Manual at the chapter on plane crashes. However those spirited Icelanders were only joshing and, like a scene from Catch 22, they are soon dive bombing us on their way Blighty bound [*Surely Iceland bound – Ed?*].

Left in the arctic stillness our intrepid fellows rapidly dig in, pitch camp and there follows a masterclass from Glorious leader in the use of the first world war 'anti polar bear' rifle during which a perfidious cardboard box experiences the full wrath of Britain's finest [*ahem, and Ireland and Germany – Ed.*].

Day 2

With the sun shining, as it did all night, the entire team decide on a reconnaissance trip into *Terra Incognita*. Glorious leader leads from the fore [*big chap, good for testing snow bridges!*], whilst Technical meister is soon instructing in the latest techniques for wearing skis, harnesses, sunglasses and probing for crevasses. Following the swift luncheon [*detrimental for the digestion!*], and not for the last time, the team splits. Appropriately, Team Tech meister decide on a technical ascent of the closest peak. Team twin cheeks opt for the open glacier approach. Not for the last time Twin cheeks is disgusted with the lack of stiff resolve and dedication exhibited by the boys and hence the 'Wuss glacier' is eponymously named. Such a slur is not accepted lightly and Glorious leader and the Quiet man decide to chaperone the Author and Twin cheeks whilst the Irish boys revert to basecamp owing to rabid blister attacks. Undeterred by this minor setback they are discovered upon our return to camp gaily holding forth with a fine rendition of Irish folk songs and eating multiple sachets of dolphin friendly tuna.

On the ice, a rapid ascent of the first unclimbed peak is made with all the usual japery – a single axe on sheet ice, falling unroped into crevasses on cols etcetera, etcetera – just in time to appreciate the approach of team Technical meister. Reports that they may have uttered a profanity upon discovery that 'their' unclimbed peak was a virgin no more are greatly exaggerated. However, in the spirit of good sportsmanship the reunited team continued to ascend the neighbouring hill via a superb snow crested ridge. In honour of the whiteness it was named the Biancograt. A fine name for a fine ridge; one wonders if it'll ever catch on! On the second summit the assembled multitude thought to christen the peak. 'Drumglas' says the Quiet man before falling silent, and so Drumglas and its neighbour Drumglas Beag came into being!

Day 3

It snowed, all day. However spirits are kept high by the Irish boys with fine Irish folk songs and sachets of dolphin friendly tuna. The author develops a rare variant of cabin fever. This condition is cleverly diagnosed at some distance by the medical officer, in a sleeping bag, from the door of his tent. The symptoms require the sufferer to construct a fine Igloo, which is good for team morale as it keeps everyone else entertained!

Day 4

It snowed until lunchtime. But just as spirits are waning the clouds part to show the sun and a fine afternoon is spent under instruction by Technical meister in all aspects of most things including 'non-functioning MSR stove' usage and avalanche transceiver burying. The Tech meister is often heard to comment with enthusiasm, 'that is fu*king sh*te.' When elaboration is requested, in the pursuit of clarity of course, he states, 'well it's worse than sh*te, so it is therefore fu*king sh*te.' In desperate need of distraction some of our brave team determine to forge a trail to Crescent Col to dump food and fuel, in an 'exercise on prescription' type of intervention! An 1800 hours departure ensures a character building midnight return when the team particularly enjoy the bracing temperatures of minus 25° Celsius. The wind chill results in a touch of frost-nip for one 'member'.

Day 5

Despite searing sunshine, the avalanche potential engenders caution, but by the afternoon Teams Glorious leader and Technical meister ascend a nearby outlier named in honour of Glorious leaders mum, Mollytinde. Not to be outdone, Twin cheeks entertains the remainder of the expedition with considerable exposure of her twin peaks whilst sunbathing.

Day 6

Three fine first ascents are achieved and the naming of peaks after wives, girlfriends [*but not both!*] continues unabated. Cordulaspitze, 2430m, North face (AD), Jobjerg, 2330m by the South West Ridge which is a continuation of the North Ridge of Cordulaspitze and Juliasbjerge, named after a niece for a change.

Day 7

Team Twin cheeks ascend into a new glacier basin in search of a wilderness experience. There, our brave team are shocked to see signs of life. Therefore, in honour of this meeting the glacier is termed the Raven glacier. Some stout trailbreaking and further 'crevasses on ridges' tom-foolery sees another mighty first ascent; Puchwhitstinde, 2339m. A prolonged technical traverse sees a further first ascent of the adjacent peak – Hasentinde – and then its down in time for a brew.

Day 8

Spurred into action by the preceding day's activities, teams Glorious leader and Technical meister both set out to mount the final virgin peak above base camp. The race is on with team Glorious leader bravely ascending a compelling, mighty couloir whilst team Technical meister select the lengthier approach up the Wuss [*entirely in character of course!*] With the usual impeccable timing these fine fellows arrive on top of Margaretabjerge almost together where a fine luncheon is enjoyed. Subsequent tales of rocks being thrown down as a signal to the competition by the first ascent team, *a la Whymper* on the Matterhorn, are dismissed as the usual good natured banter, which is only to be expected! Later Team Tech meister realise why the Lang glacier was so named, with the lengthy overnight ski back to camp resulting in Das Boer complaining because he was not wearing underpants, he suffered intimately from the arctic cold!

Meanwhile the Irish blisters have resolved sufficiently to enable a second ascent of peak Twin cheeks. The independent line of ascent is named Snow Bunting Couloir, which while unseen from basecamp, is deduced as being a fine new line as intimated by the singing of the fine Irish folk songs emanating from above.

Day 9

The efforts of the previous day have somewhat fatigued our brave explorers and a day of R&R is required. However, Twin cheeks, disgusted by the lack of activity and stiff resolve, insists on a move of camp and shoots off in the direction of Crescent col. Your humble author, gentle reader, is obliged to follow. A fine ski tour follows with much entertainment being provided by the pulks on the ascents, descents and flat sections. Finally team Twin cheeks inexplicably settle on a shady site up the flamboyantly named Gully Glacier for the new camp as the evening cool draws in.

Day 10

Exhibiting stiff resolve Team Twin cheeks finally emerges into the morning cool to explore the intriguing Gully Glacier. Mightily impressed by the crevassed nature of the surrounding glaciers, mischievously tagged 'Certain Death Crevasse Alley,' they return chastened to the cool of camp in time to greet the remainder of the team who arrive in the usual dribs and drabs. Rip roaring tales of entertainment with pulks are shared and everyone settles down to a pleasantly cool evening.

Day 11

Undeterred by the first look down the glacier Twin cheeks insists on a further trip through the 'Certain Death Crevasse Alley'. Miraculously our brave team emerge intact out the other end and hot foot it up a new glacier heading for the most likely line up a virgin peak. A fine line up a snowy gully is spotted and our team sally forth. However, considerable sallying forth is required to ascent the infernal gully [*surely Eternal – Ed*] however it does leave but a short scramble to the summit. Another mighty peak Himmelstinde is conquered. An obvious line of black ice and tottering rock up the neighbouring virgin peak is tempting but sadly the lack of daylight [*surely shome mistake in the land of the midnight sun? – Ed*] meant descent was the order of the day. So in the spirit of sharing amongst the team, the peak is left for the others. An interminable downclimb sees the team back at their skis in no time [*I think you mean 00:00hours – Ed*] and back at the camp in time for the cool of the middle of the night.

Day 12

Enthused by talk of the line of black ice and tottering rock, leading to a fine virgin summit Team Glorious leader set out for a quick sojourn up the unconquered hill. Tech meister and Das Boer bag a splendid new route up the shapely Hjornespids. The Irish boys make a fine ascent of a snowy peak' The Cold Shoulder' via the 'Certain Death Serac Alley' but sadly suffer the indignity of a wipe out on the ski descent. Not to be deterred by the near shoulder dislocation the boys entertain the team in the evening with a fine celebratory rendition of Irish folk songs and eating multiple sachets of dolphin friendly tuna. Team Twin cheeks spend the day recovering in camp and enjoy the pleasant cool of the day.

Day 13

Whilst the rest of the team sit around recovering team Twin cheeks set off on a mission to scale a mighty peak spotted from the previous summit. Twin cheeks spots an obvious buttress line but sadly the author feels he must decline the line as the minimal rack and mountain boots are woefully inadequate for the 'Half-dome-esque' tower [*such a lack of stiff resolve!*] Fortunately the author spots an alternative line which leads nicely to the summit ridge. A quick balance along the ensuing tottering ice crest sees our team top-out to a glorious view back to the original landing site from the summit of the mighty An Caisteal. Hard ice on the descent requires drilling a number of 'almost in the ice' Abalakov threads. But soon the pair are back at the planks and whizzing down an 8km descent of the virgin Puchan glacier. Roping up for skiing over the crevasses provides many face-planting opportunities – my, how one laughed once the snow was cleared from one's trachea, nostrils and mouth. The team roll into the cool of camp late in the evening and go straight to bed. No sign of the others – clearly already in bed after a lazy day.

Day 14

Gosh, what excitement. It turns out that team Glorious leader had scaled the mighty 'Archangel' peak but encountered a number of challenging situations on the descent [*Ho Ho!*] This results in a longer than expected day, two days actually, and saw the rump of the team forming the Gully glacier mountain rescue team to go and search for them. Later our brave chaps are back in camp with smiles on their faces, a virgin peak under their belts and the Quiet man sporting some intriguing frostbite blisters on each and every digit. Glorious leader revels at the opportunity to get out his Boys own first aid manual. The Quiet man doesn't say much and remains stoically quiet while the medical officer sticks a big needle and syringe into his frostbite fingers to drain the blister fluid. The soup tasted very salty that night! Although it is not referenced in the first aid manual, the medical officer also advises The Quiet man to avoid alcohol for the next 10 days and through consideration for his traumatised partner, courageously undertakes the task of finishing the whisky himself.

Meanwhile team Technical meister ascend a fine peak following Twin cheeks trail from the day before. Enigmatically they are forced into an alternative line as the avalanche debris has removed all signs of their passage. It transpires that Technical meister had fu**ing warned Twin cheeks of the bl**dy risks but she had dismissed this as him being a Wuss. Despite the obvious shoulder pain the Irish boys succeed in cheering up the sober, Quiet man somewhat, with fine Irish folk songs and proffered sachets of dolphin friendly tuna.

Day 15

While the cracked and blistered, frostbitten hands of The Quiet Man continue to fascinate resting members, Team Twin cheeks head off across a further branch of the 'Certain Death Crevasse Alley' for a look at another colossal peak. However upon reaching the base of this shapely leviathan, the black ice and rubble was enough to cause a momentary hesitation in your author. Sensing this, Twin cheeks expresses her contempt and disgust at the lack of stiff resolve and Wuss-like behaviour, but promptly agrees to retrace her steps, with little persuasion! The team roll back to camp to enjoy a cool afternoon, captivated by those frostbitten hands.

Day 16

Despite the glorious location and refreshingly cool temperatures there is growing recognition of the imperative to overcome inertia and move camp up to Col Major. So with great sadness the ice is chipped off the tents, the pulks are chipped out of the ice and the team strike camp. A fine ski tour follows with much entertainment being provided by the pulks on the ascents, descents and flat sections. Finally the col is reached and the new camp set up in a rather magnificent location below the mighty Dansketinde. Despite the late hour much comment is made on the contrasting warmth of this camp in the sunshine compared to the cool conditions on the gully glacier, and multiple layers are removed before retiring for the evening.

Day 17

The extreme high temperatures result in uncharacteristic lethargy in some team members at this splendid and beguiling camp. However, Twin cheeks, disgusted by the lack of stiff resolve and activity, garners some enthusiasm again to ascend the neighbouring rock peak. Never one to take such a slur lightly, Glorious leader enlists the Technical meister and follows in hot pursuit. Technical meister reminds the impulsive Twin cheeks not to dislodge any fu**ing rocks onto them. Rock boots are donned for the first and only time on the trip and a fine ascent is made of the turreted ridge to reach the top of Ian's Peak. An equally fine down climb is livened up by an entertaining abseil off a rock tooth and by the volley of rocks dislodged by the hybrid Glorious Leader/Technical meister team. A quick slip into a crevasse whilst approaching camp tops off an entertaining jaunt.

Day 18

Another fine day dawns and the team determine to descend the neighbouring 600metre gully to the Bersaerkerbrae glacier. Glorious leader and the Quiet man have both done this before, and with the first few 50 metre stages prepared the day before our team are confident of a swift, problem free descent. With this in mind Glorious leader disappears over the edge, not to be seen again for the remainder of the day! The Quiet man finally decides to assess the situation and is lowered down a number of metres. However the team are unable to hear his observations and a further member is lowered down. By developing this approach the members and 8 pulks are soon strewn randomly over the top 200m of the gully. Undeterred our brave team eventually manage to get all bodies and pulks down the remaining 400m in a mere 12 hour session. At the bottom Glorious leader generously suggests half the fu**ing team should proceed to set up camp instead of standing about like a…. well you get the idea! However, the result is he is left alone with only the company of 6 pulks and is later heard to mutter ungentlemanly comments about 'abandonment'. Delighted at such a swift descent Twin cheeks decides to let her sledge do the last few metres alone. The 4 gents pitching camp are initially concerned, but then suitably impressed as the errant missile accelerates directly towards them, before stopping directly outside the door to Twin cheeks own tent. Wisely, Twin cheeks declines suggestions that she should 'do that again.' Despite the effort involved everyone has clearly enjoyed their day and the team sit around for a good natured 2 minute chat before retiring to bed. The Irish boys must have put in greater than normal efforts as sadly no Irish folks songs nor sachets of dolphin friendly tuna are offered.

Day 19

A fine morning sees the team once more admiring – from a distance – the 'descent gully from hell'. Despite the general desire for a re-run of the deeds from the previous day Glorious leader recommends we strike camp then strike east down the immense Bersaerkerbrae glacier. So once more the pulks are loaded and the team set off. A fine ski tour follows with much entertainment being provided by the pulks on the ascents, descents and flat sections. Indeed, mid-tour a heavily crevassed zone sees Technical meister expertly leading two others down in a roped party. The remainder of the team follow on a single rope of 5. Despite the generous 50m rope length there are issues regarding spacing of people, pulks and increasingly that found between the ears of certain team members! Much entertainment followed with bodies and pulks strung out on the edge of crevasses and indeed physically unable to move for extended periods of time. Finally the Quiet man utters a rare vulgarism, falls silent and then unties. Your author follows suit and in no time both have surpassed the difficulties. During one of the strung out interludes Twin cheeks inspirationally shouts up that the team should just untie and ski down. Once the team are finally able to extricate themselves from the spiders web and meet her, she is noisily, generously and repeatedly thanked for her helpful insight.

The team all finally congregate once more for luncheon and to admire the sight of the unclimbed North face of Bersaerketinde. Since this is named as a possible objective Twin cheeks suggests an immediate attempt. However despite the obvious appeal of the permashade low temperatures, looming shattered serac zones and lack of descent route she is unable to find a collaborator amongst the reluctant gathering. Disgusted by the lack of stiff resolve and dedication she storms off to set up camp.

Day 20
Team Glorious leader head for an unclimbed peak back up a side glacier. A long ski approach and scramble up shattered rock of the summit ridge sees them bagging the first ascent of Skotsketinde (Scotland's Peak). Despite the obvious pain from his frostbite injuries the Quiet man remains stoically serene and climbs rather better than before! Team Twin cheeks meanwhile decide on the delights of a second ascent of a mighty summit called Panoramic peak tucked away up a side glacier. Undeterred by the 5 hour ski route they revel in the avalanche prone approach gully and shattered rock of the summit ridge. Meanwhile team Technical meister, in a rejoinder to the disdain expressed previously by Twin cheeks, head off for a reconnaissance of Bersaerketinde. Sadly they return unrewarded and with tales of permashade low temperatures, looming shattered serac zones and lack of descent route. A pleasant evening is had as the Irish boys entertain all with Irish folk songs and an ominous Mackerel Sky is seen over the shapely Bersaerkerspire to the north.

Day 21
The weather has finally broken and our team feel perplexingly at home as conditions become distinctly Scottish. Glorious leader implores us to strike camps and bravely leads the team down the glacier through the whiteout, cloud, wind and rain. A fine ski tour follows with much entertainment being provided by the pulks on the ascents, descents and flat sections. One icefall section provides particularly entertaining sport with bodies and pulks just about visible strewn all over the glacier.

Finally the glacier snout is reached. That wily old chap Glorious leader demonstrates his experience and watches sagaciously as bodies and pulks disappear in 7 different directions through rock, snow and ice – before following the least demanding line. Finally the team reconvene and cheerily ski a further few kilometres across a frozen lake to camp.

Day 22
Conditions remain distinctly Scottish as the team set off once more down the frozen Skel river towards the sea. An initial false start sees an apparent rare

glimpse of fallibility in Glorious leader, although post hoc rationalisation reveals he was simply trying to get someone else to lead over the frozen river ice to test it would support our weight! Initial pulk difficulties see a rare profanity emanating from the Quiet man. However the team are soon underway. A fine ski tour follows with much entertainment being provided by the pulks on the ascents, descents and mainly flat sections. Technical meister identifies thin ice at one point, resulting in a rapid U-turn and a diversion around the edge of the ice. The Irish boys meanwhile, engaged as they were in a rendition of fine Irish folk songs, continue straight on down the river.

The team reconvene and finally bear inland towards a hut that Glorious leader recollects from previous visits. The thought of a warming Gluhwein and piping hot Rosti keeps spirits high in the team despite the wind and rain. The rather small, dirty hut is finally spotted and camp set up outside. Sadly, neither café nor restaurant service is available out of season and so, disappointedly everyone retires immediately to bed.

Day 23

Conditions remain distinctly Scottish as the team awake. However the experienced chaps know that good things come to those who wait, and expertly fester in their tents until mid afternoon. Finally the rain eases and the team strike camp. A fine ski tour across the frozen sea ice follows with much entertainment being provided by the pulks on the ascents, descents and mainly flat sections. A pulk control issue on the final rise sees Das Boer provide a winning entry for the 'tantrum of the trip' competition before the gravel airstrip at Mestervig is reached.

An hour later the team reach the other end of the runway to be greeted by 5 howling huskies and a Danish soldier in shorts and T-shirt. Now that is what Twin Cheeks sees as stiff resolve!

'Come in. Come in. The dogs could smell you from some way off! We have baked you a cake' he says. What a pleasant welcome from this fine fellow who diplomatically ignores the pong as we all warm up! 'Would you like some beer – we have so much Carlsberg we can't drink it all'

Probably the best end to an expedition in the World!

Brian Whitworth and Colwyn Jones

[Please note: the Ed in this piece is not the Hon. Ed.—Hon. Ed.]

SCOTTISH MOUNTAINEERING TRUST – 2007

The Trustees met on 16th February, 1st June and 13th November 2007.

During the course of these meetings support was given to the Victoria Longhurst to assist her in financing a place on the British Schools Exploring Society Greenland Expedition 2007, to Lorraine Nicholson for a course at Glenmore Lodge for Visually Impaired Persons, to Heather Morning for a MSC in Managing Sustainable Mountain Development, to Mr A.L. Stewart in support of the Dundee Mountain Film Festival, to the Jonathon Conville Memorial Trust for Scottish Winter Courses 2007/2008, to Active Schools (Mr Tony Wade) in support of a programme for traversing climbing walls in schools in the Western Isles, to the Junior Mountaineering Club of Scotland for works to the Loch Coruisk Hut, to the Culag Community Woodland Trust (Little Assynt Estate) for footpath work, to the National Trust for Scotland for Scotland's Mountain Heritage Project, to Royal Society for Protection of Birds for Golden Eagle Conservation, to J. Maison for the Clachnaben Footpath, and to Scottish Mountaineering Club, subject to certain conditions, for the extension to the CIC Hut.

The present Trustees are A.C. Stead (Chairman), R. Aitken, R. Anderson, J.T.H. Allen, P.V. Brian, C.M. Huntley, A. Macdonald, C.R. Ravey, R.J.C. Robb, and D.N. Williams. J. Morton Shaw is the Trust Treasurer.

The present Directors of the Publications Company are R.K. Bott (Chairman), K.V. Crockett, C.M. Huntley, W.C. Runciman, M.G.D. Shaw and T. Prentice (Publications Manager). C.M. Huntley is both a Trustee and a Director of the Publications Company. R. Anderson is the Convenor of the Publications Sub-Committee and attends Company Board meetings. Both provide valuable liaison between the Company and the Trust.

The Trust wishes to record its appreciation for the contributions and gratitude for services to the Trustees who have retired namely Rob Archbold, Derek Bearhop, Dave Broadhead, and Charlie Orr.

The following grants were committed by the Trustees in 2007:

Victoria Longhurst, BSES Greenland 2007	£250
Lorraine Nicholson, Visually Impaired Course	£3,000
Heather Morning, funding for MSc in Managing Sustainable Mountain Development	£528
A.L. Stewart, Dundee Mountain Film Festival	£1,000
Jonathon Conville Memorial Trust, Scottish Winter Courses 2007/08	£1,222
Active Schools, Traversing Walls	£4,580
JMCS, Loch Coruisk Hut	£2,750 (grant)
	£2,750 (loan)
Culag Community Woodland Trust, Little Assynt Estate	£9,800
National Trust for Scotland, Scotland's Mountain Heritage Project	£2,500
RSPB, Golden Eagle Conservation	£5,000
J. Maison, Clachnaben Footpath	£3,500

Scottish Mountaineering Club, CIC Hut (subject to conditions)

maximum £50,000 (grant)
maximum £50,000 (loan)

The Trustees record their gratitude for donations received from Mr Andy Brindle and Mr Donald Reid.

J.D. Hotchkis
Secretary

MUNRO MATTERS 2008

By Dave Broadhead (Clerk of the List)

I TOOK over the List from David Kirk on 1 August 2007 and would like to take this opportunity to thank him for all his work over the past six years and for ensuring a smooth transition. The Clerk now enters details directly onto the SMC website so thanks also to the Webmaster, Ken Crocket, for his assistance and patience while I have been getting to grips with the technology. Thanks also to the third member of the team, the long serving Keeper of Regalia, Gordon McAndrew, who supplies the ever popular Munroist's ties and brooches.

Over his six years tenure, my predecessor added an average of 208 Compleaters to the list each year, compared to an average of 189 registered by Chris Huntly over the previous six years. The trend continues to rise, with a record 257 for the year 1 April 2007–31 March 2008 as follows: (As before, the five columns give number, name, and the year of compleation of Munros, Tops, and Furths as appropriate. *SMC member.)

3770	Andrew Nelson	2006		3806	Jim Randell	2007	
3771	Maureen Nelson	2006		3807	John Risk	2007	
3772	Nigel Lack	2006		3808	Tom Peck	2006	
3773	Chris Green	2006		3809	Rod Allan	2006	
3774	Walter Gilchrist	2006		3810	Clare Livingston	2007	
3775	Christine Robinson	2006		3811	Martin Clarke	2007	
3776	Alex Thomson	2006		3812	Martin Morris	2007	
3777	Frank Montgomery	2006		3813	David Kermode	2007	
3778	David Malia	2007		3814	Richard Kermode	2007	
3779	Robin Paton	2007		3815	Graham Hall	2007	2006
3780	Davina Lavery	2007		3816	Ed Pirie	2007	
3781	Wyn Morgan	2007		3817	Jean Crowson	2007	
3782	Doug Fleming	2007		3818	Bernard Jarvis	2007	
3783	Alan Taylor	2007		3819	Malcolm Mowat	2007	
3784	Alastair McKeown	2007		3820	Pamela Clark	2006	
3785	Jim Robertson	2007		3821	George L. May	2007	
3786	Douglas Stuart	2007		3822	Andrew Angus	2007	
3787	Leo John Petch	2007		3823	Clive Darlow	2007	
3788	Andy Colledge	2007		3824	Brian McKenna	2007	
3789	Stewart Watson	2007		3825	David De Pomerai	2007	
3790	Alan J. Isherwood	2007		3826	James Dyson	2007	
3791	Aileen Stone	2007		3827	Malcom Peart	2007	
3792	Janet Crosthwaite	2007		3828	Stephen Jung	2007	
3793	Douglas McInally	2007		3829	Tony Wood	2007	
3794	Steven Gardner	2007		3830	Stan Franklin	1995	
3795	Tish Carter	2007		3831	John Bain	2007	
3796	John L. Moses	2007		3832	Andrew Stoddart	2007	
3797	Moira Pearson	2007		3833	Murray Papworth	2001	2001
3798	Eric Murphy	2007		3834	K.M. Joy Ingram	2007	
3799	Rob Fitzgerald	2007		3835	Sarah Stark	2007	
3800	Ian McCabe	2007		3836	Bob Boyce	2007	
3801	David Beer	2007	2006	3837	Ingrid Baber	2007	
3802	Alistair Wright	2007		3838	Ken D Sinclair	2007	
3803	David Leask	2007		3839	Ray Hunter	2007	
3804	Hugo J. Allan	2007		3840	Denise C Fallas	2007	
3805	William H. Butler	2007		3841	Richard Williams	2007	

3842	Gordon M Biggar	2007	
3843	Laila Kjellstrom	2007	
3844	Steve Howe	2007	
3845	Tilly Howe	2007	
3846	Alan Forsyth	2007	
3847	Anthony Goodings	2007	
3848	Keith Bulmer	2007	
3849	Stephen Williams	2007	
3850	Maggie Carr	2007	
3851	Mike O'Donohoe	2007	
3852	Tina Humphries	2007	
3853	David Young	2007	
3854	Jim F. Callahan	2007	
3855	Ronald C. Niven	2007	
3856	Alistair Low	2007	
3857	Alan Butterworth	2007	
3858	Kevin Luton	2007	
3859	Philip Gilligan	2007	
3860	Elaine Janet Booth	2007	
3861	Peter Robertson	2007	
3862	Bryonie F. Brodie	2007	
3863	Bob Garrett	2007	
3864	Reg Abbott	2007	
3865	James Bussey	2007	
3866	D. Ronald Mitchell	2007	
3867	David Leonard	2007	
3868	Alan Wannop	2007	
3869	Nige Wheeler	2007 2007	
3870	John Steyn	2007	
3871	Alan McCaffery	2007	
3872	Anne Stronach	2007	
3873	Kay Waddell	2007	
3874	John Cheesmond	1997	2007
3875	Marion Luscombe	2007	
3876	Robin Luscombe	2007	
3877	Derek Nonhebel	2007	
3878	John McKechnie	2007	
3879	Robbie McFedries	2007	
3880	Sheila Mitchell	2007	
3881	Alistair G. Forrester	2007	
3882	Val Corry	2007	
3883	Lesley Williams	2007	
3884	Eleanor Watson	2007	
3885	Davis S. Batty	1994	
3886	Stephen C. Palmer	2007	
3887	Mary Shand	2007	
3888	William K. Ballantyne	2007	
3889	Tony Pitson	2007	
3890	Mike Croft	2007	
3891	Nigel Rose	2007	
3892	Bob Neill	2007	
3893	Janet Trythall	2007	
3894	John Trythall	2007	
3895	Alan Macdonald	2007	
3896	Bernard McNaboe	2007	
3897	Murray Elder	2007	
3898	Tom Snaith	2007	

3899	Sheena Rudkin	2007	
3900	David Campbell-Kelly	2007	
3901	David Cran	2007	
3902	Donnie MacLean	2007	
3903	Krystina Lotoczko	2007	
3904	Ian Robertson	2007	
3905	Jan Pye	2007	
3906	Graham Pye	2007	
3907	Dave Hewitt	2007	
3908	Laurence Kelly	2007	
3909	Thomas H. White	2007	
3910	John Colin Smith	2007	
3911	Dave I. Cummins	2006	
3912	Rose Wallace	2007	
3913	Gary Venter	2007	
3914	Sue Allen	2007	
3915	Duncan Tamsett	2007	
3916	Brian Morrison	2007	1999
3917	Mark Richford	2007	
3918	Bill Wheeler	2007	
3919	Callum Edwards	2007	
3920	Iain H. Carrick	2005	
3921	Wraight Shepherd	2007	
3922	R.N. Croupe	2007	
3923	Alan Greer	2007	
3924	Nicholas S. Edwards	2007	
3925	Ian Crossland	2007	
3926	Ken Matthewson	2007	
3927	David R. Murray	2007	
3928	David C. Hutchings	2007	
3929	Edward Jones	2006	
3930	Colin Nelson	2007	
3931	Graeme Nelson	2007	
3932	Ruth Swanson	1996	
3933	Derek Mountain	2007	
3934	Alastair H. Govan	2007	
3935	Jonathan Massey	2007	
3936	Audrey Malicki	2007	
3937	Eddie Malicki	2007	
3938	Martyn Goodwin	2007	
3939	Robert Grieve	2007	
3940	Sue Dalton	2007 2007	
3941	Ian D. Thomas	2007 2007	
3942	John Swanson	2007	
3943	John R. G. Rogerson	2006	
3944	Elizabeth Young	2007	
3945	John Young	2007	
3946	Gerena Sumen	2007	
3947	Shaun Breen	2007	
3948	Ali Little	2007	
3949	Kenny Little	2007	
3950	Charles Stuart	2007	
3951	Gerard Simpson	2007	
3952	J.A.S. Stewart	2007	
3953	Stuart Meek	2007	
3954	Richard E. Braithwaite	2007	
3955	Pauline Inghammar	2007	2007

3956	Ake Inghammar	2007	2007	3992	Mike Smith	2007	2007
3957	Frances Lawrie	2007		3993	Hilary Tillett	2007	
3958	Jenny Shepherd	2007		3994	Andrew Tillett	2007	
3959	Steve Shepherd	2007		3995	Andrew Duguid	2007	
3960	Nigel Earp	2007		3996	Timothy G. L. Ferrari	2007	
3961	Mark Beaton	2007		3997	Jeff Breen	2007	
3962	W. Bell	2007		3998	Linda Ross	2007	
3963	Frances Rickus	2007		3999	William A. Ross	2007	
3964	Brian Fraser	2007		4000	Moira Yeoman	2005	
3965	Trevor Williams	2007		4001	Robert Herd	2007	
3966	Sandra Wallace	1994		4002	Chris Osmond	1982	2002
3967	Lawrence Mitchell	2007		4003	Bill Cook	1990	
3968	Bob Barlow	2007		4004	Roderick McKay	2007	
3969	Donald McMillan	2007		4005	Neil Deveney	2007	
3970	Alex J. King	2007		4006	Chris Pine	2007	
3971	Richard Cheslin	2007		4007	Dave Habgood	2007	
3972	Stephen Clark	2007		4008	Rodney Crawford	2007	
3973	Jim McKay	2007		4009	George Meikleham	2007	
3974	Andy Brydie	2007		4010	Brian Endicott	2007	
3975	Geoff Thompson	2007		4011	Rob Clipsham	2007	
3976	William Venn	2007		4012	John Carey	2007	
3977	Jonathan Venn	2007		4013	David Thomas	2007	
3978	Andrew L.G. Drummond	2007		4014	Pamela Foord	2004	
3979	James R. Stewart	2007		4015	Colin Foord	2004	
3980	*Stuart Campbell	2007		4016	Roslyn Bruce	1994	
3981	Andrew Faulk	2007		4017	Bill Bruce	1994	
3982	Graham P. Nash	2002		4018	Tom Cuthbert	2007	
3983	Sarah Muirhead	2007		4019	Colin R. Marshall	1991	
3984	Francis Hughes	2007		4020	Eugene Ward	2007	
3985	Ian Wasson	2007		4021	Daniel Shanks	2007	
3986	Alan Bilsland	2007		4022	Martin Dinnage	2008	
3987	Colin Lees	2004		4023	Paul Hannon	2007	1998
3988	Janet Tyler	2007		4024	Mike Buchanan	2003	
3989	John Whiteman	2007		4025	Derek Grieve	2006	
3990	Christine Gordon	1998 2000 2007		4026	David Roeder	2006	
3991	Ron Elliott	1998		4027	Graham Tomlinson	2008	

One of the main incentives of taking on the duties of Clerk is the prospect of receiving a steady flow of fascinating letters. The rules for registration are very simple, with the minimum requirement being a signed statement confirming that all 284 summits have been climbed. There is no application form or evidence required, though there are some guidelines on the Website which suggest that a few more details are appreciated, such as first and last summits, time taken, age, future projects. Fortunately, such a momentous occasion achieved after so many years of hard toil makes most Compleatists quite reflective and more than willing to share their thoughts and feelings and recount a few interesting stories.

So what is the average Munroist really like? Answering this simple question has become one of my little projects and already a picture is emerging from the contents of their correspondence. Based on a sample of 165 received since August, 81% are male, average age 54 years, and 64% live in Scotland. Average time to Compleate is 23 years, with an average of 16 people joining the summit celebrations. 18% Compleat at the same time as their partner.

Over the years, there have been many attempts to explain why people go to the hills and Munroists give a variety of reasons. John Risk (3807) wrote: 'It all started back in September 1978, escaping my home town of Dundee as far as the bus would take us and not aware for a while what Munros were.' Brian Endicott (4010) started in exactly the same way as myself: 'I owe my introduction to our great outdoors to the Boys Brigade in the late sixties.' For others such as Andy Brydie (3974) it was clearly part of family life: 'My first Munro was Cairngorm in August 1977, taken there as a small child by my father, Jim Brydie [99].' Tony Goodings (3847) '… bought *The Munros* and started using them as a basis for walking the dogs (one did 104 and another 77).' Celebrities occasionally play a part, as reported by Stan Franklin (3830) who '… started them at the age of fifteen on a sunny day when the whole of Gartocharn where I lived was taken up Ben Lomond by Tom Weir who lived in the village.' Colin R. Marshall (4019) recalled, '… my 2nd and 3rd Munros done in 1957-58 with the Edinburgh University Mountaineering Club, including Robin Smith.' Going to the hills is sometimes considered as 'character building', though not apparently by many Munroists. Ronald Mitchell (3866) commented that: 'Many of these early trips were with groups from Youth Camps from deprived areas of Aberdeen – first and probably the last Munro for many of these teenagers.' While Edward Jones (3929) remembered: 'My personal Munro round started when I was sixteen on an Outward Bound course at Loch Eil.'

Many Compleaters recognise the unique nature of Munro bagging, combining as it does the pleasures of hillwalking with the compulsion of working through a list. Christine Robinson (3775) admitted: 'I never realised at the time it was going to become such an obsession', a feeling shared by Eddie Malicki (3937) who confessed 'I wanted the "tick" but did not want to finish bagging, such was the addiction!' Fortunately, the thrill of ticking is easily balanced with other pleasures. Sue Dalton (3940) & Ian D. Thomas (3941) explained 'Lists are a wonderful incentive to explore new hills, but we equally love travelling through the landscape and camping wild in the most beautiful country on earth. Our first Scottish mountain was Ben Nevis … and we have had 21 "Munro bagging" holidays in Scotland since – mostly backpacking across the Highlands for two or three weeks in May, posting on supplies and collecting Munros and tops as we went. These have been some of our best holidays.' Presumably with a view to 'putting something back' James Bussey (3865) described how: 'All of my Munro round was completed during my service in the Royal Air Force Regiment. We also spend several weekends at voluntary conservation activities each year, on John Muir Trust properties. We consider these to be an important part of our mountain activities.'

Having started collecting Munros, there seem to be many and varied targets for Compleation. Mike Croft (3890) is just one of many who wanted to tie in with one of life's milestones: 'Having walked 30 or 40 Munros over the years without really noticing it, I took it into my head to do them all after my 60th birthday.' There may, of course, be many obstacles on the way, such as Nigel Lack (3772) who '… was not always sure I would climb all the Munros as I have a real fear of heights.' On a more serious note, one of the most satisfying and uplifting aspects of being Clerk is receiving reports from people who have used their round as a route to better health, and even overcome serious health problems to Compleat. Alan Bilsland (3986) '… was medically retired with heart problems back in 1999 … I started to target the Munros in line with a general attempt to improve and maintain good health. I am delighted to say that this was an extremely good strategy and I feel healthier today than I did eight years ago.' John Colin Smith (3910) wrote: 'In 1999 I had triple by-pass surgery and since then have climbed 175 Munros plus 24 repeats.' However, the most remarkable triumph was recounted by Murray Elder (3897) who '… had reached 82 – Dreish, but could not go on to Mayar – heart problems. In 1988 I had a heart transplant and climbed Stuic an Lochain in 1989. I completed this year (2007) … my heart surgeon was also present.' Lord Elder, as he should more properly be addressed, also informed me 'There are now three Munroists in the House of Lords. Chris Smith and Alan Haworth compleated before joining the Lords.', making him the first Peer to compleat. Keep an eye out for ermine-trimmed cagoules!

A number of Compleaters send copies of fascinating databases and spread-sheets detailing their entire round, while others choose to highlight some facts they consider significant. Wraight Shepherd (3921) did not have to travel very far, as apparently 'From my house below Stirling Castle I can see 13 Munros and I have just identified another Top in front of Ben More.' Others made light of much more arduous journeys just to reach the hills, such as Jonathan Massey (3935) who noted 'Most of my Munros have been climbed on weekend raids North of the Border, and I have counted that I have made 88 Munro bagging trips to compleat my quest!' Anyone just starting their round and wondering what they might be letting themselves in for might like to consider the following:

It has taken me 54 trips to Scotland (from Reading) to do the round, and it involved 170 hill days. I estimate I walked for around 950 hours covering 2490km and climbing 171,350m. I also used a bike for around 160km in total. Alan McCaffery (3871)

106 days walking in 4 years and 9 days.
1359 miles walked or cycled and 509,476 feet ascended.
Most Munros in 1 day 9.
Number of aborted walks 1.
Number of times climbed wrong mountain 1. Ken Mathewson (3926)

58 trips to Scotland from South Yorkshire.
Walked 1,800 miles.
Climbed 720,000 feet over 153 days in 24 years. Martyn Goodwin (3938)

To achieve the compleation I have walked some 1704 miles, climbed 565,337ft (169,601m) and spent 1,075 hours on the hills. I have never stayed overnight on the hills which meant some long days. J.A.S. Stewart (3952)

- It has taken me 13 years to complete the round
- Average number completed per year = 22
- Most climbed in one year = 55
- Least climbed in one year = 4
- I have made 50 trips from Surrey to Scotland
- Have spent a total of 156 days on the hills
- I am still married! Richard Braithwaite (3954)

All the more remarkable then are the achievements of those Compleaters from overseas, such as Stephan Jung (3828): 'Being German I could visit the Highlands only for an average three weeks holidays…. walking all these hills was a special experience I will never rue, even though I now live in the German Alps.' Not content with the Munros, Johan de Jong (1423) from Holland has finished the Corbetts and started on the Donalds. Most foreigners make things a bit easier for themselves, like Laila Kjellstrom (3843), '… Swedish but have been living in Edinburgh for 22 years.' Fellow Swedes Pauline (3955) and Ake Inghammar (3956) wondered 'My husband Ake seems to be the first Swede who has completed the Munros and Furths? By the way, what do you call a Munroist who has completed the Furths?!!' Living in Beauly helps and this delightful couple dropped their details off in person, just in time to join the Clerk for afternoon tea. Another couple, Bob Boyce (3836) and Ingrid Baber (3837) wondered 'Ingrid is German and I am Canadian, are we the first foreign couple to do all the Munros together? However, both of us have been living in Scotland longer than Germany or Canada!' This is clearly an area with a lot of potential for achieving 'firsts', but the Clerk is too busy adding to and amending the List to keep such records, so was also unable to help Maggie Carr (3850) who '… was born in Zimbabwe. We do not expect that she is the first from this country to Compleat, but would be interested to know how many others there have been.'

Climbing Munros has of course always been popular with couples, and the correspondence indicates that this continues to be a romantic activity. Note that in keeping with good manners, the Clerk has adopted a 'ladies first' policy when allocating numbers to Compleate couples. Kevin Luton (3858) '… proposed to Susan at the summit of Seana Bhraigh in 2005 and we were married in 2006.' Things developed a bit more slowly for Robbie McFedries (3880) and Sheila Mitchell (3879) who described how 'I climbed my first Munro and developed a real love for the outdoors. A year later, I met a girl who, when we climbed our first Munro together (her first hill), I was delighted to note she also shared the love of the hills. We married a few years later and slowly we began to believe that maybe one day we could compleat the Munros.' In the best romantic tradition this story had a happy ending when, on Compleation, 'I kissed my wife THEN we kissed the cairn.' Jenny (3958) and Steve Shepherd (3959) also planned a happy ending as 'Jenny's 1st Munro was Steve's 49th and all previous 48 were then repeated to enable Jenny to catch up (true love runs deep!).' Roderick McKay (4004) found an interesting way of showing the effect of a non-climbing wife on his progress: 'This graph just shows you – getting married slows up everything!'

When the day of Compleation finally arrives, and a triumphant party gather around the final summit cairn, there are often noteworthy moments. A celebratory alcoholic drink is usually shared and drams enjoyed this year included Bowmore, Lagavulin and Tobermory. Mike Smith (3992) and his party chose an unusual way to celebrate. 'On the way down, when we found a relatively flat piece of ground, we played boulles, the girls winning by a short head.' Unfortunately, the generally poor summer weather dampened a number of celebrations. Derek Nonhebel (3877) seems to have been particularly unlucky and complained 'From a weather point of view it (Bynack More) was the worst weather I have experienced on any of the Munros.' Ben More (Mull) remains a popular finish and proved a highlight of the round for Robin Paton (3779), 'Flying my own aircraft from Strathallan airfield, Perthshire to Glenforsa airstrip on Mull, making a rapid ascent/descent of Ben More and flying back – all within 8 hours.' Friends of John Rogerson (3943) composed and recited a very entertaining poem which started thus:

Auld hill-baggers hang aboot,
But needna' fade awa',
If time an' tide permit them still,
Tae face the wind an' sna'.

Foor life doesna' end on yon last Top,
There's plenty left tae dae,
Just close yer eyes an' tell yersel'
Auld Munroists nivver dee.

For friends of James R. Stewart (3979), things did not turn out quite as expected: 'A memorable day, slightly spoiled by one of the two drivers being booked for speeding, driving out of Fort William on the way home!'

Once all the fuss is over and the new Munroist sits down to notify the Clerk of the List, mulling over future hill plans produces an interesting variety of responses. Davina Lavery (3780) is fairly typical: 'Climbing all the Munros has been a fantastic journey. I feel so lucky to have got to parts of Scotland that I might not have otherwise visited. I look forward to seeing even more of Scotland as I try to complete the Corbetts.' For some, there is a hint that their new challenges may not be met with quite the same enthusiasm. Alex Thomson (3776) noted with some regret: 'I have also begun to climb the Corbetts and now wish I had had the foresight to climb more of them in passing.' Dave Malia (3778) is set on greater things and reported 'I have at last walked all the Munros.... I have no intention of doing them again or the Corbetts.... I climbed Ama Dablam last October and hope to go to Argentina over Christmas to walk Aconcagua.' Dave Hewitt (3907) editor of *The Angry Corrie* clearly likes a focus for his bagging: 'Perhaps the most unusual feature of an otherwise fairly mundane round was that the Saddle (Compleation) was also my 1000th Munro. The landmark I'm working towards just now is a calendar round on Ben Cleuch – to have been up it on every date. Currently have 39 "gaps".' Many Compleaters seem content to sit back and enjoy the feeling of satisfaction neatly summed up by Richard Williams (3841):

Cost, around the price of an average brand new car!! Plus £10,000 worth of knee surgery (both worth every penny.) Commitment – difficult (that rain/mist, them midges, that long drive home to Wales, them pronunciations!). Generally some of the best scenery in the country. Don't think my age and knees will last for all the Corbetts, but will do some of them. Have now completed the three M's Matterhorn, Mount Blanc, Munros.

Thanks to all who have made the effort to write and notify the Clerk. Sadly, a significant number of Munroists prefer to remain unlisted, though some eventually have a change of heart, like Chris Osmond (4002) who admitted '... after much thought, I have finally decided to "come clean" and own up to being a compleater. I have completed the Munros twice and the Furths once.' Some write immediately, while others are a bit slower off the mark, like Bill Cook (4003) who explained 'I saw from a recent item in *The Angry Corrie* that you have taken over as the keeper of the list. It reminded me that perhaps it was time to put my name down – a little late. I completed on 6 May 1990.' Most choose to receive tangible evidence of their achievement, like Ruth Swanson (3932): 'As instructed, I am enclosing a SAE. I would like a certificate, please. (Simply to have something to show off to my grandchildren!)' Unfortunately, the new postal rates for A4 envelopes has caused some confusion, so please check!

In the last batch of letters received someone, who will remain nameless, sent back his certificate and asked to be removed from the List, while David Roeder (4026) finished with my favourite summary for the year of what it is all about.

> I've walked with family, friends, solo or just shared a route with strangers were going the same way at the same pace providing companionship and conversation, particularly welcome in times of poor visibility. I've seen the inside of many a cloud, had just one poor Brocken Spectre and one temperature inversion (Bens Hope and Klibreck). I've slept at 900m, awoken covered in ice (in June) and not seen a soul in 46 hours. Having visited them all, the Munros are like old friends, but always remember that you visit on their terms and they might just bite back.

Once the Clerk has finished with them, all the correspondence is passed on to the archive in the National Library of Scotland in Edinburgh. So please keep the letters coming and take your place in history.

AMENDMENTS

The following have added to their original entries on the List. Each Munroist's record is shown in full. The six columns give number, name, and year of Compleation of Munros, Tops, Furths and Corbetts. *SMC member.

Number	Name	Munros	Tops	Furths	Corbetts
2199	R. Keith Gault	1999			
		2007			
2226	E. David S. Ellis	1999	1999	1996	2007
555	Robin Howie	1982	1984	1987	
		1984	1987		
		1987	1992		
		1990			
		1992			
		1995			
		1999			
		2002			
		2007			
3440	Thomas Campbell McGee	2005		2007	
2893	Tommy Hunter	2003		2007	
3439	Donald Wooley	2005		2007	
1878	Bill Walker	1997		2007	
951	Andy Harrison	1991			2007
1150	David I. Nixon	1993	1994		
		1998			
989	W. A. Simpson	1988	1994		

1351	Margaret Beattie	1994			2007
		2000			
		2005			
1221	John F. Wilson	1993	1997		
		1999			
		2007			
118	Diane Standring	1973	2006	2007	2004
		2006			
258	Iain R. W. Park	1981			
		1997			
2750	Peter Goodwin	2002	2006	2005	
288	Jim Braid	1982	1982		
		2007	2007		
1133	Wattie Ramage	1992			
		2001			
		2007			
3073	Ian G. McCrae	2003		2007	
2540	D. W. Horner	2001		2007	
957	George Herraghty	1991			2006
375	Robert H. MacDonald	1984	1989		
		1987			
		1990			
		1992			
		1995			
		2002			
		2007			
474	Stephen Stobie	1986			
		1989			
2784	*Reg Pillinger	2002		2007	
462	Roger Booth	1986	1996	1993	2007
267	Martin Hudson	1981	1981	1982	
		2007			
2462	Elizabeth Reid	2000			2006
203	David Foster	1979	1999		1986
		1999			
3556	Chris Dodd	2006	2006		
1423	Johan De Jong	1995		1995	2007
3158	David Bunting	2004		2007	
1512	*Neil H. Martin	1995	2006	2007	
1513	Joan S. Lamb	1995	1995		
		2007	2007		
1397	Douglas R. Macleod	1995	1997	1998	2007
		2000	2002	2003	
2698	Alan Whatley	1987	1987	2002	2006
		2007			
1889	Gordon Paterson	1997			
		2007			
2057	Alan J. Murray	1998		2005	

No.	Name					
		2007				
384	J. M. Gear	1985	1985	2007	1996	
		1996				2005
		2005				
3857	Alan Butterworth	2007	2007	2007		
2754	David Flatman	2002	2007			
1798	Colin Watts	1997		2003	2007	
2579	Isabel Watts	2001		2003	2007	
2351	Brian Maguire	2000	2006	2007		
3481	Rick Salter	2005		2007		
3523	Jenny Hatfield	2005		2007		
422	George Wostenholm	1985	1982			2002
2888	Steve Marsh	2003	2007			
2862	John Edward Casson	2002		2007		
1387	Ian H. Anderson	1994		1999		
2003	Bob Macdonald	1998	2006	2006		
259	*Derek Bearhop	1981	1988			
		1988				
		1994				
		2007				
1258	Michael Hanlin	1993	1998			
3339	Elizabeth McDonald	2005		2007		
763	Brian D. Curle	1990	1991	1991	1992	
		2005				
707	Robert Gibson	1989	1996			

This information is of course also available at **www.smc.org.uk** along with the increasingly popular Munroists Photo Gallery. To register a Compleation or amendment, please write to Dave Broadhead, Cul Mor, Drynie Park North, Muir of Ord, IV6 7RP. If you would like to receive a certificate for either Munro or Corbett Compleation, please enclose an A4 sae (with the correct postage please). Once you have received a number, a Compleation photo can be posted or emailed to the Webmaster.

Enjoy your hills.

Dave Broadhead,
Clerk of the List.

The Munro Society

DURING THIS last year the Society took steps to settle two controversies which have rumbled on for too many years. The disputes concerned the heights of Foinaven and Beinn Dearg (Torridon), both marked on the OS maps as 914m. Neither of them has a trig. point and so within the variances allowed for by the OS, it was possible they exceeded 914.4m (i.e. 3,000ft). In the case of Foinaven, it was alleged, *inter alia*, that the marked height was at the *lower* end of the summit ridge. Modern surveying techniques involving the use of satellites make it possible to measure heights to within ±30mm; clearly technology could solve the controversy.

Having decided to try and settle the matter, the problem facing The Munro Society was that of cost. Hiring complex surveying equipment and the surveyors to operate it is expensive, certainly beyond the Society's resources. However, four surveying firms were approached to see if there was any way in which costs could be reduced and one, CMCR Ltd. of Larbert, offered to carry out the surveys at no cost to the Society, its return being the resultant publicity.

After one false start due to atrocious weather, the heightings were carried out and the results were checked and accepted by the OS. Foinaven was found to be 911.046m (2,988.96ft) and Beinn Dearg 913.675m (2,997.58ft), thus the controversy has been eliminated and the lists of Munros and Corbetts remain unaltered.

It was alleged by some that the Society was motivated solely to increase the number of Munros. We take the view that, at 284, there are quite enough to be going on with. What the Society would claim is that it is following on in the tradition of Sir Hugh Munro and his cohort who took great pains to check and recheck the heights of mountains. All that has changed is the technology. Whether further heightings, e.g. of the 915m Munros, will take place is a matter now under consideration.

This last year also saw the publication of the first number of *The Munro Society Journal*. This has been well received and a review will be found elsewhere in this journal.

The annual dinner was held at the Ben Wyvis Hotel, Strathpeffer where the speaker was Society member, R.H. Chris Smith (Lord Smith of Finsbury). With an expanding membership, the Society is facing the welcome problem of finding Highland hotels large enough to take our numbers at the annual dinner.

Copies of the Society's DVD, *In the Beginning*, are still available. This consists of interviews with early Munroists and their recollections of the Scottish hills in the 1950s and 1960s. The cost is £11 including p & p (cheques made out to The Munro Society), available from John Burdin, Tayview, 15 Ardestie Place, Monifieth, Angus, DD5 4PS.

Communications concerning the Society should be addressed to:

Hon. Secretary, 12 Randolph Court, Stirling, FK8 2AL

or

<themunrosociety@usa.net>

Iain A. Robertson

IN MEMORIAM

MALCOLM SLESSER j. 1948

WHEN THIS appears Malcolm, my friend of a lifetime, will of necessity be dead, unless of course there has been a dreadful Editorial Error. I may well be dead too. You see we have agreed to write each other's obituary notice for the Journal while we are both still alive. I am writing this in the year 2002 so the statistical probability of it appearing in the next ten years is quite high.

I have an impossible task. Malcolm's life was full of complex endeavour. From the beginning he was involved in so many initiatives, so many parallel projects, so many bold, convoluted ploys, so many ways of maximising whatever resources were available. He was adept at pushing a quart into a pint pot. This was a difficult exercise even for him and frequently the pot would fail to take the strain and break. Sometime this would leave Malcolm looking puzzled and his friends dismayed, other times he would not notice the pot had broken and this would leave his friends feeling puzzled as well as dismayed. Not infrequently, however, the pot held and a bold enterprise would come off.

I met him at the first Sunday morning meet of the EUMC I attended at the little quarry on Blackford Hill in October 1946. I was a first year medical student aged 18. Malcolm aged 20 was already a PhD student. Edinburgh Academy, the school he attended, was designed to educate middle of the road people with malleable minds and was unable to cope with this brilliant but obtuse schoolboy. To solve this problem the school had expedited his admission to university; probably the school and university bent several rules to do so. Such things were possible in those less bureaucratic days. When I met him he had already his own lab at King's Buildings. It was filled to capacity with surrealistically arranged flasks, retorts, tubing, condenser spirals, gas cylinders, furnaces, books, papers and, of course, climbing gear. After he left, it took years to clear it up; maybe they are still working on it to this day.

In 1948 I accompanied Malcolm and the differently endowed, but equally difficult genius Geoff Dutton to the Swiss Alps. As the junior member of this trio I was suitably deferential as, even then, they were both obviously men of destiny. (This friendship, in spite of mutual exasperation, lasted until death did us part.) Getting to the Alps at that time was not a simple exercise. Continental train tickets were only issued in London. The rail system was still recovering from wartime disruption. Only a restricted number of tickets were available. Malcolm's sister who lived in London queued for hours to get them. His other sister, a surgeon in Leicester, was alerted to arrange accommodation for us in her mess at the hospital, on our journey south. I mention this to illustrate his ability to organise the available resources was an inbuilt characteristic. We hitch-hiked down, of course. Dutton sported an Africa Corps cap which led one establishment lady to remark that it was a disgrace that German prisoners were allowed to go on holiday. Switzerland was undamaged by war and had a generous rationing system. Butter and sugar were lavish compared to home. The catch was, however, that you could only take 25 pounds sterling per annum out of the country which made for modest living amidst the abundance. We spent a week at Grindelwald climbing the Fiescherhorn and the Wetterhorn, climbs well within our ability. We didn't know this of course until afterwards. We assumed that the ascent of any Alp would be a duel with death. It is embarrassing to think back on these days of inexperience, limited horizons and tight economic constraints.

Then there was the motorbike period. Memories raise of Tam o' Shanter-like drives on Sunday nights from the Coe on third-hand temperamental bikes that had to be nursed home like invalids, making running repairs and economising on rationed petrol. Malcolm, later, was a prime mover in establishing the Edinburgh Bus Meets (SMCJ 1961, XXVII, 152, 153–6). During the subsequent private car period no one thought of going anywhere without fare paying passengers. It was just too expensive. Petrol for example was 20p a gallon. I don't think I knew anyone wealthy enough to have his car repaired in a garage. Things are better now.

He and Geoff Dutton were competent, sensitive pipers in those student days Malcolm's party piece was a creditable rendering of 'John MacDonald of Glencoe'. He kept up his skill into this century by switching to the cauldwind pipes and an electronic version of the piob mhor.

After getting his PhD he went to work for Shell in Trinidad. I remember his farewell party at the Wee Windaes restaurant which ended with a traverse of the window sills above the High Street. He took his skis to Trinidad assuming that he could have weekends skiing in the Andes. After all on the map the Andes of Columbia were not all that far away: even he did not manage that one. A year later he was back in the High Street and then off the next summer to West Greenland as a member of one of Harald Drever's Geology Expeditions. Norman Tennent was the other lay member. They made some good ascents when allowed off the scientific leash. Harald Drever also survived the experience quite well although it is said, like many others, he had to take counselling.

In 1952 he was a member of the British North Greenland Expedition and overwintered at Britannia Lake about latitude 78 degrees north. He learned to drive a tracked vehicle and travelled far onto the icecap. He also learned to drive dogs and drove his own team for several hundred miles from Daneborg north to Britannia Lake. These were among the last of the old style expeditions.

With this experience behind him he organised his first major independent expedition, the 1958 Scottish North East Greenland Expedition. This was a major achievement In those far-off days expeditions did not often originate from Scotland. Most were 'British' and were organised somewhere in the south. Organising something from Scotland was unusual, almost bad form. Bill Murray, Tom MacKinnon, Tom Weir and by no means least the 'real' Dougie Scott had pioneered the way with the Scottish Himalayan Expedition of 1950. In the 1958 expedition we all helped, but the real drive for fund-raising and organisation came from Malcolm. Maybe the expedition did not merit a book but it did merit an RSGS lecture at the Usher Hall. At any rate the hall was full.

Many Club luminaries were on that trip: Doug Scott, Len Lovat, Donald Bennet, Ken Bryan, Charlie Rose. Equally illustrious were Stan Paterson and Roddie Cameron but they never condescended to join the Club. On this expedition Stan started his glaciological research studying the movement of the Seftstrom Glacier and eventually became the author of the definitive textbook on the Mass Balance of Glaciers which was translated into many languages. Roddie became a maker of baroque flutes, the foremost in the world as it happens. He also became the de facto Cultural Ambassador for Scotland in California.

I make no apology for this digression. Malcolm was the rocket that put many of us into orbit. Without Malcolm's energy and creative drive I and many, many others would have lived less interesting lives. He may have knocked things over and trod on tender feelings (somehow I don't mind mixing a metaphor when I think of my good friend) but that was because he was walking towards a goal, didn't take his eye off it and, thus, didn't notice the people or feelings in the way. It was not his fault if they allowed his often impossible behaviour to spoil the experience. No one takes a personal affront at other forms of moving energy like thunderstorms or squalls of wind, uncomfortable though they be: his friends learned to regard him as belonging to this class of phenomenon. However, he shared all his enterprises bountifully. The various charter flights he organised to Greenland were offered at cost, all he got for his considerable investment in time and worry was a free trip for himself. He was no selfish loner.

In 1960 he was in Greenland again with John Hunt's curious youth club expedition when he made major, epic ascents of the Hjørnespids and Berserker Spire with Macnaught Davis (SMCJ 1961, XXVII, 152, 124–30). I remember he set off on the long trek up the Berserkerbrae glacier carrying an 80lb rucksack and a boil on the back of his neck as big as a fried egg with the yolk about to burst. He did not bend under adversity.

The expedition to Russia is fully related in his book Red Peak – see the book itself and also SMCJ 1963, XXVII, 154, 353–5) and review in SMCJ 1964, XXVIII, 155, 61–3 or Red Pique as it is sometimes referred to – see Patey's pastiche of the Alpine Club song in SMCJ 1966, XXVIII, 157, 197–8. He fought the corner for Scottish equal representation on that expedition to the best of his ability. He and Graeme Nicol were the last of the caravan to reach the top of Peak of Communism and did so at the end of their resources in a heroic final trudge, watched dispassionately by the oxygen-starved earlier arrivals collapsed around the summit cairn. There was no team-spirit in the Russian climbing ethos. If you didn't get to the top without help you were nobody. If you got to the top you got a large medal. That expedition, you remember, was marred by the death of Robin Smith and his companion Wilfred Noyce.

Malcolm was not a big-time mountaineer à la Bonington. The metier of siege-master requires single-minded dedication and a correspondingly restricted outlook. He was much more interesting than that. He was too 'multipotential' to be only one thing. He was nevertheless a bold, competent and imaginative all-round mountaineer with a long list of good climbs to his credit in Scotland and in various parts of the world furth of the Kingdom. I can't face the task of cataloguing the wide spectrum of his mountaineering experience on rock, ice and ski. He was also an adventurous scientist, entrepreneur, participant in contemporary culture, pater familias, bon viveur and, as they say, much, much else beside.

He was abundantly resourceful in the face of unexpected difficulties and frank emergencies. Then he was at his best and could supply leadership. He could think on his feet and apply logic in the field. I remember him telling of an accident he had when his canoe capsized and got swamped in the Sound of the Cumbraes. He told me he tried to drydock it by blowing up an inflatable lilo underneath it. It didn't work but it was a good idea. Another time in Spitzbergen, not so long ago, towards the end of a long day, our snowmobiles and trailers sank through the ice of a thawing, crotch-deep river. We were tired, wet, and cold and unable to think straight. We rigged up a complicated system of ropes and pulleys. Malcolm was the only one who understood the dynamics of the cat's cradle we had created. We followed his instructions and against all expectations the skidoo came out and we could continue our journey.

One of his boldest trips on which I was a member was the 1969 attempt to take a small boat a hundred miles down the Blosseville Coast of East Greenland to climb the isolated Mount Mikkelsen (SMCJ 1970, XXIX, 161, 256–9). This meant committing ourselves to the coastal pack ice which can often be a one way valve. His contingency plan for this involved leaving food dumps along the coast so we could walk back if the boat got stuck and then wait on the south side of Scoresby Sound until the sea froze and we could walk back across the twenty miles to the only airstrip where we could be picked up. That would have been a couple of months later. It was very important for us to rescue ourselves if anything went wrong.

He and Bill Wallace were a symbiotic pair who competitively extracted the most out of any given opportunity. In the Alps they generally skied a system non-stop from first to last lift, then in the gathering dusk traversing with rucksacks to the nearest hut, climbing something the next day and so on ad infinitum; if you weren't moving you weren't living. It was hard for a normal person like me to keep up when I was with them. They were both extraordinarily competent all-terrain skiers, able to handle everything from ice to wet heather and slopes of intimidating steepness carrying heavy rucksacks.

He was extremely kind to his friends and would go to tremendous lengths to help them in adversity. For example the duality between the competent, directly focused Malcolm and the less-than competent, impractical, oblique and wildly romantic Norman Tennent was an intriguing exercise in toleration by opposites (See 'Missing the Last Post' in SMCJ 1960, XXVII, 151, 27–32 and Norman's Obituary in SMCJ 1993, XXXV, 184, 341–2). I remember Norman once failed in some task set by Malcolm which was too devious for anyone, let alone Norman, to follow. It involved staying in Malcolm's house while the owner was away. Following the inevitable bust-up when Malcolm returned, Norman ruefully remarked, 'I don't think he found me a very good tenant'. Nevertheless, they were good for each other and I remember with respect the touching farewell speech Malcolm gave at Norman's funeral in the little church at Arisaig. Another contrast in opposites was with the equally dynamic and enterprising Graham Tiso. Malcolm was essentially a romantic who tried to be a business man. Graham, on the other hand, got it the right way round and was able to be romantic from a successful business base. Nevertheless, although it is difficult to believe looking at the flourishing Tiso empire of today, Malcolm once employed Graham as a leader on one of the trips offered by 'Exploration and Travel', Malcolm's own short-lived travel firm. I wish I had kept the documentary proof of this. Malcolm once went down to Falmouth to crew for Graham in taking his (Graham's) new yacht up to Oban. To no one's surprise and everyone's amusement Malcolm jumped ship at Holyhead. I once was the nominal leader of an expedition of which Malcolm was a ranker. When Graham heard this he couldn't restrain his hilarity. 'You!', he exclaimed, choking on his laughter, 'You? You are going to lead Malcolm!' In the event it certainly turned out to be an unbelievably devious exercise.

Malcolm's own sailing exploits were considerable both in Scotland as far as St Kilda and Shetland and in other areas as remote as the Seychelles, Thailand and the English Channel.

He was of course subject to a lot of criticisms and, if any of his schemes went wrong, frank hilarity. I am thinking of the time during the Centennial Yacht Meet when his boat, the 'Souple Jade', dried out at low tide in Loch Scresort in full view of the anchored fleet. A wave of unconcealed delight swept through the anchorage. Malcolm and his crew did not notice because by the time they got back the boat had refloated. Everyone looked forward to the next low tide, but eventually some decent soul broke radio silence and the repeat performance was cancelled. The incident is recorded as a sequence of drawings dividing up the paragraphs in the account of the meet in the Journal (SMCJ 1998, XXXVI, 189, 744–53). Only technical problems prevented the drawings appearing on the top right hand corner of each page so they would give a moving picture when the pages were flicked. Malcolm could take such mishaps and jokes at his expense in his stride and in so doing increased everyone's already considerable respect and affection. I cannot remember him harbouring resentment or a grudge for very long; he had more interesting things to do with his time.

Like most of us he was a creative nationalist, believing that Scotland should contribute directly to the world rather than through the quagmire to the south of us. He not only talked about it but actually did something. He stood twice for Parliament. His political career was doomed partly from his unintentional ability to antagonise but mainly for the simple reason that he understood the laws of thermodynamics. Burdened by intellectual baggage like that he had no hope of arguing with ill-numerate, subjectively-thinking people who were trained in purely debating skills. It is difficult to have rational discussions with people who are trained to prove that, should the need arise, black and white are the same colour or even worse those who produce a conclusion that will win approval from the groundling press.

Latterly his great contribution was in the theory and application of energy-based economics. Along with Jane King he published several seminal books on the subject. One was matter-of-factly entitled 'The Management of Greed'. Many people will doubtless make careers based on this fundamental work and their considerable efforts to make it accessible to a wider public.

Malcolm and Geoff Dutton were the two giants who immeasurably expanded my life. The bold Malcolm was gloriously, clumsily and publicly fallible, Geoff fastidious, careful, shrewd and completely infallible. It was a great privilege for me to be the straight man for this extraordinary pair of gifted eccentrics. I wish I had the courage to end this with the dreadful, but accurate, solecism 'when shall we see their likes again'.

I have left this unchanged; it was part of the agreement. We both felt that death, being inevitable should be treated as just another irreversible move in the scheme of things. My friend died with his boots on on June 2007 on a steep slope above Loch Ailort. His body stopped; Malcolm probably kept climbing on without noticing, as if death was just another inconvenience to be overcome.

Iain Smart

DEREK HODGSON j. 1979

DEREK DIED in May 2007 whilst walking the Fells near his home in Grasmere with his wife Julie. He was 74 years old. Like a number of club members of late he simply dropped on the hill without warning.

Derek left school aged 14 and studied Electrical Engineering at night school. His perseverance gained him a job with I.B.M. and he worked his way up to management level.

When we first met in the mid-seventies we were both pushing middle age, but it never occurred to us at the time. A Geordie (I called him a 'posh' Geordie much to his annoyance) living in Largs and working in I.B.M. Greenock. His large company car and unlimited free petrol was but a small factor in our climbing friendship.

Derek was a very steady second man, capable of climbing almost anything. Not tall, yet he could reach any hold a long streak like me could reach. I don't know how he did that. Only once did he refuse to follow and that was on the first pitch of *Carnivore*. I wouldn't second it myself. Five years older than me he was active during the early days of aid climbing and got his revenge for *Carnivore* by dragging me up the main overhang at Malham Cove. We only did free climbing after that.

We did many of the best routes in Glen Coe by high speed, often mid-week, day trips when the weather was favourable. This included *Trapeze* which I now see as the most enjoyable rock climb we ever did together. Everything was just right and the variety of pitches appealed to us greatly.

A similar dash north took in *Yo-Yo*, in bone dry conditions. Derek phoned from Kingshouse on our way back and was told he had to catch a late train to London on I.B.M. business. That drive home sticks in the mind as much as the memorable climb. He later told me that sitting pin-striped and briefcased in the train, he wondered what his fellow travellers would have thought had they seen him six hours earlier on *Yo-Yo*. A different world.

Derek was a keen skier, as were his wife and three daughters. They made many trips to the Alps to indulge in this pastime. Eventually his job meant moving back to the South and I moved further north.

Derek retired in 1988 and the family went to live in Grasmere so our climbing trips were much reduced. Nevertheless we had some good outings in the Lake District and up north when we exchanged visits. Age of course was now a factor, but he never gave up the hills and rock climbing.

Derek was never a big player in club matters, He moved around a lot in his career and free time was limited. He was a club member for 27 years and I last met him at Sand in Applecross during a rendezvous when he and Julie were holidaying in Gairloch. He had never been to Sand before and we enjoyed a day of blue sky and rolling breakers. A last day at the best kept secret place in the Northwest.

My sympathies go out to Julie, her daughters Jane, Susan and Gillian and their children. Derek will always be remembered by all who knew him.

W.S.

I FIRST met Derek when he moved to Largs in his work for IBM in Greenock. Although I did not climb often with the Gourock team of Bill Skidmore, Jim Crawford, John Gillespie, John Madden, Dave Dawson and Bob Richardson it was always at least 4 or 5 times a year. It was on one of these occasions that Bill introduced me to Derek. We then travelled north in Derek's large car – the rest of us had much smaller and slower ones. Jim also came along. We drove to Binnein Shuas and two ropes ascended *Ardverikie Wall*. It was a memorable day of some dry rock and some wet rock and of course mist. However, the mist cleared and we all walked over the top of the hill to finish the day.

Soon, however, Derek moved south to Harpenden – a long way from the hills of any description let alone the Highlands. I was living in Derbyshire at the time and Derek became a regular climbing partner for many years from the early '80s to recently. One very memorable visit was made to Eagle Crag in Birkness Coombe, Buttermere. Dry rock enabled us to do the two classic routes of the crag, *Carnival* a fine E1 and *Eagle Front*, a three star VS. Coming down on a high, we visited the Fish Hotel for a quick pint to celebrate but ended up having several too many and unable to drive we sat in Derek's even larger new car completely tripped out listening to Dark Side of the Moon until dawn appeared.

Visits were made to Gogarth where we made an ascent of *Central Park* a superb HVS. Whilst I was enthralled with the climbing and approaching the crux – at the top of the route – the rope decided to become a tangled web. I was panicking as the rope couldn't be fed through the Sticht plate fast enough but Derek coolly and calmly slowly undid the tangled mess before I was committed to the final moves. Visits were made to the grit heartland of Derbyshire where many happy days were spent tearing skin off knuckles. Derek was at home on any rock type and although not a Munro bagger his heart was always longing to be in the hills.

Derek was a great guy to be with on the mountain crags or valley crags. Although he did not lead very much he could always get up anything. He was always reliable, safe and had a great dry humour. He did not suffer fools. It was a joy to visit him after his retirement to Grasmere. He was always welcoming, always a cup of tea and cake as well as a story.

When his wife Julie phoned to say that Derek had died suddenly during a short walk out, it was with disbelief and incredulity that it could have happened. He seemed fit, always cycling and wanting to be on the crags. In fact the last day out we had in Langdale some months ago we reached the crag after some 'Derek-high bracken bashing'. He was shorter than me and followed in the depths of the bracken stems hoping that I was heading in the right direction. We had a great day having found the crag, doing the majority of the routes there. It was fun and a joy to climb with him whether it was some long Scottish climb, a sea cliff or gritstone route or even an esoteric Welsh climb on an obscure cliff. He was at home on it all.

D.M.

DONALD GREEN j. 1963

DON, WHO was born on 5 December 1922 in Blairgowrie, commenced his journalistic career with DC Thomson in 1940.

During the Second World War he served with the RAF as a bomb aimer and on active service flew against Japanese targets in Burma and Siam. After demob he rejoined DC Thomson and, in all, he was employed by them for a total of 47 years, retiring in 1987 as Editorial Manager.

His love of the hills and wild places was a constant theme throughout his 85 years.

Don joined the Grampian Club in 1949 and quickly became a more than competent performer as hill walker and rock and ice climber. As a winter climber, he never owned a pair of crampons and stuck to tricouni-shod boots which he reckoned were more versatile in most situations. He completed the Munros on Beinn Dorain in 1966 being the 69th recorded person to do so. He finished the Furths in Ireland three years later and was the 46th recorded person to complete the Corbetts in 1992, commencing with Morrone in 1949 and finishing on Beinn Odhar.

Not content with this impressive list he began an ascent of the Donalds with Ben Cleuch in 1992 and completed on Tinto Hill in 1998, the 60th Compleater.

In addition to his membership of the Grampian Club, Don often climbed with the Perth section of the JMCS, climbing with John Proom.

Over the years, Don had climbing trips to The Lakes and The Isle of Skye, where he stayed with the McRaes at Glen Brittle House. On many of these expeditions his companion was Gilbert Little a fellow member of the SMC. Many club members will remember him by his regular attendance at the AGM and Dinner.

He was also an enthusiastic founder member of the Munro Society and was one of five climbers who appeared in a DVD produced by the Society featuring Early Munroists.

In the course of his long climbing career Don amassed a large collection of slides and photographs – many of the highest quality and several have been reproduced in various climbing guide books. As befits his training as a first-rate journalist, his photographs, as were his climbing log books and diaries, were catalogued meticulously and are an object lesson in how such information should be presented. Don contributed many articles on climbing and the outdoor scene to several publications, articles written in his inimical style with beautifully constructed phrases and with absolutely no grammatical infelicities!

When the Grampian Club rented Inbhirfhaolain, their climbing cottage in Glen Etive from the Forestry Commission in 1962, Don volunteered his services as the first Custodian, a post he was to hold for 20 years. In recognition of his and his wife Jean's contribution to the cottage they were elected Honorary Members. As an additional accolade Don was elected to the post of Honorary President in 1982, succeeding the legendary JHB Bell in that capacity.

He continued hill walking, albeit at a slower pace, right up to the end and his final ascent of a Munro was on Tuesday, 27th March 2007, when he, with several dozen others, on the 80th anniversary of the first outdoor meet of the Grampian Club, went to the summit of Mayar, in Glen Doll.

Derek Hodgson and his dog Nic Photo: Des Marshall
Don Green Photo: Bill Jones

Don died peacefully in his sleep on the morning of 26th December 2007.

The respect by which Don was held by fellow climbers, ex-work colleagues and family friends was emphasised by the large numbers who attended a Celebration of his life which was held in Discovery Point, Dundee on Saturday 19th January when various people, both friends and family, spoke publicly of the affection in which they held Don.

He will be sadly missed as a husband, father, and grandfather and as a climbing companion with whom it was always a pleasure to be with on the hill.

Q.C./W.H.J.

Through an unfortunate error a large part of an obituary for Tom Weir in last year's journal was omitted by mistake. Rather than print the missing section by itself, the obituary is reproduced here in its entirety.

TOM WEIR, MBE j. 1945

It was on a JMCS Novice Meet in February, 1957 that I first met Tom, and although on that occasion I didn't climb with him he soon had my address and where I worked. Tom lived at that time in Springburn on the north side of Glasgow, the centre of the Scottish railway locomotive construction and maintenance industry. Serving my apprenticeship in that industry in Springburn, Tom would look out for me at the end of the working day or hear on the radio that industrial strife was to occur, enabling him to make plans for us to go into the hills. From these small beginnings a lifelong friendship developed. Initially, I was very much the novice; Tom had the great gift of putting one at ease and also passing on his knowledge of climbing and his passionate enthusiasm for the Scottish hills and for Scotland.

In those days, Tom had a wee fawn-coloured Morris van, a great asset when the ownership of a private vehicle was rare, but necessary for Tom to gather material to build his career as a writer and photographer and to travel the country giving talks. That same wee van took Tom and I on many a venture, the camp kit packed in the back. More often than not, we headed up the Lomondside road to Glen Coe or the Arrochar Alps.

Rock and winter climbing equipment was very basic in these days, just a rope and a few slings, but that didn't stop Tom taking on climbs in difficult conditions. He was always concerned for the safety of others in the party if conditions proved particularly difficult. It wasn't unusual when conditions were marginal, the rocks wet and greasy, for Tom, determined to finish a climb, to get the spare socks out of the sack, fit them over his boots and continue up the climb.

Tom loved to talk to the people he met, especially hill and rock enthusiasts and when ever the opportunity arose, he would strike up a conversation, finding out what climbs and hills they were doing, what was new to the hill scene and the crags that were being explored. This was the Tom who loved to be immersed in climbing and countryside issues and valued what people had to say about what was happening in the Highlands, especially if it was new.

When the weather was particularly poor for climbing, Tom always came up with something and always managed not to be stuck indoors. An example of this was a mid morning in Torridon, the clouds well down in the glen, the rain hammering on the hut windows: "Not a day for the high hill today," says he "but I know of a chasm up on Sgurr Dubh that would give us an interesting scramble in this sort of weather." After a short walk we arrived at the foot of the sharply defined chasm, water cascading down its sidewalls into an already swollen burn. Very soon, we had forgotten how poor the day had started out as we scrambled up the chasm, water pouring down on us from its walls, navigating round some of the heavier falls or traversing the walls to avoid some of the larger pools in its bed. We emerged from the top of the route several hundred feet above the start quite soaked but satisfied that we had got out despite the weather.

A favourite pastime of Tom's was birdwatching, and I and many others, owe much to him for his knowledge and enthusiasm for 'birding'. Many a day on the hill, be it wet or dry, the field glasses would come into play to identify a bird – maybe just a quick call from a secluded perch – and Tom would announce the bird's identity without breaking step or conversation.

Tom loved nothing better than being among hills and hill people. There was a day we had in the Arrochar Alps when Glasgow and most of the Central Belt were covered by a thick sulpherous fog. We only broke through it on the highest tops, emerging into clear skies and warm sun and were met by a solitary climber, Joe Griffin, emerging out of the fog as if a door had just been opened.

Or, at the other end of the spectrum, on a day of hard frost and almost alpine conditions Tom and I found ourselves climbing up to one of two lines that Tom had sought out; he indicated that they had potential for a good new climb high on A' Chrois. After climbing some steep ground and shallow gullies we stood on an airy stance at the foot of two iced up cracks.

Tom made two attempts at the pitch first by the crack direct and then by a steep ramp leading into the crack higher up. He managed to gain some height to a stance and fix a peg belay. Determined as ever he attempted an overhanging shelf, gateway to the continuation of the crack system. After some difficult climbing he had to retreat, but was not ready to give in. So we changed positions and, using the ice axe to stand on, and higher up standing on the peg, I climbed into a small corner. From here I lead on and climbed up to the base of the second crack system on poor snow and ice. On closer inspection the second crack rose steeply with insufficient good snow or ice in or around it to climb with a safety margin, so disappointed, we made a long and difficult descent back to the corrie.

Disappointment never lasted long with Tom and he was soon on a high and full of the merits of winter climbing again after a day of wild weather and superb ice in Glen Coe on a great climb up Crowberry Gully .

Over the years Tom and I climbed many of the classic winter and summer routes. One day I received a telegram from Tom, that winter conditions were great on the hill and, if free, to hurry down to Gartocharn on Friday evening after work.

We left early on Saturday morning, dropping off Rhona in Strathyre before continuing to Bridge of Orchy and round to Forest Lodge. Stob Ghabhar, its summit covered in early morning mist and its slopes well coated in snow, looked superb as we crossed the bealach from Coire Toaig into Coirein Lochan. We traversed into the corrie well-filled with firm snow to the foot of the Lower Couloir.

After a quick bite we continued up the couloir and up the steep intermediate slopes to the foot of the Upper Couloir. It was with a little apprehension that Tom had climbed up to the Upper Couloir, as it was on a similar winter's day, some years previously, that he had taken a long slide from these slopes. As we entered the foot of the couloir a party was busy cutting steps up the first few feet of the big ice pitch. Disappointed at not having the climb to ourselves we fixed a belay at the foot of the pitch and attempted to keep warm in the strengthening wind.

Very shortly the leader of the party returned to the foot of the climb indicating that it had become too difficult for him and that they were going to descend. Tom felt their disappointment and immediately offered them a rope if they were prepared to wait while we climbed the pitch. The offer of a rope was accepted, and with them safely belayed I set off up the pitch while Tom, keeping an eye on my rope, chatted to the two climbers.

Cutting steps took a little time, but once above a big ice bulge, I fixed a belay, allowing Tom and the other party to come on. The wind was now racing up the couloir, spindrift and ice cuttings stinging the face and so not a time to be hanging around. Tom led on to easier ground and so out of the couloir and its icy blast.

Typical of some of our summer days out on the hill was an occasion when Tom and I had found a wonderful midge free campsite, just north of Inverlair in Glen Spean, and after a leisurely tea of soup and fried steaks, that Tom always cooked, we discussed the morrow's climbing options. It was July, the days were long and dry and the climbing possibilities great. Routes on the Ben and the crags of Glen Coe were considered, but Tom was for Ardverikie Wall on Binnein Shuas, a climb still to be visited by him.

We parked up at the bridge at the Luiblea road end, the morning fine and warm for a day out on the crags. Ardverikie Wall, high on the southern side of Binnein Shuas, overlooking Lochan na h-Earba was soon reached. Tom, as ever, was keen to get to grips with the climb, as the line of the route looked good and the rock warm. After a few feet of climbing Tom was in his element and with every few moves, enthusiastic comments drifted down.

Pitch followed pitch up this fine 600ft slab, Tom leading most of the better ones, singing their praises at each belay stance. 'What a climb!' commented Tom on reaching the top of the climb, 'The best yet', and 'What a day', as we descended to the track for the walk back to the car.

In time I moved to the far north and our visits to the hills together were not quite so frequent, but when we made it the Tom Weir enthusiasm for a climb or getting out the camp kit was always there. On returning to his home Rhona was full of life and always welcoming with a warm house and a fine meal, Tom summing up the day with 'Aye, a great climb, just out the Top Drawer'.

My few words are about a man who looked after me in what can be a hazardous period for a young climber starting out. I was more than fortunate in meeting Tom at that time and in many ways he was like a second father to me.

But as Tom said, not long before his ninetieth birthday, 'Years ago that was what I did; now you are looking after me'.

It was a fine, warm July day, the start of a prolonged spell of good weather. Friends, climbers and walkers from all airts came to say their Cheerios to Tom and no doubt Tom would have made his customary comment: 'Aye you should be out on the crags on a day like this'.

Afterwards my wife and I were motoring back from Gartocharn on the way home up through Glen Coe, the sun was streaming down over the crags of the Buachaille one of his favourite 'Peaks' and into the glen. I'm sure my close friend Tom is still there.

Roger JC Robb

PROCEEDINGS OF THE CLUB

The following new members were admitted and welcomed to the Club in 2007/8.

DAVID M. AMOS, (59), Local Government Officer, Edinburgh.

NEIL J. BOYD, (42), School-teacher, Edinburgh.

STUART BURNS, (30), IT Consultant, Fintry, Stirlingshire.

RICK CAMPBELL, (44), Joiner, Edinburgh.

DAVID CRAWFORD, (35), Registered Nurse, Paisley.

MICHAEL DIXON, (47), Teacher, Inverness.

HELEN G.S. FORDE, (62), Professional Artist, Edinburgh.

JAMES M. GRAHAM, (50), Firefighter, Dunblane, Perthshire.

RUTH LOVE, (46), Dentist, Edinburgh.

ANDREW D. MACDONALD, (54), Shop manager, Inchree, Inverness.

NEIL MCGOUGAN, (51), Building contractor, Taynuilt, Argyll.

COLIN MCGREGOR, (31), Injection moulder, Glenrothes, Fife.

JOHN SANDERS, (58), Businessman, Edinburgh.

NEIL R. SMITH, (44), Field engineer, Kyle of Lochalsh.

ANDREW J. TURNER, (37), Outdoor instructor, Disley, Stockport.

The One-Hundreth-and-Nineteenth AGM and Dinner

AFTER a number of years in Fort William the Club 119th AGM and Dinner moved to the Ben Wyvis Hotel in Strathpeffer. The weather was reasonable, but many member cut short a day in the hills to benefit from a very enjoyable talk and slide show by Des Rubens as he took us through his summer exploits in Waddington Range of British Columbia.

This was followed by the AGM at which the lengthiest discussion was on the funding of the upgrading to the CIC Hut. Reassurances were sort that the contingency was adequate for the work proposed. All other club business seemed to be going well and the members appeared happy to leave the decisions to the committee and office bearers!

Then a short break before the Dinner. We had 143 seated at a range of table sizes to suit the requests of the members and their dining guests. It was good to see all sections of the club well represented. Our after dinner entertainment came from President Paul Brian who summarised the Club year and then generously poked fun at Robin Campbell and himself, before handing over to Bill McKerrow to toast the guests from our Kindred Clubs. Our Principal Guest was John Cleare, who is well known to most members either as a climber or for his photography. With ease he name dropped and reminisced, as he talked through so many famous names and climbs – Tom Patey, Dougal Haston, the filming of the Old Man of Hoy, filming the Eiger Sanction and so on.

Sunday was another fine day and members dispersed over the Northern Highlands to complete an early winter weekend.

Chris M. Huntley

Easter Meet 2008 – Kinlochewe

At Kinlochewe Hotel the early Easter promised snow for the first time in a number of years. Members had agreed to continue holding the meet on the weekend following Easter and as we travelled north on Thursday the snow covered hills sparkled in the strong sun under a clear sky. The weather looked very promising. Sadly, when we woke next morning the hills were shrouded in low cloud. The adventurous members went up into the clouds and the others settled for lower walks.

On Friday evening John Hay treated members to a feast at his house in Torridon where we enjoyed wine and spirits and a splendid meal, salads, cullen skink, roast venison, venison casserole, mussels followed by cheese and coffee. John's wet suit was draped over the garden wall – a reminder of his unproductive attempts to add scallops to the menu. This huge effort by John ensured that everyone had a wonderful evening.

Saturday weather was improved. During the day the cloud level rose revealing the mountains. We climbed in a cold wind, through variable snow, to summits with fine views of distant hills. Others enjoyed rock climbing. The usual enjoyable Saturday evening dinner was proceeded by a group photograph in the style of the 1896 Easter Meet photo. The picture is destined to join the other Kinlochewe meet photographs on the bar wall.

Sunday, when most members departed, was again overcast and those who remained settled for relaxing low level walks and Inverewe gardens. By way of a reminder Monday was another clear sunny day.

The meet had been a social success but the climbing opportunities were quite disappointing.

Walks and climbs included, Slioch, Meall a'Ghuibhais, Fionn Bheinn, Glen Bianasdail, Glen Lair, Beinn a' Mhuinidh, Traverse of the Oban and Beinn Sheildaig. Rock routes were climbed on Boc Beag near Kintail, Ardheslaig, Raven's Crag near Gairloch and on the Inveralligin sea cliffs.

Members attending were President Paul Brian, Robin Campbell, Peter MacDonald and guest Calum Anton, Iain Smart, Colin Stead, Dick Allen, Peter Biggar, Robin Chalmers, John Fowler and guest Helen Forde, Phil Gribbon, John Hay, Andrew James, Dougie Niven, Roger Robb, Charlie Rose, Bill Skidmore, David Stone, John Wood and guest Ken Brannan.

Dick Allen

Ski Mountaineering Meet 2008

Lagangarbh, Glencoe, 1st–2nd March 2008.
Members present: David Eaton, Colwyn Jones, Ann MacDonald, Heike Puchan, Chris Ravey, Brian Shackleton, Brian Whitworth.
Guests: Nielsen Craig, Matt Munro, Nick Walmsley.

Blown from the various corners of Scotland The Team drifted convivially to settle at Lagangarbh Cottage in Glencoe. Hadrian's Wall failed to resist the strong southerly airstream as one individual was swept over from England to land, skis in hand, at Glasgow before continuing north. It is assumed some members were unable to open their front doors, so strong was the force of the wind, as the final number was smaller than expected. One member was pretending to teach winter skills to novices the day before so that she could reconnoitre conditions. The skills taught that day were that sometimes it is better to stay in the pub/bed/teashop; or perhaps all three!

The overnight conditions in Glencoe remained unpleasant with driving rain and stormforce winds but Lagangarbh was still in position when a watery dawn broke on Saturday morning. After a leisurely breakfast there was the dawning realisation that some one had to make the first move.

Eventually, inertia was overcome and the majority moved east to the White Corries where they attempted to set a new record for consumption of cups of tea and coffee. Having failed in the attempt, and being outnumbered by brightly clad 'yoofs' more skilled in loafing; skis were strapped to rucksacks in eager anticipation of snow.

Carrying skis the A-team walked up from the car park to the 600m contour, where snow was indeed found. The Innuit have 30 different words for snow, but would struggle to define this peculiar variety. However, the piste bashers had earlier tried to groom the boiler plate ice which encased the mountain. Undeterred the group snapped into bindings for a steady skin up to the summit of Meall A' Bhuiridh in what can be understated as rather windy conditions. The Scottish definition of 'steady' has 30 different meanings, 5 of which applied in this instance. They were:

1. Steady – the progression from one garden shed (liftie hut) to another;
2. Steady – the ability to ski backwards down an ice slope;
3. Steady – the involuntary application of one's face to the slope assisted by a 'steady' wind;
4. Steady – the requirement to refuel at set intervals to ensure 'steady' progress can be maintained;
5. Steady – the ability to stand on a wind blown summit braced by ski poles.

From the summit, a magnificent descent on variable snow, drift and ice lead back to the Kingshouse Hotel for a rejuvenating pint of local ale.

Meanwhile the hard core mountaineers bravely surmounted a mighty Corbett above Loch Leven in blazing sunshine before migrating for an invigorating session on the plastic at the Ice Factor, Kinlochleven.

Sunday dawned warmer with moderating winds. The consensual target was Stob Coire Nan Lochan – without skis – for a mass ascent of Dorsal Arête. It was noted that the early ascentionists didn't do the route properly as they avoided the Pinnacles at the top. Those eschewing the undoubted pleasures of Dorsal Arête climbed Twisting Gully. Again, it proved to be windy on top.

Meanwhile, Ravey and Walmsley were of the opinion that an SMC ski meet should be just that! The fact that travel arrangements from Gloucestershire had precluded the carrying of anything other than ski equipment helped force the decision to go skiing. With Saturday's hard won knowledge regarding local snow conditions, height was considered to be an essential ingredient. However, tight time schedules for evening flights resulted in the use of the only obvious method of gaining height; the Aonach Mor Gondola. Whilst skis had to be carried to the bottom chairlift, the 'Goose' gully had reasonable snow cover. Four runs down the 'Goose' were enjoyed before rapidly worsening weather forced a retreat to Fort William for coffee, cakes and retail therapy.

Colwyn Jones

JMCS REPORTS

Edinburgh section: JMCS members continue to be active in all aspects of mountaineering. Rock and winter climbing are the most popular activities, but activities in evidence at our annual slide night included walking, skiing, cycling, sailing, and horse riding.

Regular midweek meets are held every Wednesday. During the winter these are either at Heriot-Watt University climbing wall or at Ratho. In summer the club visits many of the local outdoor venues; sometimes venturing further afield to Dunkeld or Northumberland. There is a regular contingent of members at Alien Rock on Mondays.

Summer meets had the usual mixture of good and bad weather, but were generally well attended. Destinations ranged as far south as North Wales and north to the CIC hut on Ben Nevis. The best attended meet was the bouldering and barbecue meet to Gullane Beach where Tai Chi, windsurfing and swimming were added to the range of activities taken part in by JMCS members.

Winter meets also had a wide variety of weather. Most were well attended, even when the forecast was poor. High points included the January meet to Muir of Inverey, blessed with good conditions and benign weather. The low point for several members was probably being blown off the duck-boards in the dark by gale force winds and landing in several feet of freezing cold water while 'walking' in to Inver Croft at Achnasheen. In spite of the difficulties on Friday night, several members enjoyed two reasonable days walking on the Saturday and Sunday.

Further afield, members have penetrated as far as the Ruwenzori mountains in Uganda, and 'hot rock' trips to the continent were popular once again.

Officials elected: *Honorary President*, John Fowler; *Honorary Vice-President*, Euan Scott; *President*, Patrick Winter; *Vice President and Smiddy Custodian*, Helen Forde (30 Reid Terrace, Edinburgh, EH3 5JH, 0131 332 0071); *Secretary*, Robert Fox (10/3 South Gyle Loan, Edinburgh, EH12 9EN, 0131 334 5582, <secretary@edinburghjmcs.org.uk>); *Treasurer*, Bryan Rynne; *Meets Secretary*, Sue Marvell; *The Cabin Custodian*, Ali Borthwick.

Robert Fox

Glasgow Section: JMCS members found the winter to be disappointingly warm, especially those restricted to weekend activity. Often a midweek snowfall would be followed by strong winds and then heavy rain so that the hills were green again by the weekend. The general warmth and lack of snow meant that little climbing activity took place, the notable exception being on Ben Nevis where over the course of the winter, but particularly in two weekends in March, members found a number of routes in excellent icy condition including Astral Highway, Orion Direct, Zero Gully, Point Five, Indicator Wall, Albatross, Psychedelic Wall, Smith's, Quickstep and Two Step Corner. In contrast, the two club winter meets held at the CIC hut yielded no climbing whatsoever – the first at least featured freezing temperatures, but also gales which did not allow one to stand up outside the hut, let alone get up the hill and climb – the second had similar gales, but also heavy rain.

The poor climbing conditions at least allowed many club members to add to their tally of Corbetts and Munros, and to complete some long mountain bike trips. Several club members made winter trips abroad for skiing in France and Switzerland – including a ski ascent of Rosablanche, and ice climbing in Norway and Italy.

A warm and sunny spring helped compensate for the poor winter, and members were out rock climbing by mid March from Am Buachaille and Glen Nevis to Bosigran in Cornwall. Although the Easter meet location of Elphin must have been the only part of the country with wet weather that weekend. Early summer meets in Dundonnell and Speyside were well attended – on the first May bank holiday weekend four JMCS members had Carnmore crag to themselves in glorious sunshine, while in June six members were the only people observed climbing in the Loch A'an basin in similar conditions.

Persistent wet weather limited many members' activities over the summer, although hills were still climbed and crags visited as the rain allowed. Notable ascents in Scotland by club members included King Kong on Ben Nevis. Foreign trips were undertaken by members to the French Alps, Provence, Canada, and the Dolomites. Three members joined the SMC Greenland expedition in May, bagging 16 new peaks and returning with smiles and sunburn. A large contingent visited Kalymnos in September, featuring more members than attended some of the Scottish hut meets!

Midweek summer evening meets were held this year to various destinations around Glasgow, and included cragging, biking (both on and off road), running, and the traditional midsummer's night meet on the Cobbler which was unusually dry and midge-free.

The Section continues to hold weekend meets on a fortnightly basis, to meet at the Ibrox climbing wall midweek, and at the Three Judges pub in Partick on alternate Thursday evenings.

Office bearers for 2008 are as follows: *President & Treasurer*, Richard Jewell (33 Holyknowe Road, Lennoxtown, 01360 310 314); *Secretary*, Paul Hammond (Flat 2/1, 88 Leslie Street, Glasgow, 0141 423 7505).

For others and for further information see the website:
   www.glasgowjmcs.org.uk

Jeremy Morris

Lochaber Mountaineering Club (JMCS Lochaber Section): The Lochaber section of the JMCS enjoyed a reasonably healthy and active year throughout 2007. The membership of the section currently stands at just under sixty, that's in number not age. It comprises members resident in the Lochaber area and others spread throughout the country.

The section's main activities revolve around the organised meets that are held on a regular basis to various venues. The meets are usually well attended and not just by the same old faces. There were no Munro completions in 2007, but several members are teetering on the edge in the low single figures.

In 2007 the section held its annual dinner at the Stage Coach Inn, Cairndow. Over thirty members and guests attended and all enjoyed the excellent facilities and hospitality on offer. For the first time, the section held its AGM at the dinner meet and it proved to be a resounding success with many members being able to enter in the club's debates for the first time.

Steall Cottage in Glen Nevis continues to provide the main income for the section and its revenue helps to subsidise the club's activities. Over the last few years there has been a steady decline in bookings for the hut and the income for 2007 was half of what was generated as recently as 2005. Through informal discussions with other organisations, it seems this is a general trend and not just relating to Steall. Are we as mountaineers getting soft and looking for more comfortable options as we take to the hills or is there a decline in the sport? We don't know. The club are actively looking at ways to raise the profile of Steall and it will be interesting to see if this has any effect.

Office bearers for 2007/2008 are as follows: *Honorary Members*, Hamish MacInnes and Douglas Scott; *Honorary President*, Iain Sutherland; *President*, James Cameron; *Vice President*, Ewen Kay; *Secretary*, Kenny Foggo (01397 706 299); *Treasurer*, George Bruce; *Hut Custodian*, John Matheson (01397 772 599); *General Committee*, Iain Donaldson, Kenny Scoular and Iain MacLeod.

Kenny Foggo

London Section: Highlights for the year were the trip to Annapurna and climb on Chulu Far East – see separate account from John Steele in this journal – and Chris Comerie and Marcus Harvey's visit to La Berarde in the Ecrins, which resulted in 89 pitches and 2600 metres of climbing during two weeks in July. For the rest of us it was more mundane stuff – a mixture of climbing, walking, mountain biking and sailing. The meets programme was characterised by the variety of locations. We visited Glencoe, the Yorkshire Dales, Peak District, Lake District and North Wales where the club hut in Bethesda was well used. There was sailing in the Hebrides including visits to Pabbay and Berneray and climbing on the sea-cliffs of Pembroke.

The year culminated in a successful and well-attended club dinner in Coniston – special thanks to John Steele and Andy Hughes for the slide show – and to our hosts at Coniston YHA – an excellent location for club dinners. We were delighted that Peter Whitechurch and Hugh Jordan were able to join us, each having been in the club longer than they care to remember but almost certainly in excess of 50 years.

Work continues on making our hut in Bethesda fire-compliant and there have been several other improvements including new windows. Membership now stands at 37-plus life members.

Office bearers are as follows: *President*, Steve Senior; *Secretary*, John Firmin; *Treasurer*, David Hughes; *Hut Custodian*, Rod Kleckham.

John Firmin

Perth Mountaineering Club (JMCS Perth Section): The PMC's year started with a very blustery meet to Roy Bridge where various members struggled against the elements for two days. The weather didn't improve for the December day meet which, in the end, had to be cancelled due to 'truly horrendous' conditions. It would have been hard enough to get out of the car let alone climb a hill! Things didn't improve much for the January meet to Glen Etive on which members coped with the most atrocious conditions. However, a very agreeable time was had by all and a communal Burns Supper was enjoyed in the basic but comfortable Smiddy surrounded by dripping gear!

Reasonable winter conditions were had on the February meet to the Raeburn hut, with some members enjoying the classic Raeburn's Gully on the Saturday.

The next two meets to Kintail and Glen Lyon were successful despite the weather but things definitely took a turn for the better for the very successful camping meet to Glen Rosa on Arran. Great days were had by all including classic climbs, ridge walks and cycling with wall to wall sunshine. However, the good weather was temporary as the next meet to Coruisk, Skye, was hampered by very high winds to such an extent that the boat from Elgol could not set sail and it was too windy to walk in past the 'bad step' so the intrepid members decided to walk in from Sligachan. No Munros were attempted and the Dubh Slabs were thought best avoided in the windy conditions but all the same an enjoyable time was had by all and the wind and rain abated in time for the long walk out.

Members on the next trip to Elphin took advantage of the fantastic weather to enjoy an outstanding day on the Saturday, some on Foinaven and some on Arkle. However the conditions were not quite so favourable the next day so some opted for a trip to the Bone Caves and then home, while others combined this with a walk up Breabag.

In between the weekend meets some great day meets were had, in particular, a trip to Arrochar and a sporting ascent of the Cobbler's South Peak, a true mountaineering day to Garbh Choire, Braeraich and the North-East ridge of Angel's Peak and a classic traverse from Kingshouse to Inveroran.

Wednesday evening climbing meets were a bit hit and miss this year due to the weather but most meets were attended even if some climbs were attempted in the rain. Some new venues were visited including the Aberdeen sea cliffs and Kirrie Quarry which no doubt will be on the meets list in 2008.

The Annual Dinner was 'at home' this year and held at The Royal Hotel, Comrie, which was a delightful venue and a great evening was had by all. A few members also enjoyed a day on the local hills on the Saturday.

This year's PSNS Annual Lecture was given by Alasdair and Pamela Dutton who described their 6 months sabbatical to New Zealand with a wonderful accompanying slide show.

Office bearers for 2007/2008 are: *President*, Trish Reed; *Vice President*, Rhod Watt; *Secretary*, Lucy Garthwaite; *Treasurer*, Pamela Dutton; *Meets Secretary*, Clare and Mike Aldridge; *Newsletter Editor*, Des Bassett; *Committee Members*, Donald Barrie, Karen Carnson, Den Underwood and Derek Queenan.

Lucy Garthwaite

SMC AND JMCS ABROAD

Himalaya

JOHN STEELE REPORTS: The JMCS London Section mounted a second expedition to Nepal, in the spring of 2007, taking in the Annapurna Circuit and Chulu Peak.

The team started off in mid April from Pokhara with a 1200m ascent on the first day, followed by a dawn ascent of Poon Hill (3200m) to catch the sunrise over Dhaulagiri. This was trumped by a 2000m descent into the Kali Gandaki gorge and a bathe in the natural hot springs at Tatopani.

The next week saw us moving north into Mustang and visiting the temples at Muktinath, sheltering below the Thorung La pass at 5416m. Crossing (the wrong way?) at nearly 18,000ft was not a problem and we eagerly wanted to see our peak, Chulu Far East (6050m), having warmed up on the Annapurna Circuit.

Several dusty campsites and prudent ascent days found us poised to climb the ice peak on 10 May 2007. A good early start, hastened by reports of a snow leopard prowling around the tents, saw us poised below the summit slopes at sunrise. However we were thwarted about six rope-lengths below the summit by a band of hard ice – so hard that no protection could be inserted. The decision was made to quit; however we reckoned all eight climbers and two local guides would have made the top under normal conditions. Another great trip supported by Dan Tamang of Bluesky and the porters of Salle village.

Team members: John Steele(leader), Barbara Gibbons, Trevor Burrows, Andy Hughes, Jamie Ward, Paz Parish, Bob Fick and Graham Emmet.

Africa

COLWYN JONES REPORTS: On 29 December 2007 members Ann MacDonald and Colwyn Jones climbed Mount Kilimanjaro (5898m) in Tanzania by the Machame route arriving at the summit at 6.30 a.m. Then 9 days later they reached the top of Mount Kenya (5188m), completing the normal (south face/ridge) route from the Lewis Glacier in 6.5 hours. They noted that the Lewis glacier was tiny compared to 12 years ago when they last visited, a probable result of global warming.

They report that climbing Kilimanjaro first certainly helped with acclimatisation for the technical rock climbing on Mount Kenya. The rock was excellent quality, which gave confidence, but there was a lot of new snow before they made their summit attempt. They also elected to spend a night in the small bivouac shelter, the Howell Hut, on the summit of Nelion, which was surprisingly comfortable, and that night they had no headache!

The descent was routine involving multiple abseils down the huge south face of the peak. However, they had met a pair of Italian climbers who were having difficulties so helped them overnight and on the long descent. Thankfully, they all descended safely.

Up in the mountains it was very quiet with no problems after the elections in Kenya. They even went on a Safari for a few days where they saw lots of animals but no other tourists. It was reported as a fantastic trip to Africa with a final night at a luxurious floodlit waterhole watching big game animals. They also had their safari van charged by a trumpeting elephant!

North America

The Scottish Coast Range Expedition 2007

DES RUBENS REPORTS: Expedition is perhaps rather a grandiose title where members are flown in to a base half an hour's scramble from their first unclimbed summit. However the alternative, 'trip', seemed to lack the appropriate dignity.

Our team consisted of Billy Hood, Bob Hamilton, Billy Hood, Steve Kennedy, Neil McGougan, Dave Ritchie and myself.

Steve Kennedy and I had come up with the idea of visiting the Waddington Range, swayed by Simon Richardson's passion for the area. We considered going as a two until we discovered that Mike King, the helicopter pilot for the area, had recently purchased a larger beast and costs had proportionately increased. We cast around for further quarry.

Several days later, to my consternation, Steve had rounded up a fair proportion of the outdoor folk of Argyll, a few of whom were fairly new to this game and thus extremely enthusiastic. Despite my respect for Steve's judge of character, I had a few misgivings, not least as they were all west-coasters. As it turned out, I could not have spent time with a finer bunch of folk. We had become a party of six: educationalists, engineers, a lawyer and a prawn fisherman, mostly on the wrong side of fifty. All were from the Glasgow side of Scotland apart from myself from classier Edinburgh. Despite this deep gulf, we all got on remarkably well.*

You can't go wrong with the Waddington Range. Don Serl's fine new guide minimised research efforts and the only major decision was whether to go for classic but known routes around Waddington itself or for the unknown on an outlying area with the risk of possible disappointment. The unknown won out and we were bound for some exploratory mountaineering in the vicinity of Mount Geddes, monarch of the Frontier Range, a few miles north-west of Waddington.

I warmed up with my brother Clive's family at Canmore while the others disported themselves at Squamish. I was picked up from Kamloops in one of two well loaded hire cars for the journey to White Saddle. We enjoyed splendid hospitality from the Kings and were amused how Lori King was especially taken with six different Scottish accents. Hey, we're supposed to be the world travellers recording the idiosyncrasies of quaint foreigners, not the objects of curiosity!

Next morning, I found myself alone on the glacier below the North Face of Mount Geddes with a mountain of gear. A cautious approach regarding victuals had lead to an excess of weight and difficulty in unloading the helicopter, and Steve and Dave Ritchie had been abandoned temporarily on a neighbouring glacier whilst I had unloaded the stacks of gear. Awaiting their return, a discontinuity of memory and reality caused me to re-examine the map. I then had to confess to the others that we'd been dropped at the wrong ridge. Map reading had been a bit difficult, what with lots of glacier, crevasses and bits of crag rushing up at a fast pace, as well as being pinned down in flight by a

---

*cf. the cementing of relations on the Anglo-Scottish Peru trip, sorry expedition, of 2004.

substantial quantity of equipment. Flying over such grand terrain was an unusual experience for me. Glen Coe or Ben Nevis don't quite prepare one for the tremendous scenery of the Waddington Range.

Fortunately for me, no one was much bothered about this error. We were about a kilometre away from the planned drop-off and ultimately it turned out for the best.

Two days of poor weather were enlivened by the digging of a kitchen snowhole, a job generating a little tension due to the presence of not one but two engineers in the party. When the weather improved, we set out for the North Face of Geddes. I had spotted a possible route in the guide dropping from the summit of Geddes, taking the line of three beautiful snow arêtes, interspersed with mixed ground. Accessing the initial gully necessitated an exposed traverse in high above a glacier and then a grand climb up exposed gullies and the arêtes, with a hidden chimney concealing the final way through to the summit. Constant exclamations of delight accompanied the ascent. The snow and ice was in good condition, perhaps testament to the heavy snow of the previous winter. The cloud rose with us and from the summit we glimpsed only the occasional view of Waddington itself. A chilly abseil descent was made down the rocks to the side of Hourglass Couloir, with an Abalakov thread to finish. We had broken our duck and *Caledonia* (D+) was climbed.

Our two bottles of whisky (one Islay, one Speyside) had both survived the flights from Scotland and the Canadian meltwater seemed to complement the robust tastes surprisingly well (much to our relief – the compatibility of Canadian meltwater with our national drink had been a source of some anxiety to us). Naturally with supplies strictly limited, drams had to be rationed to very special occasions. However, the first ascent of *Caledonia* was a worthy candidate.

A day's rest was enlivened by rock ascents on Mount Haworth and a nearby unclimbed tower. The tower gave us an easy scramble to an exposed summit with spectacular views down over the Roover's Glacier. It was impossible not to be impressed with so much untrodden ground around us. There was then discussion as to our next moves. Those of an exploratory bent won out and we resolved to go as a large and jolly party to attempt the unclimbed Roover's Needle. As we were two ridges, a glacier and an unclimbed peak away from the objective, it was perhaps a mite ambitious for a day out. I argued that the lay of the land suggested the possibility of easy snow slopes on the far side of the south-east ridge of our objective.

We departed early and gained the ridge of Camp Inspiration of the pioneers of 1948 and the originally intended site of our base camp. We discovered no trace of their camp, nor, indeed, of the promised water source. We then continued round the west end of Polydactyl Ridge and trod delicately along the snow arête forming Propyleum Pass to gain an unclimbed snow dome. Steve, with a yearning perhaps for the misty Bens of his native land, suggested for this peak the Gaelic name 'Mam Beag', meaning *small breast* (although it seemed quite large to me). This was not just a sad old man's pathos (although I'm not disputing this is a possibility), but honoured the resemblance of this peak to those of our native land. I digress. We looked onward to our objective and three of the party expressed less than outright optimism at the prospects of success.

There was an amicable parting of the ways and Steve, Bob and I continued. The south-east ridge of Roover's Needle proved to be devoid of snow slopes and too time-consuming for success, but gave us some good rock climbing (amidst, it has to be conceded, generally pretty loose terrain). I asked Bob, the oldest and most venerated member of our party, how he was enjoying the Alpine experience and invited him to make comparisons with previous trips. 'Oh wonderful' he replied, then disclosed that this was the first time he'd climbed in an Alpine environment. In honour of his great age and inauguration into such territory, we christened the highest rock tower of our ascent 'Sgurr Hamilton'. The loose rock was not entirely bad as the retreat was enlivened by some of the finest trundling we have had the pleasure to engage in. At home, such simple pleasures are disappointingly hard to come by nowadays, due to the all embracing presence of Health and Safety (never mind the environmental outcries). Our pleasure had the incidental benefit of improving the ground for future parties and, in geological terms, was 'nobbut a ba' hair's' moment from occurring anyway. Steve's boyish delight as he strained against yet another unstable piece of British Columbia, his features lighting up as he successfully separated yet another muckle boulder from its socket and dispatched it, accompanied by a whiff of cordite, to the Roover's Glacier, was a highlight of the day. We celebrated our return to Mam Beag with an hour's doze and then retraced our steps, reaching the chilly comfort of the kitchen snowhole at sunset. Although the final summit had eluded us, the joy of carefree exploration, of constant movement in such fine country in perfect weather, of uncertainty of outcome and the high spiritedness of the party made for an unforgettable day out.

Meanwhile, Billy, Dave and Neil had made the probable first ascent of the highest peak on the Umbra Ridge which gave great views over Scimitar Glacier to the heart of the Waddington Range. This peak had given a fine climb on rock of about 300m. Sheepishly, they admitted to crossing the tracks of a large ungulate on the way, leading to unkind remarks as to whether they had left any gates open. I am sorry to report that this schoolboy humour continued to the end of the trip.

During our return, Steve had spotted a further route on Geddes, which took a fine traverse on the buttress below the central peak and thus became, prosaically, *Central Buttress* (TD-). On this occasion, the weather was again exceptional and we moved together up the lower part of the face as the sun turned the snows a soft pink. The highlight was an easy but exposed traverse – vertical above and undercut below. Higher up, a steep chimney gave us a fine steep mixed pitch after which we moved together to the summit.

Range after range of glaciated scenery spread out before us. Waddington itself took on a Himalayan demeanour. We basked in golden rays for an hour or so. The pleasure was heightened by dozy reminiscences of shadowy short winter days at home accompanied by wind and the icy blast of spindrift cooling the cheeks and neck.

Even more surprising to us was how seldom these peaks were ascended. According to the register, the last ascent of Geddes had been made five years previously. In the Alps, such a mountain would have been first climbed in the latter part of the nineteenth century and would now receive several, if not

Base Camp in the Frontier Group of the Waddington Range, Scottish Coast Range Expedition 2007. Photo: Des Rubens.

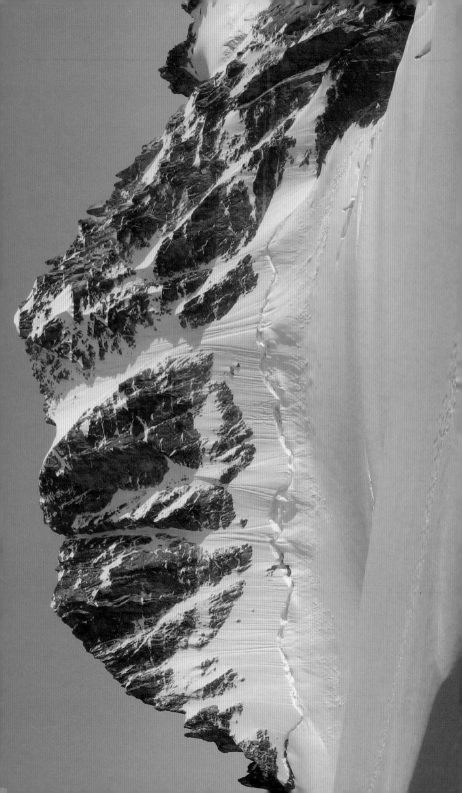

several hundred, ascents daily through the summer season. Obviously access, expense and a miniscule population is part of the reason for the lack of climbers, but it still surprised us that more do not come to such wonderful mountains.

We did a little more exploratory wandering. On our final day, we visited, en masse, Hermit Peak, first ascended by the ubiquitous Beckey. We had some fun on the final pinnacle and admired Waddington again and the chaotic icefalls on the upper part of Scimitar Glacier. We returned to dismantle base camp and then awaited our flight out in the evening. It was an experience to hear the helicopter coming in on a greying evening sky, the pilot on radio using GPS as it was his first visit to the area, the splendid Bell's peak in the background.

Our routes are, of course, modest by modern standards (or even old standards, you may say, unkindly). However, for us, it was an unforgettable experience to have had ten days of high altitude wandering in such unspoiled and untrodden country. In more frequented parts, such as Squamish, we greatly appreciated the friendliness of Canadian climbers. Perhaps you'll see a few more Scots tourists as word spreads! However, don't worry too much as we'll keep the news to us few Scots and a secret from the English. Nice enough folk in their own way, but there's an awful lot of them down there.

Thanks to both Don Serl and Simon Richardson for generously given advice.

Greenland

The Scottish Mountaineering Club East Greenland Expedition 2007

COLWYN JONES REPORTS: The human element of the expedition departed in two waves from across Europe. On Friday 27 April 2007 two SMC members, Brian Shackleton and Heike Puchan-Whitworth flew from Glasgow to Keflavik with Icelandair. They stayed overnight in Reykjavik and on Saturday 28th they flew from Reykjavik to Constable Point.

On Sunday 29 April three expedition members flew from Glasgow to Keflavik with Icelandair and three via London (from Munich, Cork and Gloucester) with British Airways to Keflavik. From Reykjavik domestic airport they flew to an unusually warm Akureyri, arriving in the late afternoon sunshine.

On 30 April the 'Akureyri six' awoke to a bright morning and, in a chartered Air Iceland ski-equipped Twin Otter aircraft, were flown from Akureyri in Iceland to Constable Point in Greenland. Here they were united with the two other expedition members and the food and gear they had freighted out about a month beforehand. They also collected 50 litres of Jet A1 fuel for cooking and a rifle and ammunition they had hired locally.

The Twin Otter took off into a stunningly clear blue sky followed by a short flight with an exciting landing on the Lang Glacier arriving early afternoon. Basecamp was at 1390m (N71°59'43" W024°48'44.2"). After digging the plane out of the snow and cheering it back into the air, they erected the tents and made themselves comfortable. One problem was that the two new MSR Whisperlite and the dragonfly stoves would not light! This could have been a disaster. The two MSR GSK II stoves worked well.

On 1 May they climbed the first new peaks. **Peak 1** was named *Drumglas Beag*, 2060m (N71°59'22.3" W024°53'02.2"). **Peak 2** *Drumglas*, 2330m

North Face of Mount Geddes. 'Central Buttress' takes a L to R ledge halfway up the buttress to the L of the wide couloir. 'Caledonia' takes the snow arêtes which culminate at the summit of Mt Geddes.. Photo: Des Rubens.

(N71°58'41.5" W024°52'49.5"), was climbed by the north ridge, appropriately named the *Biancograt* and graded AD. The 14 hour day was felt to be a good start to the trip.

Light snow and low cloud were allowed to restrict climbing activity on 2–4 May. On 4 May a team of four members did a nine hour ski tour to dump half of the food and fuel at Crescent Col, 1984m (N72°03'47.2" W024°55'42.0"). The food and fuel dump was strategically placed for the return journey to the coast.

On 5 May **Peak 3** was climbed and named *Mollytinde,* 1670m (N71°59'21.1" W024°50'47"), F+. The surrounding glacier was named the *BASCD Glacier*. BASCD is an abbreviation for the 'British Association for the Study of Community Dentistry' and the then President of the association in May 2007 was the expedition leader.

On 6 May three new peaks were climbed. **Peak 4** was named *Cordulaspids*, 2430m (N71°58'41.9" W024°54'28.1"), and was climbed from the Wuss glacier. The descent used from Drumglas on 1 May (grade AD), was reversed to the LoLa Col, then the *East Ridge* was followed to the summit, PD+. **Peak 5** *Jobjerg*, 2330m (N71°59'0.3" W024°55'17.1"), was climbed by the *South-West Ridge* which is a continuation of the north ridge of Cordulaspids. The descent was the reverse of the ascent, as was often the case, to retrieve skis. **Peak 6**, named *Juliasbjerge*, 2058m (N71°59'35.8" W024°55'16.6"), was climbed by a wide couloir from the west side of the Wuss glacier onto a col on the south ridge.

On 7 May **Peak 7**, named *Puchwhitstinde*, 2339m (N72°00'38.8" W024°45'39.1"), east of base camp was ascended by the north flank from a col between it and peak 8 (Hasentinde). The glacier on the approach was called the *Raven Glacier* for an obvious ornithological reason. On 8 May this peak was also climbed from the newly explored *O'Sullivan/Moore Glacier* by a couloir on the south face named *Snowbunting Couloir*, PD. **Peak 8**, named *Hasentinde*, 2376m (N72°01' 24.5" W024°47' 08.4"), was also ascended on 7 May by the south ridge from a col between peaks 7 and 8. The south ridge was named *Igel Ridge* (Hedgehog Ridge).

On 8 May **Peak 9**, named *Margretabjerge*, 2430m (N71°58'34.7" W024°50'58.0"), was ascended by two routes. One via the South Flank and SW Ridge (PD). The large subsidiary glacier west off the Lang glacier was explored and named the *MåL Glacier*. The second route was from the newly-named *Witches Cauldron Glacier* via the *Presidential Couloir* (SE Gully) with an exciting cornice to exit, AD.

On 10 May they moved camp from the Lang glacier over Crescent Col – collecting food and fuel – to a camp on the Gully Glacier named The Refrigerator Base Camp, 1680m (N72°05'27.4" W024°58'42.8").

On 11 May **Peak 10**, named *Himmelstinde* (Heavens Peak), 2492m (N72°04'51.8" W025°05'22.5"), was ascended by the appropriately-named *Eternal Couloir*. The previously unnamed glacier used in approach was called the *Puchan Glacier*.

On 12 May **Peak 11**, named *Archangel Peak*, 2558m (N72°04'31.5" W025°05'23.5"), gave a D ascent. From the summit the climbers descended onto the very crevassed glacier on the west of the peak named, with hindsight, the *Devil's Own Glacier*. The difficult terrain encountered forced a reascent to the summit and descent via the ascent route. **Peak 12**, named *The Cold Shoulder*,

2450m (estimated lat/long N72°04'32.4" W024°54'12"), was climbed by the
West Ridge, PD. The summit is on the west ridge leading from the summit of
C.F. Knoxtinde. *Hjornespids*, 2870m, was also climbed by a new route – the
Laubscher-Litterick Gully on the south-west flank of the peak, D, 600m. The
route then followed the *West Ridge* to the summit. They believe this is the sixth
ascent of, and the fourth route on, this fine peak.

On 13 May **Peak 13**, named *An Caisteal* (The Castle), 2614m (N72°03'31.9"
W024°59'52.6"), was ascended by a face and gully on the east flank then up the
North Ridge, TD⁻.

On 15 May *Crescentinde*, 2455m (N72°03'38.0" W024°57'15.0"), was
ascended by a new route; the *North-East Face*, PD. **Peak 14** was named
Ebensbjerge, 2510m (N72°03'34.9" W024°58'05.8"), and was climbed from
Daleens Col (between Ebensbjerge and Crescentinde) via the *North-East Face*,
AD.

The second move of base camp on 16 May was to a magnificent site on the
top of Col Major, 2130m (N72°06'53.1" W024°55'07.0").

On 17 May **Peak 15**, named *Ian's Peak*, 2607m (N72°07'13.3" W024°55'01.3"),
was climbed by the established South Ridge route (MVS) and a new route
named the *Accessory Rib* (VS, 4c).

The long descent of the couloir from Col Major was done over 18 May with a
camp on the flat upper reaches of the Bersaerkerbrae glacier below, 1655m
(N72°06'36.6" W024°54'04.0").

On 19 May they descended the enormous Bersaerkerbrae glacier to camp at
the branch which extends to below the north face of Bersaerkertinde, 1025m
(N72°06'11.8" W024°42'19.7").

On 20 May **Peak 16**, named *Skotsketinde* (Scotland's Peak), 1775m
(N72°07'36.6" W024°45'20.4"), was climbed by the shattered summit ridge. It
was approached via the east flank to a point where skis were left at 1585m
(N72°07'34.2" W024°44'56"). The ascent then followed the *East Ridge*, PD+.
Panoramic Peak main top was climbed with a corrected altitude of 1988m
(N72°06'27.9" W024°4'35.3"). The ascent was by a gully on the south-east flank
to the south ridge, AD⁻.

On 21 May, in a whiteout, they skied down the Bersaerkerbrae and safely off
the snout to Camp 6 next to the river in the Skeldal, 80m (N72°11'59"
W024°19'43.6").

On 22 May, in typically Scottish conditions, they skied north along the Skel to
Camp 7 adjacent to the old hunters' hut (Fangsthytte) close to the mouth of the
Skel, altitude five metres (N72°17'15" W024°07'30").

They skied over sea ice to the gravel airstrip at Mestersvig arriving late on 23
May. Poor weather in the form of high winds prevented the chartered aircraft
from flying until 25 May when just after midday they flew back to Constable
Point, then Akureyri and subsequently Reykjavik that evening. They spent 26
May in Iceland with a swim in the Blue Lagoon and flew back to the UK on 27
May 2007 after a very successful trip.

SMC members; Colwyn Jones, leader and medical officer, Brian Shackleton,
quartermaster, Mark Litterick, Heike Puchan and Brian Whitworth. Plus others
Laubie Laubscher, Kenneth Moore and Stephen O'Sullivan.

REVIEWS

Mount Everest, The Reconnaissance 1935: Tony Astill, (Published by the author, 2005, hardback, 360pp, 125 illus., 10 maps, ISBN 978-0-9549201-0-4, £30).

Tony Astill's book has been privately produced and is a joy to handle. There is a double dustcover, strong and striking, based on the reconnaissance survey of the northern face of Mount Everest. Inside are sketch maps old and new; high quality paper is matched by fine printing; and of the wealth of photographs from the expedition many are enhanced to modern clarity.

A reconnaissance of a mountain is not a summit bid. It may well be more fun. This 1935 party aimed to be light-weight and to move more freely than earlier more ponderous expeditions; and to reconnoitre is always to be flexible, with time built into the programme to explore, and in exploring to enjoy. Likely leads arise and must be followed. There will be comings and goings with the climbers regrouping. The ensuing record may have many different strands.

The people are fundamental. Each member of the group is introduced with a short section in the text from some other writer, so that justice is done to them as individuals before they are merged into a team. The 1935 expedition had well-known climbing names in the leader Eric Shipton and in H.W. Tilman but all members of the team were distinct personalities, whilst the Sherpas and their close cousins the Tibetans were just as strongly individual. There is the story of the young Tensing turning sadly from the line of applicants when he wrongly thought he had been rejected – a passing incident to chill one's thinking – and then, called back and accepted, honing his skills and his techniques. Later, letters and diaries of the expedition members are widely used and well blended into the narrative to light up personal reactions and plot the hardships and the joys. This makes a fine involvement for the reader.

Some readers will seize on accounts of the many fresh peaks that were climbed. Others will appreciate the careful progress of the survey – Michael Spender's diary is a fine record of his task. Many perhaps will treasure most of all the Sherpa characters and the Tibetan people in their villages. Eric Shipton, above all, blended without effort into other ways of life. A light expedition which did not aim for the summit had a good chance to link with those who lived nearby.

Readers will make their own selections and there is much to be enjoyed.

Jennifer Bourdillon

Great British Rock Climbs – Classic Rock: compiled by Ken Wilson, (Baton Wicks, 2007, hardback, 296pp, ISBN 978-1-898573-70-8, £32).

This is larger, longer and better than the superb original of 1979, which was derived from the highly innovative and successful Hard Rock. These have been well reviewed, so let me tell you what else is new. It retains the same format, style and many of the original descriptions, but some are by new authors. What is strikingly fresh is the predominance of large colour photographs of climbers in action, in comparison with the exclusively monochrome original. However, there are added many fascinating old portraits and action shots of great historical value, complete with boxes of contextual information. This complements the special character of classic rock routes in Britain. Their pioneers really did use clinker nailed boots, or gutties (with socks over them if the rock was wet), hemp ropes and token belays, woollen sports jackets. But they had enormous talent and enthusiasm. The original 55 sets of descriptions of 79 routes are still there, from Ben Nevis to Lands End, although the order is no longer North–South, but progresses generally from small to big cliffs region by region. Thus fittingly this new edition now ends with Long Climb. This series of books were never intended as guidebooks, but the topo diagrams, descriptions and photos are actually very helpful, specially when visiting a new crag. The crucial achievement and place of this series for British mountaineering is in alerting climbers to the delights available outside their local crags. Ken Wilson rounds off the descriptions with an Appendix of other similar routes, the notorious comparative grades table, and a plea for the climbers of SE England that they be provided, at public expense, with plastic replicas of Kyloe and Stanage to climb on – ever the polemicist!

The focus of these routes is big cliffs in the mountains and by the sea. The tone and message of the book is that this style of route is the bedrock and foundation of the sport as practised in Britain. No in-situ gear, no markers, complex cliffs, difficult descents, fickle weather, vegetation and patches of loose rock: wonderful! Many modern climbers may bypass this, going direct from indoor wall to extremes on outcrops. They do not know what they are missing and hopefully will discover, for relaxation between harder climbs, or as their muscles fade, the superb delights of these Classics. If you have the original, the new edition will enhance your memories, if you have not then this is well worth its price.

Finally, as an inspiration and a tribute, the text of a postcard sent to me a decade ago in thanks for a day on Long Crack, Archer Ridge and Crypt Route in pouring rain. 'Classic rock challenge, in aid of John Muir Trust: time 52 days, 1501 miles of cycling, completed 78 of 79 routes (ring ouzels nesting at Hen Cloud!), quickest 75 sec Powder Monkey Parade, slowest 4hr 50min Cuillin, solo 35, roped 44, best bit putting – bike on train at Kyle, worst bit – midges in Glencoe. [signed] Jamie Fisher.'

Alan Walker

Happy Climbing Tells No Tales:[*] Judith Brown, (Open Mountain, 2007, paperback, 124pp, ISBN 978-0-9554980-0-8, £5.95).
The cover of this slim volume informs us that the vast majority of climbers just bumble about, having fun and that the authoress numbers herself amongst this motley swarm. Very true and we all have stories to tell – tragic, embossed, comic – if we've knocked about long enough but whether they're worth relating to anyone else depends entirely upon the imagination and narrative skills of the essayist. Judith Brown has chosen the most challenging of genres; that of turning her mountain experiences into a collection of fictional short stories. The big problem, of course, is that fabricating a yarn only works if the plot is entertaining, well-told and plausible, otherwise it's about as riveting as listening to someone recount their dreams of the previous night. In addition, she has compounded the stumbling-blocks for herself by the use of large amounts of

---

[*] [Shortlisted for The Boardman Tasker Prize 2007—Hon. Ed.]

dialogue, notoriously difficult to get right but so easy to make exasperating. I have to admit that I came to read her stories with a prejudice, suspecting that writers use these literary techniques as smoke-screens, hiding behind the posturing of their manufactured characters, but also because fiction is seldom as potent as the truth.

In this compilation the writer succeeds particularly in capturing the feel of the rock-climber's world, self-centred as it often is, its camaraderie and vanity. In Troll Climb, for all its silly story about amoeboid rock, it is clear that she has experienced fear on a big, wet cliff as the chilling mist numbs rational thought. I like the Tolkien-inspired fantasy The Precious and her choice of Callum as the perfidious climbing partner but, even as a flight of fancy, it loses the plot. In Once Upon A Mountain, the contrast between the banal reality of a hospital room, with its dismal view, and the thrill of snowy summits is full of awful meaning and well created. The Bear will make you look for the hidden answer – it's in a name – and we are left to ponder whether faithful relationships will become the victims of physical desire. The final story, Happy Climbing Tells No Tales, is self-explanatory; a great day on a great Lakeland cliff followed by a thirst-quenching pint in the Wasdale Head as the ghosts of O.G. Jones and F. Botterill smile with pleasure … a simple rock-climbing day relished and filed away in the memory. It's the simplest and best evocation in the book and, in that context, this tale wags the dog.

Although there are passages of well-expressed description the overall effect is spoilt by inappropriate similes such as: '… the mountain had pitched and rolled in the maelstrom like a ship in full sail about to break its moorings and tear across the sky.'[1] This feels confused and very contrived to me; in my experience, when the world about you breaks loose in violent storm, it is the very solidity of the mountain that provides your only reference point, unless you are hopelessly drunk. Any matelot, too, could have told her that a moored ship would not be under full sail, let alone sprouting wings. There are incoherent metaphors such as: 'The wind was the sound of silence, howling around mountains, making the deep-throated roar of emptiness.'[2] Really? In this particular case, I think I know what she's trying to portray but I find too many inconsistencies in her attempts at inventive and dramatic composition to feel much sympathy for her cause.

Perhaps the most irritating feature of the book is the overplayed use of swear-words by her characters. It smacks of vacuous affectation, à la Gordon Ramsay rather than the ease of Billy Connelly, and of impotence in being able to create mood through vivid prose. Of the twelve stories, nine of them include oaths of one sort or another, from 'Shit' he thought 'It's night'[3] to 'You silly bastard f**cker!'[4] If anyone could have justified the use of the language of the working man, moving freely in that world, then it would surely have been a writer of the calibre of Robin Smith, yet Geoff Dutton wrote, '…he calmly achieves his most cathartically black effects without a single oath.'[5] Ms Brown, like most of us, is

---

[1] Page 63
[2] Page 83
[3] Page 85
[4] Page 68
[5] *High Endeavours* by Jimmy Cruikshank, p145.

not in that league and, if she wished to use the f-word to try to inject some perceived macho-realism into her characters' speech, then why did she then back-off and give us f**kings, f**ks and f**kers ... for fuck's sake, in this day and age, let's call a star an expletive and have done with it.

What I like in a book are either thought-provoking nuances that resonate with my own feelings, so that I can re-read a sentence several times in contemplation, or straightforward, engrossing drama. In neither sense, I'm afraid, did this book engage my attention for long, despite its claim to 'explore the reasons why climbers do it.' Last year I had the pleasure of reviewing an anthology of Jim Perrin's essays; it is with reluctance that it leaves my bookshelf to join the SMC's Library in Glasgow. I wish I could say the same about this one.

There are twelve stories in the book which is published in soft-back by 'Open Mountain', Cockermouth at £5.95, which seems relatively poor value for just over 100 pages. I counted several typographical errors/omissions which should have been picked up by careful proof-reading. The author lives in Cumbria and is not to be confused with the identically named compiler of 'Immodest Acts: The Life of a Lesbian Nun in Renaissance Italy.' What a pity.

Mike Jacob

The Stone Country Guide to Bouldering in Scotland: Edited by John Watson, (Stone Country Press, 2008, paperback, 192pp, ISBN 978-0-9548779-2-7, £21.95).

At last we have a selective guidebook to bouldering in Scotland and one I'm sure a lot of boulderers have been waiting for. John Watson, a keen boulderer himself, has made a formidable job of cataloguing many of the best boulder venues and problems across the country. The book is split into eleven regions, each accompanied by an appetite-whetting introduction and maps of how to get to the areas. The boulders are easy to locate and follow with clearly marked photo topos, problems described and star rated. In addition the pages are littered with some great action shots. Simple, effective page design makes the book easy to use, whilst John's creative writing skills ensure a good and interesting read.

The book is inspiring and makes obvious the great wealth of bouldering here in Scotland. Venues include the hulk of a boulder at Ruthven, this sit alone rock offers gneiss at its best; the mass of excellent granite boulders at the Shelterstone give class problems in the most spectacular setting; Dumbarton's now famous basalt boulders hold some of the hardest problems in the country; the impressive prow of the Ship Boulder is Torridonian sandstone at its best; Cummingston's intricate and technical pocket problems and traverses offer a uniqueness of their own, and the imposing rough gabbro rocks in Coire Laggan will give days of pleasure. These venues may not be as well known as the Peak or Northumberland, but in my mind they equal in quality and surpass in setting! No crowds here either, the boulderer visiting will often be in complete solitude.

I hope this guide will inspire climbers to venture further afield to sample some of the most remote and beautiful island and mountain regions in Scotland, to explore and taste some of the incredible locations, rock types and world-class boulder problems.

It may seem a tad expensive at £21.95, however this little guide will ensure hours, months if not years of fun, so I'd say it's worth every penny.

Joanna George.

The Munro Society Journal: 50pp, £4.

Although not a paid-up member, the Clerk of the List works closely with the Munro Society and sends membership details to all Compleaters, now they are at last eligible to join. Founded in 2001 under the principal of 'give something back to the mountains', this is their first Journal, published at the end of 2007. Comprising exactly 50 pages of text, this slender A5 volume is packed with a remarkable variety of content around the common Munro-bagging theme.

President Iain Robertson reviews the gestation, birth and growth of the new Society, and describes how he sees it fitting in with the many other 'conservation organisations'. Production of the Society's popular video of early Munroists, 'In the Beginning' is described by Jim Closs. Delving even further back, Robin Campbell gives a brief biographical sketch of 'An Early Enthusiast: Edred Moss Corner'. This interesting gentleman joined the SMC in 1897 and had a particular penchant for Tops, way ahead of his time. Still on a historical theme, Raymond Lamont-Brown describes the evolution of the role of 'The Queens Messengers', whose assignments were taken up on several occasions by Sir Hugh himself. Ian Collie reflects on the Rev. Thomas Grierson's book 'Autumnal Rambles in the Scottish Mountains', published in 1848. Capturing some of the spirit of contemporary bagging, Robin Howie shares his enthusiasm for Sgurr na Ciche and its neighbours, while Grahame Downer describes a number of unsuccessful attempts on the elusive Sgurr nan Ceathreamhnan before finally earning his tick. On the darker side of the sport, Charles Murray recalls some mountain rescue experiences from the 1970s and Irvine Butterfield recounts a tragedy on Schiehallion in 1874. Not forgetting the finer points of Munrology, Dave Hewitt examines the concept of 'the round' by comparing what he describes as the 'Golfers method' with the 'Cumulative total'. This is of particular interest to the reviewer, who recently discovered himself well over half way through his second cumulative round. To help speed fellow baggers on their way, Frank Johnstone highlights 'the 102 Munros that can be walked in groups of six or more in one day by the reasonably fit'. For those willing to dip a toe into the challenging waters of deep ecology, Rob McMorran from the Centre for Mountain Studies at Perth College has a very interesting and accessible analysis of 'Scottish wild landscapes: Wild nature or wild experience?' Finally, John Burdin gives an update on one of the Munro Societies most useful projects, compiling Mountain Quality Indicators which now cover 240 out of the 284 Munros. Filling up the spaces between these articles are a number of short and some longer pieces of poetry, mostly by the excellent Tom Rix.

Plenty of gems here, with only one small niggle over the cover, which will immediately remind SMC members of our own Journal of bygone days. Having opted for a simple pale blue cover with the familiar Munro crest, the editors have added eight pages of sixteen glossy colour photos to the centre fold. The results are rather tiny and do not do justice to the images. A striking colour photo for the cover and fewer, larger pictures inside would have made a more attractive publication. Otherwise, highly recommended. Copies available for £4 (including p&p) from Hon. Secretary, 12 Randolph Court, Stirling FK8 2AL.

Dave Broadhead

ERRATA

1. Volume Numbers

For many years each **Volume** of the Journal has consisted of **three** issues. An index has been produced for each new volume – with the same dimensions as the Journal – to allow members to include it if they decide to have their Journal Volumes bound.

The last two complete Volumes have been as follows:

Volume XXXVIII [38]
2002 (Pages 1–282)
2003 (Pages 283–516)
2004 (Pages 517–710)

Volume XXXIX [39]
2005 (Pages 1–240)
2006 (Pages 241–460)
2007 (Pages 461–682)

Unfortunately this numbering system has gone awry in recent Journals.

On the title page of the **2004** Journal the Volume Number was shown as XXXIX when it should have been XXXVIII.

On the title page of the **2006** Journal the Volume Number was shown as XXXX when it should have been XXXIX.

On the title page of the **2007** Journal the Volume Number was shown as XL when it should have been XXXIX.

Stickers are being supplied with this issue to remedy these errors.

In view of the increased size of current Journals it has been decided to have just **two issues** per Volume in future years. So Volume XL [40] will include just the 2008 and 2009 issues.

2. SMCJ 2006

In the article entitled *Man-Eater* (pp.251–61) jointly written by Ken Crocket and John Mackenzie paragraphs 2–7 are all italicised, indicating that they were all written by KVC. In fact, the paragraphs should run:
pp.251–2
2   KVC
3   JM
4   KVC
5   JM
6   JM
7   KVC

Also on p.254
para.1 KVC

OFFICE BEARERS 2007-08

Honorary President: W.D. Brooker
Honorary Vice-Presidents: D. Scott and G.S. Peet
President: Paul V. Brian
Vice-Presidents: Brian S. Findlay and Charles J Orr

Honorary Secretary: John R.R. Fowler, 4 Doune Terrace, Edinburgh, EH3 6DY. **Honorary Treasurer:** John A. Wood, Spout Close, Millbeck, Keswick, CA12 4PS. **Membership Secretary:** Campbell Forrest, Strathview, Fintry Road, Kippen, Stirling, FK8 3HL. **Honorary Meets Secretary:** E.R.(Dick) Allen, Croft Head, Kentmere, Kendal, LA8 9JH. **Honorary Editor of Journal:** D. Noel Williams, Solus Na Beinne, Happy Valley, Torlundy, Fort William, PH33 6SN. **Honorary Librarian:** John Hunter, 2 Lorraine Road, Glasgow, G12 9NZ. **Honorary Archivist:** Robin N. Campbell, Glynside, Kippen Road, Fintry, Glasgow, G63 0LW. **Honorary Custodian of Slides:** David Stone, 30 Summerside Street, Edinburgh, EH6 4NU. **SMC Webmaster:** Kenneth V. Crocket, Glenisla, Long Row, Menstrie, FK11 7EA. **Convener of Publications Sub-Committee:** Rab Anderson, 24 Paties Road, Edinburgh, EH14 1EE. **Convener of Huts Sub-Committee:** William H. Duncan, Kirktoun, Eastend, Lochwinnoch, PA12 4ER. **Committee:** Campbell Forrest, Gillian E. Irvine, Clifford D. Smith, James Beaton, Peter J. Biggar, Andrew M. James, Joanna M George, Alan R Walker, David Whalley.

Journal Information

Editor:	Noel Williams, Solus Na Beinne, Happy Valley, Torlundy, Fort William, PH33 6SN. **e-mail** <noel@beinne.plus.com>
New Routes Editor:	Andy Nisbet, 20 Craigie Avenue, Boat of Garten, PH24 3BL. **e-mail** <anisbe@globalnet.co.uk>
Photos Editor:	Andy Tibbs, Crown Cottage, 4 Crown Circus, Inverness, IV2 3NQ. **e-mail** <teamtibbs@hotmail.com>
Distribution:	Dougie Lang, Hillfoot Hey, 580 Perth Road, Dundee, DD2 1PZ. **e-mail** <douglas.lang@btinternet.com>

INSTRUCTIONS TO CONTRIBUTORS

The Editor welcomes contributions from members and non-members alike. Priority will be given to articles relating to Scottish mountaineering. Articles should be submitted before the end of March if they are to be considered for inclusion in the Journal of the same year. Material is preferred in electronic form and should be sent by e-mail direct to the Editor.

Acceptable file formats in order of preference are (best) Open Document Format (odt), Rich Text Format (rtf), Plain Text (txt) or MS Word (doc/docx). *Open Office* is an open-source, multi-platform productivity suite which is free for individuals to download from http://www.openoffice.org/

Those without access to e-mail can send hard copy (typewritten and double-spaced) by post to the Editor's home address.

SCOTTISH MOUNTAINEERING CLUB JOURNAL BACK NUMBERS

	Year
£5.00	1972
	1977
	1978
	1979
	1980
	1983
£5.50	1985
£5.70	1986
	1987
	1989
	1990
	1991
	1992
£6.95	1993
	1994
	1995
£8.95	1996
	1997
	1998
£11.95	1999
£12.95	2000
	2001
	2002
	2003
	2004
£13.95	2005
	2006
	2007

Post & Packaging is extra.

Please contact: David 'Heavy' Whalley
Fuar Tholl
47 Grant St
Burghead
IV30 5UE

e-mail: <heavy_whalley@hotmail.com>
tel: 01343-835 338   mob: 07754 595 740

SCOTTISH MOUNTAINEERING CLUB HUTS

CHARLES INGLIS CLARK MEMORIAL HUT, BEN NEVIS
Location: (NN 167 722) On the north side of Ben Nevis by the Allt a' Mhuilinn. This hut was erected by Dr and Mrs Inglis Clark in memory of their son Charles who was killed in action in the 1914–18 War.
Custodian: Robin Clothier, 35 Broompark Drive, Newton Mearns, Glasgow, G77 5DZ.
tel (work) Mon to Fri only 0800–1800hrs 01560-600 811; mob (0800–2200hrs) 07836 637 842;
e-mail <cichutbennevis@hotmail.co.uk>

LAGANGARBH HUT, GLEN COE
Location: (NN 221 559) North of Buachaille Etive Mor near the River Coupall.
Custodian: Bernard Swan, 16 Knowes View, Faifley, Clydebank, G81 5AT.
tel 01389-875 505; answering service 01389-800 478; mob 07710 785 227; e-mail <bswan99686@aol.com>.

LING HUT, GLEN TORRIDON
Location: (NG 958 562) On the south side of Glen Torridon.
Custodian: Bill Skidmore, 1 Kirkton Drive, Lochcarron, Strathcarron, IV54 8UD.
tel 01520-722 434; mob 07780 786 601.

NAISMITH HUT, ELPHIN
Location: (NC 216 118) In the community of Elphin on the east side of the A835.
Custodian: Bill McKerrow, Scotsburn House, Drummond Road, Inverness, IV2 4NA.
tel 01463-223 917;
e-mail <billmckerrow@btinternet.com>.

RAEBURN HUT, LAGGAN
Location: (NN 636 909) On the north side of the A889 between Dalwhinnie and Laggan.
Custodian: Heather Morning, Duach Mills, Nethybridge, PH25 3DH.
tel 01479-821 448; mob 07788 861 431;
e-mail <heather_morning@hotmail.com>.

SMC Web Site

For a wealth of information about
mountaineering in Scotland
including the latest news about
SMC guidebooks, huts and
Munro compleaters
visit the SMC Web Site

www.smc.org.uk

Full details of these publications can be found on the Scottish Mountaineering Club Web Site (www.smc.org.uk) where they can also be purchased online direct from the suppliers. If you have any queries please complete the 'feedback form' available on the *Contacts* page.

Distributed by: Cordee, 3a De Montfort Street, Leicester LE1 7HD
Tel: Leicester 0116 254 3579 Fax: 0116 247 1176
www.cordee.co.uk

These publications are also available from bookshops and mountain equipment suppliers.

All profit from the sale of SMC climbing and hillwalking guides goes to the **Scottish Mountaineering Trust** and provides much of the Trust's revenue. The Trust is a grant awarding Charity, which for more than 40 years has been helping people enjoy and appreciate mountains and mountain environments, both in Scotland and throughout the world.

In the past 10 years grants totalling over £600,000 have been made. Some of the major areas which have benefited are; footpath repair and maintenance, land purchase, wildlife studies, and mountaineering education and training.

For further information about the Scottish Mountaineering Trust see the *Trust* section on the SMC Web Site.

Dave MacLeod leading Echo Wall, Ben Nevis, 28 July 2008. HiRes video still: Claire MacLeod.
A film of this ascent will be available in late October 2008.